Thomas Carlyle
The French Revolution, Vol. II

Édition de Grand Luxe

The French Revolution

A History

By
Thomas Carlyle

With a Critical and Biographical Introduction
by William Edward Hartpole Lecky

Illustrated
Volume II

Μέγας ὁ ἀγὼν ἔστι, θεῖον γὰρ ἔργον· ὑπὲρ βασι-
λείας, ὑπὲρ ἐλευθερίας, ὑπὲρ εὐροίας, ὑπὲρ ἀταραξίας.
ARRIANUS
Δόγμα γὰρ αὐτῶν τίς μεταβάλλει; χωρὶς δὲ δογ-
μάτων μεταβολῆς, τί ἄλλο ἢ δουλεία στενόντων καὶ
πείθεσθαι προσποιουμένων; ANTONINUS

New York
D. Appleton and Company
1900

CONTENTS

BOOK XII

PARLIAMENT FIRST

CHAPTER   PAGE

   I. Grande Acceptation 491
  II. The Book of the Law 499
 III. Avignon 507
 IV. No Sugar 515
  V. Kings and Emigrants 519
 VI. Brigands and Jalès 529
 VII. Constitution will not march . . . 533
VIII. The Jacobins 538
 IX. Minister Roland 542
  X. Pétion-National-Pique 546
 XI. The Hereditary Representative . . . 549
 XII. Procession of the Black Breeches . . . 553

BOOK XIII

THE MARSEILLESE

   I. Executive that does not act 561
  II. Let us march 568
 III. Some Consolation to Mankind . . . 571
 IV. Subterranean 576
  V. At Dinner 579
 VI. The Steeples at Midnight 583
 VII. The Swiss 591
VIII. Constitution burst in Pieces 598

BOOK XIV

SEPTEMBER

 I. The Improvised Commune 605
II. Danton 616

iii

CHAPTER   PAGE

III. Dumouriez 621
IV. September in Paris 625
V. A Trilogy 634
VI. The Circular 641
VII. September in Argonne 650
VIII. Exeunt 659

BOOK XV

REGICIDE

I. The Deliberative 669
II. The Executive 678
III. Discrowned 682
IV. The Loser pays 685
V. Stretching of Formulas 688
VI. At the Bar 694
VII. The Three Votings 702
VIII. Place de la Révolution 708

BOOK XVI

THE GIRONDINS

I. Cause and Effect 717
II. Culottic and Sansculottic 723
III. Growing Shrill 728
IV. Fatherland in Danger 732
V. Sansculottism accoutred 740
VI. The Traitor 744
VII. In Fight 748
VIII. In Death-Grips 751
IX. Extinct 757

BOOK XVII

TERROR

I. Charlotte Corday 765
II. In Civil War 773
III. Retreat of the Eleven 777
IV. O Nature 782
V. Sword of Sharpness 787
VI. Risen against Tyrants 791
VII. Marie-Antoinette 795
VIII. The Twenty-two 798

CONTENTS

BOOK XVIII

TERROR THE ORDER OF THE DAY

CHAPTER   PAGE

I. Rushing down 805
II. Death 810
III. Destruction 817
IV. Carmagnole complete 826
V. Like a Thunder-Cloud 833
VI. Do thy Duty 837
VII. Flame-Picture 844

BOOK XIX

THERMIDOR

I. The Gods are Athirst 851
II. Danton, no Weakness 857
III. The Tumbrils 863
IV. Mumbo-Jumbo 869
V. The Prisons 873
VI. To finish the Terror 876
VII. Go down to 881

BOOK XX

VENDÉMIAIRE

I. Decadent 891
II. La Cabarus 895
III. Quiberon 900
IV. Lion not Dead 904
V. Lion sprawling its Last 908
VI. Grilled Herrings 914
VII. The Whiff of Grapeshot 918
VIII. Finis 924

Book XII

PARLIAMENT FIRST

CHAPTER I

GRANDE ACCEPTATION

IN the last nights of September, when the autumnal equinox is past, and gray September fades into brown October, why are the Champs Elysées illuminated; why is Paris dancing, and flinging fireworks? They are gala-nights, these last of September; Paris may well dance, and the Universe: the Edifice of the Constitution is completed! Completed; nay revised, to see that there was nothing insufficient in it; solemnly proffered to his Majesty; solemnly accepted by him, to the sound of cannon-salvoes, on the fourteenth of the month. And now by such illumination, jubilee, dancing and fire-working, do we joyously handsel the new Social Edifice, and first raise heat and reek there, in the name of Hope.

The Revision, especially with a throne standing on its vertex, has been a work of difficulty, of delicacy. In the way of propping and buttressing, so indispensable now, something could be done; and yet, as is feared, not enough. A repentant Barnave Triumvirate, our Rabauts, Duports, Thourets, and indeed all Constitutional Deputies did strain every nerve: but the Extreme Left was so noisy; the People were so suspicious, clamorous to have the work ended: and then the loyal Right Side sat feeble-petulant all the while, and as it were pouting and petting; unable to help, had they even been willing. The Two Hundred and Ninety had solemnly made scission, before that, and departed, shaking the dust off their feet. To such transcendency of fret, and desperate hope that worsening of the bad might the sooner end it and bring back the good, had our unfortunate loyal Right Side now come![1]

However, one finds that this and the other little prop has been added, where possibility allowed. Civil-list and Privy-purse were from of old well cared for. King's Constitutional Guard, Eighteen hundred loyal men from the Eighty-three

Departments, under a loyal Duke de Brissac; this, with trust-worthy Swiss besides, is of itself something. The old loyal Bodyguards are indeed dissolved, in name as well as in fact; and gone mostly toward Coblentz. But now also those Sans-culottic violent Gardes Françaises, or Centre Grenadiers, shall have their mittimus: they do ere long, in the Journals, not without a hoarse pathos, publish their Farewell; "wishing all Aristocrats the graves in Paris which to us are denied." [2] They depart, these first soldiers of the Revolution; they hover very dimly in the distance for about another year; till they can be remodelled, new-named, and sent to fight the Aus-trians; and then History beholds them no more. A most notable Corps of men; which has its place in World-History—though to us, so is History written, they remain mere rubrics of men; nameless; a shaggy Grenadier Mass, crossed with buff-belts. And yet might we not ask: What Argonauts, what Leonidas' Spartans had done such a work? Think of their destiny: since that May morning, some three years ago, when they, unparticipating, trundled off D'Espréménil to the Ca-lypso Isles; since that July evening, some two years ago, when they, participating and sacreing with knit brows, poured a volley into Besenval's Prince de Lambesc! History waves them her mute adieu.

So that the Sovereign Power, these Sansculottic Watch-dogs, more like wolves, being leashed and led away from his Tuileries, breathes freer. The Sovereign Power is guarded henceforth by a loyal Eighteen Hundred—whom Contrivance, under various pretexts, may gradually swell to Six Thousand; who will hinder no journey to Saint-Cloud. The sad Varennes business has been soldered up; cemented, even in the blood of the Champ-de-Mars, these two months and more; and indeed ever since, as formerly, Majesty has had its privileges, its "choice of residence," though, for good reasons, the royal mind "prefers continuing in Paris." Poor royal mind, poor Paris; that have to go mumming; enveloped in speciosities, in falsehood which knows itself false; and to enact mutually your sorrowful farce-tragedy, being bound to it; and on the whole, to hope always, in spite of hope!

Nay, now that his Majesty has accepted the Constitution, to the sound of cannon-salvoes, who would not hope? Our good King was misguided, but he meant well. Lafayette has

moved for an Amnesty, for universal forgiving and forgetting
of Revolutionary faults; and now surely the glorious Revolution, cleared of its rubbish, is complete! Strange enough, and
touching in several ways, the old cry of " Vive le Roi!" once
more rises round King Louis the Hereditary Representative.
Their Majesties went to the Opera; gave money to the Poor:
the Queen herself, now when the Constitution is accepted,
hears voice of cheering. Bygone shall be bygone; the New
Era shall begin! To and fro, amid those lamp-galaxies of
the Elysian Fields, the Royal Carriage slowly wends and rolls;
everywhere with vivats, from a multitude striving to be glad.
Louis looks out, mainly on the variegated lamps and gay
human groups, with satisfaction enough for the hour. In her
Majesty's face, " under that kind graceful smile a deep sadness
is legible." [3] Brilliancies, of valour and of wit, stroll here
observant: a Dame de Staël, leaning most probably on the
arm of her Narbonne. She meets Deputies; who have built
this Constitution; who saunter here with vague communings,
not without thoughts whether it will stand. But as yet melodious fiddle-strings twang and warble everywhere, with rhythm
of light fantastic feet; long lamp-galaxies fling their coloured
radiance; and brass-lunged Hawkers elbow and bawl, " Grande
Acceptation, Constitution Monarchique ": it behooves the Son
of Adam to hope. Have not Lafayette, Barnave, and all Con-
stitutionalists set their shoulders handsomely to the inverted
pyramid of a throne? Feuillans, including almost the whole
Constitutional Respectability of France, perorate nightly from
their tribune; correspond through all Post-offices; denouncing
unquiet Jacobinism; trusting well that its time is nigh done.
Much is uncertain, questionable; but if the Hereditary Representative be wise and lucky, may one not, with a sanguine
Gaelic temper, hope that he will get in motion better or worse;
that what is wanting to him will gradually be gained and
added?

For the rest, as we must repeat, in this building of the Constitutional Fabric, especially in this Revision of it, nothing
that one could think of to give it new strength, especially to
steady it, to give it permanence, and even eternity, has been
forgotten. Biennial Parliament, to be called Legislative,
Assemblée Législative; with Seven Hundred and Forty-five
Members, chosen in a judicious manner by the " active citi-

zens " alone, and even by electing of electors still more active:
this, with privileges of Parliament, shall meet, self-authorized
if need be, and self-dissolved; shall grant money-supplies and
talk; watch over the administration and authorities; discharge
forever the functions of a Constitutional Great Council, Collective Wisdom and National Palaver—as the Heavens will
enable. Our First biennial Parliament, which indeed has been
a-choosing since early in August, is now as good as chosen.
Nay it has mostly got to Paris: it arrived gradually—not without pathetic greeting to its venerable Parent, the now moribund Constituent; and sat there in the Galleries, reverently
listening; ready to begin, the instant the ground were clear.

Then as to changes in the Constitution itself? This, impossible for any Legislative, or common biennial Parliament,
and possible solely for some resuscitated Constituent or National Convention, is evidently one of the most ticklish points.
The august moribund Assembly debated it for four entire days.
Some thought a change, or at least a reviewal and new approval, might be admissible in thirty years, some even went
lower, down to twenty, nay to fifteen. The august Assembly
had once decided for thirty years; but it revoked that, on better
thoughts; and did not fix any date of time, but merely some
vague outline of a posture of circumstances, and, on the whole,
left the matter hanging.[4] Doubtless a National Convention
can be assembled even within the thirty years: yet one may
hope, not; but that Legislatives, biennial Parliaments of the
common kind, with their limited faculty, and perhaps quiet
successive additions thereto, may suffice for generations, or
indeed while computed Time runs.

Furthermore, be it noted that no member of this Constituent has been, or could be, elected to the new Legislative. So
noble-minded were these Law-makers! cry some: and Solon-
like would banish themselves. So splenetic! cry more: each
grudging the other, none daring to be outdone in self-denial
by the other. So unwise in either case! answer all practical
men. But consider this other self-denying ordinance, That
none of us can be King's Minister, or accept the smallest
Court Appointment, for the space of four, or at lowest (and
on long debate and Revision) for the space of two years! So
moves the incorruptible seagreen Robespierre; with cheap
magnanimity he; and none dare be outdone by him. It was

such a law, not superfluous then, that sent Mirabeau to the
gardens of Saint-Cloud, under cloak of darkness, to that colloquy of the gods; and thwarted many things. Happily and
unhappily there is no Mirabeau now to thwart.

Welcomer meanwhile, welcome surely to all right hearts, is
Lafayette's chivalrous Amnesty. Welcome too is that hard-
wrung Union of Avignon; which has cost us, first and last,
" thirty sessions of debate," and so much else : may it at length
prove lucky ! Rousseau's statue is decreed : virtuous Jean-
Jacques, Evangelist of the Contrat Social. Not Drouet of
Varennes; not worthy Lataille, master of the old world-
famous Tennis-Court in Versailles, is forgotten; but each has
his honourable mention, and due reward in money.[5] Whereupon, things being all so neatly winded up, and the Deputations, and Messages, and royal and other ceremonials having
rustled by; and the King having now affectionately perorated
about peace and tranquillization, and members having answered " Oui ! Oui ! " with effusion, even with tears—President Thouret, he of the Law Reforms, rises, and, with a
strong voice, utters these memorable last-words : " The National Constituent Assembly declares that it has finished its
mission; and that its sittings are all ended." Incorruptible
Robespierre, virtuous Pétion are borne home on the shoulders
of the people; with vivats heaven-high. The rest glide quietly
to their respective places of abode. It is the last afternoon
of September 1791 ; on the morrow morning the new Legislative will begin.

So, amid glitter of illuminated streets and Champs Elysées,
and crackle of fireworks and glad deray, has the first National
Assembly vanished; dissolving, as they well say, into blank
Time; and is no more. National Assembly is gone, its work
remaining; as all Bodies of men go, and as man himself goes :
it had its beginning, and must likewise have its end. A
Phantasm-Reality born of Time, as the rest of us are; flitting
ever backward now on the tide of Time; to be long remembered of men. Very strange Assemblages, Sanhedrims, Am-
phictyonics, Trades-Unions, Ecumenic Councils, Parliaments
and Congresses, have met together on this Planet, and dispersed again; but a stranger Assemblage than this august
Constituent, or with a stranger mission, perhaps never met

there. Seen from the distance, this also will be a miracle. Twelve Hundred human individuals, with the Gospel of Jean-Jacques Rousseau in their pocket, congregating in the name of Twenty-five Millions, with full assurance of faith, to " make the Constitution " : such sight, the acme and main product of the Eighteenth Century, our World can witness once only. For Time is rich in wonders, in monstrosities most rich ; and is observed never to repeat himself, or any of his Gospels— surely least of all, this Gospel according to Jean-Jacques. Once it was right and indispensable, since such had become the Belief of men ; but once also is enough.

They have made the Constitution, these Twelve Hundred Jean-Jacques Evangelists ; not without result. Near twenty-nine months they sat, with various fortune ; in various capacity —always, we may say, in that capacity of car-borne Carroccio, and miraculous Standard of the Revolt of Men, as a Thing high and lifted up ; whereon whosoever looked might hope healing. They have seen much, cannons levelled on them ; then suddenly, by interposition of the Powers, the cannons drawn back ; and a wargod Broglie vanishing, in thunder not his own, amid the dust and downrushing of a Bastille and Old Feudal France. They have suffered somewhat : Royal Session, with rain and Oath of the Tennis-Court ; Nights of Pentecost ; Insurrections of Women. Also have they not done somewhat ? Made the Constitution, and managed all things the while ; passed, in these twenty-nine months, " twenty-five hundred Decrees," which on the average is some three for each day, including Sundays ! Brevity, one finds, is possible, at times : had not Moreau de St. Méry to give three thousand orders before rising from his seat ?—There was valour (or value) in these men ; and a kind of faith, were it only faith in this, That cobwebs are not cloth ; that a Constitution could be made. Cobwebs and chimeras ought verily to disappear ; for a Reality there is. Let formulas, soul-killing, and now grown body-killing, insupportable, begone, in the name of Heaven and Earth !—Time, as we say, brought forth these Twelve Hundred ; Eternity was before them, Eternity behind : they worked, as we all do, in the confluence of Two Eternities ; what work was given them. Say not that it was nothing they did. Consciously they did somewhat ; unconsciously how much ! They had their giants and their dwarfs, they accom-

plished their good and their evil; they are gone, and return
no more. Shall they not go with our blessing, in these circumstances; with our mild farewell?

By post, by diligence, on saddle or sole; they are gone:
toward the four winds. Not a few over the marches, to rank
at Coblentz. Thither wended Maury, among others; but in
the end toward Rome—to be clothed there in red Cardinal
plush; in falsehood as in a garment; pet son (her last born?)
of the Scarlet Woman. Talleyrand-Périgord, excommunicated
Constitutional Bishop, will make his way to London: to be
Ambassador, spite of the Self-denying Law; brisk young
Marquis Chauvelin acting as Ambassador's-Cloak. In London
too, one finds Pétion the virtuous; harangued and haranguing,
pledging the winecup with Constitutional Reform-Clubs, in
solemn tavern-dinner. Incorruptible Robespierre retires for
a little to native Arras: seven short weeks of quiet; the last
appointed him in this world. Public Accuser in the Paris
Department, acknowledged highpriest of the Jacobins; the
glass of incorruptible thin Patriotism, for his narrow emphasis
is loved of all the narrow—this man seems to be rising,
somewhither? He sells his small heritage at Arras; accompanied by a Brother and a Sister, he returns, scheming out
with resolute timidity a small sure destiny for himself and
them, to his old lodging, at the Cabinet-maker's, in the Rue
St. Honoré: O resolute-tremulous incorruptible seagreen man,
toward what a destiny!

Lafayette, for his part, will lay down the command. He
retires Cincinnatus-like to his hearth and farm; but soon leaves
them again. Our National Guard, however, shall henceforth
have no one Commandant; but all Colonels shall command
in succession, month about. Other Deputies we have met, or
Dame de Staël has met, " sauntering in a thoughtful manner ";
perhaps uncertain what to do. Some, as Barnave, the Lameths,
and their Duport, will continue here in Paris; watching the
new biennial Legislative, Parliament the First; teaching it to
walk, if so might be; and the Court to lead it.

Thus these: sauntering in a thoughtful manner; travelling
by post or diligence—whither Fate beckons. Giant Mirabeau
slumbers in the Pantheon of Great Men: and France? and
Europe?—the brass-lunged Hawkers sing " Grand Acceptation, Monarchic Constitution " through these gay crowds: the

Morrow, grandson of Yesterday, must be what it can, as To-day its father is. Our new biennial Legislative begins to. constitute itself on the first of October 1791.

NOTES

[1] Toulongeon, ii, 56, 59.
[2] " Hist. Parl.," xiii, 73.
[3] De Staël, " Considérations," i, c. 23.
[4] " Choix de Rapports," etc. (Paris, 1825), vi, 239–317.
[5] " Moniteur " (in " Hist. Parl.," xi, 473).

CHAPTER II

THE BOOK OF THE LAW

IF the august Constituent Assembly itself, fixing the regards of the Universe, could, at the present distance of time and place, gain comparatively small attention from us, how much less can this poor Legislative! It has its Right Side and its Left; the less Patriotic and the more, for Aristocrats exist not here or now: it spouts and speaks; listens to Reports, reads Bills and Laws; works in its vocation, for a season: but the History of France, one finds, is seldom or never there. Unhappy Legislative, what can History do with it; if not drop a tear over it, almost in silence? First of the two-year Parliaments of France, which, if Paper Constitution and oft-repeated National Oath could avail aught, were to follow in softly-strong indissoluble sequence while Time ran—it had to vanish dolefully within one year; and there came no second like it. Alas! your biennial Parliaments in endless indissoluble sequence; they, and all that Constitutional Fabric, built with such explosive Federation Oaths, and its top-stone brought out with dancing and variegated radiance, went to pieces, like frail crockery, in the crash of things; and already, in eleven short months, were in that Limbo near the Moon, with the ghosts of other Chimeras. There, except for rare specific purposes, let them rest, in melancholy peace.

On the whole, how unknown is a man to himself; or a public Body of men to itself! Æsop's fly sat on the chariot-wheel, exclaiming, What a dust I do raise! Great Governors, clad in purple with fasces and insignia, are governed by their valets, by the pouting of their women and children; or, in Constitutional countries, by the paragraphs of their Able Editors. Say not, I am this or that; I am doing this or that! For thou knowest it not, thou knowest only the name it as yet goes by. A purple Nebuchadnezzar rejoices to feel

himself now verily Emperor of this great Babylon which he
has builded; and is a nondescript biped-quadruped, on the eve
of a seven-years course of grazing! These Seven Hundred
and Forty-five elected individuals doubt not but they are the
first biennial Parliament, come to govern France by parliamentary eloquence: and they are what? And they have come
to do what? Things foolish and not wise!

It is much lamented by many that this First Biennial had
no members of the old Constituent in it, with their experience
of parties and parliamentary tactics; that such was their foolish Self-denying Law. Most surely, old members of the Constituent had been welcome to us here. But, on the other
hand, what old or what new members of any Constituent under
the Sun could have effectually profited? There are first biennial Parliaments so postured as to be, in a sense, beyond
wisdom; where wisdom and folly differ only in degree,
and wreckage and dissolution are the appointed issue for
both.

Old-Constituents, your Barnaves, Lameths, and the like, for
whom a special Gallery has been set apart, where they may
sit in honour and listen, are in the habit of sneering at these
new Legislators;[1] but let not us! The poor Seven Hundred
and Forty-five, sent together by the active citizens of France,
are what they could be; do what is fated them. That they are
of Patriot temper we can well understand. Aristocrat Noblesse had fled over the marches, or sat brooding silent in
their unburned Châteaus; small prospect had they in Primary
Electoral Assemblies. What with Flights to Varennes, what
with Days of Poniards, with plot after plot, the People are
left to themselves; the People must needs choose Defenders
of the People, such as can be had. Choosing, as they also will
ever do, "if not the ablest man, yet the man ablest to be
chosen"! Fervour of character, decided Patriot-Constitu-
tional feeling; these are qualities: but free utterance, master-
ship in tongue-fence; this is the quality of qualities. Accordingly one finds, with little astonishment, in this First Biennial,
that as many as Four hundred Members are of the Advocate
or Attorney species. Men who can speak, if there be aught
to speak: nay here are men also who can think, and even act.
Candour will say of this ill-fated First French Parliament,
that it wanted not its modicum of talent, its modicum of hon-

esty; that it, neither in the one respect nor in the other, sank below the average of Parliaments, but rose above the average. Let average Parliaments, whom the world does not guillotine, and cast forth to long infamy, be thankful not to themselves but to their stars!

France, as we say, has once more done what it could: fervid men have come together from wide separation; for strange issues. Fiery Max Isnard is come, from the utmost Southeast; fiery Claude Fauchet, Te-Deum Fauchet Bishop of Calvados, from the utmost Northwest. No Mirabeau now sits here, who had swallowed formulas: our only Mirabeau now is Danton, working as yet out of doors; whom some call " Mirabeau of the Sansculottes."

Nevertheless we have our gifts—especially of speech and logic. An eloquent Vergniaud we have; most mellifluous yet most impetuous of public speakers; from the region named Gironde, of the Garonne: a man unfortunately of indolent habits; who will sit playing with your children, when he ought to be scheming and perorating. Sharp-bustling Guadet; considerate grave Gensonné; kind-sparkling mirthful young Ducos; Valazé doomed to a sad end: all these likewise are of that Gironde or Bordeaux region: men of fervid Constitutional principles; of quick talent, irrefragable logic, clear respectability; who will have the Reign of Liberty establish itself, but only by respectable methods. Round whom others of like temper will gather; known by and by as Girondins, to the sorrowing wonder of the world. Of which sort note Condorcet, Marquis and Philosopher; who has worked at much, at Paris Municipal Constitution, Differential Calculus, Newspaper " Chronique de Paris," Biography, Philosophy; and now sits here as two-years Senator: a notable Condorcet, with stoical Roman face and fiery heart; " volcano hid under snow"; styled likewise, in irreverent language, " mouton enragé," peaceablest of creatures bitten rabid! Or note, lastly, Jean-Pierre Brissot; whom Destiny, long working noisily with him, has hurled hither, say, to have done with him. A biennial Senator he too; nay, for the present, the king of such. Restless, scheming, scribbling Brissot; who took to himself the style de Warville, heralds know not in the least why—unless it were that the father of him did, in an unexceptionable manner, perform Cookery and Vintnery in the Village of Ouar-

ville? A man of the windmill species, that grinds always, turning toward all winds; not in the steadiest manner.

In all these men there is talent, faculty to work; and they
will do it: working and shaping, not without effect, though
alas not in marble, only in quicksand!—But the highest faculty
of them all remains yet to be mentioned; or indeed has yet
to unfold itself for mention: Captain Hippolyte Carnot, sent
hither from the Pas de Calais; with his cold mathematical
head, and silent stubbornness of will: iron Carnot, far-plan-
ning, imperturbable, unconquerable; who, in the hour of need,
shall not be found wanting. His hair is yet black; and it
shall grow gray, under many kinds of fortune, bright and
troublous; and with iron aspect, this man shall face them all.

Nor is Côté Droit, and band of King's friends, wanting:
Vaublanc, Dumas, Jaucourt the honoured Chevalier; who love
Liberty, yet with Monarchy over it; and speak fearlessly
according to that faith—whom the thick-coming hurricanes
will sweep away. With them let a new military Théodore
Lameth be named—were it only for his two Brothers' sake,
who look down on him, approvingly there, from the Old-
Constituents' Gallery. Frothy professing Pastorets, honey-
mouthed conciliatory Lamourettes, and speechless nameless
individuals sit plentiful, as Moderates, in the middle. Still less
is a Côté Gauche wanting: extreme Left; sitting on the topmost benches, as if aloft on its speculatory Height or Mountain, which will become a practical fulminatory Height, and
make the name of Mountain famous-infamous to all times and
lands.

Honour waits not on this Mountain; nor as yet even loud
dishonour. Gifts it boasts not, nor graces, of speaking or of
thinking; solely this one gift of assured faith, of audacity that
will defy the Earth and the Heavens. Foremost here are the
Cordelier Trio: hot Merlin from Thionville, hot Bazaire,
Attorneys both; Chabot, disfrocked Capuchin, skilful in agio.
Lawyer Lacroix, who wore once as subaltern the single
epaulette, has loud lungs and a hungry heart. There too is
Couthon, little dreaming what he is—whom a sad chance has
paralyzed in the lower extremities. For, it seems, he sat once
a whole night, not warm in his true-love's bower (who indeed
was by law another's), but sunken to the middle in a cold
peat-bog, being hunted out from her; quaking for his life, in

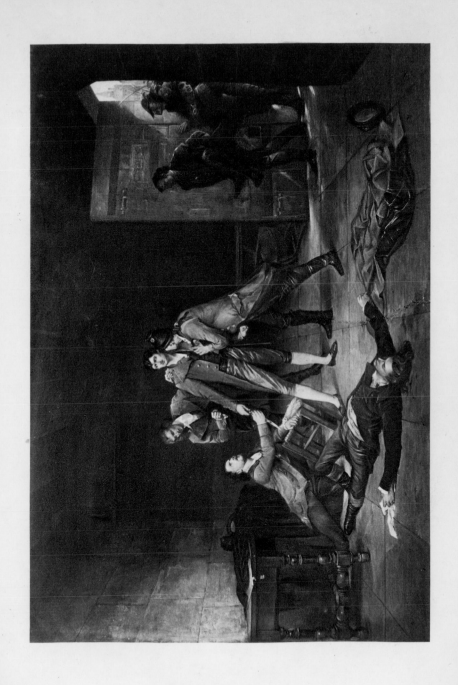

the cold quaking morass;[2] and goes now on crutches to the
end. Cambon likewise, in whom slumbers undeveloped such
a finance-talent for printing of Assignats; Father of Paper-
money; who, in the hour of menace, shall utter this stern
sentence, "War to the Manor-house, peace to the Hut, Guerre
aux Châteaux, paix aux Chaumières!"[3] Lecointre, the intrepid Draper of Versailles, is welcome here; known since the
Opera-Repast and Insurrection of Women. Thuriot too;
Elector Thuriot, who stood in the embrasures of the Bastille,
and saw Saint-Antoine rising in mass; who has many other
things to see. Last and grimmest of all, note old Ruhl, with
his brown dusky face and long white hair; of Alsatian Lu-
theran breed; a man whom age and book-learning have not
taught; who, haranguing the old men of Rheims, shall hold
up the Sacred Ampulla (Heaven-sent, wherefrom Clovis and
all Kings have been anointed) as a mere worthless oil-bottle,
and dash it to shreds on the pavement there; who, alas! shall
dash much to shreds, and finally his own wild head by pistol-
shot, and so end it.

Such lava welters redhot in the bowels of this Mountain;
unknown to the world and to itself! A mere commonplace
Mountain hitherto; distinguished from the Plain chiefly by
its superior barrenness, its baldness of look: at the utmost it
may, to the most observant, perceptibly smoke. For as yet
all lies so solid, peaceable; and doubts not, as was said, that
it will endure while Time runs. Do not all love Liberty
and the Constitution? All heartily—and yet with degrees.
Some, as Chevalier Jaucourt and his Right Side, may love
Liberty less than Royalty, were the trial made; others, as
Brissot and his Left Side, may love it more than Royalty.
Nay again, of these latter some may love Liberty more than
Law itself; others not more. Parties will unfold themselves;
no mortal as yet knows how. Forces work within these men
and without: dissidence grows opposition; ever widening;
waxing into incompatibility and internecine feud; till the
strong is abolished by a stronger; himself in his turn by a
strongest! Who can help it? Jaucourt and his Monarchists,
Feuillans, or Moderates; Brissot and his Brissotins, Jacobins,
or Girondins; these, with the Cordelier Trio, and all men,
must work what is appointed them, and in the way appointed them.

And to think what fate these poor Seven Hundred and Forty-five are assembled, most unwittingly, to meet! Let no heart be so hard as not to pity them. Their soul's wish was to live and work as the First of the French Parliaments; and make the Constitution march. Did they not, at their very instalment, go through the most affecting Constitutional ceremony, almost with tears? The Twelve eldest are sent solemnly to fetch the Constitution itself, the printed Book of the Law. Archivist Camus, an Old-Constituent appointed Archivist, he and the Ancient Twelve, amid blare of military pomp and clangour, enter, bearing the divine Book: and President and all Legislative Senators, laying their hand on the same, successively take the Oath, with cheers and heart-effusion, universal three-times-three.[4] In this manner they begin their Session. Unhappy mortals! For, that same day, his Majesty having received their Deputation of welcome, as seemed, rather drily, the Deputation can not but feel slighted, can not but lament such slight: and thereupon our cheering swearing First Parliament sees itself, on the morrow, obliged to explode into fierce retaliatory sputter of anti-royal Enactment as to how they, for their part, will receive Majesty; and how Majesty shall not be called Sire any more, except they please: and then, on the following day, to recall this Enactment of theirs, as too hasty, and a mere sputter, though not unprovoked.

An effervescent well-intentioned set of Senators; too combustible, where continual sparks are flying! Their History is a series of sputters and quarrels; true desire to do their function, fatal impossibility to do it. Denunciations, reprimandings of King's Ministers, of traitors supposed and real; hot rage and fulmination against fulminating Emigrants; terror of Austrian Kaiser, of "Austrian Committee" in the Tuileries itself; rage and haunting terror, haste and doubt and dim bewilderment!—Haste, we say; and yet the Constitution had provided against haste. No Bill can be passed till it have been printed, till it have been thrice read, with intervals of eight days—"unless the Assembly shall beforehand decree that there is urgency." Which, accordingly the Assembly, scrupulous of the Constitution, never omits to do: Considering this, and also considering that, and then that other, the Assembly decrees always "qu'il y a urgence"; and thereupon "the Assembly, having decreed that there is urgence," is free to decree—what indispensable distracted thing seems best to it. Two thousand and odd decrees, as men reckon, within Eleven months![5] The haste of the Constituent seemed great; but this is treble-quick. For the time itself is rushing treble-quick; and they have to keep pace with that. Unhappy Seven Hundred and Forty-five: true-patriotic, but so combustible; being fired, they must needs fling fire: Senate of touchwood and rockets, in a world of smoke-storm, with sparks wind-driven continually flying!

Or think, on the other hand, looking forward some months, of what scene they call Baiser de Lamourette! The dangers of the country are now grown imminent, immeasurable; National Assembly, hope of France, is divided against itself. In such extreme circumstances, honey-mouthed Abbé Lamourette, new Bishop of Lyons, rises, whose name, l'amourette, signifies the sweetheart, or Delilah doxy—he rises, and, with pathetic honeyed eloquence, calls on all august Senators to forget mutual griefs and grudges, to swear a new oath, and unite as brothers. Whereupon they all, with vivats, embrace and swear; Left Side confounding itself with Right; barren Mountain rushing down to fruitful Plain, Pastoret into the arms of Condorcet, injured to the breast of injurer, with tears: and all swearing that whosoever wishes either Feuillant Two-Chamber Monarchy or Extreme-Jacobin Republic, or anything but the Constitution and that only, shall be anathema maranatha.[6] Touching to behold! For, literally on the morrow morning, they must again quarrel, driven by Fate; and their sublime reconcilement is called derisively the Baiser de Lamourette, or Delilah Kiss.

Like fated Eteocles-Polynices Brothers, embracing, though in vain; weeping that they must not love, that they must hate only, and die by each other's hands! Or say, like doomed Familiar Spirits; ordered, by Art Magic under penalties, to do a harder than twist ropes of sand: "to make the Constitution march." If the Constitution would but march! Alas! the Constitution will not stir. It falls on its face; they tremblingly lift it on end again: march, thou gold Constitution! The Constitution will not march.—"He shall march, by ——!" said kind Uncle Toby, and even swore.

34

The Corporal answered mournfully: "He will never march in this world."

A Constitution, as we often say, will march when it images, if not the old Habits and Beliefs of the Constituted, then accurately their Rights, or better indeed their Mights—for these two, well understood, are they not one and the same? The old Habits of France are gone: her new Rights and Mights are not yet ascertained, except in Paper-theorem; nor can be, in any sort, till she have tried. Till she have measured herself, in fell death-grip, and were it in utmost preternatural spasm of madness, with Principalities and Powers, with the upper and the under, internal and external; with the Earth and Tophet and the very Heaven! Then will she know. —Three things bode ill for the marching of this French Constitution: the French People; the French King; thirdly, the French Noblesse and an assembled European World.

NOTES

[1] Dumouriez, ii, 150, etc.
[2] Ibid., ii, 370.
[3] "Choix de Rapports," xi, 25.
[4] "Moniteur," Séance du 4 Octobre, 1791.
[5] Montgaillard, iii, 1, 237.
[6] "Moniteur," Séance du 6 Juillet, 1792.

CHAPTER III

AVIGNON

BUT quitting generalities, what strange Fact is this, in the far Southwest, toward which the eyes of all men do now, in the end of October, bend themselves? A tragical combustion, long smoking and smouldering unluminous, has now burst into flame there.

Hot is that Southern Provençal blood: alas, collisions, as was once said, must occur in a career of Freedom; different directions will produce such; nay, different velocities in the same direction will! To much that went on there, History, busied elsewhere, would not specially give heed: to troubles of Uzez, troubles of Nismes, Protestant and Catholic, Patriot and Aristocrat; to troubles of Marseilles, Montpellier, Arles; to Aristocrat Camp of Jalès, that wondrous real-imaginary Entity, now fading pale-dim, then always again glowing forth deep-hued (in the imagination mainly)—ominous magical, " an Aristocrat picture of war done naturally "! All this was a tragical deadly combustion, with plot and riot, tumult by night and by day; but a dark combustion not luminous, not noticed; which now, however, one can not help noticing.

Above all places, the unluminous combustion in Avignon and the Comtat Venaissin was fierce. Papal Avignon, with its Castle rising sheer over the Rhone-stream; beautifulest Town, with its purple vines and gold-orange groves; why must foolish old rhyming Réné, the last Sovereign of Provence, bequeath it to the Pope and Gold Tiara, not rather to Louis Eleventh with the Leaden Virgin in his hatband? For good and for evil! Popes, Antipopes, with their pomp, have dwelt in that Castle of Avignon rising sheer over the Rhone-stream: there Laura de Sade went to hear mass; her Petrarch twang-

507

ing and singing by the Fountain of Vaucluse hard by, surely in a most melancholy manner. This was in the old days.

And now in these new days such issues do come from a squirt of the pen by some foolish rhyming Réné, after centuries—this is what we have: Jourdan Coupe-tête, leading to siege and warfare an Army, from three to fifteen thousand strong, called the Brigands of Avignon; which title they themselves accept, with the addition of an epithet, " The brave Brigands of Avignon! " It is even so. Jourdan the Headsman fled hither from that Châtelet Inquest, from that Insurrection of Women; and began dealing in madder: but the scene was rife in other than dye-stuffs; so Jourdan shut his madder-shop, and has risen, for he was the man to do it. The tile-beard of Jourdan is shaven off; his fat visage has got coppered and studded with black carbuncles; the Silenus trunk is swollen with drink and high living: he wears blue National uniform with epaulettes, " an enormous sabre, two horse-pistols crossed in his belt, and other two smaller sticking from his pockets "; styles himself General, and is the tyrant of men.[1] Consider this one fact, O Reader; and what sort of facts must have preceded it, must accompany it! Such things come of old Réné; and of the question which has risen, Whether Avignon can not now cease wholly to be Papal, and become French and free?

For some twenty-five months the confusion has lasted. Say three months of arguing; then seven of raging; then finally some fifteen months now of fighting, and even of hanging. For already in February 1790, the Papal Aristocrats had set up four gibbets, for a sign; but the People rose in June, in retributive frenzy; and, forcing the public Hangman to act, hanged four Aristocrats, on each Papal gibbet a Papal Haman. Then were Avignon Emigrations, Papal Aristocrats, emigrating over the Rhone River; demission of Papal Consul, flight, victory: re-entrance of Papal Legate, truce, and new onslaught; and the various turns of war. Petitions there were to National Assembly; Congresses of Townships; threescore and odd Townships voting for French Reunion and the blessings of Liberty; while some twelve of the smaller, manipulated by Aristocrats, gave vote the other way: with shrieks and discord! Township against Township, Town against Town:

Carpentras, long jealous of Avignon, is now turned out in
open war with it—and Jourdan Coupe-tête, your first General
being killed in mutiny, closes his dye-shop; and does there
visibly, with siege-artillery, above all with bluster and tumult,
with the "brave Brigands of Avignon," beleaguer the rival
Town, for two months, in the face of the world.

Feats were done, doubt it not, far-famed in Parish History;
but to Universal History unknown. Gibbets we see rise, on
the one side and on the other; and wretched carcasses swinging there, a dozen in the row; wretched Mayor of Vaison
buried before dead.[2] The fruitful seedfields lie unreaped, the
vineyards trampled down; there is red cruelty, madness of
universal choler and gall. Havoc and anarchy everywhere; a
combustion most fierce, but unlucent, not to be noticed here!
—Finally, as we saw, on the 14th of September last, the
National Constituent Assembly—having sent Commissioners
and heard them;[3] having heard Petitions, held Debates,
month after month ever since August 1789; and on the whole
"spent thirty sittings" on this matter—did solemnly decree
that Avignon and the Comtat were incorporated with France,
and his Holiness the Pope should have what indemnity was
reasonable.

And so hereby all is amnestied and finished? Alas! when
madness of choler has gone through the blood of men, and
gibbets have swung on this side and on that, what will a
parchment Decree and Lafayette Amnesty do? Oblivious
Lethe flows not above ground! Papal Aristocrats and Patriot
Brigands are still an eye-sorrow to each other; suspected,
suspicious, in what they do and forbear. The august Constituent Assembly is gone but a fortnight, when, on Sunday
the Sixteenth morning of October 1791, the unquenched
combustion suddenly becomes luminous. For Anti-constitu-
tional Placards are up, and the Statue of the Virgin is said
to have shed tears, and grown red.[4] Wherefore, on that
morning, Patriot l'Escuyer, one of our "six leading Patriots,"
having taken counsel with his brethren and General Jourdan,
determines on going to Church, in company with a friend or
two: not to hear mass, which he values little; but to meet
all the Papalists there in a body, nay, to meet that same weeping Virgin, for it is the Cordeliers Church; and give them

a word of admonition. Adventurous errand; which has the fatalest issue! What L'Escuyer's word of admonition might be, no History records; but the answer to it was a shrieking howl from the Aristocrat Papal worshippers, many of them women. A thousand-voiced shriek and menace; which, as L'Escuyer did not fly, became a thousand-handed hustle and jostle; a thousand-footed kick, with tumblings and tramplings, with the pricking of sempstress stilettoes, scissors and female pointed instruments. Horrible to behold; the ancient Dead, and Petrarchan Laura, sleeping round it there:[5] high Altar and burning tapers looking down on it; the Virgin quite tearless, and of the natural stone-colour!—L'Escuyer's friend or two rush off, like Job's Messengers, for Jourdan and the National Force. But heavy Jourdan will seize the Town-Gates first; does not run treble-fast, as he might: on arriving at the Cordeliers Church, the Church is silent, vacant; L'Escuyer, all alone, lies there, swimming in his blood, at the foot of the high Altar; pricked with scissors, trodden, massacred— gives one dumb sob, and gasps out his miserable life forever-more.

Sight to stir the heart of any man; much more of many men, self-styled Brigands of Avignon! The corpse of L'Escuyer, stretched on a bier, the ghastly head girt with laurel, is borne through the streets; with many-voiced unmelodious Nenia; funeral-wail still deeper than it is loud! The copper-face of Jourdan, of bereft Patriotism, has grown black. Patriot Municipality despatches official Narrative and tidings to Paris; orders numerous and innumerable arrestments for inquest and perquisition. Aristocrats male and female are haled to the Castle; lie crowded in subterranean dungeons there, bemoaned by the hoarse rushing of the Rhone; cut out from help.

So lie they; waiting inquest and perquisition. Alas! with a Jourdan Headsman for Generalissimo, with his copper-face grown black, and armed Brigand Patriots chanting their Nenia, the inquest is likely to be brief. On the next day and the next, let Municipality consent or not, a Brigand Court-Martial establishes itself in the subterranean stories of the Castle of Avignon; Brigand Executioners, with naked sabre, waiting at the door for a Brigand verdict. Short judgment, no appeal! There is Brigand wrath and vengeance; not un-refreshed by brandy. Close by is the Dungeon of the Glacière, or Ice-Tower: there may be deeds done—? For which language has no name!—Darkness and the shadow of horrid cruelty envelops these Castle Dungeons, that Glacière Tower: clear only that many have entered, that few have returned. Jourdan and the Brigands, supreme now over Municipals, over all authorities Patriot or Papal, reign in Avignon, waited on by Terror and Silence.

The result of all which is, that, on the 15th of November 1791, we behold friend Dampmartin, and subalterns beneath him, and General Choisi above him, with Infantry and Cavalry, and proper cannon-carriages rattling in front, with spread banners, to the sound of fife and drum, wend, in a deliberate formidable manner, toward that sheer Castle Rock, toward those broad Gates of Avignon; three new National-Assembly Commissioners following at safe distance in the rear.[6] Avignon, summoned in the name of Assembly and Law, flings its Gates wide open; Choisi with the rest, Dampmartin and the "Bons Enfans, Good Boys, of Baufremont"—so they name these brave Constitutional Dragoons, known to them of old—do enter amid shouts and scattered flowers. To the joy of all honest persons; to the terror only of Jourdan Headsman and the Brigands. Nay, next we behold carbuncled swollen Jourdan himself show copper-face, with sabre and four pistols; affecting to talk high; engaging, meanwhile, to surrender the Castle that instant. So the Choisi Grenadiers enter with him there. They start and stop, passing that Glacière, snuffing its horrible breath; with wild yell, with cries of "Cut the Butcher down!"—and Jourdan has to whisk himself through secret passages, and instantaneously vanish.

Be the mystery of iniquity laid bare, then! A Hundred and Thirty Corpses, of men, nay, of women and even children (for the trembling mother, hastily seized, could not leave her infant), lie heaped in that Glacière; putrid, under putridities: the horror of the world. For three days there is mournful lifting out, and recognition; amid the cries and movements of a passionate Southern people, now kneeling in prayer, now storming in wild pity and rage: lastly there is solemn sepulture, with muffled drums, religious requiem, and all the people's wail and tears. Their Massacred rest now in holy ground; buried in one grave.

And Jourdan Coupe-tête? Him also we behold again, after a day or two: in flight, through the most romantic Petrarchan hill-country; vehemently spurring his nag; young Ligonnet, a brisk youth of Avignon, with Choisi Dragoons, close in his rear! With such swollen mass of a rider no nag can run to advantage. The tired nag, spur-driven, does take the River Sorgue; but sticks in the middle of it; firm on that chiaro fondo di Sorga; and will proceed no farther for spurring! Young Ligonnet dashes up; the Copper-face menaces and bellows, draws pistol, perhaps even snaps it; is nevertheless seized by the collar; is tied firm, ankles under horse's belly, and ridden back to Avignon, hardly to be saved from massacre on the streets there.[7]

Such is the combustion of Avignon and the Southwest, when it becomes luminous. Long loud debate is in the august Legislative, in the Mother Society, as to what now shall be done with it. Amnesty, cry eloquent Vergniaud and all Patriots: let there be mutual pardon and repentance, restoration, pacification, and, if so might anyhow be, an end! Which vote ultimately prevails. So the Southwest smoulders and welters again in an "Amnesty," or Non-remembrance, which, alas, can not but remember, no Lethe flowing above ground! Jourdan himself remains unhanged; gets loose again, as one not yet gallows-ripe; nay, as we transiently discern from the distance, is "carried in triumph through the cities of the South."[8] What things men carry!

With which transient glimpse, of a Copper-faced Portent faring in this manner through the cities of the South, we must quit these regions—and let them smoulder. They want not their Aristocrats; proud old Nobles, not yet emigrated. Arles has its "Chiffonne," so, in symbolical cant, they name that Aristocrat Secret-Association; Arles has its pavements piled up, by and by, into Aristocrat barricades. Against which Rebecqui, the hot-clear Patriot, must lead Marseillese with cannon. The Bar of Iron has not yet risen to the top in the Bay of Marseilles; neither have these hot Sons of the Phoceans submitted to be slaves. By clear management and hot instance, Rebecqui dissipates that Chiffonne, without bloodshed; restores the pavement of Arles. He sails in Coast-barks, this Rebecqui, scrutinizing suspicious Martello-towers, with the keen eye of Patriotism; marches overland with despatch, singly, or in force; to City after City; dim scouring far and wide [9]—argues, and if it must be, fights. For there is much to do; Jalès itself is looking suspicious. So that Legislator Fauchet, after debate on it, has to propose Commissioners and a Camp on the Plain of Beaucaire; with or without result.

Of all which, and much else, let us note only this small consequence, that young Barbaroux, Advocate, Town-Clerk of Marseilles, being charged to have these things remedied, arrives at Paris in the month of February 1792. The beautiful and brave: young Spartan, ripe in energy, not ripe in wisdom; over whose black doom there shall flit nevertheless a certain ruddy fervour, streaks of bright Southern tint, not wholly swallowed of Death! Note also that the Rolands of Lyons are again in Paris; for the second and final time. King's Inspectorship is abrogated at Lyons, as elsewhere: Roland has his retiring-pension to claim, if attainable; has Patriot friends to commune with; at lowest, has a Book to publish. That young Barbaroux and the Rolands came together; that elderly Spartan Roland liked, or even loved the young Spartan, and was loved by him, one can fancy: and Madame ——? Breathe not, thou poison-breath, Evil-speech! That soul is taintless, clear as the mirror-sea. And yet if they two did look into each other's eyes, and each, in silence, in tragical renunciance, did find that the other was all-too lovely? Honi soit! She calls him " beautiful as Antinous ": he " will speak elsewhere of that astonishing woman."—A Madame d'Udon (or some such name, for Dumont does not recollect quite clearly) gives copious breakfast to the Brissotin Deputies and us Friends of Freedom, at her House in the Place Vendôme; with temporary celebrity, with graces and wreathed smiles; not without cost. There, amid wide babble and jingle, our plan of Legislative Debate is settled for the day, and much counselling held. Strict Roland is seen there, but does not go often.[10]

NOTES

[1] Dampmartin, "' Evénemens," i, 267.
[2] Barbaroux, " Mémoires," p. 26.
[3] Lescène Desmaisons, " Compte rendu à l'Assemblée Nationale," September 10, 1791 (" Choix des Rapports," vii, 273–293).

[4] " Procès-verbal de la Commune d'Avignon," etc. (in " Hist.
Parl.," xii, 419–423).

[5] Ugo Foscolo, " Essay on Petrarch," p. 35.

[6] Dampmartin, i, 251–294.

[7] Ibid., ubi suprà.

[8] " Deux Amis " (Paris, 1797), vii, pp. 59–71.

[9] Barbaroux, p. 21; " Hist. Parl.," xiii, 421–424.

[10] Dumont, " Souvenirs," p. 374.

CHAPTER IV

NO SUGAR

SUCH are our inward troubles; seen in the Cities of the South; extant, seen or unseen, in all cities and districts, North as well as South. For in all are Aristocrats, more or less malignant; watched by Patriotism; which again, being of various shades, from light Fayettist-Feuillant down to deep-sombre Jacobin, has to watch even itself.

Directories of Departments, what we call County Magistracies, being chosen by Citizens of a too "active" class, are found to pull one way; Municipalities, Town Magistracies, to pull the other way. In all places too are Dissident Priests; whom the Legislative will have to deal with: contumacious individuals, working on that angriest of passions; plotting, enlisting for Coblentz; or suspected of plotting: fuel of a universal unconstitutional heat. What to do with them? They may be conscientious as well as contumacious: gently they should be dealt with, and yet it must be speedily. In unilluminated La Vendée the simple are like to be seduced by them; many a simple peasant, a Cathelineau the wooldealer wayfaring meditative with his woolpacks, in these hamlets, dubiously shakes his head! Two Assembly Commissioners went thither last Autumn; considerate Gensonné, not yet called to be a senator; Gallois, an editorial man. These Two, consulting with General Dumouriez, spake and worked, softly, with judgment; they have hushed down the irritation, and produced a soft Report—for the time.

The General himself doubts not in the least but he can keep peace there; being an able man. He passes these frosty months among the pleasant people of Niort, occupies "tolerably handsome apartments in the Castle of Niort," and tempers the minds of men.[1] Why is there but one Dumouriez? Elsewhere you find, South or North, nothing but untempered

515

obscure jarring; which breaks forth ever and anon into open
clangour of riot.   Southern Perpignan has its tocsin, by torchlight; with rushing and onslaught: Northern Caen, not less,
by daylight; with Aristocrats ranged in arms at Places of
Worship; Departmental compromise proving impossible;
breaking into musketry and a Plot discovered![2]   Add Hunger too: for bread, always dear, is getting dearer: not so much
as Sugar can be had; for good reasons.   Poor Simoneau,
Mayor of Etampes, in this Northern region, hanging out his
Red Flag in some riot of grains, is trampled to death by a
hungry exasperated People.   What a trade this of Mayor, in
these times!   Mayor of Saint-Denis hung at the Lanterne,
by Suspicion and Dyspepsia, as we saw long since; Mayor of
Vaison, as we saw lately, buried before dead; and now this
poor Simoneau the Tanner, of Etampes—whom legal Constitu-
tionalism will not forget.

With factions, suspicions, want of bread and sugar, it is
verily what they call déchiré, torn asunder, this poor country:
France and all that is French.   For, over seas too come bad
news.   In black Saint-Domingo, before that variegated Glitter
in the Champs Elysées was lit for an Accepted Constitution,
there had risen, and was burning contemporary with it, quite
another variegated Glitter and nocturnal Fulgor, had we
known it: of molasses and ardent-spirits; of sugar-boil-
eries, plantations, furniture, cattle and men: sky-high;
the Plain of Cap Français one huge whirl of smoke and
flame!

What a change here, in these two years; since that first
" Box of Tricolor Cockades " got through the Custom-house
and atrabiliar Creoles too rejoiced that there was a levelling
of Bastilles!   Levelling is comfortable, as we often say: levelling, yet only down to one's self.   Your pale-white Creoles
have their grievances—and your yellow Quarteroons?   And
your dark-yellow Mulattoes?   And your Slaves soot-black?
Quarteroon Ogé, Friend of our Parisian-Brissotin Friends of
the Blacks, felt, for his share too, that Insurrection was the
most sacred of duties.   So the tricolor Cockades had fluttered
and swashed only some three months on the Creole hat, when
Ogé's signal conflagrations went aloft; with the voice of rage
and terror.   Repressed, doomed to die, he took black .powder
or seedgrains in the hollow of his hand, this Ogé; sprinkled

a film of white ones on the top, and said to his Judges, " Behold, they are white "; then shook his hand, and said, " Where are the whites, Où sont les blancs? "

So now, in the Autumn of 1791, looking from the sky-windows of Cap Français, thick clouds of smoke girdle our horizon, smoke in the day, in the night fire; preceded by fugitive shrieking white women, by Terror and Rumour. Black demonized squadrons are massacring and harrying, with nameless cruelty. They fight and fire " from behind thickets and coverts," for the Black man loves the Bush; they rush to the attack, thousands strong, with brandished cutlasses and fusils, with caperings, shoutings and vociferation — which, if the White Volunteer Company stands firm, dwindle into staggerings, into quick gabblement, into panic flight at the first volley, perhaps before it.[3] Poor Ogé could be broken on the wheel; this fire-whirlwind too can be abated, driven up into the Mountains: but Saint-Domingo is shaken, as Ogé's seedgrains were; shaking, writhing in long horrid death-throes, it is Black without remedy; and remains, as African Haiti, a monition to the world.

O my Parisian Friends, is not this, as well as Regraters and Feuillant Plotters, one cause of the astonishing dearth of Sugar! The Grocer, palpitant, with drooping lip, sees his Sugar taxé; weighed out by female Patriotism, in instant retail, at the inadequate rate of twenty-five sous, or thirteen pence a pound. " Abstain from it? " Yes, ye Patriot Sections, all ye Jacobins, abstain! Louvet and Collot-d'Herbois so advise; resolute to make the sacrifice; though " how shall literary men do without coffee? " Abstain, with an oath; that is the surest![4]

Also, for like reason, must not Brest and the Shipping Interest languish? Poor Brest languishes, sorrowing, not without spleen; denounces an Aristocrat Bertrand-Moleville, traitorous Aristocrat Marine-Minister. Do not her Ships and King's Ships lie rotting piecemeal in harbour; Naval Officers mostly fled, and on furlough too, with pay? Little stirring there; if it be not the Brest Galleys, whip-driven, with their Galley-Slaves—alas, with some Forty of our hapless Swiss Soldiers of Château-Vieux, among others! These Forty Swiss, too mindful of Nanci, do now, in their red wool caps, tug sorrowfully at the oar; looking into the Atlantic brine, which reflects only their own sorrowful shaggy faces; and seem forgotten of Hope.

But, on the whole, may we not say, in figurative language, that the French Constitution which shall march is very rheumatic, full of shooting internal pains, in joint and muscle; and will not march without difficulty?

NOTES

[1] Dumouriez, ii, 129.
[2] " Hist. Parl.," xii, 131, 141; xiii, 114, 417.
[3] " Deux Amis," x, 157.
[4] " Débats des Jacobins," etc. (" Hist. Parl.," xiii, 92–98, 171).

CHAPTER V

KINGS AND EMIGRANTS

EXTREMELY rheumatic Constitutions have been known to march, and keep on their feet, though in a staggering sprawling manner, for long periods, in virtue of one thing only: that the Head were healthy. But this Head of the French Constitution! What King Louis is and can not help being, Readers already know. A King who can not take the Constitution, nor reject the Constitution: nor do anything at all, but miserably ask, What shall I do? A King environed with endless confusions; in whose own mind is no germ of order. Haughty implacable remnants of Noblesse struggling with humiliated repentant Barnave-Lameths; struggling in that obscure element of fetchers and carriers, of Half-pay braggarts from the Café Valois, of Chambermaids, whisperers, and subaltern officious persons; fierce Patriotism looking on all the while, more and more suspicious, from without: what, in such struggle, can they do? At best, cancel one another, and produce zero. Poor King! Barnave and your Senatorial Jaucourts speak earnestly into this ear; Bertrand-Moleville, and Messengers from Coblentz, speak earnestly into that: the poor Royal Head turns to the one side and to the other side; can turn itself fixedly to no side. Let Decency drop a veil over it: sorrier misery was seldom enacted in the world. This one small fact, does it not throw the saddest light on much? The Queen is lamenting to Madame Campan: "What am I to do? When they, these Barnaves, get us advised to any step which the Noblesse do not like, then I am pouted at; nobody comes to my card-table; the King's Couchee is solitary." [1] In such a case of dubiety, what is one to do? Go inevitably to the ground!

The King has accepted this Constitution, knowing beforehand that it will not serve: he studies it, and executes it in the hope mainly that it will be found inexecutable. King's Ships lie rotting in harbour, their officers gone; the Armies disorganized; robbers scour the Highways, which wear down unrepaired; all Public Service lies slack and waste: the Executive makes no effort, or an effort only to throw the blame on the Constitution. Shamming death, " faisant la mort! " What Constitution, use it in this manner, can march? " Grow to disgust the Nation," it will truly,[2] unless you first grow to disgust the Nation! It is Bertrand de Moleville's plan, and his Majesty's; the best they can form.

Or if, after all, this best-plan proved too slow; proved a failure? Provident of that too, the Queen, shrouded in deepest mystery, " writes all day, in cipher, day after day, to Coblentz "; Engineer Goguelat, he of the Night of Spurs, whom the Lafayette Amnesty has delivered from Prison, rides and runs. Now and then, on fit occasion, a Royal familiar visit can be paid to that Salle de Manége, an affecting encouraging Royal Speech (sincere, doubt it not, for the moment) can be delivered there, and the Senators all cheer and almost weep— at the same time Mallet du Pan has visibly ceased editing, and invisibly bears abroad a King's Autograph, soliciting help from the Foreign Potentates.[3] Unhappy Louis, do this thing or else that other—if thou couldst!

The thing which the King's Government did do was to stagger distractedly from contradiction to contradiction; and wedding Fire to Water, envelope itself in hissing and ashy steam. Danton and needy corruptible Patriots are sopped with presents of cash: they accept the sop; they rise refreshed by it, and—travel their own way.[4] Nay, the King's Government did likewise hire Hand-clappers, or claqueurs, persons to applaud. Subterranean Rivarol has Fifteen Hundred Men in King's pay, at the rate of some 10,000l. sterling per month; what he calls " a staff of genius ": Paragraph-writers, Placard Journalists; " two hundred and eighty Applauders, at three shillings a day ": one of the strangest Staffs ever commanded by man—the muster-rolls and account-books of which still exist.[5] Bertrand-Moleville himself, in a way he thinks very dexterous, contrives to pack the Galleries of the Legislative; gets Sansculottes hired to go thither, and applaud at a signal given, they fancying it was Pétion that bade them: a device which was not detected for almost a week. Dexterous enough;

as if a man, finding the Day fast decline, should determine on altering the Clock-hands: that is a thing possible for him.

Here too let us note an unexpected apparition of Philippe d'Orléans at Court: his last at the Levee of any King. D'Orléans, some time in the winter months seemingly, has been appointed to that old first-coveted rank of Admiral—though only over ships rotting in port. The wished-for comes too late! However, he waits on Bertrand-Moleville to give thanks: nay, to state that he would willingly thank his Majesty in person; that, in spite of all the horrible things men have said and sung, he is far from being his Majesty's enemy; at bottom, how far! Bertrand delivers the message, brings about the royal Interview, which does pass to the satisfaction of his Majesty; D'Orléans seeming clearly repentant, determined to turn over a new leaf. And yet, next Sunday, what do we see? "Next Sunday," says Bertrand, "he came to the King's Levee; but the Courtiers ignorant of what had passed, the Crowd of Royalists who were accustomed to resort thither on that day specially to pay their court, gave him the most humiliating reception. They came pressing round him; managing, as if by mistake, to tread on his toes, to elbow him toward the door, and not let him enter again. He went downstairs to her Majesty's Apartments, where cover was laid; so soon as he showed face, sounds rose on all sides, ' Messieurs, take care of the dishes,' as if he had carried poison in his pockets. The insults, which his presence everywhere excited, forced him to retire without having seen the Royal Family: the crowd followed him to the Queen's staircase; in descending, he received a spitting (crachat) on the head, and some others on his clothes. Rage and spite were seen visibly painted on his face ": [6] as indeed how could they miss to be? He imputes it all to the King and Queen, who know nothing of it, who are even grieved at it; and so descends to his Chaos again. Bertrand was there at the Château that day himself, and an eye-witness to these things.

For the rest, Non-jurant Priests, and the repression of them, will distract the King's conscience; Emigrant Princes and Noblesse will force him to double-dealing: there must be veto on veto; amid the ever-waxing indignation of men. For Patriotism, as we said, looks on from without, more and more suspicious. Waxing tempest, blast after blast, of Patriotic

35

indignation, from without; dim inorganic whirl of Intrigues, Fatuities, within! Inorganic, fatuous; from which the eye turns away. De Staël intrigues for her so gallant Narbonne, to get him made War-Minister; and ceases not, having got him made. The King shall fly to Rouen; shall there, with the gallant Narbonne, properly "modify the Constitution." This is the same brisk Narbonne, who, last year, cut out from their entanglement, by force of dragoons, those poor fugitive Royal Aunts: men say he is at bottom their Brother, or even more, so scandalous is scandal. He drives now, with his De Staël, rapidly to the Armies, to the Frontier Towns; produces rose-coloured Reports, not too credible; perorates, gesticulates; wavers poising himself on the top, for a moment, seen of men; then tumbles, dismissed, washed away by the Time-flood.

Also the fair Princess de Lamballe intrigues, bosom-friend of her Majesty: to the angering of Patriotism. Beautiful Unfortunate, why did she ever return from England? Her small silver-voice, what can it profit in that piping of the black World-tornado? which will whirl her, poor fragile Bird of Paradise, against grim rocks. Lamballe and De Staël intrigue visibly, apart or together: but who shall reckon how many others, and in what infinite ways, invisibly! Is there not what one may call an "Austrian Committee," sitting invisible in the Tuileries; centre of an invisible Anti-National Spiderweb, which, for we sleep among mysteries, stretches its threads to the ends of the Earth? Journalist Carra has now the clearest certainty of it: to Brissotin Patriotism, and France generally, it is growing more and more probable.

O Reader, hast thou no pity for this Constitution? Rheumatic shooting pains in its members; pressure of hydrocephale and hysteric vapours on its Brain: a Constitution divided against itself; which will never march, hardly even stagger! Why were not Drouet and Procureur Sausse in their beds, that unblessed Varennes Night? Why did they not, in the name of Heaven, let the Korff Berline go whither it listed? Nameless incoherency, incompatibility, perhaps prodigies at which the world still shudders, had been spared.

But now comes the third thing that bodes ill for the marching of this French Constitution: besides the French

1791-'92]   KINGS AND EMIGRANTS   523

People, and the French King, there is thirdly—the assembled
European World. It has become necessary now to look at that
also. Fair France is so luminous: and round and round it, is
troublous Cimmerian Night. Calonnes, Breteuils hover dim,
far-flown; overnetting Europe with intrigues. From Turin
to Vienna; to Berlin, and utmost Petersburg in the frozen
North! Great Burke has raised his great voice long ago;
eloquently demonstrating that the end of an Epoch is come,
to all appearance the end of Civilized Time. Him many answer: Camille Desmoulins, Clootz, Speaker of Mankind, Paine
the rebellious Needleman, and honourable Gaelic Vindicators
in that country and in this: but the great Burke remains un-
answerable; "the Age of Chivalry is gone," and could not
but go, having now produced the still more indomitable Age
of Hunger. Altars enough, of the Dubois-Rohan sort, changing to the Gobel-and-Talleyrand sort, are faring by rapid
transmutations to—shall we say, the right Proprietor of them?
French Game and French Game-Preservers did alight on the
Cliffs of Dover, with cries of distress. Who will say that the
end of much is not come? A set of mortals has risen, who
believe that Truth is not a printed Speculation, but a practical
Fact; that Freedom and Brotherhood are possible in this
Earth, supposed always to be Belial's, which "the Supreme
Quack" was to inherit! Who will say that Church, State,
Throne, Altar are not in danger; that the Sacred Strongbox
itself, last Palladium of effete Humanity, may not be blasphe-
mously blown upon, and its padlocks undone?

The poor Constituent Assembly might act with what delicacy and diplomacy it would; declare that it abjured med-
dling with its neighbours, foreign conquest, and so forth; but
from the first this thing was to be predicted: that old Europe
and new France could not subsist together. A Glorious Revolution, oversetting State-Prisons and Feudalism; publishing,
with outburst of Federative Cannon, in face of all the Earth,
that Appearance is not Reality, how shall it subsist amid
Governments which, if Appearance is not Reality, are—one
knows not what? In death-feud, and internecine wrestle and
battle, it shall subsist with them; not otherwise.

"Rights of Man," printed on Cotton Handkerchiefs, in various dialects of human speech, pass over to the Frankfort Fair.[7]
What say we, Frankfort Fair? They have crossed Euphrates,

and the fabulous Hydaspes; wafted themselves beyond the
Ural, Altai, Himalayah; struck off from wood stereotypes, in
angular Picture-writing, they are jabbered and jingled of in
China and Japan. Where will it stop? Kien-Lung smells
mischief; not the remotest Dalai-Lama shall now knead his
dough-pills in peace.—Hateful to us, as is the Night! Bestir
yourselves, ye Defenders of Order! They do bestir themselves: all Kings and Kinglets, with their spiritual temporal
array, are astir; their brows clouded with menace. Diplomatic emissaries fly swift; Conventions, privy Conclaves
assemble; and wise wigs wag, taking what counsel they can.

Also, as we said, the Pamphleteer draws pen, on this side
and that: zealous fists beat the Pulpit-drum. Not without
issue! Did not iron Birmingham, shouting " Church and
King," itself knew not why, burst out, last July, into rage,
drunkenness and fire; and your Priestleys, and the like, dining
there on that Bastille day, get the maddest singeing; scandalous to consider! In which same days, as we can remark,
High Potentates, Austrian and Prussian, with Emigrants, were
faring toward Pilnitz in Saxony; there, on the 27th of August,
they, keeping to themselves what further " secret Treaty "
there might or might not be, did publish their hopes and their
threatenings, their Declaration that it was " the common cause
of Kings."

Where a will to quarrel is, there is a way. Our readers
remember that Pentecost-Night, Fourth of August 1789, when
Feudalism fell in a few hours? The National Assembly, in
abolishing Feudalism, promised that " compensation " should
be given; and did endeavour to give it. Nevertheless the
Austrian Kaiser answers that his German Princes, for their
part, can not be unfeudalized; that they have Possessions in
French Alsace, and Feudal Rights secured to them, for which
no conceivable compensation will suffice. So this of the Possessioned Princes, " Princes possessionés," is bandied from
Court to Court; covers acres of diplomatic paper at this day:
a weariness to the world. Kaunitz argues from Vienna;
Delessarts responds from Paris, though perhaps not sharply
enough. The Kaiser and his Possessioned Princes will too
evidently come and take compensation—so much as they can
get. Nay, might one not partition France, as we have done
Poland, and are doing; and so pacify it with a vengeance?

From South to North! For actually it is "the common cause of Kings." Swedish Gustav, sworn Knight of the Queen of France, will lead Coalized Armies—had not Ankarström treasonously shot him; for, indeed, there were griefs nearer home.[8] Austria and Prussia speak at Pilnitz; all men intensely listening. Imperial Rescripts have gone out from Turin; there will be secret Convention at Vienna. Catherine of Russia beckons approvingly; will help, were she ready. Spanish Bourbon stirs amid his pillows; from him too, even from him, shall there come help. Lean Pitt, "the Minister of Preparatives," looks out from his watch-tower in Saint James's, in a suspicious manner. Councillors plotting, Calonnes dim-hovering—alas! Sergeants rub-a-dubbing openly through all manner of German market-towns, collecting ragged valour![9] Look where you will, immeasurable Obscurantism is girdling this fair France; which, again, will not be girdled by it. Europe is in travail; pang after pang, what a shriek was that of Pilnitz! The birth will be: War.

Nay, the worst feature of the business is this last, still to be named; the Emigrants at Coblentz. So many thousands ranking there, in bitter hate and menace: King's Brothers, all Princes of the Blood except wicked D'Orléans; your duelling De Castries, your eloquent Cazalès; bull-headed Malseigne, a wargod Broglie; Distaff Seigneurs, insulted Officers, all that have ridden across the Rhine-stream—D'Artois welcoming Abbé Maury with a kiss, and clasping him publicly to his own royal heart! Emigration, flowing over the Frontiers, now in drops, now in streams, in various humours of fear, of petulance, rage and hope, ever since those first Bastille days when D'Artois went, "to shame the citizens of Paris"— has swollen to the size of a Phenomenon for the world. Coblentz is become a small extra-national Versailles; a Versailles in partibus: briguing, intriguing, favouritism, strumpetocracy itself, they say, goes on there; all the old activities, on a small scale, quickened by hungry Revenge.

Enthusiasm, of loyalty, of hatred and hope, has risen to a high pitch; as, in any Coblentz tavern you may hear, in speech and in singing. Maury assists in the interior Council; much is decided on: for one thing, they keep lists of the dates of your emigrating; a month sooner, or a month later, determines your greater or your less right to the coming Division of the Spoil. Cazalès himself, because he had occasionally spoken with a Constitutional tone, was looked on coldly at first: so pure are our principles.[10] And arms are a-hammering at Liége; "three thousand horses" ambling hitherward from the Fairs of Germany: Cavalry enrolling; likewise Foot-soldiers, "in blue coat, red waistcoat and nankeen trousers."[11] They have their secret domestic correspondences, as their open foreign: with disaffected Crypto-Aristocrats, with contumacious Priests, with Austrian Committee in the Tuileries. Deserters are spirited over by assiduous crimps; Royal-Allemand is gone almost wholly. Their route of march, toward France and the Division of the Spoil, is marked out, were the Kaiser once ready. "It is said, they mean to poison the sources; but," adds Patriotism making report of it, "they will not poison the source of Liberty"; whereat on applaudit, we can not but applaud. Also they have manufactories of False Assignats; and men that circulate in the interior, distributing and disbursing the same; one of these we denounce now to Legislative Patriotism: "a man Lebrun by name; about thirty years of age, with blonde hair and in quantity; has," only for the time being surely, "a black-eye, œil poché; goes in a wiski with a black horse,"[12] always keeping his Gig!

Unhappy Emigrants, it was their lot, and the lot of France! They are ignorant of much that they should know: of themselves, of what is around them. A Political Party that knows not when it is beaten, may become one of the fatalest of things, to itself, and to all. Nothing will convince these men that they can not scatter the French Revolution at the first blast of their war-trumpet; that the French Revolution is other than a blustering Effervescence, of brawlers and spouters, which, at the flash of chivalrous broadswords, at the rustle of gallows-ropes, will burrow itself, in dens the deeper the welcomer. But, alas! what man does know and measure himself, and the things that are round him—else where were the need of physical fighting at all? Never, till they are cleft asunder, can these heads believe that a Sansculottic arm has any vigour in it: cleft asunder, it will be too late to believe.

One may say, without spleen against his poor erring brothers of any side, that above all other mischiefs, this of the

Emigrant Nobles acted fatally on France. Could they have known, could they have understood! In the beginning of 1789, a splendour and a terror still surrounded them: the Conflagration of their Châteaus, kindled by months of obstinacy, went out after the Fourth of August; and might have continued out, had they at all known what to defend, what to relinquish as indefensible. They were still a graduated Hierarchy of Authorities, or the accredited similitude of such: they sat there, uniting King with Commonalty; transmitting and translating gradually, from degree to degree, the command of the one into the obedience of the other; rendering command and obedience still possible. Had they understood their place, and what to do in it, this French Revolution, which went forth explosively in years and in months, might have spread itself over generations; and not a torture-death but a quiet euthanasia have been provided for many things.

But they were proud and high, these men; they were not wise to consider. They spurned all from them in disdainful hate, they drew the sword and flung away the scabbard. France has not only no Hierarchy of Authorities, to translate command into obedience; its Hierarchy of Authorities has fled to the enemies of France; calls loudly on the enemies of France to interfere armed, who want but a pretext to do that. Jealous Kings and Kaisers might have looked on long, meditating interference, yet afraid and ashamed to interfere: but now do not the King's Brothers, and all French Nobles, Dignitaries and Authorities that are free to speak, which the King himself is not—passionately invite us, in the name of Right and of Might? Ranked at Coblentz, from Fifteen to Twenty thousand stand now brandishing their weapons, with the cry: "On, on!" Yes, Messieurs, you shall on—and divide the spoil according to your dates of emigrating.

Of all which things a poor Legislative Assembly, and Patriot France, is informed: by denunciant friend, by triumphant foe. Sulleau's Pamphlets, of the Rivarol Staff of Genius, circulate; heralding supreme hope. Durosoy's Placards tapestry the walls; "Chant du Coq" crows day, pecked at by Talien's "Ami des Citoyens." King's-Friend Royou, "Ami du Roi," can name, in exact arithmetical ciphers, the contingents of the various Invading Potentates; in all, Four hundred and

nineteen thousand Foreign fighting men, with Fifteen thousand Emigrants.   Not to reckon these your daily and hourly
desertions, which an Editor must daily record, of whole Companies, and even Regiments, crying " Vive le Roi, Vive la
Reine!" and marching over with banners spread [13]—lies all,
and wind; yet to Patriotism not wind; nor, alas, one day, to
Royou! Patriotism, therefore, may brawl and babble yet a
little while: but its hours are numbered: Europe is coming
with Four hundred and nineteen thousand and the Chivalry
of France; the gallows, one may hope, will get its own.

NOTES

[1] Campan, ii, 177, 202.
[2] Bertrand-Moleville, i, c. 4.
[3] Ibid., i, 370.
[4] Ibid., i, c. 17.
[5] Montgaillard, iii, 41.
[6] Bertrand-Moleville, i, 177.
[7] Toulongeon, i, 256.
[8] March 30, 1792 (" Annual Register," p. 11).
[9] Toulongeon, ii, 100–117.
[10] Montgaillard, iii, 5–17; Toulongeon, ubi suprà.
[11] See " Hist. Parl.," xiii, 11–38, 41–61, 358, etc.
[12] " Moniteur," Séance du 2 Novembre, 1791 (" Hist. Parl.," xiii, 212).
[13] " Ami du Roi " Newspaper (in " Hist. Parl.," xiii, 175).

CHAPTER VI

BRIGANDS AND JALÈS

WE shall have War, then; and on what terms! With an Executive "pretending," really with less and less deceptiveness now, "to be dead"; casting even a wishful eye toward the enemy: on such terms we shall have War.

Public Functionary in vigorous action there is none; if it be not Rivarol with his Staff of Genius and Two hundred and eighty Applauders. The Public Service lies waste; the very Taxgatherer has forgotten his cunning: in this and the other Provincial Board of Management (Directoire de Département) it is found advisable to retain what Taxes you can gather, to pay your own inevitable expenditures. Our Revenue is Assignats; emission on emission of Paper-money. And the Army; our Three grand Armies, of Rochambeau, of Lückner, of Lafayette? Lean, disconsolate hover these Three grand Armies, watching the Frontiers there; three Flights of long-necked Cranes in moulting-time—wrecked, disobedient, disorganized; who never saw fire; the old Generals and Officers gone across the Rhine. War-Minister Narbonne, he of the rose-coloured Reports, solicits recruitments, equipments, money, always money; threatens, since he can get none, to "take his sword," which belongs to himself, and go serve his country with that.[1]

The question of questions is: What shall be done? Shall we, with a desperate defiance which Fortune sometimes favours, draw the sword at once, in the face of this inrushing world of Emigration and Obscurantism; or wait, and temporize and diplomatize, till, if possible, our resources mature themselves a little? And yet again, are our resources growing toward maturity; or growing the other way? Dubious: the ablest Patriots are divided; Brissot and his Brissotins, or Girondins,

in the Legislative, cry aloud for the former defiant plan;
Robespierre, in the Jacobins, pleads as loud for the latter dilatory one: with responses, even with mutual reprimands; dis-
tracting the Mother of Patriotism.   Consider also what agitated
Breakfasts there may be at Madame d'Udon's in the Place
Vendôme! The alarm of all men is great. Help, ye Patriots;
and O at least agree; for the hour presses. Frost was not yet
gone, when in that "tolerably handsome apartment of the
Castle of Niort," there arrived a Letter: General Dumouriez
must to Paris. It is War-Minister Narbonne that writes; the
General shall give counsel about many things.[2] In the month
of February 1792, Brissotin friends welcome their Dumouriez
Polymetis—comparable really to an antique Ulysses in modern
costume; quick, elastic, shifty, insuppressible, a "many-counselled man."

Let the Reader fancy this fair France with a whole Cimmerian Europe girdling her, rolling in on her, black, to burst
in red thunder of War; fair France herself hand-shackled and
foot-shackled in the weltering complexities of this Social
Clothing, or Constitution, which they have made for her; a
France that, in such Constitution, can not march! And Hunger too; and plotting Aristocrats, and excommunicating Dissident Priests: "the man Lebrun by name" urging his black
wiski, visible to the eye; and, still more terrible in his invisibility, Engineer Goguelat, with Queen's cipher, riding and
running!
     The excommunicatory Priests give new trouble in the
Maine and Loire; La Vendée, nor Cathelineau the wool-dealer,
has not ceased grumbling and rumbling. Nay, behold Jalès
itself once more: how often does that real-imaginary Camp of
the Fiend require to be extinguished! For near two years
now, it has waned faint and again waxed bright, in the bewildered soul of Patriotism: actually, if Patriotism knew it,
one of the most surprising products of Nature working with
Art. Royalist Seigneurs, under this or the other pretext,
assemble the simple people of these Cevennes Mountains; men
not unused to revolt, and with heart for fighting, could their
poor heads be got persuaded. The Royalist Seigneur harangues; harping mainly on the religious string: "True Priests
maltreated, false Priests intruded, Protestants (once dragooned)

now triumphing, things sacred given to the dogs "; and so produces, from the pious Mountaineer throat, rough growlings: " Shall we not testify, then, ye brave hearts of the Cevennes; march to the rescue? Holy Religion; duty to God and the King? "—" Si fait, si fait, Just so, just so," answer the brave hearts always: " Mais il y a de bien bonnes choses dans la Révolution, But there are main good things in the Revolution too! "—And so the matter, cajole as we may, will only turn on its axis, not stir from the spot, and remains theatrical merely.[3]

Nevertheless deepen your cajolery, harp quick and quicker, ye Royalist Seigneurs; with a dead-lift effort you may bring it to that. In the month of June next, this Camp of Jalès will step forth as a theatricality suddenly become real; Two thousand strong, and with the boast that it is Seventy thousand: most strange to see; with flags flying, bayonets fixed; with Proclamation, and D'Artois Commission of civil war! Let some Rebecqui, or other the like hot-clear Patriot; let some " Lieutenant-Colonel Aubry," if Rebecqui is busy elsewhere, raise instantaneous National Guards, and disperse and dissolve it; and blow the Old Castle asunder,[4] that so, if possible, we hear of it no more!

In the Months of February and March, it is recorded, the terror, especially of rural France, had risen even to the transcendental pitch: not far from madness. In Town and Hamlet is rumour, of war, massacre: that Austrians, Aristocrats, above all, that The Brigands are close by. Men quit their houses and huts; rush fugitive, shrieking, with wife and child, they know not whither. Such a terror, the eye-witnesses say, never fell on a Nation; nor shall again fall, even in Reigns of Terror expressly so called. The Countries of the Loire, all the Central and Southeast regions, start up distracted, " simultaneously as by an electric shock "—for indeed grain too gets scarcer and scarcer. " The people barricade the entrances of Towns, pile stones in the upper stories, the women prepare boiling water; from moment to moment, expecting the attack. In the Country, the alarm-bell rings incessant; troops of peasants, gathered by it, scour the highways, seeking an imaginary enemy. They are armed mostly with scythes stuck in wood; and, arriving in wild troops at the barricaded Towns, are themselves sometimes taken for Brigands." [5]

So rushes old France : old France is rushing down. What the end will be is known to no mortal ; that the end is near all mortals may know.

NOTES

[1] " Moniteur," Séance du 23 Janvier, 1792; " Biographie des Ministres," § Narbonne.

[2] Dumouriez, ii, c. 6.

[3] Dampmartin, i, 201.

[4] " Moniteur," Séance du 15 Juillet, 1792.

[5] Newspapers, etc. (in " Hist. Parl.," xiii, 325).

CHAPTER VII

CONSTITUTION WILL NOT MARCH

TO all which our poor Legislative, tied up by an unmarching Constitution, can oppose nothing, by way of remedy, but mere bursts of parliamentary eloquence! They go on, debating, denouncing, objurgating: loud weltering Chaos, which devours itself.

But their two thousand and odd Decrees? Reader, these happily concern not thee, nor me. Mere Occasional-Decrees, foolish and not foolish; sufficient for that day was its own evil! Of the whole two thousand there are not now half a score, and these mostly blighted in the bud by royal Veto, that will profit or disprofit us. On the 17th January, the Legislative, for one thing, got its High Court, its Haute Cour, set up at Orléans. The theory had been given by the Constituent, in May last, but this is the reality: a Court for the trial of Political Offences; a Court which can not want work. To this it was decreed that there needed no royal Acceptance, therefore that there could be no Veto. Also Priests can now be married; ever since last October. A patriotic adventurous Priest had made bold to marry himself then; and not thinking this enough, came to the bar with his new spouse; that the whole world might hold honeymoon with him, and a Law be obtained.

Less joyful are the Laws against Refractory Priests; and yet not less needful! Decrees on Priests and Decrees on Emigrants: these are the two brief Series of Decrees, worked out with endless debate, and then cancelled by Veto, which mainly concern us here. For an august National Assembly must needs conquer these Refractories, Clerical or Laic, and thumbscrew them into obedience: yet, behold, always as you turn your legislative thumbscrew, and will press and even crush till Refractories give way—King's Veto steps in with magical paralysis; and your thumbscrew, hardly squeezing, much less crushing, does not act!

Truly a melancholy Set of Decrees, a pair of Sets; paralyzed by Veto! First, under date the 28th of October 1791, we have Legislative Proclamation, issued by herald and billsticker; inviting Monsieur, the King's Brother, to return within two months, under penalties. To which invitation Monsieur replies nothing; or indeed replies by Newspaper Parody, inviting the august Legislative " to return to common sense within two months," under penalties. Whereupon the Legislative must take stronger measures. So, on the 9th of November, we declare all Emigrants to be " suspect of conspiracy "; and, in brief, to be " outlawed," if they have not returned at Newyear's-day—Will the King say Veto? That " triple impost " shall be levied on these men's Properties, or even their Properties be " put in sequestration," one can understand. But further, on Newyear's-day itself, not an individual having " returned," we declare, and with fresh emphasis some fortnight later again declare, That Monsieur is déchu, forfeited of his eventful Heirship to the Crown; nay, more, that Condé, Calonne, and a considerable List of others are accused of high treason; and shall be judged by our High Court of Orléans: Veto!—Then again as to Non-jurant Priests: it was decreed, in November last, that they should forfeit what Pensions they had; be " put under inspection, under surveillance," and, if need were, be banished: Veto! A still sharper turn is coming; but to this also the answer will be, Veto.

Veto after Veto; your thumbscrew paralyzed! Gods and men may see that the Legislative is in a false position. As, alas! who is in a true one? Voices already murmur for a " National Convention." [1] This poor Legislative, spurred and stung into action by a whole France and a whole Europe, can not act; can only objurgate and perorate; with stormy " motions," and motion in which is no way; with effervescence, with noise and fuliginous fury!

What scenes in that National Hall! President jingling his inaudible bell; or, as utmost signal of distress, clapping on his hat; " the tumult subsiding in twenty minutes," and this or the other indiscreet Member sent to the Abbaye Prison for three days! Suspected Persons must be summoned and questioned; old M. de Sombreuil of the Invalides has to give account of himself, and why he leaves his Gates open.   Unusual smoke rose from the Sèvres Pottery, indicating conspiracy; the Potters explained that it was Necklace-Lamotte's "Mémoires," bought up by her Majesty, which they were endeavouring to suppress by fire,[2] which nevertheless he that runs may still read.

Again, it would seem, Duke de Brissac and the King's Constitutional-Guard are "making cartridges secretly in the cellars": a set of Royalists, pure and impure; black cutthroats many of them, picked out of gaming-houses and sinks; in all Six thousand instead of Eighteen hundred; who evidently gloom on us every time we enter the Château.[3]   Wherefore, with infinite debate, let Brissac and King's Guard, be disbanded.   Disbanded accordingly they are; after only two months of existence, for they did not get on foot till March of this same year.   So ends briefly the King's new Constitutional Maison Militaire; he must now be guarded by mere Swiss and blue Nationals again.   It seems the lot of Constitutional things.   New Constitutional Maison Civile he would never even establish, much as Barnave urged it; old resident Duchesses sniffed at it, and held aloof; on the whole her Majesty thought it not worth while, the Noblesse would so soon be back triumphant.[4]

Or, looking still into this National Hall and its scenes, behold Bishop Torné, a Constitutional Prelate, not of severe morals, demanding that "religious costumes and such caricatures" be abolished.   Bishop Torné warms, catches fire; finishes by untying, and indignantly flinging on the table, as if for gage or bet, his own pontifical cross.   Which cross, at any rate, is instantly covered by the cross of Te-Deum Fauchet, then by other crosses and insignia, till all are stripped; this clerical Senator clutching off his skull-cap, that other his frill-collar—lest Fanaticism return on us.[5]

Quick is the movement here!   And then so confused, unsubstantial, you might call it almost spectral: pallid, dim, inane, like the Kingdoms of Dis!   Unruly Linguet, shrunk to a kind of spectre for us, pleads here some cause that he has; amid rumour and interruption, which excel human patience: he "tears his papers, and withdraws," the irascible adust little man.   Nay, honourable Members will tear their papers, being effervescent: Merlin of Thionville tears his papers, crying:

"So, the People can not be saved by you!" Nor are Deputations wanting: Deputations of Sections; generally with complaint and denouncement, always with Patriot fervour of sentiment: Deputation of Women, pleading that they also may be allowed to take Pikes, and exercise in the Champ-de-Mars. Why not, ye Amazons, if it be in you? Then occasionally, having done our message and got answer, we "defile through the Hall singing ' Ça-ira ' "; or rather roll and whirl through it, "dancing our ronde patriotique the while" —our new Carmagnole, or Pyrrhic war-dance and liberty-dance. Patriot Huguenin, Ex-Advocate, Ex-Carbineer, Ex-Clerk of the Barriers, comes deputed, with Saint-Antoine at his heels; denouncing Anti-patriotism, Famine, Forestalment and Man-eaters; asks an august Legislative: "Is there not a tocsin in your hearts against these mangeurs d'hommes!" [6]

But above all things, for this is a continual business, the Legislative has to reprimand the King's Ministers. Of his Majesty's Ministers we have said hitherto, and say, next to nothing. Still more spectral these! Sorrowful; of no permanency any of them, none at least since Montmorin vanished: the "eldest of the King's Council" is occasionally not ten days old.[7] Feuillant-Constitutional, as your respectable Cahier de Gerville, as your respectable unfortunate Delessarts; or Royalist-Constitutional, as Montmorin last Friend of Necker; or Aristocrat, as Bertrand-Moleville: they flit there phantom-like, in the huge simmering confusion; poor shadows, dashed in the racking winds; powerless, without meaning—whom the human memory need not charge itself with.

But how often, we say, are these poor Majesty's Ministers summoned over; to be questioned, tutored; nay, threatened, almost bullied! They answer what, with adroitest simulation and casuistry, they can: of which a poor Legislative knows not what to make. One thing only is clear, That Cimmerian Europe is girdling us in; that France (not actually dead, surely?) can not march. Have a care, ye Ministers! Sharp Guadet transfixes you with cross-questions, with sudden Advocate-conclusions; the sleeping tempest that is in Vergniaud can be awakened. Restless Brissot brings up Reports, Accusations, endless thin Logic; it is the man's highday even now. Condorcet redacts, with his firm pen, our "Address of the Legislative Assembly to the French Nation." [8] Fiery Max

Isnard, who, for the rest, will " carry not Fire and Sword " on those Cimmerian Enemies, " but Liberty "—is for declaring " that we hold Ministers responsible; and that by responsibility we mean death, nous entendons la mort."

For verily it grows serious: the time presses, and traitors there are. Bertrand-Moleville has a smooth tongue, the known Aristocrat; gall in his heart. How his answers and explanations flow ready; jesuitic, plausible to the ear! But perhaps the notablest is this, which befell once when Bertrand had done answering and was withdrawn. Scarcely had the august Assembly begun considering what was to be done with him, when the Hall fills with smoke. Thick sour smoke: no oratory, only wheezing and barking—irremediable; so that the august Assembly has to adjourn![9] A miracle? Typical miracle? One knows not: only this one seems to know, that " the Keeper of the Stoves was appointed by Bertrand " or by some underling of his!—O fuliginous confused Kingdom of Dis, with thy Tantalus-Ixion toils, with thy angry Fire-floods, and Streams named of Lamentation, why hast thou not thy Lethe too, that so one might finish?

NOTES

[1] December, 1791 (" Hist. Parl.," xii, 257).

[2] " Moniteur," Séance du 28 Mai, 1792; Campan, ii, 196.

[3] Dumouriez, ii, 168.

[4] Campan, ii, c. 19.

[5] " Moniteur," du 7 Avril, 1792; " Deux Amis," vii, 111.

[6] See " Moniteur," Séances (in " Hist. Parl.," xiii, xiv).

[7] Dumouriez, ii, 137.

[8] February 16, 1792 (" Choix des Rapports," viii, 375–392).

[9] " Courrier de Paris," 14 Janvier, 1792 (Gorsas's Newspaper), in " Hist. Parl.," xiii, 83.

CHAPTER VIII

THE JACOBINS

NEVERTHELESS let not Patriotism despair. Have we not, in Paris at least, a virtuous Pétion, a wholly Patriotic Municipality? Virtuous Pétion, ever since November, is Mayor of Paris: in our Municipality, the Public, for the Public is now admitted too, may behold an energetic Danton; further an epigrammatic slow-sure Manuel; a resolute unrepentant Billaud-Varennes, of Jesuit breeding; Tallien able-editor; and nothing but Patriots, better or worse. So ran the November Elections: to the joy of most citizens; nay, the very Court supported Pétion rather than Lafayette. And so Bailly and his Feuillants, long waning like the Moon, had to withdraw then, making some sorrowful obeisance,[1] into extinction—or indeed into worse, into lurid half-light, grimmed by the shadow of that Red Flag of theirs, and bitter memory of the Champ-de-Mars. How swift is the progress of things and men! Not now does Lafayette, as on that Federation-day, when his noon was, "press his sword firmly on the Fatherland's Altar," and swear in sight of France: ah no; he, waning and setting ever since that hour, hangs now, disastrous, on the edge of the horizon; commanding one of those Three moulting Crane-flights of Armies, in a most suspected, unfruitful, uncomfortable manner.

But, at worst, can not Patriotism, so many thousands strong in this Metropolis of the Universe, help itself? Has it not right-hands, pikes? Hammering of Pikes, which was not to be prohibited by Mayor Bailly, has been sanctioned by Mayor Pétion; sanctioned by Legislative Assembly. How not, when the King's so-called Constitutional Guard "was making cartridges in secret"? Changes are necessary for the National Guard itself; this whole Feuillant-Aristocrat Staff of the Guard must be disbanded. Likewise, citizens without uniform may surely rank in the Guard, the pike beside the musket, in such a time: the "active" citizen and the passive who can fight for us, are they not both welcome?—Oh my Patriot friends, indubitably Yes! Nay, the truth is, Patriotism throughout, were it never so white-frilled, logical, respectable, must either lean itself heartily on Sansculottism, the black, bottomless; or else vanish, in the frightfulest way, to Limbo! Thus some, with upturned nose, will altogether sniff and disdain Sansculottism; others will lean heartily on it; nay, others again will lean what we call heartlessly on it: three sorts; each sort with a destiny corresponding.

In such point of view, however, have we not for the present a Volunteer Ally, stronger than all the rest; namely, Hunger? Hunger; and what rushing of Panic Terror this and the sumtotal of our other miseries may bring! For Sansculottism grows by what all other things die of. Stupid Peter Baille almost made an epigram, though unconsciously, and with the Patriot world laughing not at it but at him, when he wrote: "Tout va bien ici, le pain manque, All goes well here, food is not to be had." [2]

Neither, if you knew it, is Patriotism without her Constitution that can march; her not impotent Parliament; or call it, Ecumenic Council, and General-Assembly of the Jean-Jacques Churches: the Mother Society, namely! Mother Society with her three hundred full-grown Daughters; with what we can call little Grand-daughters trying to walk, in every village of France, numerable, as Burke thinks, by the hundred thousand. This is the true Constitution; made not by Twelve hundred august Senators, but by Nature herself; and has grown, unconsciously, out of the wants and the efforts of these Twenty-five Millions of men. They are "Lords of the Articles," our Jacobins; they originate debates for the Legislative; discuss Peace and War; settle beforehand what the Legislative is to do. Greatly to the scandal of philosophical men, and of most Historians—who do in that judge naturally, and yet not wisely. A Governing power must exist: your other powers here are simulacra; this power is it.

Great is the Mother Society; she has had the honour to be denounced by Austrian Kaunitz; [3] and is all the dearer to Patriotism. By fortune and valour she has extinguished Feuillantism itself, at least the Feuillant Club. This latter,

high as it once carried its head, she, on the 18th of February,
has the satisfaction to see shut, extinct; Patriots having gone
thither, with tumult, to hiss it out of pain.   The Mother
Society has enlarged her locality, stretches now over the whole
nave of the Church.   Let us glance in, with the worthy Toulongeon, our old Ex-Constituent Friend, who happily has eyes
to see.   "The nave of the Jacobins Church," says he, "is
changed into a vast Circus, the seats of which mount up circularly, like an amphitheatre to the very groin of the domed
roof.   A high Pyramid of black marble, built against one of the
walls, which was formerly a funeral monument, has alone been
left standing: it serves now as back to the Office-bearers'
Bureau.   Here on an elevated Platform sit President and Secretaries, behind and above them the white Busts of Mirabeau,
of Franklin, and various others, nay, finally of Marat.   Facing
this is the Tribune, raised till it is midway between floor and
groin of the dome, so that the speaker's voice may be in the
centre.   From that point thunder the voices which shake all
Europe: down below, in silence, are forging the thunderbolts
and the fire-brands.   Penetrating into this huge circuit, where
all is out of measure, gigantic, the mind can not repress some
movement of terror and wonder; the imagination recalls those
dread temples which Poetry, of old, had consecrated to the
Avenging Deities." [4]

Scenes too are in this Jacobin Amphitheatre—had History
time for them.   Flags of the "Three Free Peoples of the
Universe," trinal brotherly flags of England, America, France,
have been waved here in concert; by London Deputation, of
Whigs or Wighs and their Club, on this hand, and by young
French Citoyennes on that; beautiful sweet-tongued Female
Citizens, who solemnly send over salutation and brotherhood,
also Tricolor stitched by their own needle, and finally Ears of
Wheat; while the dome rebellows with "Vivent les trois peuples
libres!" from all throats—a most dramatic scene.   Demoiselle
Théroigne recites, from that Tribune in mid air, her perse-
cutions in Austria; comes leaning on the arm of Joseph
Chénier, Poet Chénier, to demand Liberty for the hapless
Swiss of Château-Vieux.[5]   Be of hope, ye forty Swiss; tugging
there, in the Brest waters; not forgotten!

Deputy Brissot perorates from that Tribune; Desmoulins,
our wicked Camille, interjecting audibly from below, "Co-

quin!" Here, though oftener in the Cordeliers, reverberates
the lion-voice of Danton; grim Billaud-Varennes is here;
Collot d'Herbois, pleading for the forty Swiss, tearing a
passion to rags. Apophthegmatic Manuel winds up in this
pithy way: "A Minister must perish!"—to which the Amphitheatre responds: "Tous, Tous, All, All!" But the Chief
Priest and Speaker of this place, as we said, is Robespierre, the
long-winded incorruptible man. What spirit of Patriotism
dwelt in men in those times, this one fact, it seems to us, will
evince: that fifteen hundred human creatures, not bound to it,
sat quiet under the oratory of Robespierre; nay, listened
nightly, hour after hour, applausive; and gaped as for the
word of life. More insupportable individual, one would say,
seldom opened his mouth in any Tribune. Acrid, implacable-
impotent, dull-drawling, barren as the Harmattan wind. He
pleads, in endless earnest-shallow speech, against immediate
War, against Woollen Caps or Bonnets Rouges, against many
things; and is the Trismegistus and Dalai-Lama of Patriot
men. Whom nevertheless a shrill-voiced little man, yet with
fine eyes and a broad beautifully sloping brow, rises respectfully to controvert; he is, say the Newspaper Reporters,
"M. Louvet, Author of the charming Romance of Faublas."
Steady, ye Patriots! Pull not yet two ways; with a France
rushing panic-stricken in the rural districts, and a Cimmerian
Europe storming in on you!

NOTES

[1] "Discours de Bailly, Réponse de Pétion" ("Moniteur" du 20
Novembre, 1791).
[2] Barbaroux, p. 94.
[3] "Moniteur," Séance du 20 Mars, 1792.
[4] Toulongeon, ii, 124.
[5] "Débats des Jacobins" ("Hist. Parl.," xiii, 259, etc.).

CHAPTER IX

MINISTER ROLAND

ABOUT the vernal equinox, however, one unexpected gleam of hope does burst forth on Patriotism: the appointment of a thoroughly Patriot Ministry. This also his Majesty, among his innumerable experiments of wedding fire to water, will try. Quod bonum sit. Madame d'Udon's Breakfasts have jingled with a new significance; not even Genevese Dumont but had a word in it. Finally, on the 15th and onward to the 23d day of March 1792, when all is negotiated—this is the blessed issue; this Patriot Ministry that we see.

General Dumouriez, with the Foreign Portfolio, shall ply Kaunitz and the Kaiser, in another style than did poor Delessarts; whom indeed we have sent to our High Court of Orléans for his sluggishness. War-Minister Narbonne is washed away by the Time-flood; poor Chevalier de Grave, chosen by the Court, is fast washing away: then shall austere Servan, able Engineer-Officer, mount suddenly to the War Department. Genevese Clavière sees an omen realized; passing the Finance Hôtel, long years ago, as a poor Genevese exile, it was borne wondrously on his mind that he was to be Finance-Minister; and now he is it—and his poor Wife, given up by the Doctors, rises and walks, not the victim of nerves but their vanquisher.[1] And above all, our Minister of the Interior? Roland de la Platrière, he of Lyons! So have the Brissotins, public or private Opinion, and Breakfasts in the Place Vendôme, decided it. Strict Roland, compared to a Quaker endimanché, or Sunday Quaker, goes to kiss hands at the Tuileries, in round hat and sleek hair, his shoes tied with mere riband or ferrat. The Supreme Usher twitches Dumouriez aside: "Quoi, Monsieur! No buckles to his shoes?"—"Ah, Monsieur," answers Dumouriez, glancing toward the ferrat: "All is lost, Tout est perdu."[2]

And so our fair Roland removes from her upper-floor in the Rue Saint-Jacques, to the sumptuous saloons once occupied by Madame Necker. Nay, still earlier, it was Calonne that did all this gilding; it was he who ground these lustres, Venetian mirrors; who polished this inlaying, this veneering and or-moulu; and made it, by rubbing of the proper lamp, an Aladdin's Palace—and now behold, he wanders dim-flitting over Europe; half-drowned in the Rhine-stream, scarcely saving his Papers! Vos non vobis.—The fair Roland, equal to either fortune, has her public Dinner on Fridays, the Ministers all there in a body: she withdraws to her desk (the cloth once removed), and seems busy writing; nevertheless loses no word: if, for example, Deputy Brissot and Minister Clavière get too hot in argument, she, not without timidity, yet with a cunning gracefulness, will interpose. Deputy Brissot's head, they say, is getting giddy, in this sudden height; as feeble heads do.

Envious men insinuate that the Wife Roland is Minister, and not the Husband: it is happily the worst they have to charge her with. For the rest, let whose head soever be getting giddy, it is not this brave woman's. Serene and queenly here, as she was of old in her own hired garret of the Ursulines Convent! She who has quietly shelled French-beans for her dinner; being led to that, as a young maiden, by quiet insight and computation; and knowing what that was, and what she was: such a one will also look quietly on or-moulu and veneering, not ignorant of these either. Calonne did the veneering: he gave dinners here, old Besenval diplomatically whispering to him; and was great: yet Calonne we saw at last " walk with long strides." Necker next; and where now is Necker? Us also a swift change has brought hither; a swift change will send us hence. Not a Palace but a Caravansera!

So wags and wavers this unrestful World, day after day, month after month. The streets of Paris, and all Cities, roll daily their oscillatory flood of men; which flood does nightly disappear, and lie hidden horizontal in beds and truckle-beds; and awakes on the morrow to new perpendicularity and movement. Men go their roads, foolish or wise—Engineer Goguelat to and fro, bearing Queen's cipher. A Madame de Staël is busy; can not clutch her Narbonne from the Time-flood: a Princess de Lamballe is busy; can not help her Queen.

Barnave, seeing the Feuillants dispersed, and Coblentz so brisk, begs by way of final recompense to kiss her Majesty's hand; "augurs not well of her new course"; and retires home to Grenoble, to wed an heiress there. The Café Valois and Méot the Restaurateur's hear daily gasconade; loud babble of Half-pay Royalists, with or without poniards. Remnants of Aristo-crat saloons call the new Ministry "Ministère-Sansculotte." A Louvet, of the Romance "Faublas," is busy in the Jacobins. A Cazotte, of the Romance "Diable Amoureux," is busy else-where: better wert thou quiet, old Cazotte; it is a world, this, of magic become real! All men are busy; doing they only half guess what—flinging seeds, of tares mostly, into the "Seed-field of Time": this, by and by, will declare wholly what.

But Social Explosions have in them something dread, and as it were mad and magical; which indeed Life always secretly has: thus the dumb Earth (says Fable), if you pull her man-drake-roots, will give a dæmonic mad-making moan. These Explosions and Revolts ripen, break forth like dumb dread Forces of Nature; and yet they are Men's forces; and yet we are part of them: the Dæmonic that is in man's life has burst out on us, will sweep us too away!—One day here is like another, and yet it is not like but different. How much is growing; silently resistless, at all moments! Thoughts are growing; forms of Speech are growing, and Customs and even Costumes; still more visibly are actions and transactions grow-ing, and that doomed Strife of France with herself and with the whole world.

The word Liberty is never named now except in conjunc-tion with another: Liberty and Equality. In like manner, what, in a reign of Liberty and Equality, can these words, "Sir," "Obedient Servant," "Honour to be," and such-like, signify? Tatters and fibres of old Feudality; which, were it only in the Grammatical province, ought to be rooted out! The Mother Society has long since had proposals to that effect: these she could not entertain; not, at the moment. Note too how the Jacobin Brethren are mounting new Symbolical head-gear: the Woollen Cap or Nightcap, bonnet de laine, better known as bonnet rouge, the colour being red. A thing one wears not only by way of Phrygian Cap-of-Liberty, but also for convenience-sake, and then also in compliment to the Lower-class Patriots and Bastille Heroes; for the Red Nightcap combines all the three properties. Nay, cockades themselves begin to be made of wool, of tricolor yarn: the riband-cockade, as a symptom of Feuillant Upper-class temper, is becoming suspicious. Signs of the times.

Still more, note the travail-throes of Europe: or rather, note the birth she brings; for the successive throes and shrieks, of Austrian and Prussian Alliance, of Kaunitz Anti-Jacobin Despatch, of French Ambassadors cast out, and so forth, were long to note. Dumouriez corresponds with Kaunitz, Metternich, or Cobentzel, in another style than Delessarts did. Strict becomes stricter; categorical answer, as to this Coblentz work and much else, shall be given. Failing which? Failing which, on the 20th day of April 1792, King and Ministers step over to the Salle de Manége; promulgate how the matter stands; and poor Louis, "with tears in his eyes," proposes that the Assembly do now decree War. After due eloquence, War is decreed that night.

War, indeed! Paris came all crowding, full of expectancy, to the morning, and still more to the evening, session. D'Orléans with his two sons is there; looks on, wide-eyed, from the opposite gallery.[3] Thou canst look, O Philippe: it is a War big with issues, for thee and for all men. Cimmerian Obscurantism and this thrice-glorious Revolution shall wrestle for it, then: some Four-and-Twenty years; in immeasurable Briareus wrestle; trampling and tearing; before they can come to any, not agreement, but compromise, and approximate ascertainment each of what is in the other.

Let our Three Generals on the Frontiers look to it, therefore; and poor Chevalier de Grave, the War-Minister, consider what he will do. What is in the three Generals and Armies we may guess. As for poor Chevalier de Grave, he, in this whirl of things all coming to a press and pinch upon him, loses head, and merely whirls with them, in a totally distracted manner; signing himself at last, " De Grave, Mayor of Paris "; whereupon he demits, returns over the Channel, to walk in Kensington Gardens;[4] and austere Servan, the able Engineer-Officer, is elevated in his stead. To the post of Honour? To that of Difficulty, at least.

NOTES

[1] Dumont, c. 20, 21.
[2] Madame Roland, ii, 80–115.
[3] " Deux Amis," vii, 146–166.
[4] Dumont, c. 19, 21.

CHAPTER X

PÉTION-NATIONAL-PIQUE

AND yet, how, on dark bottomless Cataracts there plays the foolishest fantastic-coloured spray and shadow; hiding the Abyss under vapoury rainbows! Alongside of this discussion as to Austrian-Prussian War, there goes on not less but more vehemently a discussion, Whether the Forty or Two-and-Forty Swiss of Château-Vieux shall be liberated from the Brest Galleys? And then, Whether, being liberated, they shall have a public Festival, or only private ones?

Théroigne, as we saw, spoke; and Collot took up the tale. Has not Bouillé's final display of himself, in that final Night of Spurs, stamped your so-called " Revolt of Nanci " into a " Massacre of Nanci," for all Patriot judgments? Hateful is that massacre; hateful the Lafayette-Feuillant " public thanks " given for it! For indeed, Jacobin Patriotism and dispersed Feuillantism are now at death-grips; and do fight with all weapons, even with scenic shows. The walls of Paris, accordingly, are covered with Placard and Counter-Placard, on the subject of Forty Swiss blockheads. Journal responds to Journal; Player Collot to Poetaster Roucher; Joseph Chénier the Jacobin, squire of Théroigne, to his Brother André the Feuillant; Mayor Pétion to Dupont de Nemours: and for the space of two months, there is nowhere peace for the thought of man—till this thing be settled.

Gloria in excelsis! The Forty Swiss are at last got " amnestied." Rejoice, ye Forty; doff your greasy wool Bonnets, which shall become Caps of Liberty. The Brest Daughter Society welcomes you from on board, with kisses on each cheek: your iron Handcuffs are disputed as Relics of Saints; the Brest Society indeed can have one portion, which it will beat into Pikes, a sort of Sacred Pikes; but the other portion must belong to Paris, and be suspended from the dome there, along with the Flags of the Three Free Peoples! Such a goose is man; and cackles over plush-velvet Grand Monarques and woollen Galley-slaves; over everything and over nothing— and will cackle with his whole soul, merely if others cackle!

On the ninth morning of April, these Forty Swiss block-heads arrive. From Versailles; with vivats heaven-high; with the affluence of men and women. To the Townhall we con-duct them; nay, to the Legislative itself, though not without difficulty. They are harangued, bedinnered, begifted—the very Court, not for conscience-sake, contributing something; and their Public Festival shall be next Sunday. Next Sunday accordingly it is.[1] They are mounted into a " triumphal Car resembling a ship "; are carted over Paris, with the clang of cymbals and drums, all mortals assisting applausive; carted to the Champ-de-Mars and Fatherland's Altar; and finally carted, for Time always brings deliverance—into invisibility for evermore.

Whereupon dispersed Feuillantism, or that Party which loves Liberty yet not more than Monarchy, will likewise have its Festival: Festival of Simoneau, unfortunate Mayor of Etampes, who died for the Law; most surely for the Law, though Jacobinism disputes; being trampled down with his Red Flag in the riot about grains. At which Festival the Public again assists, unapplausive: not we.

On the whole, Festivals are not wanting; beautiful rainbow-spray when all is now rushing treble-quick toward its Niagara Fall. National Repasts there are; countenanced by Mayor Pétion; Saint-Antoine, and the Strong Ones of the Halles defiling through Jacobin Club, " their felicity," according to Santerre, " not perfect otherwise "; singing many-voiced their " Ça-ira," dancing their ronde patriotique. Among whom one is glad to discern Saint-Huruge, expressly " in white hat," the Saint-Christopher of the Carmagnole. Nay, a certain Tam-bour, or National Drummer, having just been presented with a little daughter, determines to have the new Frenchwoman christened, on Fatherland's Altar, then and there. Repast once over, he accordingly has her christened; Fauchet the Te-Deum Bishop acting in chief, Thuriot and honourable persons stand-ing gossips: by the name, Pétion-National-Pique![2] Does this remarkable Citizeness, now past the meridian of life, still walk the Earth? Or did she die perhaps of teething? Universal History is not indifferent.

NOTES

[1] Newspapers of February, March, April, 1792; "Iambe d'André Chénier sur la Fête des Suisses," etc., etc. (in "Hist. Parl.," xiii, xiv).

[2] "Patriote-Français" (Brissot's Newspaper), in "Hist. Parl.," xiii, 451.

CHAPTER XI

THE HEREDITARY REPRESENTATIVE

AND yet it is not by carmagnole-dances, and singing of
" Ça-ira," that the work can be done. Duke Brunswick
is not dancing carmagnoles, but has his drill-sergeants busy.

On the Frontiers, our Armies, be it treason or not, behave
in the worst way. Troops badly commanded, shall we say?
Or troops intrinsically bad? Unappointed, undisciplined,
mutinous; that, in a thirty-years peace, have never seen fire?
In any case, Lafayette's and Rochambeau's little clutch, which
they made at Austrian Flanders, has prospered as badly as
clutch need do: soldiers starting at their own shadow; suddenly shrieking, " On nous trahit," and flying off in wild
panic, at or before the first shot—managing only to hang
some two or three prisoners they had picked up, and massacre
their own Commander, poor Theobald Dillon, driven into a
granary by them in the Town of Lille.

And poor Gouvion: he who sat shiftless in that Insurrection of Women! Gouvion quitted the Legislative Hall and
Parliamentary duties, in disgust and despair, when those
Galley-slaves of Château-Vieux were admitted there. He said,
" Between the Austrians and the Jacobins there is nothing
but a soldier's death for it ";[1] and so, " in the dark stormy
night," he has flung himself into the throat of the Austrian
cannon, and perished in the skirmish at Maubeuge on the ninth
of June. Whom Legislative Patriotism shall mourn, with
black mort-cloths and melody in the Champ-de-Mars: many a
Patriot shiftier, truer none. Lafayette himself is looking altogether dubious; in place of beating the Austrians, is about
writing to denounce the Jacobins. Rochambeau, all disconsolate, quits the service: there remains only Lückner, the
babbling old Prussian Grenadier.

Without Armies, without Generals! And the Cimmerian Night has gathered itself; Brunswick preparing his proclamation; just about to march! Let a Patriot Ministry and Legislative say, what in these circumstances it will do? Suppress internal enemies, for one thing, answers the Patriot Legislative; and proposes, on the 24th of May, its Decree for the Banishment of Priests. Collect also some nucleus of determined internal friends, adds War-Minister Servan; and proposes, on the 7th of June, his Camp of Twenty-thousand. Twenty-thousand National Volunteers; Five out of each Canton, picked Patriots, for Roland has charge of the Interior: they shall assemble here in Paris; and be for a defence, cunningly devised, against foreign Austrians and domestic Austrian Committee alike. So much can a Patriot Ministry and Legislative do.

Reasonable and cunningly devised as such Camp may, to Servan and Patriotism, appear, it appears not so to Feuillantism; to that Feuillant-Aristocrat Staff of the Paris Guard; a Staff, one would say again, which will need to be dissolved. These men see, in this proposed Camp of Servan's, an offence; and even, as they pretend to say, an insult. Petitions there come, in consequence, from blue Feuillants in epaulettes; ill received. Nay, in the end, there comes one Petition, called " of the Eight-thousand National Guards ": so many names are on it, including women and children. Which famed Petition of the Eight-thousand is indeed received: and the Petitioners, all under arms, are admitted to the honours of the sitting—if honours or even if sitting there be; for the instant their bayonets appear at the one door, the Assembly " adjourns," and begins to flow out at the other.[2]

Also, in these same days, it is lamentable to see how National Guards, escorting Fête-Dieu or Corpus-Christi ceremonial, do collar and smite down any Patriot that does not uncover as the Hostie passes. They clap their bayonets to the breast of Cattle-butcher Legendre, a known Patriot ever since the Bastille days; and threaten to butcher him; though he sat quite respectfully, he says, in his Gig, at a distance of fifty paces, waiting till the thing were by. Nay, orthodox females were shrieking to have down the Lanterne on him.[3]

To such height has Feuillantism gone in this Corps. For indeed, are not their Officers creatures of the chief Feuillant,

Lafayette? The Court too has, very naturally, been tamper-
ing with them; caressing them, ever since that dissolution of
the so-called Constitutional Guard. Some Battalions are altogether " pétris, kneaded full " of Feuillantism, mere Aristocrats at bottom: for instance, the Battalion of the Filles-Saint-
Thomas, made up of your Bankers, Stockbrokers, and other
Full-purses of the Rue Vivienne. Our worthy old Friend
Weber, Queen's Foster-brother Weber, carries a musket in
that Battalion—one may judge with what degree of Patriotic
intention.

Heedless of all which, or rather heedful of all which, the
Legislative, backed by Patriot France and the feeling of
Necessity, decrees this Camp of Twenty-thousand. Decisive
though conditional Banishment of malign Priests it has already decreed.

It will now be seen, therefore, Whether the Hereditary
Representative is for us or against us? Whether or not, to
all our other woes, this intolerablest one is to be added; which
renders us not a menaced Nation in extreme jeopardy and
need, but a paralytic Solecism of a Nation; sitting wrapped
as in dead cerements, of a Constitutional-Vesture that were
no other than a winding-sheet; our right hand glued to our
left: to wait there, writhing and wriggling, unable to stir from
the spot, till in Prussian rope we mount to the gallows? Let
the Hereditary Representative consider it well: The Decree
of Priests? The Camp of Twenty-thousand?—By Heaven, he
answers, Veto! Veto!—Strict Roland hands-in his " Letter to
the King "; or rather it was Madame's Letter, who wrote it
all at a sitting; one of the plainest-spoken Letters ever handed-
in to any King. This plain-spoken Letter King Louis has
the benefit of reading overnight. He reads, inwardly digests;
and next morning, the whole Patriot Ministry finds itself
turned out. It is the 13th of June 1792.[4]

Dumouriez the many-counselled, he, with one Duranthon
called Minister of Justice, does indeed linger for a day or two;
in rather suspicious circumstances; speaks with the Queen,
almost weeps with her: but in the end, he too sets off for the
Army; leaving what Un-Patriot or Semi-Patriot Ministry and
Ministries can now accept the helm, to accept it. Name them
not; new quick-changing Phantasms, which shift like magic-
lantern figures; more spectral than ever!

Unhappy Queen, unhappy Louis! The two Vetos were so natural: are not the Priests martyrs; also friends? This Camp of Twenty-thousand, could it be other than of stormfulest Sansculottes? Natural; and yet, to France, unendurable. Priests that co-operate with Coblentz must go elsewhither with their martyrdom: stormful Sansculottes, these and no other kind of creatures will drive back the Austrians. If thou prefer the Austrians, then, for the love of Heaven, go join them. If not, join frankly with what will oppose them to the death. Middle course is none.

Or, alas! what extreme course was there left now for a man like Louis? Underhand Royalists, Ex-Minister Bertrand-Moleville, Ex-Constituent Malouet, and all manner of unhelpful individuals, advise and advise. With face of hope turned now on the Legislative Assembly, and now on Austria and Coblentz, and round generally on the Chapter of Chances, an ancient Kingship is reeling and spinning, one knows not whitherward, on the flood of things.

NOTES

[1] Toulongeon, ii, 149.
[2] " Moniteur," Séance du 10 Juin, 1792.
[3] " Débats des Jacobins " (in " Hist. Parl.," xiv, 429).
[4] Madame Roland, ii, 115.

CHAPTER XII

PROCESSION OF THE BLACK BREECHES

BUT is there a thinking man in France who, in these circumstances, can persuade himself that the Constitution will march? Brunswick is stirring; he, in few days now, will march. Shall France sit still, wrapped in dead cerements and grave-clothes, its right hand glued to its left, till the Brunswick Saint-Bartholomew arrive; till France be as Poland, and its Rights of Man become a Prussian Gibbet?

Verily it is a moment frightful for all men. National Death; or else some preternatural convulsive outburst of National Life—that same dæmonic outburst! Patriots whose audacity has limits had, in truth, better retire like Barnave; court private felicity at Grenoble. Patriots whose audacity has no limits must sink down into the obscure; and, daring and defying all things, seek salvation in stratagem, in Plot of Insurrection. Roland and young Barbaroux have spread out the Map of France before them, Barbaroux says " with tears ": they consider what Rivers, what Mountain-ranges are in it: they will retire behind this Loire-stream, defend these Auvergne stone-labyrinths; save some little sacred Territory of the Free; die at least in their last ditch. Lafayette indites his emphatic Letter to the Legislative against Jacobinism; [1] which emphatic Letter will not heal the unhealable.

Forward, ye Patriots whose audacity has no limits; it is you now that must either do or die! The Sections of Paris sit in deep counsel; send out Deputation after Deputation to the Salle de Manége, to petition and denounce. Great is their ire against tyrannous Veto, Austrian Committee, and the combined Cimmerian Kings. What boots it? Legislative listens to the " tocsin in our hearts "; grants us honours of the sitting, sees us defile with jingle and fanfaronade; but the Camp of Twenty-thousand, the Priest-Decree, be-vetoed by Majesty,

are become impossible for Legislative. Fiery Isnard says,
" We will have Equality, should we descend for it to the tomb."
Vergniaud utters, hypothetically, his stern Ezekiel-visions of
the fate of Anti-national Kings. But the question is: Will
hypothetic prophecies, will jingle and fanfaronade demolish
the Veto; or will the Veto, secure in its Tuileries Château,
remain undemolishable by these? Barbaroux, dashing away
his tears, writes to the Marseilles Municipality, that they must
send him " Six hundred men who know how to die, qui savent
mourir." [2] No wet-eyed message this, but a fire-eyed one—
which will be obeyed!

Meanwhile the Twentieth of June is nigh, anniversary of
that world-famous Oath of the Tennis-Court: on which day,
it is said, certain citizens have in view to plant a Mai or Tree
of Liberty in the Tuileries Terrace of the Feuillants; perhaps
also to petition the Legislative and Hereditary Representative
about these Vetos—with such demonstration, jingle and evo-
lution, as may seem profitable and practicable. Sections have
gone singly, and jingled and evolved: but if they all went,
or great part of them, and there, planting their Mai in these
alarming circumstances, sounded the tocsin in their hearts?

Among King's Friends there can be but one opinion as to
such a step: among Nation's Friends there may be two. On
the one hand, might it not by possibility scare away these
unblessed Vetos? Private Patriots and even Legislative Deputies may have each his own opinion, or own no-opinion: but
the hardest task falls evidently on Mayor Pétion and the Municipals, at once Patriots and Guardians of the public Tranquil-
lity. Hushing the matter down with the one hand; tickling it
up with the other! Mayor Pétion and Municipality may lean
this way; Department-Directory with Procureur-Syndic Rœderer, having a Feuillant tendency, may lean that. On the
whole, each man must act according to his one opinion or to
his two opinions, and all manner of influences, official repre-
sentations cross one another in the foolishest way. Perhaps
after all, the Project, desirable and yet not desirable, will dissipate itself, being run athwart by so many complexities; and
come to nothing?

Not so; on the Twentieth morning of June, a large Tree
of Liberty, Lombardy Poplar by kind, lies visibly tied on its
car, in the Suburb Saint-Antoine. Suburb Saint-Marceau too,

in the uttermost Southeast, and all that remote Oriental region, Pikemen and Pikewomen, National Guards, and the unarmed curious are gathering—with the peaceablest intentions in the world. A tricolor Municipal arrives; speaks. Tush, it is all peaceable, we tell thee, in the way of Law: are not Petitions allowable, and the Patriotism of Mais? The tricolor Municipal returns without effect: your Sansculottic rills continue flowing, combining into brooks: toward noontide, led by tall Santerre in blue uniform, by tall Saint-Huruge in white hat, it moves westward, a respectable river, or complication of still-swelling rivers.

What Processions have we not seen: Corpus-Christi and Legendre waiting in his Gig; Bones of Voltaire with bullock chariots, and goadsmen in Roman Costume; Feasts of Château-Vieux and Simoneau; Gouvion Funerals, Rousseau Sham funeral, and the Baptism of Pétion-National-Pike! Nevertheless this Procession has a character of its own. Tricolor ribands streaming aloft from Pike-heads; ironshod batons; and emblems not a few; among which see specially these two, of the tragic and the untragic sort: a Bull's Heart transfixed with iron, bearing this epigraph, " Cœur d'Aristocrate, Aristocrat's heart "; and, more striking still, properly the standard of the host, a pair of old Black Breeches (silk, they say), extended on cross-staff, high overhead, with these memorable words: " Tremblez, tyrans; voilà les Sansculottes, Tremble, tyrants; here are the Sans-indispensables!" Also, the Procession trails two cannons.

Scarfed tricolor Municipals do now again meet it, in the Quai Saint-Bernard, and plead earnestly, having called halt. Peaceable, ye virtuous tricolor Municipals, peaceable are we as the sucking dove. Behold our Tennis-Court Mai. Petition is legal; and as for arms, did not an august Legislative receive the so-called Eight-thousand in arms, Feuillants though they were? Our Pikes, are they not of National iron? Law is our father and mother, whom we will not dishonour; but Patriotism is our own soul. Peaceable, ye virtuous Municipals—and on the whole, limited as to time! Stop we can not; march ye with us.—The Black Breeches agitate themselves, impatient; the cannon-wheels grumble: the many-footed Host tramps on.

How it reached the Salle de Manége, like an ever-waxing

river; got admittance after debate; read its Address; and de-
filed, dancing and ça-ira-ing, led by tall sonorous Santerre and
tall sonorous Saint-Huruge: how it flowed, not now a waxing
river but a shut Caspian lake, round all Precincts of the
Tuileries; the front Patriot squeezed by the rearward against
barred iron Grates, like to have the life squeezed out of him,
and looking too into the dread throat of cannon, for National
Battalions stand ranked within: how tricolor Municipals ran
assiduous, and Royalists with Tickets of Entry; and both
Majesties sat in the interior surrounded by men in black: all
this the human mind shall fancy for itself, or read in old Newspapers, and Syndic Rœderer's " Chronicle of Fifty Days." [3]

Our Mai is planted; if not in the Feuillants Terrace,
whither is no ingate, then in the Garden of the Capuchins, as
near as we could get. National Assembly has adjourned till
the Evening Session: perhaps this shut lake, finding no ingate,
will retire to its sources again; and disappear in peace? Alas!
not yet: rearward still presses on; rearward knows little what
pressure is in the front. One would wish, at all events, were
it possible, to have a word with his Majesty first!

The shadows fall longer, eastward; it is four o'clock: will
his Majesty not come out? Hardly he! In that case, Commandant Santerre, Cattle-butcher Legendre, Patriot Huguenin
with the tocsin in his heart; they, and others of authority, will
enter in. Petition and request to wearied uncertain National
Guard; louder and louder petition; backed by the rattle of
our two cannons! The reluctant Grate opens: endless Sansculottic multitudes flood the stairs; knock at the wooden
guardian of your privacy. Knocks, in such case, grow strokes,
grow smashings: the wooden guardian flies in shivers. And
now ensues a Scene over which the world has long wailed;
and not unjustly; for a sorrier spectacle, of Incongruity fronting Incongruity, and as it were recognising themselves incongruous, and staring stupidly in each other's face, the world
seldom saw.

King Louis, his door being beaten on, opens it; stands
with free bosom; asking, " What do you want?" The Sansculottic flood recoils awestruck; returns however, the rear
pressing on the front, with cries of " Veto! Patriot Ministers!
Remove Veto! "—which things, Louis valiantly answers, this
is not the time to do, nor this the way to ask him to do.

Honour what virtue is in a man. Louis does not want courage; he has even the higher kind called moral-courage; though only the passive-half of that. His few National Grenadiers shuffle back with him, into the embrasure of a window: there he stands, with unimpeachable passivity, amid the shouldering and the braying; a spectacle to men. They hand him a red Cap of Liberty; he sets it quietly on his head, forgets it there. He complains of thirst; half-drunk Rascality offers him a bottle, he drinks of it. "Sire, do not fear," says one of his Grenadiers. "Fear?" answers Louis: "feel then," putting the man's hand on his heart. So stands Majesty in Red woollen Cap; black Sansculottism weltering round him, far and wide, aimless, with inarticulate dissonance, with cries of "Veto! Patriot Ministers"!

For the space of three hours or more The National Assembly is adjourned; tricolor Municipal avail almost nothing: Mayor Pétion tarries absent; Authori y is none. The Queen with her Children and Sister Elizabeth, in tears and terror not for themselves only, are sitting behind barricaded tables and Grenadiers, in an inner room. The Men in black have all wisely disappeared. Blind lake of Sansculottism welters stagnant through the King's Château, for the space of three hours.

Nevertheless all things do end. Vergniaud arrives with Legislative Deputation, the Evening Session having now opened. Mayor Pétion has arrived; is haranguing, "lifted on the shoulders of two Grenadiers." In this uneasy attitude and in others, at various places without and within, Mayor Pétion harangues; many men harangue; finally Commandant Santerre defiles; passes out, with his Sansculottism, by the opposite side of the Château. Passing through the room where the Queen, with an air of dignity and sorrowful resignation, sat among the tables and Grenadiers, a woman offers her too a Red Cap; she holds it in her hand, even puts it on the little Prince Royal. "Madame," said Santerre, "this People loves you more than you think." [4]—About eight o'clock the Royal Family fall into each other's arms amid "torrents of tears." Unhappy Family! Who would not weep for it, were there not a whole world to be wept for?

Thus has the Age of Chivalry gone, and that of Hunger come. Thus does all-needing Sansculottism look in the face of its Roi, Regulator, King or Able-man; and find that he has nothing to give it. Thus do the two Parties, brought face to face after long centuries, stare stupidly at one another, " This verily, am I; but, good Heaven, is that Thou? "—and depart, not knowing what to make of it. And yet, Incongruities having recognised themselves to be incongruous, something must be made of it. The Fates know what.

This is the world-famous Twentieth of June, more worthy to be called the Procession of the Black Breeches. With which, what we had to say of this First French biennial Parliament, and its products and activities, may perhaps fitly enough terminate.

NOTES

[1] " Moniteur," Séance du 18 Juin, 1792.
[2] Barbaroux, p. 40.
[3] Rœderer, etc., etc. (in " Hist. Parl.," xv, 98–194).
[4] Toulongeon, ii, 173; Campan, ii, c. 20.

Book XIII

THE MARSEILLESE

CHAPTER I

EXECUTIVE THAT DOES NOT ACT

HOW could your paralytic National Executive be put "in action," in any measure, by such a Twentieth of June as this? Quite contrariwise: a large sympathy for Majesty so insulted arises everywhere; expresses itself in Addresses, Petitions, " Petition of the Twenty-thousand inhabitants of Paris," and such-like, among all Constitutional persons; a decided rallying round the throne.

Of which rallying it was though King Louis might have made something. However, he does make nothing of it, or attempt to make; for indeed his views are lifted beyond domestic sympathy and rallying, over to Coblentz mainly. Neither in itself is this same sympathy worth much. It is sympathy of men who believe still that the Constitution can march. Wherefore the old discord and ferment, of Feuillant sympathy for Royalty, and Jacobin sympathy for Fatherland, acting against each other from within; with terror of Coblentz and Brunswick acting from without—this discord and ferment must hold on its course, till a catastrophe do ripen and come. One would think, especially as Brunswick is near marching, such catastrophe can not now be distant. Busy, ye Twenty-five French Millions: ye foreign Potentates, minatory Emigrants, German drill-sergeants; each do what his hand findeth! Thou, O Reader, at such safe distance, wilt see what they make of it among them.

Consider, therefore, this pitiable Twentieth of June as a futility; no catastrophe, rather a catastasis, or heightening. Do not its Black Breeches wave there, in the Historical Imagination, like a melancholy flag of distress; soliciting help, which no mortal can give? Soliciting pity, which thou wert hardhearted not to give freely, to one and all! Other such flags, or what are called Occurrences, and black or bright

561

symbolic Phenomena will flit through the Historical Imagination; these, one after one, let us note, with extreme brevity.

The first phenomenon is that of Lafayette at the Bar of the Assembly; after a week and day. Promptly, on hearing of this scandalous Twentieth of June, Lafayette has quitted his Command on the North Frontier, in better or worse order; and got hither, on the 28th, to repress the Jacobins: not by letter now; but by oral Petition, and weight of character, face to face. The august Assembly finds the step questionable; invites him meanwhile to the honours of the sitting.[1] Other honour, or advantage, there unhappily came almost none; the Galleries all growling; fiery Isnard glooming; sharp Guadet not wanting in sarcasms.

And out of doors, when the sitting is over, Sieur Resson, keeper of the Patriot Café in these regions, hears in the street a hurlyburly; steps forth to look, he and his Patriot customers: it is Lafayette's carriage, with a tumultuous escort of blue Grenadiers, Cannoneers, even Officers of the Line, hurrahing and capering round it. They make a pause opposite Sieur Resson's door; wag their plumes at him; nay, shake their fists, bellowing " A bas les Jacobins! " but happily pass on without onslaught. They pass on, to plant a Mai before the General's door, and bully considerably. All which the Sieur Resson can not but report with sorrow, that night, in the Mother Society.[2] But what no Sieur Resson nor Mother Society can do more than guess is this, That a council of rank Feuillants, your unabolished Staff of the Guard and who else has status and weight, is in these very moments privily deliberating at the General's: Can we not put down the Jacobins by force? Next day, a Review shall be held, in the Tuileries Gardens, of such as will turn out, and try. Alas! says Toulongeon, hardly a hundred turned out. Put it off till tomorrow, then, to give better warning. On the morrow, which is Saturday, there turn out " some thirty "; and depart shrugging their shoulders![3] Lafayette promptly takes carriage again; returns musing on many things.

The dust of Paris is hardly off his wheels, the summer Sunday is still young, when Cordeliers in deputation pluck up that Mai of his: before sunset, Patriots have burned him in effigy. Louder doubt and louder rises, in Section, in National

Assembly, as to the legality of such unbidden Anti-Jacobin visit on the part of a General: doubt swelling and spreading all over France, for six weeks or so; with endless talk about usurping soldiers, about English Monk, nay, about Cromwell: O thou poor Grandison-Cromwell!—What boots it? King Louis himself looked coldly on the enterprise: colossal Hero of two Worlds, having weighed himself in the balance, finds that he is become a gossamer Colossus, only some thirty turning out.

In a like sense, and with a like issue, works our Department-Directory here at Paris; who, on the 6th of July, take upon them to suspend Mayor Pétion and Procureur Manuel from all civic functions, for their conduct, replete, as is alleged, with omissions and commissions, on that delicate Twentieth of June. Virtuous Pétion sees himself a kind of martyr, or pseudo-martyr, threatened with several things; drawls out due heroical lamentation; to which Patriot Paris and Patriot Legislative duly respond. King Louis and Mayor Pétion have already had an interview on that business of the Twentieth; an interview and dialogue, distinguished by frankness on both sides; ending on King Louis's side with the words " Taisez-vous, Hold your peace."

For the rest, this of suspending our Mayor does seem a mistimed measure. By ill chance, it came out precisely on the day of that famous Baiser de l'amourette, or miraculous reconciliatory Delilah-Kiss, which we spoke of long ago. Which Delilah-Kiss was thereby quite hindered of effect. For now his Majesty has to write, almost that same night, asking a reconciled Assembly for advice! The reconciled Assembly will not advise; will not interfere. The King confirms the suspension; then perhaps, but not till then, will the Assembly interfere, the noise of Patriot Paris getting loud. Whereby your Delilah-Kiss, such was the destiny of Parliament First, becomes a Philistine Battle!

Nay, there goes a word that as many as Thirty of our chief Patriot Senators are to be clapped in prison, by mittimus and indictment of Feuillant Justices, Juges de Paix; who here in Paris were well capable of such a thing. It was but in May last that Juge-de-Paix Larivière, on complaint of Bertrand-Moleville touching that Austrian Committee, made bold to

launch his mittimus against three heads of the Mountain,
Deputies Bazire, Chabot, Merlin, the Cordelier Trio; summoning them to appear before him, and show where that
Austrian Committee was, or else suffer the consequences.
Which mittimus the Trio, on their side, made bold to fling in
the fire: and valiantly pleaded privilege of Parliament. So
that, for his zeal without knowledge, poor Justice Larivière
now sits in the prison of Orléans, waiting trial from the Haute
Cour there. Whose example, may it not deter other rash
Justices; and so this word of the Thirty arrestments continue
a word merely?

But on the whole, though Lafayette weighed so light, and
has had his Mai plucked up, Official Feuillantism falters not
a whit; but carries its head high, strong in the letter of the
Law. Feuillants all of these men; a Feuillant Directory;
founding on high character, and such-like; with Duke de la
Rochefoucault for President—a thing which may prove dangerous for him! Dim now is the once bright Anglomania
of these admired Noblemen. Duke de Liancourt offers, out
of Normandy where he is Lord-Lieutenant, not only to receive
his Majesty, thinking of flight thither, but to lend him money
to enormous amounts. Sire, it is not a Revolt, it is a Revolution; and truly no rose-water one! Worthier Noblemen were
not in France nor in Europe than those two: but the Time
is crooked, quick-shifting, perverse; what straightest course
will lead to any goal, in it?

Another phasis which we note, in these early July days, is
that of certain thin streaks of Federate National Volunteers
wending from various points toward Paris, to hold a new
Federation-Festival, or Feast of Pikes, on the Fourteenth
there. So has the National Assembly wished it, so has the
Nation willed it. In this way, perhaps, may we still have our
Patriot Camp in spite of Veto. For can not these Fédérés,
having celebrated their Feast of Pikes, march on to Soissons;
and, there being drilled and regimented, rush to the Frontiers,
or whither we like? Thus were the one Veto cunningly
eluded!

As indeed the other Veto, about Priests, is also like to be
eluded; and without much cunning. For Provincial Assemblies, in Calvados as one instance, are proceeding, on their

own strength, to judge and banish Antinational Priests. Or
still worse, without Provincial Assembly, a desperate People,
as at Bordeaux, can "hang two of them on the Lanterne," on
the way toward judgment.[4] Pity for the spoken Veto, when
it can not become an acted one!

It is true, some ghost of a War-minister, or Home-minister,
for the time being, ghost whom we do not name, does write
to Municipalities and King's Commanders, that they shall, by
all conceivable methods, obstruct this Federation, and even
turn back the Fédérés by force of arms: a message which
scatters mere doubt, paralysis and confusion; irritates the poor
Legislature; reduces the Fédérés, as we see, to thin streaks.
But being questioned, this ghost and the other ghosts, What
it is then that they propose to do for saving the country?—
they answer, That they can not tell; that indeed they, for
their part, have, this morning, resigned in a body; and do
now merely respectfully take leave of the helm altogether.
With which words they rapidly walk out of the Hall, sortent
brusquement de la salle, the "Galleries cheering loudly," the
poor Legislature sitting "for a good while in silence"![5] Thus
do Cabinet-ministers themselves, in extreme cases, strike work;
one of the strangest omens. Other complete Cabinet-ministry
there will not be; only fragments, and these changeful, which
never get completed; spectral Apparitions that can not so
much as appear! King Louis writes that he now views this
Federation Feast with approval; and will himself have the
pleasure to take part in the same.

And so these thin streaks of Fédérés wend Paris-ward
through a paralytic France. Thin grim streaks; not thick
joyful ranks, as of old to the first Feast of Pikes! No: these
poor Federates march now toward Austria and Austrian Committee, toward jeopardy and forlorn hope; men of hard fortune
and temper, not rich in the world's goods. Municipalities,
paralyzed by War-minister, are shy of affording cash; it may
be, your poor Federates can not arm themselves, can not
march, till the Daughter Society of the place open her pocket
and subscribe. There will not have arrived, at the set day,
Three-thousand of them in all. And yet, thin and feeble as
these streaks of Federates seem, they are the only thing one
discerns moving with any clearness of aim in this strange
scene. Angry buzz and simmer; uneasy tossing and moaning

of a huge France, all enchanted, spellbound by unmarching Constitution, into frightful conscious and unconscious Magnetic-sleep; which frightful Magnetic-sleep must now issue soon in one of two things: Death or Madness! The Fédérés carry mostly in their pockets some earnest cry and Petition, to have the "National Executive put in action"; or as a step toward that, to have the King's Déchéance, King's Forfeiture, or at least his Suspension, pronounced. They shall be welcome to the Legislative, to the Mother of Patriotism; and Paris will provide for their lodging.

Déchéance, indeed: and what next? A France spell-free, a Revolution saved; and anything, and all things next! so answer grimly Danton and the unlimited Patriots, down deep in their subterranean region of Plot, whither they have now dived. Déchéance, answers Brissot with the limited: and if next the little Prince Royal were crowned, and some Regency of Girondins and recalled Patriot Ministry set over him? Alas! poor Brissot; looking, as indeed poor man does always, on the nearest morrow as his peaceable promised land; deciding what must reach to the world's end, yet with an insight that reaches not beyond his own nose! Wiser are the unlimited subterranean Patriots, who with light for the hour itself, leave the rest to the gods.

Or were it not, as we now stand, the probablest issue of all, that Brunswick, in Coblentz, just gathering his huge limbs toward him to rise, might arrive first; and stop both Déchéance, and theorizing on it? Brunswick is on the eve of marching; with Eighty-thousand, they say; fell Prussians, Hessians, feller Emigrants: a General of the Great Frederick, with such an Army. And our Armies? And our Generals? As for Lafayette, on whose late visit a Committee is sitting and all France is jarring and censuring, he seems readier to fight us than fight Brunswick. Lückner and Lafayette pretend to be interchanging corps, and are making movements, which Patriotism can not understand. This only is very clear, that their corps go marching and shuttling, in the interior of the country; much nearer Paris than formerly! Lückner has ordered Dumouriez down to him; down from Maulde, and the Fortified Camp there. Which order the many-counselled Dumouriez, with the Austrians hanging close on him, he busy meanwhile training a few thousands to stand fire and be soldiers, declares

that, come of it what will, he can not obey.[6] Will a poor
Legislative, therefore, sanction Dumouriez; who applies to it,
"not knowing whether there is any War-ministry"?   Or
sanction Lückner and these Lafayette movements?

The poor Legislative knows not what to do. It decrees,
however, that the Staff of the Paris Guard, and indeed all
such Staffs, for they are Feuillants mostly, shall be broken
and replaced. It decrees earnestly, in what manner one can
declare, that the Country is in Danger. And finally, on the
11th of July, the morrow of that day when the Ministry struck
work, it decrees that the Country be, with all despatch, declared in Danger. Whereupon let the King sanction; let the
Municipality take measures: if such Declaration will do service, it need not fail.

In Danger truly, if ever Country was! Arise, O Country;
or be trodden down to ignominious ruin! Nay, are not the
chances a hundred to one that no rising of the Country will
save it; Brunswick, the Emigrants, and Feudal Europe drawing nigh?

NOTES

[1] " Moniteur," Séance du 28 Juin, 1792.
[2] " Débats des Jacobins " (" Hist. Parl.," xv, 235).
[3] Toulongeon, ii, 180. See also Dampmartin, ii, 161.
[4] " Hist. Parl.," xvi, 259.
[5] " Moniteur," Séance du Juillet, 1792.
[6] Dumouriez, ii, 1, 5.

CHAPTER II

LET US MARCH

BUT, to our minds, the notablest of all these moving phenomena is that of Barbaroux's "Six-hundred Marseillese who know how to die."

Prompt to the request of Barbaroux, the Marseilles Municipality has got these men together: on the fifth morning of July, the Townhall says, "Marchez, abattez le Tyran, March, strike down the Tyran";[1] and they, with grim appropriate "Marchons," are marching. Long journey, doubtful errand; Enfans de la Patrie, may a good genius guide you! Their own wild heart and what faith it has will guide them: and is not that the monition of some genius, better or worse? Five-hundred and Seventeen able men, with Captains of fifties and tens; well armed all, musket on shoulder, sabre on thigh: nay, they drive three pieces of cannon; for who knows what obstacles may occur? Municipalities there are, paralyzed by War-minister; Commandants with orders to stop even Federation Volunteers: good, when sound arguments will not open a Towngate, if you have a petard to shiver it! They have left their sunny Phocean City and Seahaven, with its bustle and its bloom: the thronging Course, with high-frondent Avenues, pitchy dockyards, almond and olive groves, orange-trees on house-tops, and white glittering bastides that crown the hills, are all behind them. They wend on their wild way, from the extremity of French land, through unknown cities, toward an unknown destiny; with a purpose that they know.

Much wondering at this phenomenon, and how, in a peaceable trading City, so many householders or hearthholders do severally fling down their crafts and industrial tools; gird themselves with weapons of war, and set out on a journey of six hundred miles, to "strike down the tyrant"—you search in all Historical Books, Pamphlets and Newspapers, for some

568

light on it: unhappily without effect. Rumour and Terror
precede this march; which still echo on you; the march itself
an unknown thing. Weber, in the back-stairs of the Tuileries,
has understood that they were Forçats, Galley-slaves and mere
scoundrels, these Marseillese; that, as they marched through
Lyons, the people shut their shops—also that the number of
them was some Four Thousand. Equally vague is Blanc
Gilli, who likewise murmurs about Forçats and danger of
plunder.[2] Forçats they were not; neither was there plunder
or danger of it. Men of regular life, or of the best-filled
purse, they could hardly be; the one thing needful in them
was that they " knew how to die." Friend Dampmartin saw
them, with his own eyes, march " gradually " through his
quarters at Villefranche in the Beaujolais: but saw in the
vaguest manner; being indeed preoccupied, and himself
minded for marching just then—across the Rhine. Deep was
his astonishment to think of such a march, without appointment or arrangement, station or ration; for the rest, it was
" the same men he had seen formerly " in the troubles of the
South; " perfectly civil "; though his soldiers could not be
kept from talking a little with them.[3]

So vague are all these; " Moniteur," " Histoire Parlementaire " are as good as silent: garrulous History, as is too
usual, will say nothing where you most wish her to speak!
If enlightened Curiosity ever get sight of the Marseilles Coun-
cil-Books, will it not perhaps explore this strangest of Municipal procedures; and feel called to fish-up what of the Biog-
raphies, creditable or discreditable, of these Five-hundred and
Seventeen, the stream of Time has not yet irrevocably swallowed?

As it is, these Marseillese remain inarticulate, undistin-
guishable in feature; a black-browed Mass, full of grim fire,
who wend there, in the hot sultry weather: very singular to contemplate. They wend; amid the infinitude of doubt and dim
peril; they not doubtful: Fate and Feudal Europe, having
decided, come girdling in from without; they, having also
decided, to march within. Dusty of face, with frugal refreshment, they plod onward; unweariable, not to be turned aside.
Such march will become famous. The Thought, which works
voiceless in this black-browed mass, an inspired Tyrtæan
Colonel, Rouget de Lille, whom the Earth still holds,[4] has

38

translated into grim melody and rhythm; into his "Hymn" or "March of the Marseillese": luckiest musical-composition ever promulgated. The sound of which will make the blood tingle in men's veins; and whole Armies and Assemblages will sing it, with eyes weeping and burning, with hearts defiant of Death, Despot and Devil.

One sees well, these Marseillese will be too late for the Federation Feast. In fact, it is not Champ-de-Mars Oaths that they have in view. They have quite another feat to do: a paralytic National Executive to set in action. They must "strike down" whatsoever "Tyrant," or Martyr-Fainéant, there may be who paralyzes it; strike and be struck; and on the whole prosper, and know how to die.

NOTES

[1] Dampmartin, ii, 183.

[2] See Barbaroux, "Mémoires" (Note in pp. 40, 41).

[3] Dampmartin, ubi suprà.—As to Dampmartin himself and what became of him further, see "Mémoires de la Comtesse de Lichtenau," écrits par elle-même; traduits de l'Allemand (à Londres, 1809), i, 200–207; ii, 78–91.

[4] A. D. 1836.

CHAPTER III

SOME CONSOLATION TO MANKIND

OF the Federation Feast itself we shall say almost nothing. There are Tents pitched in the Champ-de-Mars; tent for National Assembly; tent for Hereditary Representative—who indeed is there too early, and has to wait long in it. There are Eighty-three symbolic Departmental Trees-of-Liberty; trees and mais enough: beautifulest of all, there is one huge mai, hung round with effete Scutcheons, Emblazonries and Genealogy-books, nay, better still, with Lawyers'-bags, "sacs de procédure"; which shall be burnt. The Thirty seat-rows of that famed Slope are again full; we have a bright Sun; and all is marching, streamering and blaring: but what avails it? Virtuous Mayor Pétion, whom Feuillantism had suspended, was reinstated only last night, by Decree of the Assembly. Men's humour is of the sourest. Men's hats have on them, written in chalk, "Vive Pétion"; and even, "Pétion or Death, Pétion ou la Mort."

Poor Louis, who has waited till five o'clock before the Assembly would arrive, swears the National Oath this time, with a quilted cuirass under his waistcoat which will turn pistol-bullets.[1] Madame de Staël, from that Royal Tent, stretches out the neck in a kind of agony, lest the waving multitude which received him may not render him back alive. No cry of "Vive le Roi!" salutes the ear; cries only of "Vive Pétion; Pétion ou la Mort!" The National Solemnity is as it were huddled by; each cowering off almost before the evolutions are gone through. The very Mai with its Scutcheons and Lawyers'-bags is forgotten, stands unburnt; till "certain Patriot Deputies," called by the people, set a torch to it, by way of voluntary after-piece. Sadder Feast of Pikes no man ever saw.

Mayor Pétion, named on hats, is at his zenith in this Federation: Lafayette again is close upon his nadir. Why does the storm-bell of Saint-Roch speak out, next Saturday; why do the citizens shut their shops? [2] It is Sections defiling, it is fear of effervescence. Legislative Committee, long deliberating on Lafayette and that Anti-Jacobin visit of his, reports, this day, that there is "not ground for Accusation!" Peace, ye Patriots, nevertheless; and let that tocsin cease: the Debate is not finished, nor the Report accepted; but Brissot, Isnard and the Mountain will sift it, and resift it, perhaps for some three weeks longer.

So many bells, storm-bells and noises do ring—scarcely audible; one drowning the other. For example: in this same Lafayette tocsin, of Saturday, was there not withal some faint bob-minor, and Deputation of Legislative, ringing the Chevalier Paul Jones to his long rest; tocsin or dirge now all one to him! Not ten days hence Patriot Brissot, beshouted this day by the Patriot Galleries, shall find himself begroaned by them, on account of his limited Patriotism; nay, pelted at while perorating, and "hit with two prunes." [3] It is a distracted empty-sounding world; of bob-minors and bob-majors, of triumph and terror, of rise and fall!

The more touching is this other Solemnity, which happens on the morrow of the Lafayette tocsin: Proclamation that the Country is in Danger. Not till the present Sunday could such Solemnity be. The Legislative decreed it almost a fortnight ago; but Royalty and the ghost of a Ministry held back as they could. Now, however, on this Sunday, 22d day of July 1792, it will hold back no longer; and the Solemnity in very deed is. Touching to behold! Municipality and Mayor have on their scarfs; cannon-salvo booms alarm from the Pont-Neuf, and single-gun at intervals all day. Guards are mounted, scarfed Notabilities, Halberdiers, and a Cavalcade; with streamers, emblematic flags; especially with one huge Flag, flapping mournfully: "Citoyens, la Patrie est en Danger!" They roll through the streets, with stern-sounding music, and slow rattle of hoofs; pausing at set stations, and with doleful blast of trumpet singing out through Herald's throat, what the Flag says to the eye: "Citizens, our Country is in Danger!"

Is there a man's heart that hears it without a thrill? The many-voiced responsive hum or bellow of these multitudes is not of triumph; and yet it is a sound deeper than triumph. But when the long Cavalcade and Proclamation ended; and our huge Flag was fixed on the Pont-Neuf, another like it on the Hôtel-de-Ville, to wave there till better days; and each Municipal sat in the centre of his Section, in a Tent raised in some open square, Tents surmounted with flags of " Patrie en Danger! " and topmost of all a Pike and Bonnet Rouge; and, on two drums in front of him, there lay a plank-table, and on this an open Book, and a Clerk sat, like recording-angel, ready to write the lists, or as we say to enlist! O, then, it seems, the very gods might have looked down on it. Young Patriotism, Culottic and Sansculottic, rushes forward emulous: That is my name; name, blood and life is all my country's; why have I nothing more! Youths of short stature weep that they are below size. Old men come forward, a son in each hand. Mothers themselv 3 will grant the son of their travail; send him, though w .th tears. And the multitude bellows " Vive la Patrie! " f.r reverberating. And fire flashes in the eyes of men—and at eventide, your Municipal returns to the Townhall followed by his long train of Volunteer valour; hands-in his List; says proudly, looking round, This is my day's harvest.[4] They will march, on the morrow, to Soissons, small bundle holding all their chattels.

So, with " Vive la Patrie! Vive la Liberté! " stone Paris reverberates like Ocean in his caves; day after day, Municipals enlisting in tricolor Tent; the Flag flapping on Pont-Neuf and Townhall, " Citoyens, la Patrie est en Danger! " Some Ten-thousand fighters, without discipline but full of heart, are on march in few days. The like is doing in every Town of France. —Consider, therefore, whether the Country will want defend-ers, had we but a National Executive? Let the Sections and Primary Assemblies, at any rate, become Permanent! They do become Permanent, and sit continually in Paris, and over France, by Legislative Decree, dated Wednesday the 25th.[5]

Mark contrariwise how, in these very hours, dated the 25th, Brunswick " shakes himself, s'ébranle," in Coblentz; and takes the road! Shakes himself indeed; one spoken word becomes such a shaking. Successive, simultaneous dirl of thirty-thou-sand muskets shouldered; prance and jingle of ten-thousand horsemen, fanfaronading Emigrants in the van; drum, kettle-drum; noise of weeping, swearing; and the immeasurable lumbering clank of baggage-wagons and camp-kettles that groan into motion : all this is Brunswick shaking himself; not without all this does the one man march, " covering a space of forty miles." Still less without his Manifesto, dated, as we say, the 25th; a State-Paper worthy of attention !

By this Document, it would seem great things are in store for France. The universal French People shall now have permission to rally round Brunswick and his Emigrant Seigneurs; tyranny of a Jacobin Faction shall oppress them no more; but they shall return, and find favour with their own good King; who, by Royal Declaration (three years ago) of the Twenty-third of June, said that he would himself make them happy. As for National Assembly, and other Bodies of Men invested with some temporary shadow of authority, they are charged to maintain the King's Cities and Strong Places intact, till Brunswick arrive to take delivery of them. Indeed, quick submission may extenuate many things; but to this end it must be quick. Any National Guard or other unmilitary person found resisting in arms shall be " treated as a traitor "; that is to say, hanged with promptitude. For the rest, if Paris, before Brunswick gets thither, offer any insult to the King; or, for example, suffer a Faction to carry the King away elsewhither; in that case, Paris shall be blasted asunder with cannon-shot and " military execution." Likewise all other Cities, which may witness, and not resist to the uttermost, such forced-march of his Majesty, shall be blasted asunder; and Paris and every City of them, starting-place, course and goal of said sacrilegious forced-march, shall, as rubbish and smoking ruin, lie there for a sign. Such vengeance were indeed signal, " an insigne vengeance."—O Brunswick, what words thou writest and blusterest ! In this Paris, as in old Nineveh, are so many score thousands that know not the right hand from the left, and also much cattle. Shall the very milk-cows, hard-living cadgers'-asses, and poor little canary-birds die ?

Nor is Royal and Imperial Prussian-Austrian Declaration wanting: setting forth, in the amplest manner, their Sanssouci-Schönbrunn version of this whole French Revolution, since the first beginning of it; and with what grief these high heads have seen such things done under the Sun. However, " as some small consolation to mankind," [6] they do now despatch Brunswick; regardless of expense, as one might say, or of sacrifices on their own part; for is it not the first duty to console men?

Serene Highnesses, who sit there protocolling and manifestoing, and consoling mankind! how were it if, for once in the thousand years, your parchments, formularies and reasons of state were blown to the four winds; and Reality Sans-indispensables stared you, even you, in the face; and Mankind said for itself what the thing was that would console it?—

NOTES

[1] Campan, ii, c. 20; De Staël, ii, c. 7.
[2] " Moniteur," Séance du 21 Juillet, 1792.
[3] " Hist. Parl.," xvi, 185.
[4] " Tableau de la Révolution," § Patrie en Danger.
[5] " Moniteur," Séance du 25 Juillet, 1792.
[6] " Annual Register " (1792), p. 236.

CHAPTER IV

SUBTERRANEAN

BUT judge if there was comfort in this to the Sections all sitting permanent; deliberating how a National Executive could be put in action!

High rises the response, not of cackling terror but of crowing counter-defiance, and " Vive la Nation! " young Valour streaming toward the Frontiers; " Patrie en Danger! " mutely beckoning on the Pont-Neuf. Sections are busy, in their permanent Deep; and down, lower still, works unlimited Patriotism, seeking salvation in plot. Insurrection, you would say, becomes once more the sacredest of duties? Committee, self-chosen, is sitting at the Sign of the Golden Sun; Journalist Carra, Camille Desmoulins, Alsatian Westermann friend of Danton, American Fournier of Martinique—a Committee not unknown to Mayor Pétion, who, as an official person, must sleep with one eye open. Not unknown to Procureur Manuel; least of all to Procureur-Substitute Danton! He, wrapped in darkness, being also official, bears it on his giant shoulders; cloudy invisible Atlas of the whole.

Much is invisible; the very Jacobins have their reticences. Insurrection is to be: but when? This only we can discern, that such Fédérés as are not yet gone to Soissons, as indeed are not inclined to go yet, " for reasons," says the Jacobin President, " which it may be interesting not to state," have got a Central Committee sitting close by, under the roof of the Mother Society herself. Also, what in such ferment and danger of effervescence is surely proper, the Forty-eight Sections have got their Central Committee intended " for prompt communication." To which Central Committee the Municipality, anxious to have it at hand, could not refuse an Apartment in the Hôtel-de-Ville.

Singular City! For overhead of all this, there is the cus-

tomary baking and brewing; Labour hammers and grinds.
Frilled promenaders saunter under the trees; white-muslin
promenaderess, in green parasol, leaning on your arm. Dogs
dance, and shoe-blacks polish, on that Pont-Neuf itself, where
Fatherland is in danger. So much goes its course; and yet
the course of all things is nigh altering and ending.

Look at that Tuileries and Tuileries Garden. Silent all as
Sahara; none entering save by ticket! They shut their Gates,
after the day of the Black Breeches; a thing they had the
liberty to do. However the National Assembly grumbled
something about Terrace of the Feuillants, how said Terrace
lay contiguous to the back-entrance to their Salle, and was
partly National Property; and so now National Justice has
stretched a Tricolor Riband athwart it, by way of boundary-
line; respected with splenetic strictness by all Patriots. It
hangs there, that Tricolor boundary-line; carries " satirical
inscriptions on cards," generally in verse; and all beyond this
is called Coblentz, and remains vacant; silent as a fateful
Golgotha; sunshine and umbrage alternating on it in vain.
Fateful Circuit: what hope can dwell in it? Mysterious
Tickets of Entry introduce themselves; speak of Insurrection
very imminent. Rivarol's staff of Genius had better purchase
blunderbusses; Grenadier bonnets, red Swiss uniforms may be
useful. Insurrection will come; but likewise will it not be
met? Staved off, one may hope, till Brunswick arrive?

But consider withal if the Bourne-stones and Portable-
chairs remain silent; if the Herald's College of Bill-Stickers
sleep! Louvet's " Sentinel " warns gratis on all walls; Sulleau
is busy; People's-Friend Marat and King's-Friend Royou
croak and counter-croak. For the man Marat, though long
hidden since that Champ-de-Mars Massacre, is still alive. He
has lain, who knows in what cellars; perhaps in Legendre's;
fed by a steak of Legendre's killing: but, since April, the
bull-frog voice of him sounds again; hoarsest of earthly cries.
For the present, black terror haunts him: O brave Barbaroux,
wilt thou not smuggle me to Marseilles, " disguised as a
jockey "? [1] In Palais Royal and all public places, as we read,
there is sharp activity; private individuals haranguing that
Valour may enlist; haranguing that the Executive may be put
in action. Royalist Journals ought to be solemnly burnt:
argument thereupon; debates, which generally end in single-

stick, coups de cannes.[2] Or think of this: the hour midnight;
place Salle de Manége; august Assembly just adjourning;
" Citizens of both sexes enter in a rush, exclaiming, ' Vengeance; they are poisoning our Brothers ' "—baking brayed-
glass among their bread at Soissons! Vergniaud has to speak
soothing words, How Commissioners are already sent to investigate this brayed-glass, and do what is needful therein—
till the rush of Citizens " makes profound silence "; and goes
home to its bed.

Such is Paris; the heart of a France like to it. Preternatural suspicion, doubt, disquietude, nameless anticipation,
from shore to shore—and those black-browed Marseillese
marching, dusty, unwearied, through the midst of it; not
doubtful they. Marching to the grim music of their hearts,
they consume continually the long road, these three weeks and
more; heralded by Terror and Rumour. The Brest Fédérés
arrive on the 26th; through hurrahing streets. Determined
men are these also, bearing or not bearing the Sacred Pikes
of Château-Vieux; and on the whole decidedly disinclined for
Soissons as yet. Surely the Marseillese Brethren do draw
nigher all days.

NOTES

[1] Barbaroux, p. 60.
[2] Newspapers, Narratives and Documents (" Hist. Parl.," xv, 240;
xvi, 399).

CHAPTER V

AT DINNER

IT was a bright day for Charenton, that 29th of the month, when the Marseillese Brethren actually came in sight. Barbaroux, Santerre and Patriots have gone out to meet the grim Wayfarers. Patriot clasps dusty Patriot to his bosom; there is footwashing and refection: " dinner of twelve-hundred covers at the Blue Dial, Cadran Bleu"; and deep interior consultation, that one wots not of.[1] Consultation indeed which comes to little; for Santerre, with an open purse, with a loud voice, has almost no head. Here, however, we repose this night: on the morrow is public entry into Paris.

Of which public entry the Day-Historians, Diurnalists, or Journalists as they call themselves, have preserved record enough. How Saint-Antoine male and female, and Paris generally, gave brotherly welcome, with bravo and handclapping, in crowded streets; and all passed in the peaceablest manner— except it might be our Marseillese pointed out here and there a riband-cockade, and beckoned that it should be snatched away, and exchanged for a wool one; which was done. How the Mother Society in a body has come as far as the Bastille-ground, to embrace you. How you then wend onward, triumphant, to the Townhall, to be embraced by Mayor Pétion; to put down your muskets in the Barracks of Nouvelle France, not far off—then toward the appointed Tavern in the Champs Elysées, to enjoy a frugal Patriot repast.[2]

Of all which the indignant Tuileries may, by its Tickets of Entry, have warning. Red Swiss look doubly sharp to their Château-Grates—though surely there is no danger? Blue Grenadiers of the Filles-Saint-Thomas Section are on duty there this day: men of Agio, as we have seen; with stuffed purses, riband-cockades; among whom serves Weber. A party of these latter, with Captains, with sundry Feuillant

579

Notabilities, Moreau de Saint-Méry of the three-thousand orders, and others, have been dining, much more respectably, in a Tavern hard by. They have dined, and are now drinking Loyal-Patriotic toasts; while the Marseillese, National-Patriotic merely, are about sitting down to their frugal covers of delf. How it happened remains to this day undemonstrable; but the external fact is, certain of these Filles-Saint-Thomas Grenadiers do issue from their Tavern; perhaps touched, surely not yet muddled with any liquor they have had—issue in the professed intention of testifying to the Marseillese, or to the multitude of Paris Patriots who stroll in these spaces, That they, the Filles-Saint-Thomas men, if well seen into, are not a whit less Patriotic than any other class of men whatever.

It was a rash errand! For how can the strolling multitude credit such a thing; or do other indeed than hoot at it, provoking and provoked?—till Grenadier sabres stir in the scabbard, and thereupon a sharp shriek rises: " À nous, Marseillais, Help, Marseillese! " Quick as lightning, for the frugal repast is not yet served, that Marseillese Tavern flings itself open: by door, by window; running, bounding, vault forth the Five-hundred and Seventeen undined Patriots; and, sabre flashing from thigh, are on the scene of controversy. Will ye parley, ye Grenadier Captains and Official Persons; " with faces grown suddenly pale," the Deponents say?[3] Advisabler were instant moderately swift retreat! The Filles-Saint-Thomas men retreat, back foremost; then, alas! face foremost, at treble-quick time; the Marseillese, according to a Deponent, " clearing the fences and ditches after them, like lions: Messieurs, it was an imposing spectacle."

Thus they retreat, the Marseillese following. Swift and swifter, toward the Tuileries: where the Drawbridge receives the bulk of the fugitives; and, then suddenly drawn up, saves them; or else the green mud of the Ditch does it. The bulk of them; not all; ah, no! Moreau de Saint-Méry, for example, being too fat, could not fly fast; he got a stroke, flat-stroke only, over the shoulder-blades, and fell prone—and disappears there from the History of the Revolution. Cuts also there were, pricks in the posterior fleshy parts; much rending of skirts, and other discrepant waste. But poor Sublieutenant Duhamel, innocent Change-broker, what a lot for him! He turned on his pursuer, or pursuers, with a pistol; he fired and missed; drew a second pistol, and again fired and missed; then ran: unhappily in vain. In the Rue Saint-Florentin, they clutched him; thrust him through, in red rage: that was the end of the New Era, and of all Eras, to poor Duhamel.

Pacific readers can fancy what sort of grace-before-meat this was to frugal Patriotism. Also how the Battalion of the Filles-Saint-Thomas " drew out in arms," luckily without further result; how there was accusation at the Bar of the Assembly, and counter-accusation and defence; Marseillese challenging the sentence of a free jury-court—which never got empanneled. We ask rather, What the upshot of all these distracted wildly-accumulating things may, by probability, be? Some upshot; and the time draws nigh! Busy are Central Committees, of Fédérés at the Jacobins Church, of Sections at the Townhall; Reunion of Carra, Camille and Company at the Golden Sun. Busy; like submarine deities, or call them mud-gods, working there in deep murk of waters; till the thing be ready.

And how your National Assembly, like a ship water-logged, helmless, lies tumbling; the Galleries, of shrill Women, of Fédérés with sabres, bellowing down on it, not unfrightful— and waits where the waves of chance may please to strand it; suspicious, nay, on the Left-side, conscious, what submarine Explosion is meanwhile a-charging! Petition for King's Forfeiture rises often there: Petition from Paris Section, from Provincial Patriot Towns; " from Alençon, Briançon, and the Traders at the Fair of Beaucaire." Or what of these? On the 3d of August, Mayor Pétion and the Municipality come petitioning for Forfeiture: they openly, in their tricolor Municipal scarfs. Forfeiture is what all Patriots now want and expect. All Brissotins want Forfeiture; with the little Prince Royal for King, and us for Protector over him. Emphatic Fédérés ask the Legislature: " Can you save us, or not?" Forty-seven Sections have agreed to Forfeiture; only that of the Filles-Saint-Thomas pretending to disagree. Nay, Section Mauconseil declares Forfeiture to be, properly speaking, come; Mauconseil, for one, " does from this day," the last of July, " cease allegiance to Louis," and take minute of the same before all men. A thing blamed aloud; but which will be praised aloud; and the name of " Mauconseil," of Ill-counsel, be thenceforth changed to " Bonconseil," of Good-counsel.

President Danton, in the Cordeliers Section, does another thing: invites all Passive Citizens to take place among the Active in Section-business, one peril threatening all. Thus he, though an official person; cloudy Atlas of the whole. Likewise he manages to have that black-browed Battalion of Marseillese shifted to new Barracks, in his own region of the remote Southeast. Sleek Chaumette, cruel Billaud, Deputy Chabot the Disfrocked, Huguenin with the tocsin in his heart, will welcome them there. Wherefore again and again, " O Legislators, can you save us or not? " Poor Legislators; with their Legislature water-logged, volcanic Explosion charging under it! Forfeiture shall be debated on the ninth of August; that miserable business of Lafayette may be expected to terminate on the eighth.

Or will the humane Reader glance into the Levee-day of Sunday the fifth? The last Levee! Not for a long time, " never," says Bertrand-Moleville, had a Levee been so brilliant, at least so crowded. A sad presaging interest sat on every face; Bertrand's own eyes were filled with tears. For indeed, outside of that Tricolor Riband on the Feuillants Terrace, Legislature is debating, Sections are defiling, all Paris is astir this very Sunday, demanding Déchéance.[4] Here, however, within the riband, a grand proposal is on foot, for the hundredth time, of carrying his Majesty to Rouen and the Castle of Gaillon. Swiss at Courbevoye are in readiness; much is ready; Majesty himself seems almost ready. Nevertheless, for the hundredth time, Majesty, when near the point of action, draws back; writes, after one has waited, palpitating, an endless summer day, that " he has reason to believe the Insurrection is not so ripe as you suppose." Whereat Bertrand-Moleville breaks forth " into extremity at once of spleen and despair, d'humeur et de désespoir." [5]

NOTES

[1] " Deux Amis," viii, 90–101.
[2] " Hist. Parl.," xvi, 196. See Barbaroux, pp. 51–55.
[3] " Moniteur," Séances du 30, du 31 Juillet, 1792 (" Hist. Parl.," xvi, 197–210).
[4] " Hist. Parl.," xvi, 337–339.
[5] Bertrand-Moleville, " Mémoires," ii, 129.

CHAPTER VI

THE STEEPLES AT MIDNIGHT

FOR, in truth, the Insurrection is just about ripe. Thursday is the ninth of the month August: if Forfeiture be not pronounced by the Legislature that day, we must pronounce it ourselves.

Legislature? A poor water-logged Legislature can pronounce nothing. On Wednesday the eighth, after endless oratory once again, they can not even pronounce Accusation against Lafayette; but absolve him—hear it, Patriotism!—by a majority of two to one. Patriotism hears it; Patriotism, hounded-on by Prussian Terror, by Preternatural Suspicion, roars tumultuous round the Salle de Manége, all day; insults many leading Deputies, of the absolvent Right-side; nay, chases them, collars them with loud menace: Deputy Vaublanc, and others of the like, are glad to take refuge in Guard-houses, and escape by the back window. And so, next day, there is infinite complaint; Letter after Letter from insulted Deputy; mere complaint, debate and self-cancelling jargon: the sun of Thursday sets like the others, and no Forfeiture pronounced. Wherefore in fine, To your tents, O Israel!

The Mother Society ceases speaking; groups cease haranguing: Patriots, with closed lips now, " take one another's arm "; walk off, in rows, two and two, at a brisk business-pace; and vanish afar in the obscure places of the East.[1] Santerre is ready; or we will make him ready. Forty-seven of the Forty-eight Sections are ready; nay, Filles-Saint-Thomas itself turns up the Jacobin side of it, turns down the Feuillant side of it, and is ready too. Let the unlimited Patriot look to his weapon, be it pike, be it firelock; and the Brest brethren—above all, the black-browed Marseillese, prepare themselves for the extreme hour! Syndic Rœderer knows,

and laments or not as the issue may turn, that " five-thousand
ball-cartridges, within these few days, have been distributed
to Fédérés, at the Hôtel-de-Ville." [2]

And ye likewise, gallant gentlemen, defenders of Royalty,
crowd ye on your side to the Tuileries. Not to a Levee: no,
to a Couchée; where much will be put to bed. Your Tickets
of Entry are needful; needfuler your blunderbusses!—They
come and crowd, like gallant men who also know how to die:
old Maillé the Camp-Marshal has come, his eyes gleaming
once again, though dimmed by the rheum of almost fourscore
years. Courage, Brothers! We have a thousand red Swiss;
men stanch of heart, steadfast as the granite of their Alps.
National Grenadiers are at least friends of Order; Commandant Mandat breathes loyal ardour, will " answer for it on his
head." Mandat will, and his Staff; for the Staff, though there
stands a doom and Decree to that effect, is happily never yet
dissolved.

Commandant Mandat has corresponded with Mayor Pétion; carries a written Order from him these three days, to
repel force by force. A squadron on the Pont-Neuf with
cannon shall turn back these Marseillese coming across the
River: a squadron at the Townhall shall cut Saint-Antoine
in two, " as it issues from the Arcade Saint-Jean "; drive one-
half back to the obscure East, drive the other half forward
" through the Wickets of the Louvre." Squadrons not a few,
and mounted squadrons; squadrons in the Palais Royal, in the
Place Vendôme: all these shall charge, at the right moment;
sweep this street, and then sweep that. Some new Twentieth
of June we shall have; only still more ineffectual? Or probably the Insurrection will not dare to rise at all? Mandat's
Squadrons, Horse-gendarmerie and blue Guards march, clattering, tramping; Mandat's Cannoneers rumble. Under cloud
of night; to the sound of his générale, which begins drumming when men should go to bed. It is the 9th night of
August 1792.

On the other hand, the Forty-eight Sections correspond by
swift messengers; are choosing each their " three Delegates
with full powers." Syndic Rœderer, Mayor Pétion are sent
for to the Tuileries: courageous Legislators, when the drum
beats danger, should repair to their Salle. Demoiselle Théroigne has on her grenadier-bonnet, short-skirted riding-habit;

two pistols garnish her small waist, and sabre hangs in baldric by her side.

Such a game is playing in this Paris Pandemonium, or City of All the Devils!—And yet the Night, as Mayor Pétion walks here in the Tuileries Garden, "is beautiful and calm"; Orion and the Pleiades glitter down quite serene. Pétion has come forth, the "heat" inside was so oppressive.[3] Indeed, his Majesty's reception of him was of the roughest; as it well might be. And now there is no outgate; Mandat's blue Squadrons turn you back at every Grate; nay, the Filles-Saint-Thomas Grenadiers give themselves liberties of tongue, How a virtuous Mayor "shall pay for it, if there be mischief," and the like; though others again are full of civility. Surely if any man in France is in straits this night, it is Mayor Pétion: bound, under pain of death, one may say, to smile dexterously with the one side of his face, and weep with the other—death if he do it not dexterously enough! Not till four in the morning does a National Assembly, hearing of his plight, summon him over "to give account of Paris"; of which he knows nothing: whereby, however, he shall get home to bed, and only his gilt coach be left. Scarcely less delicate is Syndic Rœderer's task; who must wait, whether he will lament or not, till he see the issue. Janus Bifrons, or Mr. Facing-both-ways, as vernacular Bunyan has it! They walk there, in the meanwhile, these two Januses, with others of the like double conformation; and "talk of indifferent matters."

Rœderer, from time to time, steps in; to listen, to speak; to send for the Department-Directory itself, he their Procureur Syndic not seeing how to act. The Apartments are all crowded; some seven-hundred gentlemen in black elbowing, bustling; red Swiss standing like rocks; ghost, or partial-ghost of a Ministry, with Rœderer and advisers, hovering round their Majesties; old Marshal Maillé kneeling at the King's feet to say, He and these gallant gentlemen are come to die for him. List! through the placid midnight; clang of the distant stormbell! So, in very sooth: steeple after steeple takes up the wondrous tale. Black Courtiers listen at the windows, opened for air; discriminate the steeple-bells:[4] this is the tocsin of Saint-Roch; that again, is it not Saint-Jacques, named de la Boucherie? Yes, Messieurs! Or even

39

Saint-Germain l'Auxerrois, hear ye it not? The same metal that rang storm, two hundred and twenty years ago; but by a Majesty's order then; on Saint-Bartholomew's Eve![5]—So go the steeple-bells; which Courtiers can discriminate. Nay, meseems, there is the Townhall itself; we know it by its sound! Yes, Friends, that is the Townhall; discoursing so, to the Night. Miraculously; by miraculous metal-tongue and man's-arm: Marat himself, if you knew it, is pulling at the rope there! Marat is pulling; Robespierre lies deep, invisible for the next forty hours; and some men have heart, and some have as good as none, and not even frenzy will give them any.

What struggling confusion, as the issue slowly draws on; and the doubtful Hour, with pain and blind struggle, brings forth its Certainty, never to be abolished!—The Full-power Delegates, three from each Section, a Hundred and forty-four in all, got gathered at the Townhall, about midnight. Mandat's Squadron, stationed there, did not hinder their entering: are they not the "Central Committee of the Sections" who sit here usually; though in greater number to-night? They are there: presided by Confusion, Irresolution, and the Clack of Tongues. Swift scouts fly; Rumour buzzes, of black Courtiers, red Swiss, of Mandat and his Squadrons that shall charge. Better put off the Insurrection? Yes, put it off. Ha, hark! Saint-Antoine booming out eloquent tocsin, of its own accord! —Friends, no: ye can not put off the Insurrection; but must put it on, and live with it, or die with it.

Swift now, therefore: let these actual Old Municipals, on sight of the Full-powers, and mandate of the Sovereign elective People, lay down their functions; and this New Hundred and Forty-four take them up! Will ye nill ye, worthy Old Municipals, go ye must. Nay, is it not a happiness for many a Municipal that he can wash his hands of such a business; and sit there paralyzed, unaccountable, till the hour do bring forth; or even go home to his night's rest?[6] Two only of the Old, or at most three, we retain: Mayor Pétion, for the present walking in the Tuileries; Procureur Manuel; Procureur-Substitute Danton, invisible Atlas of the whole. And so, with our Hundred and Forty-four, among whom are a Tocsin-Huguenin, a Billaud, a Chaumette; and Editor-Talliens, and Fabre d'Eglantines, Sergents, Panises; and in brief, either emergent or else emerged and full-blown, the entire Flower of unlimited Patriotism: have we not, as by magic, made a New Municipality; ready to act in the unlimited manner; and declare itself roundly, " in a state of Insurrection! "—First of all, then, be Commandant Mandat sent for, with that Mayor's-Order of his; also let the New Municipals visit those Squadrons that were to charge; and let the stormbell ring its loudest—and, on the whole, " Forward, ye Hundred and Forty-four; retreat is now none for you! "

Reader, fancy not, in thy languid way, that Insurrection is easy.   Insurrection is difficult: each individual uncertain even of his next neighbour; totally uncertain of his distant neighbours, what strength is with him, what strength is against him; certain only that, in case of failure, his individual portion is the gallows!   Eight hundred thousand heads, and in each of them a separate estimate of these uncertainties, a separate theorem of action conformable to that: out of so many uncertainties, does the certainty, and inevitable net-result never to be abolished, go on, at all moments, bodying itself forth—leading thee also toward civic crowns or an ignominious noose.

Could the Reader take an Asmodeus' Flight, and waving open all roofs and privacies, look down from the Tower of Notre-Dame, what a Paris were it!   Of treble-voice whimperings or vehemence, of bass-voice growlings, dubitations; Courage screwing itself to desperate defiance; Cowardice trembling silent within barred doors—and all round, Dulness calmly snoring; for much Dulness, flung on its mattresses, always sleeps.   O, between the clangour of these high-storming tocsins and that snore of Dulness, what a gamut: of trepidation, excitation, desperation; and above it, mere Doubt, Danger, Atropos, and Nox!

Fighters of this Section draw out; hear that the next Section does not; and thereupon draw in.   Saint-Antoine, on this side of the River, is uncertain of Saint-Marceau on that. Steady only is the snore of Dulness, are the Six-hundred Marseillese that know how to die.   Mandat, twice summoned to the Townhall, has not come.   Scouts fly incessant, in distracted haste; and the many-whispering voices of Rumour.   Théroigne and unofficial Patriots flit, dim-visible, exploratory, far and wide; like Night-birds on the wing.   Of Nationals some Three-thousand have followed Mandat and his générale; the rest fol-

low each his own theorem of the uncertainties: theorem, that
one should march rather with Saint-Antoine: innumerable
theorems, that in such a case the wholesomest were sleep.
And so the drums beat, in mad fits, and the stormbells peal.
Saint-Antoine itself does but draw out and draw in: Commandant Santerre, over there, can not believe that the Marseillese and Saint-Marceau will march. Thou laggard sonorous Beervat, with the loud voice and timber-head, is it time
now to palter? Alsatian Westermann clutches him by the
throat with drawn sabre: whereupon the Timber-headed believes. In this manner wanes the slow night; amid fret, uncertainty and tocsin; all men's humour rising to the hysterical pitch; and nothing done.

However, Mandat, on the third summons, does come—
come, unguarded; astonished to find the Municipality new.
They question him straitly on that Mayor's-Order to resist
force by force; on that strategic scheme of cutting Saint-
Antoine in two halves: he answers what he can: they think
it were right to send this strategic National Commandant to
the Abbaye Prison, and let a Court of Law decide on him.
Alas! a Court of Law, not Book-Law but primeval Club-Law,
crowds and jostles out of doors; all fretted to the hysterical
pitch; cruel as Fear, blind as the Night: such Court of Law,
and no other, clutches poor Mandat from his constables; beats
him down, massacres him, on the steps of the Townhall. Look
to it, ye new Municipals; ye People, in a state of Insurrection!
Blood is shed, blood must be answered for—alas! in such
hysterical humour, more blood will flow: for it is as with the
Tiger in that; he has only to begin.

Seventeen Individuals have been seized in the Champs
Elysées, by exploratory Patriotism; they flitting dim-visible,
by it flitting dim-visible. Ye have pistols, rapiers, ye Seventeen? One of those accursed "false Patrols"; that go ma-
rauding, with Anti-National intent; seeking what they can
spy, what they can spill! The Seventeen are carried to the
nearest Guardhouse; eleven of them escape by back passages.
"How is this?" Demoiselle Théroigne appears at the front
entrance, with sabre, pistols, and a train; denounces treasonous
connivance; demands, seizes, the remaining six, that the justice of the People be not trifled with. Of which six two more
escape in the whirl and debate of the Club-Law Court; the

last unhappy Four are massacred, as Mandat was: Two Ex-Bodyguards; one dissipated Abbé; one Royalist Pamphleteer, Sulleau, known to us by name, Able Editor and wit of all work. Poor Sulleau: his " Acts of the Apostles," and brisk Placard-Journals (for he was an able man) come to Finis, in this manner; and questionable jesting issues suddenly in horrid earnest! Such doings usher-in the dawn of the Tenth of August 1792.

Or think what a night the poor National Assembly has had: sitting there, " in great paucity," attempting to debate—quivering and shivering; pointing toward all the thirty-two azimuths at once, as the magnet-needle does when thunderstorm is in the air! If the Insurrection come? If it come, and fail? Alas! in that case, may not black Courtiers with blunderbusses, red Swiss with bayonets rush over, flushed with victory, and ask us: Thou undefinable, water-logged, self-distractive, self-destructive Legislative, what dost thou here unsunk?—Or figure the poor National Guards, bivouacking in " temporary tents " there; or standing ranked, shifting from leg to leg, all through the weary night; New Tricolor Municipals ordering one thing, old Mandat Captains ordering another. Procureur Manuel has ordered the cannons to be withdrawn from the Pont-Neuf; none ventured to disobey him. It seems certain, then, the old Staff, so long doomed, has finally been dissolved, in these hours; and Mandat is not our Commandant now, but Santerre? Yes, friends: Santerre henceforth—surely Mandat no more! The Squadrons that were to charge see nothing certain, except that they are cold, hungry, worn down with watching; that it were sad to slay French brothers; sadder to be slain by them. Without the Tuileries Circuit, and within it, sour uncertain humour sways these men: only the red Swiss stand steadfast. Them their officers refresh now with a slight wetting of brandy; wherein the Nationals, too far gone for brandy, refuse to participate.

King Louis meanwhile had laid him down for a little sleep; his wig when he reappeared had lost the powder on one side.[7] Old Marshal Maillé and the gentlemen in black rise always in spirits, as the Insurrection does not rise: there goes a witty saying now, " Le tocsin ne rend pas," The tocsin, like a dry milk-cow, does not yield. For the rest, could not one pro-

claim Martial Law? Not easily; for now, it seems, Mayor
Pétion is gone. On the other hand, our Interim Commandant, poor Mandat being off " to the Hôtel-de-Ville," complains that so many Courtiers in black encumber the service,
are an eyesorrow to the National Guards. To which her
Majesty answers with emphasis, That they will obey all, will
suffer all, that they are sure men these.

And so the yellow lamplight dies out in the gray of morning, in the King's Palace, over such a scene. Scene of jostling,
elbowing, of confusion, and indeed conclusion, for the thing
is about to end. Rœderer and spectral Ministers jostle in the
press; consult, in side-cabinets, with one or with both Majesties.
Sister Elisabeth takes the Queen to the window: " Sister, see
what a beautiful sunrise," right over the Jacobins Church and
that quarter! How happy if the tocsin did not yield! But
Mandat returns not; Pétion is gone: much hangs wavering
in the invisible Balance. About five o'clock, there rises from
the Garden a kind of sound; as of a shout which had become
a howl, and instead of " Vive le Roi! " were ending in " Vive la
Nation! " " Mon Dieu! " ejaculates a spectral Minister, " what
is he doing down there?" For it is his Majesty, gone down
with old Marshal Maillé to review the troops; and the nearest
companies of them answer so. Her Majesty bursts into a
stream of tears. Yet on stepping from the cabinet, her eyes
are dry and calm, her look is even cheerful. " The Austrian
lip, and the aquiline nose, fuller than usual, gave to her countenance," says Peltier,[8] " something of majesty, which they
that did not see her in these moments can not well have an
idea of." O thou Theresa's Daughter!

King Louis enters, much blown with the fatigue; but for
the rest with his old air of indifference. Of all hopes now,
surely the joyfulest were, that the tocsin did not yield.

NOTES

[1] " Deux Amis," viii, 129–188.

[2] Rœderer à la Barre (Séance du 9 Août, in " Hist. Parl.," xvi, 393).

[3] Rœderer, " Chronique de Cinquante Jours; Récit de Pétion."
Townhall Records, etc. (in " Hist. Parl.," xvi, 399–466).

[4] Rœderer, ubi suprà.

[5] August 24, 1572.

[6] Section Documents, Townhall Documents (" Hist. Parl.," ubi
suprà).   [7] Rœderer, ubi suprà.   [8] In Toulongeon, ii, 241.

CHAPTER VII

THE SWISS

UNHAPPY Friends, the tocsin does yield, has yielded! Lo ye, how with the first sunrays its Ocean-tide, of pikes and fusils, flows glittering from the far East—immeasurable; born of the Night! They march there, the grim host; Saint-Antoine on this side the River; Saint-Marceau on that, the black-browed Marseillese in the van. With hum, and grim murmur, far-heard; like the Ocean-tide, as we say: drawn up, as if by Luna and Influences, from the great Deep of Waters, they roll gleaming on; no King, Canute or Louis, can bid them roll back. Wide eddying side-currents, of onlookers, roll hither and thither, unarmed, not voiceless; they, the steel host, roll on. New-Commandant Santerre, indeed, has taken seat at the Townhall; rests there, in his halfway-house. Alsatian Westermann, with flashing sabre, does not rest; nor the Sections, nor the Marseillese, nor Demoiselle Théroigne; but roll continually on.

And now, where are Mandat's Squadrons that were to charge? Not a Squadron of them stirs: or they stir in the wrong direction, out of the way; their officers glad that they will do even that. It is to this hour uncertain whether the Squadron on the Pont-Neuf made the shadow of resistance, or did not make the shadow: enough, the black-browed Marseillese, and Saint-Marceau following them, do cross without let; do cross, in sure hope now of Saint-Antoine and the rest; do billow on, toward the Tuileries, where their errand is. The Tuileries, at sound of them, rustles responsive: the red Swiss look to their priming; Courtiers in black draw their blunderbusses, rapiers, poniards, some have even fire-shovels; every man his weapon of war.

Judge if, in these circumstances, Syndic Rœderer felt easy! Will the kind Heavens open no middle-course of refuge for a

poor Syndic who halts between two? If indeed his Majesty
would consent to go over to the Assembly! His Majesty,
above all her Majesty, can not agree to that. Did her Majesty
answer the proposal with a " Fi donc "; did she say even, she
would be nailed to the walls sooner? Apparently not. It is
written also that she offered the King a pistol; saying, Now
or else never was the time to show himself. Close eye-witnesses did not see it, nor do we. They saw only that she was
queen-like, quiet; that she argued not, upbraided not, with
the Inexorable; but, like Cæsar in the Capitol, wrapped her
mantle, as it beseems Queens and Sons of Adam to do.
But thou, O Louis! of what stuff art thou at all? Is
there no stroke in thee, then, for Life and Crown? The
silliest hunted deer dies not so. Art thou the languidest
of all mortals; or the mildest-minded? Thou art the worst-
starred.

The tide advances; Syndic Rœderer's and all men's straits
grow straiter and straiter. Fremescent clangour comes from
the armed Nationals in the Court; far and wide is the infinite
hubbub of tongues. What counsel? And the tide is now
nigh! Messengers, forerunners speak hastily through the
outer Grates; hold parley sitting astride the walls. Syndic
Rœderer goes out and comes in. Cannoneers ask him: Are
we to fire against the people? King's Ministers ask him: Shall
the King's House be forced? Syndic Rœderer has a hard
game to play. He speaks to the Cannoneers with eloquence,
with fervour; such fervour as a man can, who has to blow hot
and cold in one breath. Hot and cold, O Rœderer? We, for
our part, can not live and die! The Cannoneers, by way of
answer, fling down their linstocks.—Think of this answer, O
King Louis, and King's Ministers; and take a poor Syndic's
safe middle-course, toward the Salle de Manége. King Louis
sits, his hands leaned on his knees, body bent forward; gazes
for a space fixedly on Syndic Rœderer; then answers, looking
over his shoulder to the Queen: "Marchons!" They march;
King Louis, Queen, Sister Elisabeth, the two royal children
and governess: these, with Syndic Rœderer, and Officials of
the Department; amid a double rank of National Guards. The
men with blunderbusses, the steady red Swiss gaze mournfully,
reproachfully; but hear only these words from Syndic Rœderer: "The King is going to the Assembly; make way." It

has struck eight, on all clocks, some minutes ago: the King has left the Tuileries—forever.

O ye stanch Swiss, ye gallant gentlemen in black, for what a cause are ye to spend and be spent! Look out from the western windows, ye may see King Louis placidly hold on his way; the poor little Prince Royal " sportfully kicking the fallen leaves." Fremescent multitude on the Terrace of the Feuillants whirls parallel to him; one man in it, very noisy, with a long pole: will they not obstruct the outer Staircase, and back-entrance of the Salle, when it comes to that? King's Guards can go no farther than the bottom step there. Lo, Deputation of Legislators come out; he of the long pole is stilled by oratory; Assembly's Guards join themselves to King's Guards, and all may mount in this case of necessity; the outer Staircase is free, or passable. See, Royalty ascends; a blue Grenadier lifts the poor little Prince Royal from the press; Royalty has entered in. Royalty has vanished forever from your eyes.—And ye? Left standing there, amid the yawning abysses, and earthquake of Insurrection; without course; without command: if ye perish, it must be as more than martyrs, as martyrs who are now without a cause! The black Courtiers disappear mostly; through such issues as they can. The poor Swiss know not how to act: one duty only is clear to them, that of standing by their post; and they will perform that.

But the glittering steel tide has arrived; it beats now against the Château barriers and eastern Courts; irresistible, loud-surging far and wide—breaks in, fills the Court of the Carrousel, black-browed Marseillese in the van. King Louis gone, say you; over to the Assembly! Well and good: but till the Assembly pronounce Forfeiture of him, what boots it? Our post is in that Château or stronghold of his: there till then must we continue. Think, ye stanch Swiss, whether it were good that grim murder began, and brothers blasted one another in pieces for a stone edifice?—Poor Swiss! they know not how to act: from the southern windows, some fling cartridges, in sign of brotherhood; on the eastern outer staircase, and within through long stairs and corridors, they stand firm-ranked, peaceable and yet refusing to stir. Westermann speaks to them in Alsatian German; Marseillese plead, in hot Provençal speech and pantomime; stunning hubbub pleads and threatens, infinite, around. The Swiss stand fast, peaceable and yet immovable; red granite pier in that waste flashing sea of steel.

Who can help the inevitable issue; Marseillese and all France on this side; granite Swiss on that? The pantomime grows hotter and hotter; Marseillese sabres flourishing by way of action; the Swiss brow also clouding itself, the Swiss thumb bringing its firelock to the cock. And hark! high thundering above all the din, three Marseillese cannon from the Carrousel, pointed by a gunner of bad aim, come rattling over the roofs! Ye Swiss, therefore: " Fire!" The Swiss fire; by volley, by platoon, in rolling-fire: Marseillese men not a few, and " a tall man that was louder than any," lie silent, smashed upon the pavement—not a few Marseillese, after the long dusty march, have made halt here. The Carrousel is void; the black tide recoiling; "fugitives rushing as far as Saint-Antoine before they stop." The Cannoneers without linstock have squatted invisible, and left their cannon; which the Swiss seize.

Think what a volley: reverberating doomful to the four corners of Paris, and through all hearts; like the clang of Bellona's thongs! The black-browed Marseillese, rallying on the instant, have become black Demons that know how to die. Nor is Brest behindhand; nor Alsatian Westermann; Demoiselle Théroigne is Sibyl Théroigne: Vengeance, Victoire ou la mort! From all Patriot artillery, great and small; from Feuillants Terrace, and all terraces and places of the wide-spread Insurrectionary sea, there roars responsive a red blazing whirlwind. Blue Nationals, ranked in the Garden, can not help their muskets going off, against Foreign murderers. For there is a sympathy in muskets, in heaped masses of men: nay, are not Mankind, in whole, like tuned strings, and a cunning infinite concordance and unity; you smite one string, and all strings will begin sounding—in soft sphere-melody, in deafening screech of madness! Mounted Gendarmerie gallop distracted; are fired on merely as a thing running; galloping over the Pont Royal, or one knows not whither. The brain of Paris, grain-fevered in the centre of it here, has gone mad; what you call, taken fire.

Behold, the fire slackens not; nor does the Swiss rolling-fire slacken from within. Nay, they clutch cannon, as we

saw; and now, from the other side, they clutch three pieces
more; alas! cannon without linstock; nor will the steel-and-
flint answer, though they try it.[1]   Had it chanced to answer!
Patriot onlookers have their misgivings; one strangest Patriot
onlooker thinks that the Swiss, had they a commander, would
beat.   He is a man not unqualified to judge; the name of him
Napoleon Buonaparte.[2]   And onlookers, and women, stand
gazing, and the witty Dr. Moore of Glasgow among them,
on the other side of the River: cannon rush rumbling past
them; pause on the Pont Royal; belch out their iron entrails
there, against the Tuileries; and at every new belch, the women
and onlookers "shout and clap hands."[3]   City of all the
Devils!   In remote streets, men are drinking breakfast-coffee;
following their affairs; with a start now and then, as some
dull echo reverberates a note louder.   And here?   Marseillese
fall wounded; but Barbaroux has surgeons; Barbaroux is close
by, managing, though underhand and under cover.   Marseillese fall death-struck; bequeath their firelock, specify in which
pocket are the cartridges; and die murmuring, "Revenge me,
Revenge thy country!"   Brest Fédéré Officers, galloping in
red coats, are shot as Swiss.   Lo you, the Carrousel has burst
into flame!—Paris Pandemonium!   Nay, the poor City, as we
said, is in fever-fit and convulsion: such crisis has lasted for
the space of some half hour.

But what is this that, with Legislative Insignia, ventures
through the hubbub and death-hail, from the back-entrance of
the Manége?   Toward the Tuileries and Swiss: written Order
from his Majesty to cease firing!   O ye hapless Swiss, why
was there no order not to begin it?   Gladly would the Swiss
cease firing: but who will bid mad Insurrection cease firing?
To Insurrection you can not speak; neither can it, hydra-
headed, hear.   The dead and dying, by the hundred, lie all
around; are borne bleeding through the streets, toward help;
the sight of them, like a torch of the Furies, kindling Madness.   Patriot Paris roars; as the bear bereaved of her whelps.
On, ye Patriots: Vengeance!   Victory or death!   There are
men seen, who rush on, armed only with walking-sticks.[4]
Terror and Fury rule the hour.

The Swiss, pressed on from without, paralyzed from within,
have ceased to shoot; but not to be shot.   What shall they
do?   Desperate is the moment.   Shelter or instant death:

yet How, Where? One party flies out by the Rue de l'Échelle; is destroyed utterly, " en entier." A second, by the other side, throws itself into the Garden; " hurrying across a keen fusillade "; rushes suppliant into the National Assembly; finds pity and refuge in the back benches there. The third, and largest, darts out in column, three hundred strong, toward the Champs Elysées: " Ah, could we but reach Courbevoye, where other Swiss are! " Wo! see, in such fusillade the column " soon breaks itself by diversity of opinion," into distracted segments, this way and that—to escape in holes, to die fighting from street to street. The firing and murdering will not cease; not yet for long. The red Porters of Hôtels are shot at, be they Suisse by nature, or Suisse only in name. The very Firemen, who pump and labour on that smoking Carrousel, are shot at: why should the Carrousel not burn? Some Swiss take refuge in private houses; find that mercy too does still dwell in the heart of man. The brave Marseillese are merciful, late so wroth; and labour to save. Journalist Gorsas pleads hard with infuriated groups. Clemence the Wine-merchant stumbles forward to the Bar of the Assembly, a rescued Swiss in his hand; tells passionately how he rescued him with pain and peril, how he will henceforth support him, being childless himself; and falls a-swoon round the poor Swiss's neck: amid plaudits. But the most are butchered, and even mangled. Fifty (some say Fourscore) were marched as prisoners, by National Guards, to the Hôtel-de-Ville: the ferocious people bursts through on them, in the Place-de-Grève; massacres them to the last man. " O Peuple, envy of the universe! " Peuple, in mad Gaelic effervescence!

Surely few things in the history of carnage are painfuler. What ineffaceable red streak, flickering so sad in the memory, is that, of this poor column of red Swiss " breaking itself in the confusion of opinions "; dispersing, into blackness and death! Honour to you, brave men; honourable pity, through long times! Not martyrs were ye; and yet almost more. He was no King of yours, this Louis; and he forsook you like a King of shreds and patches: ye were but sold to him for some poor sixpence a-day; yet would ye work for your wages, keep your plighted word. The work now was to die; and ye did it. Honour to you, O Kinsmen; and may the old Deutsch Biederkeit and Tapferkeit, and Valour which is Worth and

Truth, be they Swiss, be they Saxon, fail in no age! Not bastards; true-born were these men: sons of the men of Sempach, of Murten, who knelt, but not to thee, O Burgundy! —Let the traveller, as he passes through Lucerne, turn aside to look a little at their monumental Lion; not for Thorwaldsen's sake alone. Hewn out of living rock, the Figure rests there, by the still Lake-waters, in lullaby of distant-tinkling rance-des-vaches, the granite Mountains dumbly keeping watch all round; and, though inanimate, speaks.

NOTES

[1] " Deux Amis," viii, 179–188.

[2] See " Hist. Parl.," xvii, 56; Las Cases, etc.

[3] Moore, " Journal during a Residence in France" (Dublin, 1793), i, 26.

[4] " Hist. Parl.," ubi suprà. " Rapport du Capitaine des Canonniers, Rapport du Commandant," etc. (Ibid., xvii, 300–318).

CHAPTER VIII

CONSTITUTION BURST IN PIECES

THUS is the Tenth of August won and lost. Patriotism reckons its slain by the thousand on thousand, so deadly was the Swiss fire from these windows; but will finally reduce them to some Twelve-hundred. No child's-play was it —nor is it! Till two in the afternoon the massacring, the breaking and the burning has not ended; nor the loose Bedlam shut itself again.

How deluges of frantic Sansculottism roared through all passages of this Tuileries, ruthless in vengeance; how the Valets were butchered, hewn down; and Dame Campan saw the Marseillese sabre flash over her head, but the Black-browed said, "Va-t'en, Get thee gone," and flung her from him unstruck;[1] how in the cellars wine-bottles were broken, wine-butts were staved-in and drunk; and, upward to the very garrets, all windows tumbled out their precious royal furnitures: and, with gold mirrors, velvet curtains, down of ripped feather-beds, and dead bodies of men, the Tuileries was like no Garden of the Earth—all this let him who has a taste for it see amply in Mercier, in acrid Montgaillard, or Beaulieu of the " Deux Amis." A hundred and eighty bodies of Swiss lie piled there; naked, unremoved till the second day. Patriotism has torn their red coats into snips; and marches with them at the Pike's point: the ghastly bare corpses lie there, under the sun and under the stars; the curious of both sexes crowding to look. Which let not us do. Above a hundred carts, heaped with Dead, fare toward the Cemetery of Saint-Madeleine; bewailed, bewept; for all had kindred, all had mothers, if not here, then there. It is one of those Carnage-fields, such as you read of by the name " Glorious Victory," brought home in this case to one's own door.

But the black-browed Marseillese have struck down the tyrant of the Château. He is struck down; low, and hardly again to rise. What a moment for an august Legislative was that when the Hereditary Representative entered, under such circumstances; and the Grenadier, carrying the little Prince Royal out of the press, set him down on the Assembly-table! A moment—which one had to smooth-off with oratory; waiting what the next would bring! Louis said few words: " He was come hither to prevent a great crime; he believed himself safer nowhere than here." President Vergniaud answered briefly, in vague oratory as we say, about " defence of Constituted Authorities," about dying at our post.[2] And so King Louis sat him down; first here, then there; for a difficulty arose, the Constitution not permitting us to debate while the King is present : finally he settles himself with his Family in the " Loge of the Logographe," in the Reporter's-Box of a Journalist; which is beyond the enchanted Constitutional Circuit, separated from it by a rail. To such Lodge of the Logographe, measuring some ten feet square, with a small closet at the entrance of it behind, is the King of broad France now limited : here can he and his sit pent, under the eyes of the world, or retire into their closet at intervals; for the space of sixteen hours. Such quite peculiar moment has the Legislative lived to see.

But also what a moment was that other, few minutes later, when the three Marseillese cannon went off, and the Swiss rolling-fire and universal thunder, like the crack of Doom, began to rattle! Honourable Members start to their feet; stray bullets singing epicedium even here, shivering-in with window-glass and jingle. " No, this is our post; let us die here!" They sit therefore, like stone Legislators. But may not the Loge of the Logographe be forced from behind? Tear down the railing that divides it from the enchanted Constitutional Circuit! Ushers tear and tug; his Majesty himself aiding from within: the railing gives way; Majesty and Legislative are united in place, unknown Destiny hovering over both.

Rattle, and again rattle, went the thunder; one breathless wide-eyed messenger rushing in after another: King's order to the Swiss went out. It was a fearful thunder; but, as we know, it ended. Breathless messengers, fugitive Swiss, denunciatory Patriots, trepidation; finally tripudiation!—Before four o'clock much has come and gone.

The New Municipals have come and gone; with Three Flags, Liberté, Egalité, Patrie, and the clang of vivats. Vergniaud, he who as President few hours ago talked of dying for Constituted Authorities, has moved, as Committee-Reporter, that the Hereditary Representative be suspended; that a National Convention do forthwith assemble to say what further! An able Report; which the President must have had ready in his pocket? A President, in such cases, must have much ready, and yet not ready; and Janus-like look before and after.

King Louis listens to all; retires about midnight "to three little rooms on the upper floor"; till the Luxembourg be prepared for him, and "the safeguard of the Nation." Safer if Brunswick were once here! Or, alas! not so safe? Ye hapless discrowned heads! Crowds came, next morning, to catch a glimpse of them, in their three upper rooms. Montgaillard says the august Captives wore an air of cheerfulness, even of gaiety; that the Queen and Princess Lamballe, who had joined her overnight, looked out of the opened window, "shook powder from their hair on the people below, and laughed." [3] He is an acrid distorted man.

For the rest, one may guess that the Legislative, above all that the New Municipality continues busy. Messengers, Municipal or Legislative, and swift despatches rush off to all corners of France; full of triumph, blended with indignant wail, for Twelve-hundred have fallen. France sends up its blended shout responsive; the Tenth of August shall be as the Fourteenth of July, only bloodier and greater. The Court has conspired? Poor Court: the Court has been vanquished; and will have both the scath to bear and the scorn. How the statues of Kings do now all fall! Bronze Henri himself, though he wore a cockade once, jingles down from the Pont Neuf, where Patrie floats in Danger. Much more does Louis Fourteenth, from the Place Vendôme, jingle down; and even breaks in falling. The curious can remark, written on his horse's shoe: " 12 Août 1692 "; a Century and a Day.

The tenth of August was Friday. The week is not done, when our old Patriot Ministry is recalled, what of it can be got: strict Roland, Genevese Clavière; add heavy Monge the Mathematician, once a stone-hewer; and, for Minister of Justice—Danton, "led hither," as himself says, in one of his

gigantic figures, "through the breach of Patriot cannon!"
These, under Legislative Committees, must rule the wreck
as they can : confusedly enough ; with an old Legislative water-
logged, with a new Municipality so brisk. But National Convention will get itself together; and then! Without delay,
however, let a new Jury-Court and Criminal Tribunal be set
up in Paris, to try the crimes and conspiracies of the Tenth.
High Court of Orleans is distant, slow : the blood of the
Twelve-hundred Patriots, whatever become of other blood,
shall be inquired after. Tremble, ye Criminals and Conspirators ; the Minister of Justice is Danton ! Robespierre too, after
the victory, sits in the New Municipality; insurrectionary
"improvised Municipality," which calls itself Council General
of the Commune.

For three days now, Louis and his Family have heard the
Legislative Debates in the Lodge of the Logographe; and retired nightly to their small upper rooms. The Luxembourg
and safeguard of the Nation could not be got ready : nay, it
seems the Luxembourg has too many cellars and issues; no
Municipality can undertake to watch it. The compact Prison
of the Temple, not so elegant indeed, were much safer. To
the Temple, therefore ! On Monday 13th day of August 1792,
in Mayor Pétion's carriage, Louis and his sad suspended
Household fare thither; all Paris out to look at them. As
they pass through the Place Vendôme, Louis Fourteenth's
Statue lies broken on the ground. Pétion is afraid the Queen's
looks may be thought scornful, and produce provocation; she
casts down her eyes, and does not look at all. The "press
is prodigious," but quiet: here and there, it shouts " Vive la
Nation !" but for most part gazes in silence. French Royalty
vanishes within the gates of the Temple : these old peaked
Towers, like peaked Extinguisher or Bonsoir, do cover it up—
from which same Towers, poor Jacques Molay and his Tem-
plars were burned out, by French Royalty, five centuries since.
Such are the turns of Fate below. Foreign Ambassadors,
English Lord Gower have all demanded passports; are driving
indignantly toward their respective homes.

So, then, the Constitution is over? Forever and a day!
Gone is that wonder of the Universe; First biennial Parliament, water-logged, waits only till the Convention come; and

40

will then sink to endless depths. One can guess the silent rage of Old-Constituents, Constitution-builders, extinct Feuillants, men who thought the Constitution would march! Lafayette rises to the altitude of the situation; at the head of his Army. Legislative Commissioners are posting toward him and it, on the Northern Frontier, to congratulate and perorate; he orders the Municipality of Sedan to arrest these Commissioners, and keep them strictly in ward as Rebels, till he say further. The Sedan Municipals obey.

The Sedan Municipals obey; but the Soldiers of the Lafayette Army? The Soldiers of the Lafayette Army have, as all Soldiers have, a kind of dim feeling that they themselves are Sansculottes in buff belts; that the victory of the Tenth of August is also a victory for them. They will not rise and follow Lafayette, to Paris; they will rise and send him thither! On the 18th, which is but next Saturday, Lafayette with some two or three indignant Staff-officers, one of whom is Old-Constituent Alexandre de Lameth, having first put his Lines in what order he could—rides swiftly over the marches toward Holland. Rides, alas! swiftly into the claws of Austrians! He, long wavering, trembling on the verge of the Horizon, has set, in Olmütz Dungeons; this History knows him no more. Adieu, thou Hero of two Worlds; thinnest, but compact honour-worthy man! Through long rough night of captivity, through other tumults, triumphs and changes, thou wilt swing well, " fast-anchored to the Washington Formula "; and be the Hero and Perfect-character, were it only of one idea. The Sedan Municipals repent and protest; the Soldiers shout " Vive la Nation! " Dumouriez Polymetis, from his Camp at Maulde, sees himself made Commander-in-Chief.

And, O Brunswick! what sort of " military execution " will Paris merit now? Forward, ye well-drilled exterminatory men; with your artillery-wagons, and camp-kettles jingling. Forward, tall chivalrous King of Prussia; fanfaronading Emigrants and war-god Broglie, " for some consolation to mankind," which verily is not without need of some.

NOTES

[1] Campan, ii, c. 21.
[2] " Moniteur." Séance du 10 Août 1792.
[3] Montgaillard, ii, 135–167.

Book XIV

SEPTEMBER

CHAPTER I

THE IMPROVISED COMMUNE

YE have roused her, then, ye Emigrants and Despots of the world; France is roused! Long have ye been lecturing and tutoring this poor Nation, like cruel uncalled-for pedagogues, shaking over her your ferulas of fire and steel: it is long that ye have pricked and filliped and affrighted her, there as she sat helpless in her dead cerements of a Constitution, you gathering in on her from all lands, with your armaments and plots, your invadings and truculent bullyings—and lo now, ye have pricked her to the quick, and she is up, and her blood is up. The dead cerements are rent into cobwebs, and she fronts you in that terrible strength of Nature, which no man has measured, which goes down to Madness and Tophet: see now how ye will deal with her.

This month of September 1792, which has become one of the memorable months of History, presents itself under two most diverse aspects; all of black on the one side, all of bright on the other. Whatsoever is cruel in the panic frenzy of Twenty-five million men, whatsoever is great in the simultaneous death-defiance of Twenty-five million men, stand here in abrupt contrast, near by one another. As indeed is usual when a man, how much more when a Nation of men, is hurled suddenly beyond the limits. For Nature, as green as she looks, rests everywhere on dread foundations, were we farther down; and Pan, to whose music the Nymphs dance, has a cry in him that can drive all men distracted.

Very frightful it is when a Nation, rending asunder its Constitutions and Regulations which were grown dead cerements for it, becomes transcendental; and must now seek its wild way through the New, Chaotic—where Force is not yet distinguished into Bidden and Forbidden, but Crime and Virtue welter unseparated—in that domain of what is called the

Passions; of what we call the Miracles and the Portents! It
is thus that, for some three years to come, we are to contemplate France, in this final Part of our History. Sansculottism reigning in all its grandeur and in all its hideous-
ness: the Gospel (God's-message) of Man's Rights, Man's
mights or strengths, once more preached irrefragably abroad;
along with this, and still louder for the time, the fearfulest
Devil's-Message of Man's weaknesses and sins—and all on
such a scale, and under such aspect: cloudy " death-birth of
a world ": huge smoke-cloud, streaked with rays of heaven
on one side; girt on the other as with hell-fire! History
tells us many things: but for the last thousand years and more,
what thing has she told us of a sort like this? Which therefore let us two, O Reader, dwell on willingly, for a little; and
from its endless significance endeavour to extract what may,
in present circumstances, be adapted for us.

It is unfortunate, though very natural, that the history
of this Period has so generally been written in hysterics. Exaggeration abounds, execration, wailing; and, on the whole,
darkness. But thus too, when foul old Rome had to be swept
from the Earth, and those Northmen, and other horrid sons of
Nature, came in, " swallowing formulas," as the French now
do, foul old Rome screamed execratively her loudest; so that
the true shape of many things is lost for us. Attila's Huns
had arms of such length that they could lift a stone without
stooping. Into the body of the poor Tatars execrative Roman
History intercalated an alphabetic letter; and so they continue Tartars, of fell Tartarean nature, to this day. Here, in
like manner, search as we will in these multiform innumerable
French Records, darkness too frequently covers, or sheer distraction bewilders. One finds it difficult to imagine that the
Sun shone in this September month, as he does in others.
Nevertheless it is an indisputable fact that the Sun did shine;
and there was weather and work—nay, as to that, very bad
weather for harvest-work! An unlucky Editor may do his
utmost; and after all require allowances.

He had been a wise Frenchman, who, looking close at hand
on this waste aspect of France all stirring and whirling, in
ways new, untried, had been able to discern where the cardinal
movement lay; which tendency it was that had the rule and

primary direction of it then! But at forty-four years' distance, it is different. To all men now, two cardinal movements or grand tendencies, in the September whirl, have become discernible enough: that stormful effluence toward the Frontiers; that frantic crowding toward Town-houses and Council-halls in the interior. Wild France dashes, in desperate death-defiance, toward the Frontiers, to defend itself from foreign Despots; crowds toward Townhalls and Election Committee-rooms, to defend itself from domestic Aristocrats. Let the Reader conceive well these two cardinal movements; and what side-currents and endless vortexes might depend on these. He shall judge too, whether, in such sudden wreckage of all old Authorities, such a pair of cardinal movements, half-frantic in themselves, could be of soft nature? As in dry Sahara, when the winds waken, and lift and winnow the immensity of sand! The air itself (Travellers say) is a dim sand-air; and dim looming through it, the wonderfulest uncertain colonnades of Sand-Pillars rush whirling from this side and from that, like so many mad Spinning-Dervishes, of a hundred feet in stature; and dance their huge Desert-waltz there!—

Nevertheless, in all human movements, were they but a day old, there is order, or the beginning of order. Consider two things in this Sahara-waltz of the French Twenty-five millions; or rather one thing, and one hope of a thing; the Commune (Municipality) of Paris, which is already here; the National Convention, which shall in a few weeks be here. The Insurrectionary Commune, which, improvising itself on the eve of the Tenth of August, worked this ever-memorable Deliverance by explosion, must needs rule over it—till the Convention meet. This Commune, which they may well call a spontaneous or "improvised" Commune, is, for the present, sovereign of France. The Legislative, deriving its authority from the Old, how can it now have authority when the Old is exploded by insurrection? As a floating piece of wreck, certain things, persons, and interests may still cleave to it: volunteer defenders, riflemen or pikemen in green uniform, or red night-cap (of bonnet rouge), defile before it daily, just on the wing toward Brunswick; with the brandishing of arms; always with some touch of Leonidas-eloquence, often with a fire of daring that threatens to outherod Herod—the Galleries, "especially the Ladies, never done with applauding."[1] Addresses of this

or the like sort can be received and answered, in the hearing
of all France; the Salle de Manége is still useful as a place of
proclamation. For which use, indeed, it now chiefly serves.
Vergniaud delivers spirit-stirring orations; but always with a
prophetic sense only, looking toward the coming Convention.
" Let our memory perish," cries Vergniaud; " but let France
be free!"—whereupon they all start to their feet, shouting
responsive: " Yes, yes, périsse notre mémoire, pourvu que la
France soit libre!"² Disfrocked Chabot adjures Heaven that
at least we may " have done with Kings "; and fast as powder
under spark, we all blaze-up once more, and with waved hats
shout and swear: " Yes, nous le jurons; plus de rois!"³ All
which, as a method of proclamation, is very convenient.

For the rest, that our busy Brissots, rigorous Rolands, men
who once had authority, and now have less and less; men
who love law, and will have even an Explosion explode itself
as far as possible according to rule, do find this state of
matters most unofficial-unsatisfactory—is not to be denied.
Complaints are made; attempts are made: but without effect.
The attempts even recoil; and must be desisted from, for fear
of worse: the sceptre has departed from this Legislative once
and always. A poor Legislative, so hard was fate, had let itself
be hand-gyved, nailed to the rock like an Andromeda, and
could only wail there to the Earth and Heavens; miraculously
a winged Perseus (or Improvised Commune) has dawned out
of the void Blue, and cut her loose: but whether now is it she,
with her softness and musical speech, or is it he, with his
hardness and sharp falchion and ægis, that shall have casting-
vote? Melodious agreement of vote; this were the rule! But
if otherwise, and votes diverge, then surely Andromeda's part
is to weep—if possible, tears of gratitude alone.

Be content, O France, with this Improvised Commune,
such as it is! It has the implements, and has the hands: the
time is not long. On Sunday the twenty-sixth of August,
our Primary Assemblies shall meet, begin electing of Electors;
on Sunday the second of September (may the day prove
lucky!) the Electors shall begin electing Deputies; and so
an all-healing National Convention will come together. No
marc d'argent, or distinction of Active and Passive, now insults the French Patriot: but there is universal suffrage, unlimited liberty to choose. Old-Constituents, Present-Legis-

lators, all France is eligible. Nay, it may be said, the flower of all the Universe (de l'Univers) is eligible; for in these very days we, by act of Assembly, " naturalize " the chief Foreign Friends of Humanity: Priestley, burnt out for us in Birmingham; Klopstock, a genius of all countries; Jeremy Bentham, useful Jurisconsult; distinguished Paine, the rebellious Needleman—some of whom may be chosen. As is most fit; for a Convention of this kind. In a word, Seven-hundred and Forty-five unshackled sovereigns, admired of the universe, shall replace this hapless impotency of a Legislative—out of which, it is likely, the best Members, and the Mountain in mass, may be re-elected. Roland is getting ready the Salle des Cent Suisses, as preliminary rendezvous for them; in that void Palace of the Tuileries, now void and National, and not a Palace, but a Caravansera.

As for the Spontaneous Commune, one may say that there never was on Earth a stranger Town-Council. Administration, not of a great City, but of a great Kingdom in a state of revolt and frenzy, this is the task that has fallen to it. Enrolling, provisioning, judging; devising, deciding, doing, endeavouring to do: one wonders the human brain did not give way under all this, and reel. But happily human brains have such a talent of taking up simply what they can carry, and ignoring all the rest; leaving all the rest, as if it were not there! Whereby somewhat is verily shifted for; and much shifts for itself. This Improvised Commune walks along, nothing doubting; promptly making front, without fear or flurry, at what moment soever, to the wants of the moment. Were the world on fire, one improvised tricolor Municipal has but one life to lose. They are the elixir and chosen-men of Sansculottic Patriotism; promoted to the forlorn-hope; unspeakable victory or a high gallows, this is their meed. They sit there, in the Townhall, these astonishing tricolor Municipals; in Council General; in Committee of Watchfulness (de Surveillance, which will even become de Salut Public, of Public Salvation), or what other Committees and Sub-committees are needful—managing infinite Correspondence; passing infinite Decrees: one hears of a Decree being " the ninety-eighth of the day." Ready! is the word. They carry loaded pistols in their pocket; also some improvised luncheon by way of meal. Or indeed, by and by, traiteurs contract for the supply of repasts, to be eaten on the spot—too lavishly, as it was afterward grumbled. Thus they: girt in their tricolor sashes; Municipal note-paper in the one hand, fire-arms in the other. They have their Agents out all over France; speaking in townhouses, market-places, highways and byways; agitating, urging to arm; all hearts tingling to hear. Great is the fire of Anti-aristocrat eloquence: nay, some, as Bibliopolic Momoro, seem to hint afar off at something which smells of Agrarian Law, and a surgery of the over-swoln dropsical strongbox itself—whereat indeed the bold Bookseller runs risk of being hanged, and Ex-Constituent Buzot has to smuggle him off.[4]

Governing Persons, were they never so insignificant intrinsically, have for most part plenty of Memoir-writers; and the curious, in after-times, can learn minutely their goings out and comings in: which, as men always love to know their fellow-men in singular situations, is a comfort, of its kind. Not so with these Governing Persons, now in the Townhall! And yet what most original fellow-man, of the Governing sort, high-chancellor, king, kaiser, secretary of the home or the foreign department, ever showed such a phasis as Clerk Tallien, Procureur Manuel, future Procureur Chaumette, here in this Sand-waltz of the Twenty-five millions now do? O brother mortals—thou Advocate Panis, friend of Danton, kinsman of Santerre; Engraver Sergent, since called Agate Sergent; thou Huguenin, with the tocsin in thy heart! But, as Horace says, they wanted the sacred memoir-writer (sacro vate); and we know them not. Men bragged of August and its doings, published them in high places; but of this September none now or afterward would brag. The September world remains dark, fuliginous, as Lapland witch-midnight—from which, indeed, very strange shapes will evolve themselves.

Understand this, however: that incorruptible Robespierre is not wanting, now when the brunt of battle is past; in a stealthy way the seagreen man sits there, his feline eyes excellent in the twilight. Also understand this other, a single fact worth many: that Marat is not only there, but has a seat of honour assigned him, a tribune particulière. How changed for Marat; lifted from his dark cellar into this luminous " peculiar tribune"! All dogs have their day; even rabid dogs. Sorrowful, incurable Philoctetes Marat; without whom Troy can not be taken! Hither, as a main element of the Governing

Power, has Marat been raised. Royalist types, for we have
" suppressed " innumerable Durosoys, Royous, and even
clapped them in prison—Royalist types replace the worn types
often snatched from a People's-Friend in old ill days. In our
" peculiar tribune " we write and redact: Placards, of due
monitory terror; " Amis-du-Peuple " now under the name of
" Journal de la République "); and sit obeyed of men. " Marat," says one, " is the conscience of the Hôtel-de-Ville."
Keeper, as some call it, of the Sovereign's Conscience; which
surely in such hands will not lie hid in a napkin!

Two great movements, as we said, agitate this distracted
National mind: a rushing against domestic Traitors, a rushing against foreign Despots. Mad movements both, restrain-
able by no known rule; strongest passions of human nature
driving them on: love, hatred, vengeful sorrow, braggart Nationality also vengeful—and pale Panic over all! Twelve-
hundred slain Patriots, do they not, from their dark catacombs
there, in Death's dumb-show, plead (O ye Legislators) for
vengeance? Such was the destructive rage of these Aristocrats
on the ever-memorable Tenth. Nay, apart from vengeance,
and with an eye to Public Salvation only, are there not still,
in this Paris (in round numbers), " Thirty-thousand Aristocrats," of the most malignant humour; driven now to their
last trump-card?—Be patient, ye Patriots: our new High
Court, " Tribunal of the Seventeenth," sits; each Section has
sent Four Jurymen; and Danton, extinguishing improper
judges, improper practices wheresoever found, is " the same
man you have known at the Cordeliers." With such a Minister of Justice, shall not Justice be done?—Let it be swift,
then, answers universal Patriotism; swift and sure!—
One would hope, this Tribunal of the Seventeenth is swifter
than most. Already on the 21st, while our Court is but four
days old, Collenot d'Angremont, " the Royalist enlister "
(crimp, embaucheur), dies by torchlight. For, lo, the great
Guillotine, wondrous to behold, now stands there; the Doctor's
Idea has become Oak and Iron; the huge cyclopean axe " falls
in its grooves like the ram of the Pile-engine," swiftly snuffing-
out the light of men! " Mais vous, Gualches, what have you
invented? " This?—Poor old Laporte, Intendant of the Civil
List, follows next; quietly, the mild old man. Then Durosoy,

Royalist Placarder, " cashier of all the Anti-revolutionists of
the interior " : he went rejoicing ; said that a Royalist like him
ought to die, of all days, on this day, the 25th or St. Louis's
Day. All these have been tried, cast—the Galleries shouting
approval ; and handed over to the Realized Idea, within a week.
Besides those whom we have acquitted, the Galleries murmuring, and have dismissed ; or even have personally guarded back
to Prison, as the Galleries took to howling, and even to menac-
ing and elbowing.[5] Languid this Tribunal is not.

Nor does the other movement slacken ; the rushing against
foreign Despots. Strong forces shall meet in death-grip ;
drilled Europe against mad undrilled France ; and singular
conclusions will be tried.—Conceive, therefore, in some faint
degree, the tumult that whirls in this France, in this Paris !
Placards from Section, from Commune, from Legislative, from
the individual Patriot, flame monitory on all walls. Flags of
Danger to Fatherland wave at the Hôtel-de-Ville ; on the
Pont-Neuf—over the prostrate Statues of Kings. There is
universal enlisting, urging to enlist ; there is tearful-boastful
leave-taking ; irregular marching on the Great Northeastern
Road. Marseillese sung their wild " To arms ! " in chorus ;
which now all men, all women and children have learned, and
sing chorally, in Theatres, Boulevards, Streets ; and the heart
burns in every bosom : " Aux armes ! Marchons ! "—Or think
how your Aristocrats are skulking into covert ; how Bertrand-
Moleville lies hidden in some garret " in Aubry-le-boucher
Street, with a poor surgeon who had known me." Dame de
Staël has secreted her Narbonne, not knowing what in the
world to make of him. The Barriers are sometimes open,
oftenest shut ; no passports to be had ; Townhall Emissaries,
with the eyes and claws of falcons, flitting watchful on all
points of your horizon ! In two words : Tribunal of the Seventeenth, busy under howling Galleries ; Prussian Brunswick,
" over a space of forty miles," with his war-tumbrils, and sleeping thunders, and Briarean " sixty-six thousand "[6] right hands
coming, coming !

O Heavens, in these latter days of August, he is come !
Durosoy was not yet guillotined when news had come that
the Prussians were harrying and ravaging about Metz ; in
some four days more, one hears that Longwi, our first strong-
place on the borders, is fallen " in fifteen hours." Quick there-

fore, O ye improvised Municipals; quick, and ever quicker!—
The improvised Municipals make front to this also. Enrolment urges itself; and clothing, and arming. Our very officers
have now "wool epaulettes"; for it is the reign of Equality,
and also of Necessity. Neither do men now monsieur and sir
one another; citoyen (citizen) were suitabler; we even say thou,
as "the free peoples of Antiquity did": so have Journals and
the Improvised Commune suggested; which shall be well.

Infinitely better, meantime, could we suggest, where arms
are to be found. For the present, our Citoyens chant chorally
"To arms!" and have no arms! Arms are searched for; passionately; there is joy over any musket. Moreover, entrench-
ments shall be made round Paris: on the slopes of Montmartre men dig and shovel; though even the simple suspect
this to be desperate. They dig; Tricolor sashes speak en-
couragement and well-speed-ye. Nay, finally "twelve Members of the Legislative go daily," not to encourage only, but
to bear a hand, and delve: it was decreed with acclamation.
Arms shall either be provided; or else the ingenuity of man
crack itself, and become fatuity. Lean Beaumarchais, thinking to serve the Fatherland, and do a stroke of trade in the
old way, has commissioned sixty-thousand stand of good arms
out of Holland: would to Heaven, for Fatherland's sake and
his, they were come! Meanwhile railings are torn up; hammered into pikes; chains themselves shall be welded together
into pikes. The very coffins of the dead are raised; for
melting into balls. All Church-bells must down into the furnace to make cannon; all Church-plate into the mint to make
money. Also, behold the fair swan-bevies of Citoyennes that
have alighted in Churches, and sit there with swan-neck—
sewing tents and regimentals! Nor are Patriotic Gifts wanting, from those that have aught left; nor stingily given: the
fair Villaumes, mother and daughter, Milliners in the Rue St.-
Martin, give a "silver thimble, and a coin of fifteen sous
(sevenpence halfpenny)," with other similar effects; and offer,
at least the mother does, to mount guard. Men who have not
even a thimble, give a thimbleful—were it but of invention.
One Citoyen has wrought out the scheme of a wooden cannon;
which France shall exclusively profit by, in the first instance.
It is to be made of staves, by the coopers—of almost bound-
less calibre, but uncertain as to strength! Thus they: ham-

mering, scheming, stitching, founding, with all their heart and with all their soul. Two bells only are to remain in each Parish—for tocsin and other purposes.

But mark also, precisely while the Prussian batteries were playing their briskest at Longwi in the Northeast, and our dastardly Lavergne saw nothing for it but surrender—southwestward, in remote, patriarchal La Vendée, that sour ferment about Nonjuring Priests, after long working, is ripe, and explodes: at the wrong moment for us! And so we have " eight thousand Peasants at Châtillon-sur-Sèvre " who will not be balloted for soldiers; will not have their Curates molested. To whom Bonchamps, Larochejaquelins, and Seigneurs enough of a Royalist turn, will join themselves; with Stofflets and Charettes; with Heroes and Chouan Smugglers; and the loyal warmth of a simple people, blown into flame and fury by theological and seignorial bellows! So that there shall be fighting from behind ditches, death-volleys bursting out of thickets and ravines of rivers; huts burning, feet of the pitiful women hurrying to refuge with their children on their back; seed-fields fallow, whitened with human bones—" eighty-thousand, of all ages, ranks, sexes, flying at once across the Loire," with wail borne far on the winds: and in brief, for years coming, such a suite of scenes as glorious war has not offered in these late ages, not since our Albigenses and Crusadings were over—save indeed some chance Palatinate, or so, we might have to " burn," by way of exception. The " eight-thousand at Châtillon " will be got dispelled for the moment; the fire scattered, not extinguished. To the dints and bruises of outward battle there is to be added henceforth a deadlier internal gangrene.

This rising in La Vendée reports itself at Paris on Wednesday the 29th of August—just as we had got our Electors elected; and, in spite of Brunswick and Longwi, were hoping still to have a National Convention, if it pleased Heaven. But indeed otherwise this Wednesday is to be regarded as one of the notablest Paris had yet seen: gloomy tidings come successively, like Job's messengers; are met by gloomy answers. Of Sardinia rising to invade the Southeast, and Spain threatening the South, we do not speak. But are not the Prussians masters of Longwi (treacherously yielded, one would say); and preparing to besiege Verdun? Clairfait and his

Austrians are encompassing Thionville; darkening the North. Not Metzland now, but the Clermontais is getting harried; flying hulans and hussars have been seen on the Châlons road, almost as far as Sainte-Menehould.   Heart, ye Patriots; if ye lose heart, ye lose all!

It is not without a dramatic emotion that one reads in the Parliamentary Debates of this Wednesday evening " past seven o'clock," the scene with the military fugitives from Longwi. Wayworn, dusty, disheartened, these poor men enter the Legislative, about sunset or after; give the most pathetic detail of the frightful pass they were in: Prussians billowing round by the myriad, volcanically spouting fire for fifteen hours: we, scattered sparse on the ramparts, hardly a cannoneer to two guns; our dastard Commandant Lavergne nowhere showing face; the priming would not catch; there was no powder in the bombs—what could we do?   " Mourir, Die!" answer prompt voices; [7] and the dusty fugitives must shrink elsewhither for comfort.—Yes, " Mourir," that is now the word. Be Longwi a proverb and a hissing among French strongplaces: let it (says the Legislative) be obliterated rather, from the shamed face of the Earth—and so there has gone forth Decree, that Longwi shall, were the Prussians once out of it, " be razed," to exist only as ploughed ground.

Nor are the Jacobins milder; as how could they, the flower of Patriotism?   Poor Dame Lavergne, wife of the poor Commandant, took her parasol one evening, and escorted by her Father came over to the Hall of the mighty Mother; and " reads a memoir tending to justify the Commandant of Longwi." Lafarge, Président, makes answer: " Citoyenne, the Nation will judge Lavergne; the Jacobins are bound to tell him the truth.   He would have ended his course there (terminé sa carrière), if he had loved the honour of his country." [8]

NOTES

[1] Moore's " Journal," i, 85.
[2] " Hist. Parl.," xvii, 467.
[3] Ibid., 437.
[4] " Mémoires de Buzot " (Paris, 1823), p. 88.
[5] Moore's " Journal," i, 159–168.
[6] See Toulongeon, " Hist. de France," ii, c. 5.
[7] " Hist. Parl.," xvii, 148.
[8] Ibid., xix, 300.

CHAPTER II

DANTON

BUT better than razing of Longwi, or rebuking poor dusty soldiers or soldiers' wives, Danton had come over, last night, and demanded a Decree to search for arms, since they were not yielded voluntarily. Let "Domiciliary visits," with rigour of authority, be made to this end. To search for arms; for horses—Aristocratism rolls in its carriage, while Patriotism can not trail its cannon. To search generally for munitions of war, "in the houses of persons suspect"— and even, if it seem proper, to seize and imprison the suspect persons themselves! In the Prisons their Plots will be harmless; in the Prisons they will be as hostages for us, and not without use. This Decree the energetic Minister of Justice demanded last night, and got; and this same night it is to be executed; it is being executed at the moment when these dusty soldiers get saluted with "Mourir." Two-thousand stand of arms, as they count, are foraged in this way; and some four-hundred head of new Prisoners; and, on the whole, such a terror and damp is struck through the Aristocrat heart, as all but Patriotism, and even Patriotism were it out of this agony, might pity. Yes, Messieurs! if Brunswick blast Paris to ashes, he probably will blast the Prisons of Paris too: pale Terror, if we have got it, we will also give it, and the depths of horrors that lie in it; the same leaky bottom, in these wild waters, bears us all.

One can judge what stir there was now among the "thirty-thousand Royalists": how the Plotters, or the accused of Plotting, shrank each closer into his lurking-place—like Bertrand-Moleville, looking eager toward Longwi, hoping the weather would keep fair. Or how they dressed themselves in valet's clothes, like Narbonne, and "got to England as Dr. Bollman's famulus": how Dame de Staël bestirred herself, pleading with

Manuel as a Sister in Literature, pleading even with Clerk
Tallien; a prey to nameless chagrins![1] Royalist Peltier, the
Pamphleteer, gives a touching Narrative (not deficient in
height of colouring) of the terrors of that night. From five
in the afternoon, a great city is struck suddenly silent; except
for the beating of drums, for the tramp of marching feet; and
ever and anon the dread thunder of the knocker at some door,
a Tricolor Commissioner with his blue Guards (black-guards!)
arriving. All Streets are vacant, says Peltier; beset by Guards
at each end: all Citizens are ordered to be within doors. On
the River float sentinel barges, lest we escape by water: the
Barriers hermetically closed. Frightful! The Sun shines;
serenely westering, in smokeless mackerel-sky; Paris is as if
sleeping, as if dead—Paris is holding its breath, to see what
stroke will fall on it. Poor Peltier! "Acts of Apostles," and
all jocundity of Leading-Articles, are gone out, and it is become bitter earnest instead; polished satire changed now into
coarse pike-points (hammered out of railing); all logic reduced
to this one primitive thesis, " An eye for an eye, a tooth for a
tooth! "—Peltier, dolefully aware of it, ducks low; escapes un-
scathed to England; to urge there the inky war anew—to have
Trial by Jury, in due season, and deliverance by young Whig
eloquence, world-celebrated for a day.

Of "thirty-thousand" naturally great multitudes were
left unmolested: but, as we said, some four-hundred, desig-
nated as "persons suspect," were seized; and an unspeakable
terror fell on all. Wo to him who is guilty of plotting, of
Anti-civism, Royalism, Feuillantism; who, guilty or not guilty,
has an enemy in his Section to call him guilty! Poor old
M. de Cazotte is seized; his young loved Daughter with him,
refusing to quit him. Why, O Cazotte, wouldst thou quit
romancing and "Diable Amoureux," for such reality as this?
Poor old M. de Sombreuil, he of the Invalides, is seized; a man
seen askance by Patriotism ever since the Bastille days; whom
also a fond Daughter will not quit. With young tears hardly
suppressed, and old wavering weakness rousing itself once
more—O my brothers, O my sisters!

The famed and named go; the nameless, if they have an
accuser. Necklace Lamotte's Husband is in these Prisons
(she long since squelched on the London Pavements); but
gets delivered. Gross de Morande, of the " Courrier de l'Eu-

41

rope," hobbles distractedly to and fro there: but they let him hobble out; on right nimble crutches—his hour not being yet come. Advocate Maton de la Varenne, very weak in health, is snatched off from mother and kin; Tricolor Rossignol (journeyman goldsmith and scoundrel lately, a risen man now) remembers an old Pleading of Maton's! Jourgniac de Saint-Méard goes; the brisk frank soldier: he was in the mutiny of Nanci, in that "effervescent Regiment du Roi"—on the wrong side. Saddest of all: Abbé Sicard goes; a Priest who could not take the Oath, but who could teach the Deaf and Dumb: in his Section, one man, he says, had a grudge at him; one man, at the fit hour, launches an arrest against him; which hits. In the Arsenal quarter, there are dumb hearts making wail, with signs, with wild gestures; he their miraculous healer and speech-bringer is rapt away.

What with the arrestments on this night of the Twenty-ninth, what with those that have gone on more or less, day and night, ever since the Tenth, one may fancy what the Prisons now were. Crowding and confusion; jostle, hurry, vehemence and terror! Of the poor Queen's Friends, who had followed her to the Temple, and been committed elsewhither to Prison, some, as Governess de Tourzelle, are to be let go: one, the poor Princess de Lamballe, is not let go; but waits in the strong-rooms of La Force there, what will betide further.

Among so many hundreds whom the launched arrest hits, who are rolled off to Townhall or Sectionhall, to preliminary Houses of Detention, and hurled in thither as into cattle-pens, we must mention one other: Caron de Beaumarchais, Author of "Figaro"; vanquisher of Maupeou Parlements and Goezman helldogs; once numbered among the demigods; and now—? We left him in his culminant state; what dreadful decline is this, when we again catch a glimpse of him! "At midnight" (it was but the 12th of August yet), "the servant, in his shirt, with wide-staring eyes, enters your room.—Monsieur, rise, all the people are come to seek you; they are knocking, like to break-in the door! "And they were in fact knocking in a terrible manner (d'une façon terrible). I fling on my coat, forgetting even the waistcoat, nothing on my feet but

slippers; and say to him "—And he, alas! answers mere negatory incoherences, panic interjections. And through the
shutters and crevices, in front or rearward, the dull street-
lamps disclose only streetfuls of haggard countenances; clamorous, bristling with pikes: and you rush distracted for an outlet, finding none—and have to take refuge in the crockery-
press, downstairs; and stand there, palpitating in that imperfect costume, lights dancing past your key-hole, tramp of feet
overhead, and the tumult of Satan, " for four hours and more "!
And old ladies, of the quarter, started up (as we hear next
morning); rang for their bonnes and cordial-drops, with shrill
interjections: and old gentlemen, in their shirts, " leaped gar-
den-walls "; flying while none pursued; one of whom unfortunately broke his leg.[2] Those sixty-thousand stand of Dutch
Arms (which never arrive), and the bold stroke of trade, have
turned out so ill!—

Beaumarchais escaped for this time; but not for the next
time, ten days after. On the evening of the Twenty-ninth
he is still in that chaos of the Prisons, in saddest wrestling
condition; unable to get justice, even to get audience; " Panis
scratching his head " when you speak to him, and making off.
Nevertheless let the lover of Figaro know that Procureur
Manuel, a Brother in Literature, found him, and delivered
him once more. But how the lean demigod, now shorn of
his splendour, had to lurk in barns, to roam over harrowed
fields, panting for life; and to wait under eavesdrops, and sit
in darkness " on the Boulevarde amid paving-stones and
boulders," longing for one word of any Minister, or Minister's
Clerk, about those accursed Dutch muskets, and getting none
—with heart fuming in spleen, and terror, and suppressed
canine-madness; alas! how the swift sharp hound, once fit
to be Diana's, breaks his old teeth now, gnawing mere whin-
stones; and must " fly to England "; and, returning from
England, must creep into the corner, and lie quiet, toothless
(moneyless)—all this let the lover of Figaro fancy, and weep
for. We here, without weeping, not without sadness, wave
the withered tough fellow-mortal our farewell. His Figaro
has returned to the French stage; nay, is, at this day, sometimes named the best piece there. And indeed, so long as
Man's Life can ground itself only on artificiality and aridity;
each new Revolt and Change of Dynasty turning up only a

new stratum of dry-rubbish, and no soil yet coming to view
—may it not be good to protest against such a Life, in many
ways, and even in the Figaro way?

NOTES

[1] De Staël, " Considérations sur la Révolution," ii, 67–81.
[2] Beaumarchais' Narrative, "Mémoires sur les Prisons" (Paris,
1823), i, 179–190.

CHAPTER III

DUMOURIEZ

SUCH are the last days of August 1792; days gloomy, disastrous, and of evil omen. What will become of this poor France? Dumouriez rode from the Camp of Maulde, eastward to Sedan, on Tuesday last, the 28th of the month; reviewed that so-called Army left forlorn there by Lafayette: the forlorn soldiers gloomed on him; were heard growling on him, "This is one of them, ce b——e là, that made War be declared." [1] Unpromising Army! Recruits flow in, filtering through Dépôt after Dépôt; but recruits merely: in want of all; happy if they have so much as arms. And Longwi has fallen basely; and Brunswick, and the Prussian King, with his sixty-thousand, will beleaguer Verdun; and Clairfait and Austrians press deeper in, over the Northern marches: "a hundred and fifty thousand" as fear counts, "eighty-thousand" as the returns show, do hem us in; Cimmerian Europe behind them. There is Castries-and-Broglie chivalry; Royalist foot "in red facing and nankeen trousers"; breathing death and the gallows.

And lo, finally, at Verdun on Sunday the 2d of September 1792, Brunswick is here. With his King and sixty-thousand, glittering over the heights, from beyond the winding Meuse River, he looks down on us, on our "high citadel" and all our confectionery ovens (for we are celebrated for confectionery); has sent courteous summons, in order to spare the effusion of blood!—Resist him to the death? Every day of retardation precious? How, O General Beaurepaire (asks the amazed Municipality), shall we resist him? We, the Verdun Municipals, see no resistance possible. Has he not sixty-thousand, and artillery without end? Retardation, Patriotism is good; but so likewise is peaceable baking of pastry, and sleeping in whole skin.—Hapless Beaurepaire stretches out his hands, and

pleads passionately, in the name of country, honour, of Heaven
and of Earth: to no purpose. The Municipals have, by law,
the power of ordering it—with an Army officered by Royalism
or Crypto-Royalism, such a Law seemed needful: and they
order it, as pacific Pastry-cooks, not as heroic Patriots would
—To surrender! Beaurepaire strides home, with long steps:
his valet, entering the room, sees him " writing eagerly," and
withdraws. His valet hears then, in few minutes, the report
of a pistol: Beaurepaire is lying dead; his eager writing had
been a brief suicidal farewell. In this manner died Beaurepaire, wept of France; buried in the Pantheon, with honourable Pension to his Widow, and for Epitaph these words, " He
chose Death rather than yield to Despots." The Prussians,
descending from the heights, are peaceable masters of Verdun.

And so Brunswick advances, from stage to stage: who shall
now stay him—covering forty miles of country? Foragers
fly far; the villages of the Northeast are harried; your Hessian forager has only " three sous a-day": the very Emigrants, it is said, will take silver-plate—by way of revenge.
Clermont, Sainte-Menehould, Varennes especially, ye Towns
of the Night of Spurs, tremble ye! Procureur Sausse and
the Magistracy of Varennes have fled; brave Boniface Le
Blanc of the Bras d'Or is to the woods: Mrs. Le Blanc, a
young woman fair to look upon, with her young infant, has
to live in greenwood, like a beautiful Bessy Bell of Song, her
bower thatched with rushes; catching premature rheumatism.[2]
Clermont may ring the tocsin now, and illuminate itself!
Clermont lies at the foot of its Cow (or Vache, so they name
that Mountain), a prey to the Hessian spoiler: its fair women,
fairer than most, are robbed; not of life, or what is dearer,
yet of all that is cheaper and portable; for Necessity, on three
half-pence a-day, has no law. At Sainte-Menehould the enemy has been expected more than once—our Nationals all turning out in arms; but was not yet seen. Postmaster Drouet,
he is not in the woods, but minding his Election; and will
sit in the Convention, notable King-taker, and bold Old-
Dragoon as he is.

Thus on the Northeast all roams and runs; and on a set
day, the date of which is irrecoverable by History, Brunswick
" has engaged to dine in Paris "—the Powers willing. And
at Paris, in the centre, it is as we saw; and in La Vendée

Southwest, it is as we saw; and Sardinia is in the Southeast, and Spain in the South, and Clairfait with Austria and sieged Thionville is in the North—and all France leaps distracted, like the winnowed Sahara waltzing in sand colonnades! More desperate posture no country ever stood in. A country, one would say, which the Majesty of Prussia (if it so pleased him) might partition and clip in pieces, like a Poland; flinging the remainder to poor Brother Louis—with directions to keep it quiet, or else we will keep it for him!

Or perhaps the Upper Powers, minded that a new Chapter in Universal History shall begin here and not further on, may have ordered it all otherwise? In that case, Brunswick will not dine in Paris on the set day; nor, indeed, one knows not when!—Verily, amid this wreckage, where poor France seems grinding itself down to dust and bottomless ruin, who knows what miraculous salient-point of Deliverance and New-life may have already come into existence there; and be already working there, though as yet human eye discern it not! On the night of that same twenty-eighth of August, the unpromising Review-day in Sedan, Dumouriez assembles a Council of War at his lodgings there. He spreads out the map of this forlorn war-district; Prussians here, Austrians there; triumphant both, with broad highway, and little hinderance, all the way to Paris: we scattered, helpless, here and here: what to advise? The Generals, strangers to Dumouriez, look blank enough; know not well what to advise—if it be not retreating, and retreating till our recruits accumulate; till perhaps the chapter of chances turn up some leaf for us; or Paris, at all events, be sacked at the latest day possible. The Many-counselled, who "has not closed an eye for three nights," listens with little speech to these long cheerless speeches; merely watching the speaker, that he may know him; then wishes them all good-night—but beckons a certain young Thouvenot, the fire of whose looks had pleased him, to wait a moment. Thouvenot waits: "Voilà," says Polymetis, pointing to the map! That is the Forest of Argonne, that long strip of rocky Mountain and wild Wood; forty miles long; with but five, or say even three practicable Passes through it: this, for they have forgotten it, might one not still seize, though Clairfait sits so nigh? Once seized—the Champagne called the Hungry (or worse, Campagne Pouil-

leuse) on their side of it; the fat Three Bishoprics, and willing
France on ours; and the Equinox rains not far—this Argonne
" might be the Thermopylæ of France "! [3]

O brisk Dumouriez Polymetis with thy teeming head, may
the gods grant it!—Polymetis, at any rate, folds his map
together, and flings himself on bed; resolved to try, on the
morrow morning. With astucity, with swiftness, with audacity! One had need to be a lion-fox, and have luck on
one's side.

NOTES

[1] Dumouriez, " Mémoires," ii, 383.
[2] Helen Maria Williams, " Letters from France " (London, 1791–
'93), iii, 96.
[3] Dumouriez, ii, 391.

CHAPTER IV

SEPTEMBER IN PARIS

AT Paris, by lying Rumour which proved prophetic and veridical, the fall of Verdun was known some hours before it happened. It is Sunday the second of September; handiwork hinders not the speculations of the mind. Verdun gone (though some still deny it); the Prussians in full march, with gallows-ropes, with fire and fagot! Thirty-thousand Aristocrats within our own walls; and but the merest quarter-tithe of them yet put in Prison! Nay, there goes a word that even these will revolt. Sieur Jean Julien, wagoner of Vaugirard,[1] being set in the Pillory last Friday, took all at once to crying, That he would be well avenged ere long; that the King's Friends in Prison would burst out, force the Temple, set the King on horseback, and, joined by the unimprisoned, ride roughshod over us all. This the unfortunate wagoner of Vaugirard did bawl, at the top of his lungs: when snatched off to the Townhall, he persisted in it, still bawling; yesternight, when they guillotined him, he died with the froth of it on his lips.[2] For a man's mind, padlocked to the Pillory, may go mad; and all men's minds may go mad, and " believe him," as the frenetic will do, " because it is impossible."

So that apparently the knot of the crisis and last agony of France is come? Make front to this, thou Improvised Commune, strong Danton, whatsoever man is strong! Readers can judge whether the Flag of Country in Danger flapped soothingly or distractively on the souls of men that day.

But the Improvised Commune, but strong Danton is not wanting, each after his kind. Huge Placards are getting plastered to the walls; at two o'clock the stormbell shall be sounded, the alarm-cannon fired; all Paris shall rush to the Champ-de-Mars, and have itself enrolled. Unarmed, truly,

625

and undrilled; but desperate, in the strength of frenzy. Haste, ye men; ye very women, offer to mount guard and shoulder the brown musket: weak clucking-hens, in a state of desperation, will fly at the muzzle of the mastiff; and even conquer him—by vehemence of character! Terror itself, when once grown transcendental, becomes a kind of courage; as frost sufficiently intense, according to Poet Milton, will burn.— Danton, the other night, in the Legislative Committee of General Defence, when the other Ministers and Legislators had all opined, said, It would not do to quit Paris, and fly to Saumur; that they must abide by Paris; and take such attitude as would put their enemies in fear—*faire peur;* a word of his which has been often repeated, and reprinted—in italics.[3]

At two of the clock, Beaurepaire, as we saw, has shot himself at Verdun; and, over Europe, mortals are going in for afternoon sermon. But at Paris, all steeples are clangouring not for sermon; the alarm-gun booming from minute to minute; Champ-de-Mars and Fatherland's Altar boiling with desperate terror-courage: what a miserere going up to Heaven from this once Capital of the Most Christian King! The Legislative sits in alternate awe and effervescence; Vergniaud proposing that Twelve shall go and dig personally on Montmartre; which is decreed by acclaim.

But better than digging personally with acclaim, see Danton enter—the black brows clouded, the colossus figure tramping heavy; grim energy looking from all features of the rugged man! Strong is that grim Son of France and Son of Earth; a Reality and not a Formula he too: and surely now if ever, being hurled low enough, it is on the Earth and on Realities that he rests. "Legislators!" so speaks the stentor-voice, as the Newspapers yet preserve it for us, "it is not the alarm-cannon that you hear: it is the pas-de-charge against our enemies. To conquer them, to hurl them back, what do we require? Il nous faut de l'audace, et encore de l'audace, et toujours de l'audace, To dare, and again to dare, and without end to dare!"[4]—Right so, thou brawny Titan; there is nothing left for thee but that. Old men, who heard it, will still tell you how the reverberating voice made all hearts swell, in that moment; and braced them to the sticking-place; and thrilled abroad over France, like electric virtue, as a word spoken in season.

But the Commune, enrolling in the Champ-de-Mars? But the Committee of Watchfulness, become now Committee of Public Salvation; whose conscience is Marat? The Commune enrolling enrolls many; provides tents for them in that Mars-Field, that they may march with dawn on the morrow: praise to this part of the Commune! To Marat and the Committee of Watchfulness not praise—not even blame, such as could be meted out in these insufficient dialects of ours; expressive silence rather! Lone Marat, the man forbid, meditating long in his Cellars of refuge, on his Stylites Pillar, could see salvation in one thing only: in the fall of "two-hundred and sixty thousand Aristocrat heads." With so many score of Naples Bravoes, each a dirk in his right-hand, a muff on his left, he would traverse France, and do it. But the world laughed, mocking the severe-benevolence of a People's-Friend; and his idea could not become an action, but only a fixed-idea. Lo now, however, he has come down from his Stylites Pillar to a Tribune particulière; here now, without the dirks, without the muffs at least, were it not grown possible—now in the knot of the crisis, when salvation or destruction hangs in the hour!

The Ice-Tower of Avignon was noised of sufficiently, and lives in all memories; but the authors were not punished: nay, we saw Jourdan Coupe-tête, borne on men's shoulders, like a copper Portent, "traversing the cities of the South."—What phantasms, squalid-horrid, shaking their dirk and muff, may dance through the brain of a Marat, in this dizzy pealing of tocsin-miserere and universal frenzy, seek not to guess, O Reader! Nor what the cruel Billaud "in his short brown coat" was thinking; nor Sergent, not yet Agate-Sergent; nor Panis the confidant of Danton—nor, in a word, how gloomy Orcus does breed in her gloomy womb, and fashion her monsters and prodigies of Events, which thou seest her visibly bear! Terror is on the streets of Paris; terror and rage, tears and frenzy: tocsin-miserere pealing through the air; fierce desperation rushing to battle; mothers, with streaming eyes and wild hearts, sending forth their sons to die. "Carriage-horses are seized by the bridle," that they may draw cannon; "the traces cut, the carriages left standing." In such tocsin-miserere, and murky bewilderment of Frenzy, are not Murder, Até and all Furies near at hand? On slight hint—who knows on how slight?—may not Murder come; and, with her snaky-sparkling head, illuminate this murk?

How it was and went, what part might be premeditated, what was improvised and accidental, man will never know, till the great Day of Judgment make it known. But with a Marat for keeper of the Sovereign's Conscience—And we know what the ultima ratio of Sovereigns, when they are driven to it, is! In this Paris there are as wicked men, say a hundred or more, as exist in all the Earth: to be hired, and set on; to set on, of their own accord, unhired.—And yet we will remark that premeditation itself is not performance, is not surety of performance; that it is perhaps, at most, surety of letting whosoever wills perform. From the purpose of crime to the act of crime there is an abyss; wonderful to think of. The finger lies on the pistol; but the man is not yet a murderer: nay, his whole nature staggering at such consummation, is there not a confused pause rather—one last instant of possibility for him? Not yet a murderer; it is at the mercy of light trifles whether the most fixed idea may not yet become unfixed. One slight twitch of a muscle, the death-flash bursts; and he is it, and will for Eternity be it; and Earth has become a penal Tartarus for him; his horizon girdled now not with golden hope, but with red flames of remorse; voices from the depths of Nature sounding, Wo, wo on him!

Of such stuff are we all made; on such powder-mines of bottomless guilt and criminality—" if God restrained not," as is well said—does the purest of us walk. There are depths in man that go the length of lowest Hell, as there are heights that reach highest Heaven—for are not both Heaven and Hell made out of him, made by him, everlasting Miracle and Mystery as he is?—But looking on this Champ-de-Mars, with its tent-buildings and frantic enrolments; on this murky-simmering Paris, with its crammed Prisons (supposed about to burst), with its tocsin-miserere, its mothers' tears, and soldiers' farewell shoutings—the pious soul might have prayed, that day, that God's grace would restrain, and greatly restrain; lest on slight hest or hint, Madness, Horror and Murder rose, and this Sabbathday of September became a Day black in the Annals of men.

The tocsin is pealing its loudest, the clocks inaudibly striking Three, when poor Abbé Sicard, with some thirty other

Nonjurant Priests, in six carriages, fare along the streets, from their preliminary House of Detention at the Townhall, westward toward the Prison of the Abbaye. Carriages enough stand deserted on the streets; these six move on—through angry multitudes, cursing as they move. Accursed Aristocrat Tartuffes, this is the pass ye have brought us to! And now ye will break the Prisons, and set Capet Veto on horseback to ride over us? Out upon you, Priests of Beelzebub and Moloch; of Tartuffery, Mammon and the Prussian Gallows—which ye name Mother-Church and God!—Such reproaches have the poor Nonjurants to endure, and worse; spoken-in on them by frantic Patriots, who mount even on the carriage-steps; the very Guards hardly refraining. Pull up your carriage-blinds?—No! answers Patriotism, clapping its horny paw on the carriage-blind, and crushing it down again. Patience in oppression has limits: we are close on the Abbaye, it has lasted long: a poor Nonjurant, of quicker temper, smites the horny paw with his cane; nay, finding solacement in it, smites the unkempt head, sharply and again more sharply, twice over—seen clearly of us and of the world. It is the last that we see clearly. Alas! next moment the carriages are locked and blocked in endless raging tumults; in yells deaf to the cry for mercy, which answer the cry for mercy with sabre-thrusts through the heart.[5] The thirty Priests are torn out, are massacred about the Prison-Gate, one after one—only the poor Abbé Sicard, whom one Moton a watchmaker, knowing him, heroically tried to save and secrete in the prison, escapes to tell—and it is Night and Orcus; and Murder's snaky-sparkling head has risen in the murk!—

From Sunday afternoon (exclusive of intervals and pauses not final) till Thursday evening, there follow consecutively a Hundred Hours. Which hundred hours are to be reckoned with the hours of the Bartholomew Butchery, of the Armagnac Massacres, Sicilian Vespers, or whatsoever is savagest in the annals of this world. Horrible the hour when man's soul, in its paroxysm, spurns asunder the barriers and rules; and shows what dens and depths are in it! For Night and Orcus, as we say, as was long prophesied, have burst forth, here in this Paris, from their subterranean imprisonment: hideous, dim-confused; which it is painful to look on; and yet which can not, and indeed which should not, be forgotten.

The Reader, who looks earnestly through this dim Phantasmagory of the Pit, will discern few fixed certain objects; and yet still a few. He will observe, in this Abbaye Prison, the sudden massacre of the Priests being once over, a strange Court of Justice, or call it Court of Revenge and Wild-Justice, swiftly fashion itself, and take seat round a table, with the Prison-Registers spread before it—Stanislas Maillard, Bastille hero, famed Leader of the Menads, presiding. O Stanislas, one hoped to meet thee elsewhere than here; thou shifty Riding-Usher, with an inkling of Law! This work also thou hadst to do; and then—to depart forever from our eyes. At La Force, at the Châtelet, the Conciergerie, the like Court forms itself, with the like accompaniments: the thing that one man does, other men can do. There are some Seven Prisons in Paris, full of Aristocrats with conspiracies—nay, not even Bicêtre and Salpêtrière shall escape, with their Forgers of Assignats: and there are seventy times seven hundred Patriot hearts in a state of frenzy. Scoundrel hearts also there are; as perfect, say, as the Earth holds—if such are needed. To whom, in this mood, law is as no-law; and killing, by what name soever called, is but work to be done.

So sit these sudden Courts of Wild-Justice, with the Prison-Registers before them; unwonted wild tumult howling all round; the Prisoners in dread expectancy within. Swift: a name is called; bolts jingle, a Prisoner is there. A few questions are put; swiftly this sudden Jury decides: Royalist Plotter or not? Clearly not; in that case, let the Prisoner be enlarged with "Vive la Nation!" Probably yea; then still, Let the Prisoner be enlarged, but without "Vive la Nation!" or else it may run, Let the Prisoner be conducted to La Force. At La Force again their formula is, Let the Prisoner be conducted to the Abbaye—"To La Force, then!" Volunteer bailiffs seize the doomed man; he is at the outer gate; "enlarged," or "conducted," not into La Force, but into a howling sea; forth, under an arch of wild sabres, axes and pikes; and sinks, hewn asunder. And another sinks, and another; and there forms itself a piled heap of corpses, and the kennels begin to run red. Fancy the yells of these men, their faces of sweat and blood; the crueller shrieks of these women, for there are women too; and a fellow-mortal hurled naked into it all! Jourgniac de Saint-Méard has seen battle, has seen an effer-

vescent Regiment du Roi in mutiny; but the bravest heart
may quail at this. The Swiss Prisoners, remnants of the
Tenth of August, "clasped each other spasmodically, and
hung back; gray veterans crying: "Mercy, Messieurs; ah,
mercy!" But there was no mercy. Suddenly, however, one
of these men steps forward. He had on a blue frockcoat; he
seemed about thirty, his stature was above common, his look
noble and martial. "I go first," said he, "since it must be
so: adieu!" Then dashing his hat sharply behind him:
"Which way?" cried he to the Brigands: "Show it me, then."
They open the folding gate; he is announced to the multitude.
He stands a moment motionless; then plunges forth among
the pikes, and dies of a thousand wounds." [6]

Man after man is cut down; the sabres need sharpening,
the killers refresh themselves from wine-jugs. Onward and
onward goes the butchery; the loud yells wearying down into
bass growls. A sombre-faced shifting multitude looks on; in
dull approval, or dull disapproval; in dull recognition that
it is Necessity. "An Anglais in drab greatcoat" was seen, or
seemed to be seen, serving liquor from his own dram-bottle—
for what purpose, "if not set on by Pitt," Satan and himself
know best! Witty Dr. Moore grew sick on approaching, and
turned into another street.[7]—Quick enough goes this Jury-
Court; and rigorous. The brave are not spared, nor the
beautiful, nor the weak. Old M. de Montmorin, the Minister's Brother, was acquitted by the Tribunal of the Seventeenth; and conducted back, elbowed by howling galleries; but
is not acquitted here. Princess de Lamballe has lain down
on bed: "Madame, you are to be removed to the Abbaye."
"I do not wish to remove; I am well enough here." There
is a need-be for removing. She will arrange her dress a little,
then; rude voices answer, "You have not far to go." She too
is led to the hell-gate; a manifest Queen's-Friend. She shivers
back, at the sight of bloody sabres; but there is no return:
Onward! That fair head is cleft with the axe; the neck is
severed. That fair body is cut in fragments; with indignities,
and obscene horrors of mustachio grands-lèvres, which human
nature would fain find incredible—which shall be read in the
original language only. She was beautiful, she was good, she
had known no happiness. Young hearts, generation after generation, will think with themselves: O worthy of worship,

thou king-descended, god-descended, and poor sister-woman! why was not I there; and some Sword Balmung or Thor's Hammer in my hand? Her head is fixed on a pike; paraded under the windows of the Temple; that a still more hated, a Marie Antoinette, may see. One Municipal, in the Temple with the Royal Prisoners at the moment, said, " Look out." Another eagerly whispered, " Do not look." The circuit of the Temple is guarded, in these hours, by a long stretched tricolor riband: terror enters, and the clangour of infinite tumult; hitherto not regicide, though that too may come.

But it is more edifying to note what thrillings of affection, what fragments of wild virtues turn up in this shaking asunder of man's existence; for of these too there is a proportion. Note old Marquis Cazotte: he is doomed to die; but his young Daughter clasps him in her arms, with an inspiration of eloquence, with a love which is stronger than very death: the heart of the killers themselves is touched by it; the old man is spared. Yet he was guilty, if plotting for his King is guilt: in ten days more, a Court of Law condemned him, and he had to die elsewhere; bequeathing his Daughter a lock of his old gray hair. Or note old M. de Sombreuil, who also had a Daughter: My Father is not an Aristocrat: O good gentlemen, I will swear it, and testify it, and in all ways prove it; we are not; we hate Aristocrats! " Wilt thou drink Aristocrats' blood?" The man lifts blood (if universal Rumour can be credited);[8] the poor maiden does drink. " This Sombreuil is innocent, then!" Yes, indeed—and now note, most of all, how the bloody pikes, at this news, do rattle to the ground; and the tiger-yells become bursts of jubilee over a brother saved; and the old man and his daughter are clasped to bloody bosoms, with hot tears; and borne home in triumph of " Vive la Nation!" the killers refusing even money! Does it seem strange, this temper of theirs? It seems very certain, well proved by Royalist testimony in other instances;[9] and very significant.

NOTES

[1] Moore, i, 178.
[2] " Hist. Parl.," xvii, 409.
[3] " Biographie des Ministres " (Bruxelles, 1826), p. 96.
[4] " Moniteur " (in " Hist. Parl.," xvii, 347).

[5] Félémhesi (anagram for Méhée Fils), "La Vérité tout entière sur les vrais auteurs de la journée du 2 Septembre 1792" (reprinted in "Hist. Parl.," xviii, 156–181), p. 167.

[6] Félémhesi, ut suprà, p. 173.

[7] Moore's "Journal," i, 185–195.

[8] Dulaure, "Esquisses historiques des principaux événemens de la Révolution," ii, 206 (cited in Montgaillard, iii, 205).

[9] Bertrand-Moleville ("Mém. particuliers," ii, 213), etc., etc.

CHAPTER V

A TRILOGY

AS all Delineation, in these ages, were it never so Epic,
"speaking itself and not singing itself," must either
found on Belief and provable Fact, or have no founda-
tion at all (nor, except as floating cobweb, any existence at all),
the Reader will perhaps prefer to take a glance with the very
eyes of eye-witnesses; and see, in that way, for himself, how
it was. Brave Jourgniac, innocent Abbé Sicard, judicious
Advocate Maton, these, greatly compressing themselves, shall
speak, each an instant. Jourgniac's "Agony of Thirty-eight
Hours" went through "above a hundred editions," though
intrinsically a poor work. Some portion of it may here go
through above the hundred-and-first, for want of a better.

"Toward seven o'clock" (Sunday night at the Abbaye; for
Jourgniac goes by dates): "We saw two men enter, their
hands bloody and armed with sabres; a turnkey, with a torch,
lighted them; he pointed to the bed of the unfortunate Swiss,
Reding. Reding spoke with a dying voice. One of them
paused; but the other cried, "Allons donc!" lifted the unfortunate man; carried him out on his back to the street. He
was massacred there.

"We all looked at one another in silence, we clasped each
other's hands. Motionless, with fixed eyes, we gazed on the
pavement of our prison; on which lay the moonlight, cheq-
uered with the triple stancheons of our windows."

"Three in the morning: They were breaking-in one of
the prison-doors. We at first thought they were coming to kill
us in our room; but heard, by voices on the staircase, that
it was a room where some Prisoners had barricaded themselves. They were all butchered there, as we shortly gathered."

"Ten o'clock: The Abbé Lenfant and the Abbé de Chapt-

634

Rastignac appeared in the pulpit of the Chapel, which was
our prison; they had entered by a door from the stairs. They
said to us that our end was at hand; that we must compose
ourselves, and receive their last blessing. An electric movement, not to be defined, threw us all on our knees, and we
received it. These two white-haired old men, blessing us from
their place above; death hovering over our heads, on all hands
environing us; the moment is never to be forgotten. Half
an hour after, they were both massacred, and we heard their
cries." [1]—Thus Jourgniac in his Agony in the Abbaye: how
it ended with Jourgniac, we shall see anon.

But now let the good Maton speak, what he, over in La
Force, in the same hours, is suffering and witnessing. This
" Résurrection " by him is greatly the best, the least theatrical
of these Pamphlets; and stands testing by documents:

" Toward seven o'clock," on Sunday night, " prisoners
were called frequently, and they did not reappear. Each of
us reasoned, in his own way, on this singularity: but our
ideas became calm, as we persuaded ourselves that the Memo-
rial I had drawn up for the National Assembly was producing
effect."

" At one in the morning, the grate which led to our quarter
opened anew. Four men in uniform, each with a drawn sabre
and blazing torch, came up to our corridor, preceded by a
turnkey; and entered an apartment close to ours, to investigate
a box there, which we heard them break up. This done, they
stepped into the gallery, and questioned the man Cuissa, to
know where Lamotte "(Necklace's Widower) " was. Lamotte,
they said, had some months ago, under pretext of a treasure
he knew of, swindled a sum of three-hundred livres from one
of them, inviting him to dinner for that purpose. The wretched
Cuissa, now in their hands, who indeed lost his life this night,
answered trembling, That he remembered the fact well, but
could not tell what was become of Lamotte. Determined to
find Lamotte and confront him with Cuissa, they rummaged,
along with this latter, through various other apartments; but
without effect, for we heard them say: ' Come, search among
the corpses, then; for, nom de Dieu! we must find where he is.'

" At this same time, I heard Louis Bardy, the Abbé Bardy's
name called: he was brought out; and directly massacred, as
I learned. He had been accused, along with his concubine,

five or six years before, of having murdered and cut in pieces his own Brother, Auditor of the Chambre des Comptes of Montpellier; but had by his subtlety, his dexterity, nay, his eloquence, outwitted the judges, and escaped.

"One may fancy what terror these words, 'Come search among the corpses, then,' had thrown me into. I saw nothing for it now but resigning myself to die. I wrote my last-will; concluding it by a petition and adjuration, that the paper should be sent to its address. Scarcely had I quitted the pen, when there came two other men in uniform; one of them, whose arm and sleeve up to the very shoulder, as well as his sabre, were covered with blood, said, He was as weary as a hodman that had been beating plaster."

"Baudin de la Chenaye was called; sixty years of virtues could not save him. They said, 'À l'Abbaye': he passed the fatal outer-gate; gave a cry of terror, at sight of the heaped corpses; covered his eyes with his hands, and died of innumerable wounds. At every new opening of the grate, I thought I should hear my own name called, and see Rossignol enter."

"I flung off my nightgown and cap; I put on a coarse unwashed shirt, a worn frock without waistcoat, an old round hat; these things I had sent for, some days ago, in the fear of what might happen.

"The rooms of this corridor had been all emptied but ours. We were four together; whom they seemed to have forgotten: we addressed our prayers in common to the Eternal to be delivered from this peril."

"Baptiste the turnkey came up by himself, to see us. I took him by the hands; I conjured him to save us; promised him a hundred louis, if he would conduct me home. A noise coming from the grates made him hastily withdraw.

"It was the noise of some dozen or fifteen men, armed to the teeth; as we, lying flat to escape being seen, could see from our windows. 'Up-stairs!' said they: 'Let not one remain.' I took out my penknife; I considered where I should strike myself"—but reflected "that the blade was too short," and also "on religion."

Finally, however, between seven and eight o'clock in the morning, enter four men with bludgeons and sabres!—"To one of whom Gérard my comrade whispered, earnestly, apart. During their colloquy I searched everywhere for shoes, that I might lay off the Advocate pumps (pantoufles de Palais) I had on," but could find none.—" Constant, called le Sauvage, Gérard, and a third whose name escapes me, they let clear off: as for me, four sabres were crossed over my breast, and they led me down. I was brought to their bar; to the Personage with the scarf, who sat as judge there. He was a lame man, of tall lank stature. He recognised me on the streets and spoke to me, seven months after. I have been assured that he was son of a retired attorney, and named Chepy. Crossing the Court called Des Nourrices, I saw Manuel haranguing in tricolor scarf." The trial, as we see, ends in acquittal and resurrection.[2]

Poor Sicard, from the violon of the Abbaye, shall say but a few words; true-looking, though tremulous. Toward three in the morning, the killers bethink them of this little violon; and knock from the court. " I tapped gently, trembling lest the murderers might hear, on the opposite door, where the Section Committee was sitting: they answered gruffly, that they had no key. There were three of us in this violon; my companions thought they perceived a kind of loft overhead. But it was very high; only one of us could reach it by mounting on the shoulders of both the others. One of them said to me, that my life was usefuller than theirs: I resisted, they insisted: no denial! I fling myself on the neck of these two deliverers; never was scene more touching. I mount on the shoulders of the first, then on those of the second, finally on the loft; and address to my two comrades the expression of a soul overwhelmed with natural emotions." [3]

The two generous companions, we rejoice to find, did not perish. But it is time that Jourgniac de Saint-Méard should speak his last words, and end this singular trilogy. The night had become day; and the day has again become night. Jourgniac, worn down with uttermost agitation, was fallen asleep, and had a cheering dream: he has also contrived to make acquaintance with one of the volunteer bailiffs, and spoken in native Provençal with him. On Tuesday, about one in the morning, his Agony is reaching its crisis.

" By the glare of two torches, I now descried the terrible tribunal, where lay my life or my death. The President, in gray coat, with a sabre at his side, stood leaning with his hands against a table, on which were papers, an inkstand,

tobacco-pipes and bottles. Some ten persons were around,
seated or standing; two of whom had jackets and aprons:
others were sleeping stretched on benches. Two men, in
bloody shirts, guarded the door of the place; an old turnkey
had his hand on the lock. In front of the President three
men held a Prisoner, who might be about sixty " (or seventy:
he was old Marshal Maillé, of the Tuileries and August
Tenth). " They stationed me in a corner; my guards crossed
their sabres on my breast. I looked on all sides for my
Provençal: two National Guards, one of them drunk, presented some appeal from the Section of Croix Rouge in favour
of the Prisoners; the Man in Gray answered: 'They are use-
less, these appeals for traitors.' Then the Prisoner exclaimed:
' It is frightful; your judgment is a murder.' The President
answered: ' My hands are washed of it; take M. Maillé away.'
They drove him into the street; where, through the opening of
the door, I saw him massacred.

" The President sat down to write; registering, I suppose,
the name of this one whom they had finished; then I heard
him say: ' Another, À un autre! '

" Behold me then haled before this swift and bloody
judgment-bar, where the best protection was to have no
protection, and all resources of ingenuity became null if
they were not founded on truth. Two of my guards held
me each by a hand, the third by the collar of my coat.
' Your name, your profession?' said the President. 'The
smallest lie ruins you,' added one of the Judges.—'My
name is Jourgniac Saint-Méard; I have served, as an officer, twenty years: and I appear at your tribunal with the
assurance of an innocent man, who therefore will not lie.'—
' We shall see that,' said the President: ' Do you know why
you are arrested?'—' Yes, Monsieur le Président; I am accused of editing the Journal " De la Cour et de la Ville." But
I hope to prove the falsity ' "—But no; Jourgniac's proof of
the falsity, and defence generally, though of excellent result
as a defence, is not interesting to read. It is longwinded; there
is a loose theatricality in the reporting of it, which does not
amount to unveracity, yet which tends that way. We shall
suppose him successful, beyond hope, in proving and dis-
proving; and skip largely—to the catastrophe, almost at two
steps.

"'But after all,' said one of the Judges, 'there is no smoke without kindling; tell us why they accuse you of that.' —'I was about to do so'"—Jourgniac does so; with more and more success.

"'Nay,' continued I, 'they accuse me even of recruiting for the Emigrants!' At these words there arose a general murmur. 'O Messieurs, Messieurs,' I exclaimed, raising my voice, 'it is my turn to speak; I beg M. le Président to have the kindness to maintain it for me; I never needed it more.' —'True enough, true enough,' said almost all the Judges with a laugh: 'Silence!'

"While they were examining the testimonials I had produced, a new Prisoner was brought in, and placed before the President. 'It was one Priest more,' they said, 'whom they had ferreted out of the Chapelle.' After very few questions: 'À la Force!' He flung his breviary on the table; was hurled forth, and massacred. I reappeared before the tribunal.

"'You tell us always,' cried one of the Judges, with a tone of impatience, 'that you are not this, that you are not that; what are you, then?'—'I was an open Royalist.'—There arose a general murmur; which was miraculously appeased by another of the men, who had seemed to take an interest in me: 'We are not here to judge opinions,' said he, 'but to judge the results of them.' Could Rousseau and Voltaire both in one, pleading for me, have said better?—'Yes, Messieurs,' cried I, 'always till the Tenth of August I was an open Royalist. Ever since the Tenth of August that cause has been finished. I am a Frenchman, true to my country. I was always a man of honour.'

"'My soldiers never distrusted me. Nay, two days before that business of Nanci, when their suspicion of their officers was at its height, they chose me for commander, to lead them to Lunéville, to get back the prisoners of the Regiment Mestre-de-Camp, and seize General Malseigne.'" Which fact there is, most luckily, an individual present who by a certain token can confirm.

"The President, this cross-questioning being over, took off his hat and said: 'I see nothing to suspect in this man: I am for granting him his liberty. Is that your vote?' To which all the Judges answered: 'Oui, Oui; it is just!'"

And there arose vivats within doors and without; "escort

of three," amid shoutings and embracings: thus Jourgniac
escaped from jury-trial and the jaws of death.[4]   Maton and
Sicard did, either by trial and no bill found, lank President
Chepy finding "absolutely nothing"; or else by evasion, and
new favour of Moton the brave watchmaker, likewise escape;
and were embraced and wept over; weeping in return, as
they well might.

Thus they three, in wondrous trilogy, or triple soliloquy:
uttering simultaneously, through the dread night-watches,
their Night-thoughts—grown audible to us! They Three are
become audible: but the other "Thousand and Eighty-nine,
of whom Two-hundred and two were Priests," who also had
Night-thoughts, remain inaudible; choked forever in black
Death.   Heard only of President Chepy and the Man in
Gray!—

NOTES

[1] Jourgniac Saint-Méard, "Mon Agonie de trente-huit heures" (reprinted in "Hist. Parl.," xviii, 103–135).
[2] Maton de la Varenne, "Ma Résurrection" (in "Hist. Parl.," xviii,
135–156).
[3] Abbé Sicard, "Relation adressée à un de ses amis" (in "Hist.
Parl.," xviii, 98–103).
[4] "Mon Agonie" (ut suprà, "Hist. Parl.," xviii, 128).

CHAPTER VI

THE CIRCULAR

BUT the Constituted Authorities, all this while? The Legislative Assembly; the Six Ministers; the Townhall; Santerre with the National Guard?—It is very curious to think what a City is. Theatres, to the number of some twenty-three, were open every night during these prodigies; while right-arms here grew weary with slaying, right-arms there were twiddledeeing on melodious catgut: at the very instant when Abbé Sicard was clambering up his second pair of shoulders three-men high, five hundred thousand human individuals were lying horizontal, as if nothing were amiss.

As for the poor Legislative, the sceptre had departed from it. The Legislative did send Deputation to the Prisons, to these Street-Courts; and poor M. Dusaulx did harangue there; but produced no conviction whatsoever: nay, at last, as he continued haranguing, the Street-Court interposed, not without threats; and he had to cease, and withdraw. This is the same poor worthy old M. Dusaulx who told, or indeed almost sang (though with cracked voice), the " Taking of the Bastille," to our satisfaction, long since. He was wont to announce himself, on such and on all occasions, as the Translator of Juvenal. " Good Citizens, you see before you a man who loves his country, who is the Translator of Juvenal," said he once.—" Juvenal? " interrupts Sansculottism: " Who the devil is Juvenal? One of your sacrés Aristocrates? To the Lanterne! " From an orator of this kind, conviction was not to be expected. The Legislative had much ado to save one of its own Members, or ex-Members, Deputy Jounneau, who chanced to be lying in arrest for mere Parliamentary delinquencies, in these Prisons. As for poor old Dusaulx and Company, they returned to the Salle de Manége, saying,

"It was dark; and they could not see well what was going on." [1]

Roland writes indignant messages, in the name of Order, Humanity and the Law; but there is no Force at his disposal. Santerre's National Force seems lazy to rise: though he made requisitions, he says—which always dispersed again. Nay, did not we, with Advocate Maton's eyes, see "men in uniform" too, with their "sleeves bloody to the shoulder"? Pétion goes in tricolor scarf; speaks "the austere language of the law": the killers give up, while he is there; when his back is turned, recommence. Manuel too in scarf we, with Maton's eyes, transiently saw haranguing, in the Court called of Nurses, Cour des Nourrices. On the other hand, cruel Billaud, likewise in scarf, "with that small puce coat and black wig we are used to on him," [2] audibly delivers, "standing among corpses," at the Abbaye, a short but ever-memorable harangue, reported in various phraseology, but always to this purpose: "Brave Citizens, you are extirpating the Enemies of Liberty: you are at your duty. A grateful Commune and Country would wish to recompense you adequately; but can not, for you know its want of funds. Whoever shall have worked (travaillé) in a Prison shall receive a draft of one louis, payable by our cashier. Continue your work." [3] The Constituted Authorities are of yesterday: all pulling different ways: there is properly no Constituted Authorities, but every man is his own King; and all kinglets, belligerent, allied, or armed-neutral, without king over them.

"O everlasting infamy," exclaims Montgaillard, "that Paris stood looking on in stupor for four days, and did not interfere!" Very desirable indeed that Paris had interfered; yet not unnatural that it stood even so, looking on in stupor. Paris is in death-panic, the enemy and gibbets at its door: whosoever in Paris has the heart to front death, finds it more pressing to do it fighting the Prussians, than fighting the killers of Aristocrats. Indignant abhorrence, as in Roland, may be here; gloomy sanction, premeditation or not, as in Marat and Committee of Salvation, may be there; dull disapproval, dull approval, and acquiescence in Necessity and Destiny, is the general temper. The Sons of Darkness, "two-hundred or so," risen from their lurking-places, have scope to do their work. Urged on by fever-frenzy of Patriotism, and the madness of Terror—urged on by lucre, and the gold louis of wages? Nay, not lucre; for the gold watches, rings, money of the Massacred, are punctually brought to the Townhall, by Killers sans-indispensables, who higgle afterward for their twenty shillings of wages; and Sergent sticking an uncommonly fine agate on his finger (fully "meaning to account for it") becomes Agate-Sergent. But the temper, as we say, is dull acquiescence. Not till the Patriotic or Frenetic part of the work is finished for want of material; and Sons of Darkness, bent clearly on lucre alone, begin wrenching watches and purses, brooches from ladies' necks, "to equip volunteers," in daylight, on the streets—does the temper from dull grow vehement; does the Constable raise his truncheon, and striking heartily (like a cattle-driver in earnest) beat the "course of things" back into its old regulated drove-roads. The Garde-Meuble itself was surreptitiously plundered, on the 17th of the month, to Roland's new horror; who anew bestirs himself, and is, as Sieyès says, "the veto of scoundrels," Roland veto des coquins.[4]

This is the September Massacre, otherwise called "Severe Justice of the People." These are the Septemberers (September-briseurs); a name of some note and lucency—but lucency of the Nether-fire sort; very different from that of our Bastille Heroes, who shone, disputable by no Friend of Freedom, as in Heavenly light-radiance: to such phasis of the business have we advanced since then! The numbers massacred are in the Historical fantasy, "between two and three thousand"; or indeed they are "upward of six thousand," for Peltier (in vision) saw them massacring the very patients of the Bicêtre Madhouse "with grape-shot"; nay, finally they are "twelve thousand" and odd hundreds—not more than that.[5] In Arithmetical ciphers, and Lists drawn up by accurate Advocate Maton, the number, including two-hundred and two priests, three "persons unknown," and "one thief killed at the Bernardins," is, as above hinted, a Thousand and Eighty-nine—not less than that.

A Thousand and eighty-nine lie dead, "two hundred and sixty heaped carcasses on the Pont au Change" itself—among which, Robespierre pleading afterward will "nearly weep" to reflect that there was said to be one slain innocent.[6] One; not two, O thou seagreen Incorruptible? If so, Themis Sansculotte must be lucky; for she was brief!—In the dim Registers of the Townhall, which are preserved to this day, men read, with a certain sickness of heart, items and entries not usual in Town Books. "To workers employed in preserving the salubrity of the air in the Prisons, and persons who presided over these dangerous operations," so much—in various items, nearly seven hundred pounds sterling. To carters employed to "the Burying-grounds of Clamart, Montrouge, and Vaugirard," at so much a journey, per cart; this also is an entry. Then so many francs and odd sous "for the necessary quantity of quick-lime"!⁷ Carts go along the streets; full of stripped human corpses, thrown pell-mell; limbs sticking up —seest thou that cold Hand sticking up, through the heaped embrace of brother corpses, in its yellow paleness, in its cold rigour; the palm opened toward Heaven, as if in dumb prayer, in expostulation de profundis, Take pity on the Sons of Men! —Mercier saw it, as he walked down "the Rue Saint-Jacques from Montrouge, on the morrow of the Massacres": but not a Hand; it was a Foot—which he reckons still more significant, one understands not well why. Or was it as the Foot of one spurning Heaven? Rushing, like a wild diver, in disgust and despair, toward the depths of Annihilation? Even there shall His hand find thee, and His right-hand hold thee—surely for right not for wrong, for good not evil! "I saw that Foot," says Mercier; "I shall know it again at the great Day of Judgment, when the Eternal, throned on his thunders, shall judge both Kings and Septemberers."⁸

That a shriek of inarticulate horror rose over this thing, not only from French Aristocrats and Moderates, but from all Europe, and has prolonged itself to the present day, was most natural and right. The thing lay done, irrevocable; a thing to be counted beside some other things, which lie very black in our Earth's Annals, yet which will not erase therefrom. For man, as was remarked, has transcendentalisms in him; standing, as he does, poor creature, every way "in the confluence of Infinitudes"; a mystery to himself and others: in the centre of two Eternities, of three Immensities—in the intersection of primeval Light with the everlasting Dark!— Thus have there been, especially by vehement tempers reduced to a state of desperation, very miserable things done. Sicilian

Vespers, and " eight thousand slaughtered in two hours," are a known thing. Kings themselves, not in desperation, but only in difficulty, have sat hatching, for year and day (nay, De Thou says for seven years), their Bartholomew Business; and then, at the right moment, also on an Autumn Sunday, this very Bell (they say it is the identical metal) of Saint-Germain l'Auxerrois was set a-pealing—with effect.[9] Nay, the same black boulder-stones of these Paris Prisons have seen Prison-massacres before now; men massacring countrymen, Burgundies massacring Armagnacs, whom they had suddenly imprisoned, till, as now, there were piled heaps of carcasses, and the streets ran red—the Mayor Pétion of the time speaking the austere language of the law, and answered by the Killers, in old French (it is some four hundred years old): " Maugré bieu, Sire—Sir, God's malison on your ' justice,' your ' pity,' your ' right reason.' Cursed be of God whoso shall have pity on these false traitorous Armagnacs, English; dogs they are; they have destroyed us, wasted this realm of France, and sold it to the English." [10] And so they slay, and fling aside the slain, to the extent of " fifteen hundred and eighteen, among whom are found four Bishops of false and damnable counsel, and two Presidents of· Parlement." For though it is not Satan's world this that we live in, Satan always has his place in it (underground properly); and from time to time bursts up. Well may mankind shriek, inarticulately anathematizing as they can. There are actions of such emphasis that no shrieking can be too emphatic for them. Shriek ye; acted have they.

Shriek who might in this France, in this Paris Legislative or Paris Townhall, there are Ten Men who do not shriek. A Circular goes out from the Committee of Salut Public, dated 3d of September 1792; directed to all Townhalls: a State-paper too remarkable to be overlooked. " A part of the ferocious conspirators detained in the Prisons," it says, " have been put to death by the People; and we can not doubt but the whole Nation, driven to the edge of ruin by such endless series of treasons, will make haste to adopt this means of public salvation: and all Frenchmen will cry as the men of Paris: We go to fight the enemy; but we will not leave robbers behind us, to butcher our wives and children." To which are legibly appended these signatures: Panis; Sergent; Marat,

Friend of the People;[11] with Seven others—carried down thereby, in a strange way, to the late remembrance of Antiquarians. We remark, however, that their Circular rather recoiled on themselves. The Townhalls made no use of it; even the distracted Sansculottes made little; they only howled and bellowed, but did not bite. At Rheims "about eight persons" were killed; and two afterward were hanged for doing it. At Lyons, and a few other places, some attempt was made; but with hardly any effect, being quickly put down.

Less fortunate were the Prisoners of Orléans; was the good Duke de la Rochefoucault. He journeying, by quick stages, with his Mother and Wife, toward the Waters of Forges, or some quieter country, was arrested at Gisors; conducted along the streets, amid effervescing multitudes, and killed dead " by the stroke of a paving-stone hurled through the coach-window." Killed as a once Liberal now Aristocrat; Protector of Priests, Suspender of virtuous Pétions, and most unfortunate Hot-grown-cold, detestable to Patriotism. He dies lamented of Europe; his blood spattering the cheeks of his old Mother, ninety-three years old.

As for the Orléans Prisoners, they are State Criminals: Royalist Ministers, Delessarts, Montmorins; who have been accumulating on the High Court of Orléans, ever since that Tribunal was set up. Whom now it seems good that we should get transferred to our new Paris Court of the Seventeenth; which proceeds far quicker. Accordingly hot Fournier from Martinique, Fournier l'Américain, is off, missioned by Constituted Authority; with stanch National Guards, with Lazouski the Pole; sparingly provided with road-money. These, through bad quarters, through difficulties, perils, for Authorities cross each other in this time—do triumphantly bring off the Fifty or Fifty-three Orléans Prisoners, toward Paris; where a swifter Court of the Seventeenth will do justice on them.[12] But lo, at Paris, in the interim, a still swifter and swiftest Court of the Second, and of September, has instituted itself: enter not Paris, or that will judge you!—What shall hot Fournier do? It was his duty, as volunteer Constable, had he been a perfect character, to guard those men's lives never so Aristocratic, at the expense of his own valuable life never so Sansculottic, till some Constituted Court had disposed of them. But he was an imperfect character and Constable; perhaps one of the more imperfect.

Hot Fournier, ordered to turn hither by one Authority, to turn thither by another Authority, is in a perplexing multiplicity of orders; but finally he strikes off for Versailles. His Prisoners fare in tumbrils, or open carts, himself and Guards riding and marching around; and at the last village, the worthy Mayor of Versailles comes to meet him, anxious that the arrival and locking-up were well over. It is Sunday, the ninth day of the month. Lo, on entering the Avenue of Versailles, what multitudes, stirring, swarming in the September sun, under the dull-green September foliage; the Four-rowed Avenue all humming and swarming, as if the Town had emptied itself! Our tumbrils roll heavily through the living sea; the Guards and Fournier making way with ever more difficulty; the Mayor speaking and gesturing his persuasivest; amid the inarticulate growling hum, which growls ever the deeper even by hearing itself growl, not without sharp yelpings here and there.—Would to God we were out of this strait place, and wind and separation had cooled the heat, which seems about igniting here!

And yet if the wide Avenue is too strait, what will the Street de Surintendance be, at leaving of the same? At the corner of Surintendance Street, the compressed yelpings become a continuous yell: savage figures spring on the tumbril-shafts; first spray of an endless coming tide! The Mayor pleads, pushes, half-desperate; is pushed, carried off in men's arms: the savage tide has entrance, has mastery. Amid horrid noise, and tumult as of fierce wolves, the Prisoners sink massacred—all but some eleven, who escaped into houses, and found mercy. The Prisons, and what other Prisoners they held, were with difficulty saved. The stripped clothes are burned in bonfire; the corpses lie heaped in the ditch on the morrow morning.[13] All France, except it be the Ten Men of the Circular and their people, moans and rages, inarticulately shrieking; all Europe rings.

But neither did Danton shriek; though, as Minister of Justice, it was more his part to do so. Brawny Danton is in the breach, as of stormed Cities and Nations; amid the sweep of Tenth-of-August cannon, the rustle of Prussian gallows-ropes, the smiting of September sabres; destruction all round

him, and the rushing-down of worlds: Minister of Justice is
his name; but Titan of the Forlorn Hope, and Enfant Perdu
of the Revolution, is his quality—and the man acts according
to that. "We must put our enemies in fear!" Deep fear,
is it not, as of its own accord, falling on our enemies? The
Titan of the Forlorn Hope, he is not the man that would
swiftest of all prevent its so falling. Forward, thou lost Titan
of an Enfant Perdu; thou must dare, and again dare, and without end dare; there is nothing left for thee but that! "Que
mon nom soit flétri, Let my name be blighted": what am I?
The Cause alone is great; and shall live, and not perish.—
So, on the whole, here too is a Swallower of Formulas; of
still wider gulp than Mirabeau: this Danton, Mirabeau of the
Sansculottes. In the September days, this Minister was not
heard of as co-operating with strict Roland; his business might
lie elsewhere—with Brunswick and the Hôtel-de-Ville. When
applied to by an official person, about the Orléans Prisoners,
and the risks they ran, he answered gloomily, twice over,
"Are not these men guilty?"—When pressed, he "answered
in a terrible voice," and turned his back.[14] A thousand slain
in the Prisons; horrible if you will; but Brunswick is within
a day's journey of us; and there are Five-and-twenty Millions
yet, to slay or to save. Some men have tasks—frightfuller than
ours! It seems strange, but is not strange, that this Minister
of Moloch-Justice, when any suppliant for a friend's life got
access to him, was found to have human compassion; and
yielded and granted "always"; "neither did one personal
enemy of Danton perish in these days."[15]

To shriek, we say, when certain things are acted, is proper
and unavoidable. Nevertheless, articulate speech, not shrieking, is the faculty of man: when speech is not yet possible,
let there be, with the shortest delay, at least—silence. Silence,
accordingly, in this forty-fourth year of the business, and
eighteen hundred and thirty-sixth of an "Era called Christian
as lucus à non," is the thing we recommend and practise. Nay,
instead of shrieking more, it were perhaps edifying to remark,
on the other side, what a singular thing Customs (in Latin,
Mores) are; and how fitly the Virtue, Vir-tus, Manhood or
Worth, that is in a man, is called his Morality or Customari-
ness. Fell Slaughter, one of the most authentic products of

the Pit you would say, once give it Customs, becomes War, with Laws of War; and is Customary and Moral enough; and red individuals carry the tools of it girt round their haunches, not without an air of pride—which do thou nowise blame.   While, see! so long as it is but dressed in hodden or russet; and Revolution, less frequent than War, has not yet got its Laws of Revolution, but the hodden or russet individuals are Uncustomary—O shrieking beloved brother blockheads of Mankind, let us close those wide mouths of ours; let us cease shrieking, and begin considering!

NOTES

[1] " Moniteur," Debate of September 2, 1792.
[2] Félémhesi (ut suprà, in " Hist. Parl.," xviii, p. 189).
[3] Montgaillard, iii, 191.
[4] Helen Maria Williams, iii, 27.
[5] See " Hist. Parl.," xvii, 421, 422.
[6] " Moniteur " of November 6th (Debate of November 5, 1793).
[7] " État des sommes payées par la Commune de Paris " (" Hist. Parl.," xviii, 231).
[8] Mercier, " Nouveau Paris," vi, 21.
[9] September 9 to 13, 1572 (Dulaure, " Hist. de Paris," iv, 289).
[10] Dulaure, iii, 494.
[11] " Hist. Parl.," xvii, 433.
[12] Ibid., xvii, 434.
[13] " Pièces officielles relatives au massacre des Prisonniers à Versailles " (in " Hist. Parl.," xviii, 236–249).
[14] " Biographie des Ministres," p. 97.
[15] Ibid., p. 103.

CHAPTER VII

SEPTEMBER IN ARGONNE

PLAIN, at any rate, is one thing: that the fear, whatever of fear those Aristocrat enemies might need, has been brought about. The matter is getting serious, then! Sansculottism too has become a Fact, and seems minded to assert itself as such? This huge mooncalf of Sansculottism, staggering about, as young calves do, is not mockable only, and soft like another calf; but terrible too, if you prick it; and, through its hideous nostrils, blows fire!—Aristocrats, with pale panic in their hearts, fly toward covert; and a light rises to them over several things; or rather a confused transition toward light, whereby for the moment darkness is only darker than ever. But what will become of this France? Here is a question! France is dancing its desert-waltz, as Sahara does when the winds waken; in whirl-blasts twenty-five millions in number; waltzing toward Townhalls, Aristocrat Prisons, and Election Committee-rooms; toward Brunswick and the frontiers; toward a New Chapter of Universal History; if indeed it be not the Finis, and winding-up of that!

In Election Committee-rooms there is now no dubiety; but the work goes bravely along. The Convention is getting chosen—really in a decisive spirit; in the Townhall we already date " First year of the Republic." Some Two-hundred of our best Legislators may be re-elected, the Mountain bodily: Robespierre, with Mayor Pétion, Buzot, Curate Grégoire, Rabaut, some three-score Old-Constituents; though we once had only " thirty voices." All these; and along with them, friends long known to Revolutionary fame: Camille Desmoulins, though he stutters in speech; Manuel, Tallien and Company; Journalists Gorsas, Carra, Mercier, Louvet of " Faublas "; Clootz, Speaker of Mankind; Collot d'Herbois, tearing a passion to rags; Fabre d'Eglantine, speculative Pamphleteer; Legendre, the solid Butcher; nay, Marat, though rural France can hardly believe it, or even believe that there is a Marat, except in print. Of Minister Danton, who will lay down his Ministry for a Membership, we need not speak. Paris is fervent; nor is the Country wanting to itself. Barbaroux, Rebecqui, and fervid Patriots are coming from Marseilles. Seven-hundred and forty-five men (or indeed forty-nine, for Avignon now sends Four) are gathering: so many are to meet; not so many are to part!

Attorney Carrier from Aurillac, Ex-Priest Lebon from Arras, these shall both gain a name. Mountainous Auvergne re-elects her Romme; hardy tiller of the soil, once Mathematical Professor; who, unconscious, carries in petto a remarkable " New Calendar," with Messidors, Pluvioses, and suchlike—and having given it well forth, shall depart by the death they call Roman. Sieyès Old-Constituent comes; to make new Constitutions as many as wanted: for the rest, peering out of his clear cautious eyes, he will cower low in many an emergency, and find silence safest. Young Saint-Just is coming, deputed by Aisne in the North; more like a Student than a Senator; not four-and-twenty yet; who has written Books; a youth of slight stature, with mild mellow voice, enthusiast olive-complexion and long black hair. Féraud, from the far valley D'Aure in the folds of the Pyrenees, is coming; an ardent Republican; doomed to fame, at least in death.

All manner of Patriot men are coming: Teachers, Husbandmen, Priests and Ex-Priests, Traders, Doctors; above all, Talkers, or the Attorney species. Man-midwives, as Levasseur of the Sarthe, are not wanting. Nor Artists: gross David, with the swoln cheek, has long painted, with genius in a state of convulsion; and will now legislate. The swoln cheek, choking his words in the birth, totally disqualifies him as an orator; but his pencil, his head, his gross hot heart, with genius in a state of convulsion, will be there. A man bodily and mentally swoln-cheeked, disproportionate; flabbylarge, instead of great; weak withal as in a state of convulsion, not strong in a state of composure: so let him play his part. Nor are naturalized Benefactors of the Species forgotten: Priestley, elected by the Orne Department, but declining; Paine the rebellious Needleman, by the Pas de Calais, who accepts.

Few Nobles come, and yet not none. Paul-François Barras, "noble as the Barrases, old as the rocks of Provence"; he is one. The reckless, shipwrecked man: flung ashore on the coast of the Maldives long ago, while sailing and soldiering as Indian Fighter: flung ashore since then, as hungry Parisian pleasure-hunter and half-pay, on many a Circe Island, with temporary enchantment, temporary conversion into beasthood and hoghood—the remote Var Department has now sent him hither. A man of heat and haste; defective in utterance; defective indeed in anything to utter; yet not without a certain rapidity of glance, a certain swift transient courage; who in these times, Fortune favouring, may go far. He is tall, handsome to the eye, "only the complexion a little yellow"; but "with a robe of purple, with a scarlet cloak and plume of tricolor, on occasions of solemnity," the man will look well.[1] Lepelletier Saint-Fargeau, Old-Constituent, is a kind of noble, and of enormous wealth; he too has come hither—to have the Pain of Death abolished? Hapless Ex-Parlementeer! Nay, among our Sixty Old-Constituents, see Philippe d'Orléans, a Prince of the Blood! Not now D'Orléans: for, Feudalism being swept from the world, he demands of his worthy friends the Electors of Paris, to have a new name of their choosing; whereupon Procureur Manuel, like an antithetic literary man, recommends Equality, Egalité. A Philippe Egalité therefore will sit; seen of the Earth and Heaven.

Such a Convention is gathering itself together. Mere angry poultry in moulting season; whom Brunswick's grenadiers and cannoneers will give short account of. Would the weather, as Bertrand is always praying, only mend a little![2]

In vain, O Bertrand! The weather will not mend a whit: nay, even if it did? Dumouriez Polymetis, though Bertrand knows it not, started from brief slumber at Sedan, on that morning of the 29th of August; with stealthiness, with promptitude, audacity. Some three mornings after that, Brunswick, opening wide eyes, perceives the Passes of the Argonne all seized; blocked with felled trees, fortified with camps; and that it is a most shifty swift Dumouriez this, who has outwitted him!

The manœuvre may cost Brunswick "a loss of three

weeks," very fatal in these circumstances. A Mountain-wall
of forty miles lying between him and Paris: which he should
have preoccupied—which how now to get possession of? Also
the rain it raineth every day; and we are in a hungry Champagne Pouilleuse, a land flowing only with ditch-water. How
to cross this Mountain-wall of the Argonne; or what in the
world to do with it?—There are marchings and wet splash-
ings by steep paths, with sackerments and guttural interjections; forcings of Argonne Passes—which unhappily will not
force. Through the woods, volleying War reverberates, like
huge gong-music, or Moloch's kettledrum, borne by the
echoes; swoln torrents boil angrily round the foot of rocks,
floating pale carcasses of men. In vain! Islettes Village,
with its church-steeple, rises intact in the Mountain-pass, between the embosoming heights; your forced marchings and
climbings have become forced slidings and tumblings back.
From the hill-tops thou seest nothing but dumb crags, and
endless wet moaning woods; the Clermont Vache (huge Cow
that she is) disclosing herself [3] at intervals; flinging-off her
cloud-blanket, and soon taking it on again, drowned in the
pouring Heaven. The Argonne Passes will not force: you
must skirt the Argonne: go round by the end of it.

But fancy whether the Emigrant Seigneurs have not got
their brilliancy dulled a little; whether that " Foot Regiment
in red-facings with nankeen trousers " could be in field-day
order! In place of gasconading, a sort of desperation, and
hydrophobia from excess of water, is threatening to supervene.
Young Prince de Ligne, son of that brave literary De Ligne
the Thundergod of Dandies, fell backward; shot dead in Grand-
Pré, the Northmost of the Passes: Brunswick is skirting and
rounding, laboriously, by the extremity of the South. Four
days; days of a rain as of Noah—without fire, without food!
For fire you cut down green trees, and produce smoke; for
food you eat green grapes, and produce colic, pestilential
dysentery, ὀλέκοντο δὲ λαοί. And the Peasants assassinate us,
they do not join us; shrill women cry shame on us, threaten
to draw their very scissors on us! O ye hapless dulled-bright
Seigneurs, and hydrophobic splashed Nankeens—but O, ten
times more, ye poor sackermenting ghastly-visaged Hessians
and Hulans, fallen on your backs; who had no call to die there,
except compulsion and three-halfpence a-day! Nor has Mrs.

Le Blanc of the Golden Arm a good time of it, in her bower of dripping rushes. Assassinating Peasants are hanged; Old-Constituent Honourable Members, though of venerable age, ride in carts with their hands tied: these are the woes of war.

Thus they; sprawling and wriggling, far and wide, on the slopes and passes of the Argonne—a loss to Brunswick of five-and-twenty disastrous days. There is wriggling and struggling; facing, backing and right-about facing; as the positions shift, and the Argonne gets partly rounded, partly forced—but still Dumouriez, force him, round him as you will, sticks like a rooted fixture on the ground; fixture with many hinges; wheeling now this way, now that; showing always new front, in the most unexpected manner: nowise consenting to take himself away. Recruits stream up on him: full of heart; yet rather difficult to deal with. Behind Grand-Pré, for example, Grand-Pré which is on the wrong-side of the Argonne, for we are now forced and rounded—the full heart, in one of those wheelings and showings of new front, did as it were overset itself, as full hearts are liable to do; and there rose a shriek of " sauve qui peut," and a death-panic which had nigh ruined all! So that the General had to come galloping; and, with thunder-words, with gesture, stroke of drawn sword even, check and rally, and bring back the sense of shame [4]—nay, to seize the first shriekers and ringleaders; " shave their heads and eyebrows," and pack them forth into the world as a sign. Thus too (for really the rations are short, and wet camping with hungry stomach brings bad humour) there is like to be mutiny. Whereupon again Dumouriez " arrives at the head of their line, with his staff, and an escort of a hundred hussars. He had placed some squadrons behind them, the artillery in front; he said to them: " As for you, for I will neither call you citizens, nor soldiers, nor my men (ni mes enfans), you see before you this artillery, behind you this cavalry. You have dishonoured yourselves by crimes. If you amend, and grow to behave like this brave Army which you have the honour of belonging to, you will find in me a good father. But plunderers and assassins I do not suffer here. At the smallest mutiny I will have you shivered in pieces (hacher en pièces). Seek out the Scoundrels that are among you, and dismiss them yourselves; I hold you responsible for them." [5]

Patience, O Dumouriez! This uncertain heap of shriekers, mutineers, were they once drilled and inured, will become a phalanxed mass of Fighters; and wheel and whirl, to order, swiftly like the wind or the whirlwind: tanned mustachio-figures; often bare-foot, even bare-backed; with sinews of iron; who require only bread and gunpowder: very Sons of Fire, the adroitest, hastiest, hottest ever seen perhaps since Attila's time. They may conquer and overrun amazingly, much as that same Attila did—whose Attila's-Camp and Battlefield thou now seest, on this very ground;[6] who, after sweeping bare the world, was, with difficulty, and days of tough fighting, checked here by Roman Ætius and Fortune; and his dust-cloud made to vanish in the East again!—

Strangely enough, in this shrieking Confusion of a Sol-diery, which we saw long since fallen all suicidally out of square, in suicidal collision—at Nanci, or on the streets of Metz, where brave Bouillé stood with drawn sword; and which has collided and ground itself to pieces worse and worse ever since down now to such a state: in this shrieking Confusion, and not elsewhere, lies the first germ of returning Order for France! Round which, we say, poor France nearly all ground down suicidally likewise into rubbish and Chaos, will be glad to rally; to begin growing, and new-shaping her inorganic dust; very slowly, through centuries, through Napoleons, Louis-Philippes, and other the like media and phases—into a new, infinitely preferable France, we can hope!—

These wheelings and movements in the region of the Ar-gonne, which are all faithfully described by Dumouriez him-eslf, and more interesting to us than Hoyle's or Philidor's best Game of Chess, let us nevertheless, O Reader, entirely omit—and hasten to remark two things: the first a minute private, the second a large public thing. Our minute private thing is: the presence, in the Prussian host, in that war-game of the Argonne, of a certain Man, belonging to the sort called Im-mortal; who, in days since then, is becoming visible more and more in that character, as the Transitory more and more van-ishes: for from of old it was remarked that when the Gods appear among men, it is seldom in recognisable shape; thus Admetus's neatherds give Apollo a draught of their goatskin whey-bottle (well if they do not give him strokes with their oxrungs), not dreaming that he is the Sun-god! This man's name is Johann Wolfgang von Goethe. He is Herzog Weimar's Minister, come with the small contingent of Weimar; to do insignificant unmilitary duty here; very irrecognisable to nearly all! He stands at present, with drawn bridle, on the height near Sainte-Menehould, making an experiment on the " cannon-fever "; having ridden thither against persuasion, into the dance and firing of the cannon-balls, with a scientific desire to understand what that same cannon-fever may be: " The sound of them," says he, " is curious enough; as if it were compounded of the humming of tops, the gurgling of water and the whistle of birds. By degrees you get a very uncommon sensation; which can only be described by similitude. It seems as if you were in some place extremely hot, and at the same time were completely penetrated by the heat of it; so that you feel as if you and this element you are in were perfectly on a par. The eyesight loses nothing of its strength or distinctness; and yet it is as if all things had got a kind of brown-red colour, which makes the situation and the objects still more impressive on you." [7]

This is the cannon-fever, as a World-Poet feels it.—A man entirely irrecognisable! In whose irrecognisable head, meanwhile, there verily is the spiritual counterpart (and call it complement) of this same huge Death-Birth of the World; which now effectuates itself, outwardly in the Argonne, in such cannon-thunder; inwardly, in the irrecognisable head, quite otherwise than by thunder! Mark that man, O Reader, as the memorablest of all the memorable in this Argonne Campaign. What we say of him is not dream, nor flourish of rhetoric, but scientific historic fact; as many men, now at this distance, see or begin to see.

But the large public thing we had to remark is this: That the Twentieth of September 1792 was a raw morning covered with mist; that from three in the morning, Sainte-Menehould, and those Villages and homesteads we know of old, were stirred by the rumble of artillery-wagons, by the clatter of hoofs and many-footed tramp of men: all manner of military, Patriot and Prussian, taking up positions, on the heights of La Lune and other Heights; shifting and shoving—seemingly in some dread chess-game; which may the Heavens turn to good! The Miller of Valmy has fled dusty under ground;

his Mill, were it never so windy, will have rest to-day. At seven in the morning the mist clears off: see Kellermann, Dumouriez' second in command, with "eighteen pieces of cannon," and deep-serried ranks, drawn up round that same silent Windmill, on his knoll of strength; Brunswick, also with serried ranks and cannon, glooming over to him from the Height of La Lune: only the little brook and its little dell now parting them.

So that the much-longed-for has come at last! Instead of hunger and dysentery, we shall have sharp shot; and then!— Dumouriez, with force and firm front, looks on from a neighbouring height; can help only with his wishes, in silence. Lo, the eighteen pieces do bluster and bark, responsive to the bluster of La Lune; and thunder-clouds mount into the air; and echoes roar through all dells, far into the depths of Argonne Wood (deserted now); and limbs and lives of men fly dissipated, this way and that. Can Brunswick make an impression on them? The dulled-bright Seigneurs stand biting their thumbs; these Sansculottes seem not to fly like poultry! Toward noontide a cannon-shot blows Kellermann's horse from under him; there bursts a powder-cart high into the air, with knell heard over all: some swagging and swaying observable—Brunswick will try! "Camarades," cries Kellermann, "Vive la Patrie! Allons vaincre pour elle, Come let us conquer for her." "Live the Fatherland!" rings responsive to the welkin, like rolling-fire from side to side: our ranks are as firm as rocks; and Brunswick may recross the dell, ineffectual; regain his old position on La Lune; not unbattered by the way. And so, for the length of a September day—with bluster and bark; with bellow far-echoing! The cannonade lasts till sunset; and no impression made. Till an hour after sunset, the few remaining Clocks of the District striking Seven; at this late time of day Brunswick tries again. With not a whit better fortune! He is met by rock-ranks, by shout of "Vive la Patrie!" and driven back, not unbattered. Whereupon he ceases; retires "to the Tavern of La Lune"; and sets to raising a redoute lest he be attacked!

Verily so, ye dulled-bright Seigneurs, make of it what ye may. Ah, and France does not rise round us in mass; and the Peasants do not join us, but assassinate us; neither hanging nor any persuasion will induce them! They have lost their old distinguishing love of King and King's-cloak—I fear, altogether; and will even fight to be rid of it: that seems now their humour.   Nor does Austria prosper, nor the siege of Thionville.   The Thionvillers, carrying their insolence to the epigrammatic pitch, have put a Wooden Horse on their walls, with a bundle of Hay hung from him, and this Inscription: "When I finish my hay, you will take Thionville." [8] To such height has the frenzy of mankind risen.

The trenches of Thionville may shut; and what though those of Lille open?   The Earth smiles not on us, nor the Heaven; but weeps and blears itself, in sour rain, and worse. Our very friends insult us; we are wounded in the house of our friends: "His Majesty of Prussia had a greatcoat, when the rain came; and (contrary to all known laws) he put it on, though our two French Princes, the hope of their country, had none"!   To which indeed, as Goethe admits, what answer could be made? [9]—Cold and Hunger and Affront, Colic and Dysentery and Death; and we here, cowering redouted, most unredoubtable, amid the "tattered cornshocks and deformed stubble," on the splashy Height of La Lune, round the mean Tavern de la Lune!—

This is the Cannonade of Valmy; wherein the World-Poet experimented on the cannon-fever; wherein the French Sansculottes did not fly like poultry.   Precious to France!   Every soldier did his duty, and Alsatian Kellermann (how preferable to old Lückner the dismissed!) began to become greater; and Égalité Fils, Equality Junior, a light gallant Field-Officer, distinguished himself by intrepidity—it is the same intrepid individual who now, as Louis-Philippe, without the Equality, struggles, under sad circumstances, to be called King of the French for a season.

NOTES

1 " Dictionnaire des Hommes Marquans," § Barras.
2 Bertrand-Moleville, " Mémoires," ii, 225.
3 See Helen Maria Williams, " Letters," iii, 79–81.
4 Dumouriez, " Mémoires," iii, 29.
5 Ibid., iii, 55.
6 Helen Maria Williams, iii, 32.
7 Goethe, " Campagne in Frankreich " (" Werke," xxx, 73).
8 " Hist. Parl.," xix, 177.
9 Goethe, xxx, 49.

CHAPTER VIII

B UT this Twentieth of September is otherwise a great day. For, observe, while Kellermann's horse was flying blown from under him at the Mill of Valmy, our new National Deputies, that shall be a National Convention, are hovering and gathering about the Hall of the Hundred Swiss: with intent to constitute themselves!

On the morrow, about noontide, Camus the Archivist is busy "verifying their powers"; several hundreds of them already here. Whereupon the Old Legislative comes solemnly over, to merge its old ashes phœnix-like in the body of the new—and so forthwith, returning all solemnly back to the Salle de Manége, there sits a National Convention, Seven-hundred and Forty-nine complete, or complete enough; presided by Pétion—which proceeds directly to do business. Read that reported afternoon's-debate, O Reader; there are few debates like it: dull reporting "Moniteur" itself becomes more dramatic than a very Shakspeare. For epigrammatic Manuel rises, speaks strange things; how the President shall have a guard of honour, and lodge in the Tuileries—rejected. And Danton rises and speaks; and Collot d'Herbois rises, and Curate Grégoire, and lame Couthon of the Mountain rises; and in rapid Melibœan stanzas, only a few lines each, they propose motions not a few. That the corner-stone of our new Constitution is, Sovereignty of the People; that our Constitution shall be accepted by the People or be null; further that the People ought to be avenged, and have right Judges; that the Imposts must continue till new order; that Landed and other Property be sacred forever; finally that "Royalty from this day is abolished in France": Decreed all, before four o'clock strike, with acclamation of the world![1] The

tree was all so ripe; only shake it, and there fall such yellow
cartloads.

And so over in the Valmy Region, as soon as the news
come, what stir is this, audible, visible from our muddy Heights
of La Lune?[2]   Universal shouting of the French on their opposite hill-side; caps raised on bayonets: and a sound as of
" République: Vive la République! " borne dubious on the
winds!—On the morrow morning, so to speak, Brunswick
slings his knapsacks before day, lights any fires he has; and
marches without tap of drum.   Dumouriez finds ghastly symp-
toms in that camp; " latrines full of blood "![3]   The chivalrous
King of Prussia—for he, as we saw, is here in person—may long
rue the day; may look colder than ever on these dulled-bright
Seigneurs, and French Princes their Country's hope—and, on
the whole, put on his greatcoat without ceremony, happy that
he has one.   They retire, all retire with convenient despatch,
through a Champagne trodden into a quagmire, the wild
weather pouring on them: Dumouriez, through his Keller-
manns and Dillons, pricking them a little in the hinder parts.
A little, not much; now pricking, now negotiating: for Brunswick has his eyes opened; and the Majesty of Prussia is a
repentant Majesty.

Nor has Austria prospered; nor the Wooden Horse of
Thionville bitten his hay; nor Lille City surrendered itself.
The Lille trenches opened on the 29th of the month; with
balls and shells, and redhot balls; as if not trenches but
Vesuvius and the Pit had opened.   It was frightful, say all
eye-witnesses; but it is ineffectual.   The Lillers have risen
to such temper; especially after these news from Argonne
and the East.   Not a Sans-indispensables in Lille that would
surrender for a King's ransom.   Redhot balls rain, day and
night; " six-thousand," or so, and bombs " filled internally
with oil of turpentine which splashes up in flame "—mainly
on the dwellings of the Sansculottes and Poor; the streets of
the Rich being spared.   But the Sansculottes get water-pails;
form quenching regulations: " The ball is in Peter's house! "
" The ball is in John's! "   They divide their lodging and substance with each other; shout " Vive la République! " and
faint not in heart.   A ball thunders through the main chamber
of the Hôtel-de-Ville while the Commune is there assembled:
" We are in permanence," says one coldly, proceeding with his

business; and the ball remains permanent too, sticking in the wall, probably to this day.[4]

The Austrian Archduchess (Queen's Sister) will herself see red artillery fired: in their over-haste to satisfy an Archduchess, " two mortars explode and kill thirty persons." It is in vain; Lille, often burning, is always quenched again; Lille will not yield. The very boys deftly wrench the matches out of fallen bombs: " a man clutches a rolling ball with his hat, which takes fire; when cool, they crown it with a bonnet rouge." Memorable also be that nimble Barber, who when the bomb burst beside him, snatched up a shred of it, introduced soap and lather into it, crying, " Voilà mon plat à barbe, My new shaving-dish!" and shaved " fourteen people " on the spot. Bravo, thou nimble Shaver; worthy to shave old spectral Redcloak, and find treasures!—On the eighth day of this desperate siege, the sixth day of October, Austria, finding it fruitless, draws off, with no pleasurable consciousness; rapidly, Dumouriez tending thitherward; and Lille too, black with ashes and smoulder, but jubilant skyhigh, flings its gates open. The Plat à barbe became fashionable; " no Patriot of an elegant turn," says Mercier several years afterward, " but shaves himself out of the splinter of a Lille bomb."

Quid multa, Why many words? The Invaders are in flight; Brunswick's Host, the third part of it gone to death, staggers disastrous along the deep highways of Champagne; spreading out also into " the fields of a tough spongy red-coloured clay "—" like Pharaoh through a Red Sea of mud," says Goethe; " for here also lay broken chariots, and riders and foot seemed sinking around." [5] On the eleventh morning of October, the World-Poet, struggling Northward out of Verdun, which he had entered Southward, some five weeks ago, in quite other order, discerned the following Phenomenon and formed part of it:

" Toward three in the morning, without having had any sleep, we were about mounting our carriage, drawn up at the door; when an insuperable obstacle disclosed itself: for there rolled on already, between the pavement-stones which were crushed up into a ridge on each side, an uninterrupted column of sick-wagons through the Town, and all was trodden as into a morass. While we stood waiting what could be made of it, our Landlord the Knight of Saint-Louis pressed past us, without salutation." He had been a Calonne's Notable in 1787, an Emigrant since; had returned to his home, jubilant, with the Prussians; but must now forth again into the wide world, "followed by a servant carrying a little bundle on his stick."

"The activity of our alert Lisieux shone eminent, and on this occasion too brought us on: for he struck into a small gap of the wagon-row; and held the advancing team back till we, with our six and our four horses, got intercalated; after which, in my light little coachlet, I could breathe freer. We were now under way; at a funeral pace, but still under way. The day broke; we found ourselves at the outlet of the Town, in a tumult and turmoil without measure. All sorts of vehicles, few horsemen, innumerable foot-people, were crossing each other on the great esplanade before the Gate. We turned to the right, with our Column, toward Estain, on a limited highway, with ditches at each side. Self-preservation, in so monstrous a press, knew now no pity, no respect of aught. Not far before us there fell down a horse of an ammunition-wagon; they cut the traces, and let it lie. And now as the three others could not bring their load along, they cut them also loose, tumbled the heavy-packed vehicle into the ditch; and with the smallest retardation, we had to drive on right over the horse, which was just about to rise; and I saw too clearly how its legs, under the wheels, went crashing and quivering.

"Horse and foot endeavoured to escape from the narrow laborious highway into the meadows: but these too were rained to ruin; overflowed by full ditches, the connection of the footpaths everywhere interrupted. Four gentleman-like, handsome, well-dressed French soldiers waded for a time beside our carriage; wonderfully clean and neat: and had such art of picking their steps, that their foot-gear testified no higher than the ankle to the muddy pilgrimage these good people found themselves engaged in.

"That under such circumstances one saw, in ditches, in meadows, in fields and crofts, dead horses enough, was natural to the case: by and by, however, you found them also flayed, the fleshy parts even cut away; sad token of the universal distress.

"Thus we fared on; every moment in danger, at the small-

est stoppage on our own part, of being ourselves tumbled over-
board; under which circumstances, truly, the careful dexterity
of our Lisieux could not be sufficiently praised. The same
talent showed itself at Estain; where we arrived toward noon;
and descried, over the beautiful well-built little Town, through
streets and on squares, around and beside us, one sense-con-
fusing tumult: the mass rolled this way and that; and, all struggling forward, each hindered the other. Unexpectedly our
carriage drew up before a stately house in the market-place;
master and mistress of the mansion saluted us in reverent
distance." Dexterous Lisieux, though we knew it not, had
said we were the King of Prussia's Brother!

   " But now, from the ground-floor windows, looking over
the whole market-place, we had the endless tumult lying, as it
were, palpable. All sorts of walkers, soldiers in uniform,
marauders, stout but sorrowing citizens and peasants, women
and children, crushed and jostled each other, amid vehicles of
all forms: ammunition-wagons, baggage-wagons; carriages,
single, double and multiplex; such hundredfold miscellany of
teams, requisitioned or lawfully owned, making way, hitting
together, hindering each other, rolled here to right and to
left. Horned-cattle too were struggling on; probably herds
that had been put in requisition. Riders you saw few; but the
elegant carriages of the Emigrants, many-coloured, lackered,
gilt and silvered, evidently by the best builders, caught your
eye.[6]

   " The crisis of the strait, however, arose farther on a little;
where the crowded market-place had to introduce itself into a
street—straight indeed and good, but proportionately far too
narrow. I have, in my life, seen nothing like it: the aspect
of it might perhaps be compared to that of a swoln river
which has been raging over meadows and fields, and is now
again obliged to press itself through a narrow bridge, and flow
on in its bounded channel. Down the long street, all visible
from our windows, there swelled continually the strangest tide:
a high double-seated travelling coach towered visible over the
flood of things. We thought of the fair Frenchwomen we
had seen in the morning. It was not they, however; it was
Count Haugwitz; him you could look at, with a kind of sardonic malice, rocking onward, step by step, there."[7]

   In such untriumphant Procession has the Brunswick Mani-

festo issued! Nay, in worse, " in Negotiation with these mis-
creants "—the first news of which produced such a revulsion
in the Emigrant nature, as put our scientific World-Poet " in
fear for the wits of several." [8]   There is no help: they must
fare on, these poor Emigrants, angry with all persons and
things, and making all persons angry in the hapless course
they struck into.   Landlord and landlady testify to you, at
tables-d'hôte, how insupportable these Frenchmen are: how,
in spite of such humiliation, of poverty and probable beggary,
there is ever the same struggle for precedence, the same for-
wardness and want of discretion.   High in honour, at the
head of the table, you with your own eyes observe not a
Seigneur, but the automaton of a Seigneur fallen into dotage;
still worshipped, reverently waited on and fed.   In miscellaneous seats is a miscellany of soldiers, commissaries, adven-
turers; consuming silently their barbarian victuals.   " On all
brows is to be read a hard destiny; all are silent, for each
has his own sufferings to bear, and looks forth into misery
without bounds."   One hasty wanderer, coming in, and eating
without ungraciousness what is set before him, the landlord
lets off almost scot-free.   " He is," whispered the landlord to
me, " the first of these cursed people I have seen condescend
to taste our German black bread." [9]

And Dumouriez is in Paris; lauded and feasted; paraded
in glittering saloons, floods of beautifulest blonde-dresses and
broadcloth-coats flowing past him, endless, in admiring joy.
One night, nevertheless, in the splendour of one such scene,
he sees himself suddenly apostrophized by a squalid unjoyful
Figure, who has come in uninvited, nay, despite of all lackeys;
an unjoyful Figure!   The Figure is come " in express mission
from the Jacobins," to inquire sharply, better then than later,
touching certain things: " Shaven eyebrows of Volunteer
Patriots, for instance?"   Also, " your threats of shivering in
pieces?"   Also, " why you have not chased Brunswick hotly
enough?"   Thus, with sharp croak, inquires the Figure.—
" Ah, c'est vous qu'on appelle Marat, You are he they call
Marat!" answers the General, and turns coldly on his heel.[10]
—" Marat!"   The blonde-gowns quiver like aspens; the dress-
coats gather round; Actor Talma (for it is his house), Actor
Talma, and almost the very chandelier-lights, are blue: till

this obscene Spectrum, swart unearthly Visual-Appearance, vanish, back into its native Night.

General Dumouriez, in few brief days, is gone again, toward the Netherlands; will attack the Netherlands, winter though it be. And General Montesquiou, on the Southeast, has driven in the Sardinian Majesty; nay, almost without a shot fired, has taken Savoy from him, which longs to become a piece of the Republic. And General Custine, on the Northeast, has dashed forth on Spires and its Arsenal; and then on Electoral Mentz, not uninvited, wherein are German Democrats and no shadow of an Elector now: so that in the last days of October, Frau Forster, a daughter of Heyne's, somewhat democratic, walking out of the Gate of Mentz with her Husband, finds French soldiers playing at bowls with cannon-balls there. Forster trips cheerfully over one iron bomb, with " Live the Republic! " A black-bearded National Guard answers: " Elle vivra bien sans vous, It will probably live independently of you." [11]

NOTES

[1] " Hist. Parl.," xix, 19.
[2] Williams, iii, 71.
[3] October 1, 1792: Dumouriez, iii, 73.
[4] " Bombardement de Lille " (in " Hist. Parl.," xx, 63–71).
[5] " Campagne in Frankreich," p. 103.
[6] See " Hermann und Dorothea " (also by Goethe), Buch " Kalliope."
[7] " Campagne in Frankreich," Goethe's " Werke " (Stuttgart, 1829), xxx, 133.
[8] Ibid., p. 152.
[9] Ibid., pp. 210–212.
[10] Dumouriez, iii, 115.—Marat's account, in the " Débats des Jacobins " and " Journal de la République " (" Hist. Parl.," xix, 317–321), agrees to the turning on the heel, but strives to interpret it differently.
[11] Johann Georg Forster's " Briefwechsel " (Leipzig, 1829), i, 88.

BOOK XV

REGICIDE

CHAPTER I

THE DELIBERATIVE

FRANCE therefore has done two things very completely: she has hurled back her Cimmerian Invaders far over the marches; and likewise she has shattered her own internal Social Constitution, even to the minutest fibre of it, into wreck and dissolution. Utterly it is all altered: from King down to Parish Constable, all Authorities, Magistrates, Judges, persons that bore rule, have had, on the sudden, to alter themselves, so far as needful; or else, on the sudden, and not without violence, to be altered; a Patriot "Executive Council of Ministers," with a Patriot Danton in it, and then a whole Nation and National Convention, have taken care of that. Not a Parish Constable, in the farthest hamlet, who has said "De par le Roi," and shown loyalty, but must retire, making way for a new improved Parish Constable who can say "De par la République."

It is a change such as History must beg her readers to imagine, undescribed. An instantaneous change of the whole body-politic, the soul-politic being all changed; such a change as few bodies, politic or other, can experience in this world. Say, perhaps, such as poor Nymph Semele's body did experience, when she would needs, with woman's humour, see her Olympian Jove as very Jove—and so stood, poor Nymph, this moment Semele, next moment not Semele, but Flame and a Statue of red-hot Ashes! France has looked upon Democracy; seen it face to face.—The Cimmerian Invaders will rally, in humbler temper, with better or worse luck: the wreck and dissolution must reshape itself into a social Arrangement as it can and may. But as for this National Convention, which is to settle everything, if it do, as Deputy Paine and France generally expects, get all finished "in a few months," we shall call it a most deft Convention.

In truth, it is very singular to see how this mercurial French People plunged suddenly from " Vive le Roi! " to " Vive la République! " and goes simmering and dancing, shaking off daily (so to speak), and trampling into the dust, its old social garnitures, ways of thinking, rules of existing; and cheerfully dances toward the Ruleless, Unknown, with such hope in its heart, and nothing but Freedom, Equality, and Brotherhood in its mouth. Is it two centuries, or is it only two years, since all France roared simultaneously to the welkin, bursting forth into sound and smoke at its Feast of Pikes, " Live the Restorer of French Liberty "? Three short years ago there was still Versailles and an Œil-de-Bœuf: now there is that watched Circuit of the Temple, girt with dragon-eyed Municipals, where, as in its final limbo, Royalty lies extinct. In the year 1789, Constituent Deputy Barrère " wept," in his " Break-of-Day " Newspaper, at sight of a reconciled King Louis; and now in 1792, Convention Deputy Barrère, perfectly tearless, may be considering, whether the reconciled King Louis shall be guillotined or not!

Old garnitures and social vestures drop off (we say) so fast, being indeed quite decayed, and are trodden under the National dance. And the new vestures, where are they; the new modes and rules? Liberty, Equality, Fraternity: not vestures, but the wish for vestures! The Nation is for the present, figuratively speaking, naked; it has no rule or vesture; but is naked—a Sansculottic Nation.

So far therefore, and in such manner, have our Patriot Brissots, Guadets triumphed. Vergniaud's Ezekiel-visions of the fall of thrones and crowns, which he spake hypothetically and prophetically in the Spring of the year, have suddenly come to fulfilment in the Autumn. Our eloquent Patriots of the Legislative, like strong Conjurors, by the word of their mouth, have swept Royalism with its old modes and formulas to the winds; and shall now govern a France free of formulas. Free of formulas! And yet man lives not except with formulas; with customs, ways of doing and living: no text truer than this; which will hold true from the Tea-table and Tailor's shopboard up to the High Senate-houses, Solemn Temples; nay, through all provinces of Mind and Imagination, onward to the outmost confines of articulate Being—" Ubi homines sunt modi sunt. There are modes wherever there are men."

It is the deepest law of man's nature; whereby man is a crafts-man and "tool-using animal"; not the slave of Impulse, Chance, and brute Nature, but in some measure their lord. Twenty-five millions of men, suddenly stripped bare of their modi, and dancing them down in that manner, are a terrible thing to govern!

Eloquent Patriots of the Legislative, meanwhile, have pre-cisely this problem to solve. Under the name and nickname of " statesmen, hommes d'état," of " moderate men, modéran-tins," of Brissotins, Rolandins, finally of Girondins, they shall become world-famous in solving it. For the Twenty-five millions are Gallic effervescent too—filled both with hope of the unutterable, of universal Fraternity and Golden Age; and with terror of the unutterable, Cimmerian Europe all rallying on us. It is a problem like few. Truly, if man, as the Philosophers brag, did to any extent look before and after, what, one may ask, in many cases would become of him? What, in this case, would become of these Seven-hundred and Forty-nine men? The Convention, seeing clearly before and after, were a paralyzed Convention. Seeing clearly to the length of its own nose, it is not paralyzed.

To the Convention itself neither the work nor the method of doing it is doubtful! To make the Constitution; to defend the Republic till that be made. Speedily enough, accordingly, there has been a " Committee of the Constitution" got to-gether. Sieyès, Old-Constituent, Constitution-builder by trade; Condorcet, fit for better things; Deputy Paine, foreign Benefactor of the Species, with that " red carbuncled face and the black beaming eyes"; Hérault de Séchelles, Ex-Parle-menteer, one of the handsomest men in France; these, with inferior guild-brethren, are girt cheerfully to the work; will once more "make the Constitution"; let us hope, more effectually than last time. For that the Constitution can be made, who doubts—unless the Gospel of Jean Jacques came into the world in vain? True, our last Constitution did tumble within the year, so lamentably. But what then; except sort the rubbish and boulders, and build them up again better? "Widen your basis," for one thing—to Universal Suffrage, if need be; exclude rotten materials, Royalism and such-like, for another thing. And in brief, build, O unspeakable Sieyès and Company, unwearied! Frequent perilous downrushing of scaffolding and rubblework, be that an irritation, no discouragement. Start ye always again, clearing aside the wreck; if with broken limbs, yet with whole hearts; and build, we say, in the name of Heaven—till either the work do stand; or else mankind abandon it, and the Constitution-builders be paid off, with laughter and tears! One good time, in the course of Eternity, it was appointed that this of Social Contract too should try itself out. And so the Committee of Constitution shall toil: with hope and faith—with no disturbance from any reader of these pages.

To make the Constitution, then, and return home joyfully in a few months; this is the prophecy our National Convention gives of itself; by this scientific program shall its operations and events go on. But from the best scientific program, in such a case, to the actual fulfilment, what a difference! Every reunion of men, is it not, as we often say, a reunion of incalculable Influences; every unit of it a microcosm of Influences—of which how shall Science calculate or prophesy? Science, which can not, with all its calculuses, differential, integral, and of variations, calculate the Problem of Three gravitating Bodies, ought to hold her peace here, and say only: In this National Convention there are Seven-hundred and Forty-nine very singular Bodies, that gravitate and do much else—who, probably in an amazing manner, will work the appointment of Heaven.

Of National Assemblages, Parliaments, Congresses, which have long sat; which are of saturnine temperament; above all, which are not "dreadfully in earnest," something may be computed or conjectured: yet even these are a kind of Mystery in progress—whereby accordingly we see the Journalist Reporter find livelihood: even these jolt madly out of the ruts, from time to time. How much more a poor National Convention, of French vehemence; urged on at such velocity; without routine, without rut, track or landmark; and dreadfully in earnest every man of them! It is a Parliament literally such as there was never elsewhere in the world. Themselves are new, unarranged; they are the Heart and presiding centre of a France fallen wholly into maddest disarrangement. From all cities, hamlets, from the utmost ends of this France, with its Twenty-five million vehement souls, thick-streaming influences storm-in on that same Heart, in the Salle de Ma-

nége, and storm-out again : such fiery venous-arterial circu-
lation is the function of that Heart.   Seven-hundred and
Forty-nine human individuals, we say, never sat together on
our Earth under more original circumstances.   Common individuals most of them, or not far from common : yet in virtue
of the position they occupied, so notable.   How, in this wild
piping of the whirlwind of human passions, with death, victory,
terror, valour, and all height and all depth pealing and piping
these men, left to their own guidance, will speak and act?

Readers know well that this French National Convention
(quite contrary to its own Program) became the astonishment
and horror of mankind; a kind of Apocalyptic Convention,
or black Dream become real; concerning which History seldom speaks except in the way of interjection : how it covered
France with wo, delusion, and delirium; and from its bosom
there went forth Death on the pale Horse.   To hate this poor
National Convention is easy ; to praise and love it has not been
found impossible.   It is, as we say, a Parliament in the most
original circumstances.   To us, in these pages, be it as a fuliginous fiery mystery, where Upper has met Nether, and in
such alternate glare and blackness of darkness poor bedazzled
mortals know not which is Upper, which is Nether; but rage
and plunge distractedly, as mortals in that case will do.   A
Convention which has to consume itself, suicidally; and become dead ashes—with its World!   Behoves us, not to enter
exploratively its dim embroiled deeps; yet to stand with un-
wavering eyes, looking how it welters; what notable phases
and occurrences it will successively throw up.

One general superficial circumstance we remark with
praise : the force of Politeness.   To such depth has the sense
of civilization penetrated man's life; no Drouet, no Legendre,
in the maddest tug of war, can altogether shake it off.   Debates
of Senates dreadfully in earnest are seldom given frankly to
the world; else perhaps they would surprise it.   Did not the
Grand Monarque himself once chase his Louvois with a pair
of brandished tongs?   But reading long volumes of these
Convention Debates, all in a foam with furious earnestness,
earnest many times to the extent of life and death, one is
struck rather with the degree of continence they manifest in
speech; and how in such wild ebullition, there is still a kind

of polite rule struggling for mastery, and the forms of social
life never altogether disappear. These men, though they
menace with clenched right-hands, do not clutch one another
by the collar; they draw no daggers, except for oratorical
purposes, and this not often: profane swearing is almost unknown, though the Reports are frank enough; we find only
one or two oaths, oaths by Marat, reported in all.

For the rest, that there is "effervescence" who doubts?
Effervescence enough; Decrees passed by acclamation to-day,
repealed by vociferation to-morrow; temper fitful, most rota-
tory-changeful, always headlong! The "voice of the orator is
covered with rumours"; a hundred "honourable Members
rush with menaces toward the Left side of the Hall"; President
has "broken three bells in succession"—claps on his hat, as
signal that the country is near ruined. A fiercely effervescent
Old-Gallic Assemblage!—Ah, how the loud sick sounds of
Debate, and of Life, which is a debate, sink silent one after
another: so loud now, and in a little while so low! Brennus,
and those antique Gael Captains, in their way to Rome, to
Galatia and such places, whither they were in the habit of
marching in the most fiery manner, had Debates as effervescent, doubt it not; though no "Moniteur" has reported them.
They scolded in Celtic Welsh, those Brennuses; neither were
they Sansculotte; nay, rather breeches (braccæ, say of felt or
rough-leather) were the only thing they had; being, as Livy
testifies, naked down to the haunches—and, see, it is the same
sort of work and of men still, now when they have got coats,
and speak nasally a kind of broken Latin! But, on the whole,
does not Time envelope this present National Convention; as
it did those Brennuses, and ancient august Senates in felt
breeches? Time surely: and also Eternity. Dim dusk of
Time—or noon, which will be dusk; and then there is night,
and silence; and Time with all its sick noises is swallowed in
the still sea. Pity thy brother, O son of Adam! The angriest
frothy jargon that he utters, is it not properly the whimpering
of an infant which can not speak what ails it, but is in distress
clearly, in the inwards of it; and so must squall and whimper
continually, till its Mother take it, and it get—to sleep!

This Convention is not four days old, and the melodious
Melibœan stanzas that shook down Royalty are still fresh in

our ear, when there bursts out a new diapason—unhappily
of Discord, this time.   For speech has been made of a thing
difficult to speak of well: the September Massacres.   How
deal with these September Massacres; with the Paris Commune that presided over them?   A Paris Commune hateful-
terrible; before which the poor effete Legislative had to quail,
and sit quiet.   And now if a young omnipotent Convention
will not so quail and sit, what steps shall it take?   Have a
Departmental Guard in its pay, answer the Girondins and
Friends of Order!   A Guard of National Volunteers, missioned
from all the Eighty-three or Eighty-five Departments, for that
express end; these will keep Septemberers, tumultuous Communes in a due state of submissiveness, the Convention in
a due state of sovereignty.   So have the Friends of Order
answered, sitting in Committee, and reporting; and even a
Decree has been passed of the required tenour.   Nay, certain
Departments, as the Var or Marseilles, in mere expectation
and assurance of a Decree, have their contingent of Volunteers
already on march; brave Marseillese, foremost on the Tenth
of August, will not be hindmost here: "fathers gave their
sons a musket and twenty-five louis," says Barbaroux, "and
bade them march."

Can anything be properer?   A Republic that will found
itself on justice must needs investigate September Massacres;
a Convention calling itself National, ought it not to be guarded
by a National force?—Alas!   Reader, it seems so to the eye:
and yet there is much to be said and argued.   Thou beholdest
here the small beginning of a Controversy, which mere logic
will not settle.   Two small well-springs, September, Departmental Guard, or rather at bottom they are but one and the
same small well-spring; which will swell and widen into waters
of bitterness; all manner of subsidiary streams and brooks of
bitterness flowing in, from this side and that; till it become a
wide river of bitterness, of rage and separation—which can
subside only into the Catacombs.   This Departmental Guard,
decreed by overwhelming majorities, and then repealed for
peace's sake, and not to insult Paris, is again decreed more
than once; nay, it is partially executed, and the very men
that are to be of it are seen visibly parading the Paris streets
—shouting once, being overtaken with liquor: "À bas Marat,
Down with Marat!" [1]   Nevertheless, decreed never so often, it

is repealed just as often; and continues, for some seven months
an angry noisy Hypothesis only: a fair Possibility struggling
to become a Reality, but which shall never be one; which,
after endless struggling, shall, in February next, sink into sad
rest—dragging much along with it. So singular are the ways
of men and honourable Members.

But on this fourth day of the Convention's existence, as we
said, which is the 25th of September 1792, there comes Committee Report on that Decree of the Departmental Guard,
and speech of repealing it; there come denunciations of Anarchy, of a Dictatorship—which let the incorruptible Robespierre consider: there come denunciations of a certain " Journal de la République," once called " Ami du Peuple "; and so
thereupon there comes, visibly stepping up, visibly standing
aloft on the Tribune, ready to speak—the Bodily Spectrum
of People's-Friend Marat! Shriek, ye Seven-hundred and
Forty-nine; it is verily Marat, he and not another. Marat is
no phantasm of the brain, or mere lying impress of Printer's
Types; but a thing material, of joint and sinew, and a certain
small stature; ye behold him there, in his blackness, in his
dingy squalor, a living fraction of Chaos and Old Night;
visibly incarnate, desirous to speak. " It appears," says Marat
to the shrieking Assembly, " that a great many persons here
are enemies of mine."—" All! all! " shriek hundreds of voices:
enough to drown any People's-Friend. But Marat will not
drown: he speaks and croaks explanation; croaks with such
reasonableness, air of sincerity, that repentant pity smothers
anger, and the shrieks subside, or even become applauses. For
this Convention is unfortunately the crankest of machines: it
shall be pointing eastward with stiff violence this moment;
and then do but touch some spring dexterously, the whole
machine, clattering and jerking seven-hundredfold, will whirl
with huge crash, and, next moment, is pointing westward!
Thus Marat, absolved and applauded, victorious in his turn
of fence, is, as the Debate goes on, pricked at again by some
dexterous Girondin; and then the shrieks rise anew, and Decree of Accusation is on the point of passing; till the dingy
People's-Friend bobs aloft once more; croaks once more per-
suasive stillness, and the Decree of Accusation sinks. Whereupon he draws forth—a Pistol; and setting it to his Head,
the seat of such thought and prophecy, says: " If they had

passed their Accusation Decree, he, the People's-Friend, would have blown his brains out." A People's-Friend has that faculty in him. For the rest, as to this of the two-hundred and sixty-thousand Aristocrat Heads, Marat candidly says, " C'est là mon avis, Such is my opinion." Also is it not indisputable : " No power on Earth can prevent me from seeing into traitors, and unmasking them "—by my superior originality of mind? [2] An honourable member like this Friend of the People few terrestrial Parliaments have had.

We observe, however, that this first onslaught by the Friends of Order, as sharp and prompt as it was, has failed. For neither can Robespierre, summoned out by talk of Dictatorship, and greeted with the like rumour on showing himself, be thrown into Prison, into Accusation; not though Barbaroux openly bear testimony against him, and sign it on paper. With such sanctified meekness does the Incorruptible lift his seagreen cheek to the smiter; lift his thin voice, and with jesuitic dexterity plead, and prosper; asking at last, in a prosperous manner : " But what witnesses has the Citoyen Barbaroux to support his testimony?" "Moi!" cries hot Rebecqui, standing up, striking his breast with both hands, and answering " Me!" [3] Nevertheless the Seagreen pleads again, and makes it good : the long hurly-burly, " personal merely," while so much public matter lies fallow, has ended in the order of the day. O Friends of the Gironde, why will you occupy our august sessions with mere paltry Personalities, while the grand Nationality lies in such a state?—The Gironde has touched, this day, on the foul black-spot of its fair Convention Domain; has trodden on it, and yet not trodden it down. Alas, it is a well-spring, as we said, this black-spot; and will not tread down!

NOTES

[1] " Hist. Parl.," xx, 184.

[2] " Moniteur " Newspaper, Nos. 271, 280, 294, Année première: Moore's " Journal," ii, 21, 157, etc. (which, however, may perhaps, as in similar cases, be only a copy of the Newspaper).

[3] " Moniteur," ut suprà: Séance du 25 Septembre.

CHAPTER II

THE EXECUTIVE

MAY we not conjecture therefore that round this grand enterprise of Making the Constitution, there will, as heretofore, very strange embroilments gather, and questions and interests complicate themselves; so that after a few or even several months, the Convention will not have settled everything? Alas! a whole tide of questions comes rolling, boiling; growing ever wider, without end! Among which, apart from this question of September and Anarchy, let us notice three, which emerge oftener than the others, and promise to become Leading Questions: Of the Armies; of the Subsistences; thirdly, of the Dethroned King.

As to the Armies, Public Defence must evidently be put on a proper footing; for Europe seems coalizing itself again; one is apprehensive even England will join it. Happily Dumouriez prospers in the North—nay, what if he should prove too prosperous, and become Liberticide, Murderer of Freedom!—Dumouriez prospers, through this winter season; yet not without lamentable complaints. Sleek Pache, the Swiss Schoolmaster, he that sat frugal in his Alley, the wonder of neighbours, has got lately—whither thinks the Reader? To be Minister of War! Madame Roland, struck with his sleek ways, recommended him to her husband as Clerk; the sleek Clerk had no need of salary, being of true Patriotic temper; he would come with a bit of bread in his pocket, to save dinner and time; and munching incidentally, do three men's work in a day; punctual, silent, frugal—the sleek Tartuffe that he was. Therefore Roland, in the late Overturn, recommended him to be War-Minister. And now, it would seem, he is secretly undermining Roland; playing into the hands of your hotter Jacobins and September Commune; and can not, like strict Roland, be the Veto des Coquins! [1]

How the sleek Pache might mine and undermine, one knows not well; this however one does know: that his War-Office has become a den of thieves and confusion, such as all men shudder to behold. That the Citizen Hassenfratz, as Head-Clerk, sits there in bonnet rouge, in rapine, in violence, and some Mathematical calculation; a most insolent, red-night-capped man. That Pache munches his pocket-loaf, amid head-clerks and sub-clerks, and has spent all the War-Estimates. That Furnishers scour in gigs, over all districts of France, and drive bargains. And lastly that the Army gets next to no furniture: no shoes, though it is winter; no clothes; some have not even arms; " in the Army of the South," complains an honourable Member, " there are thirty-thousand pairs of breeches wanting "—a most scandalous want.

Roland's strict soul is sick to see the course things take: but what can he do? Keep his own Department strict; re-buke, and repress wheresoever possible; at lowest, complain. He can complain in Letter after Letter, to a National Conven-tion, to France, to Posterity, the Universe; grow ever more querulous-indignant—till at last, may he not grow wearisome? For is not this continual text of his, at bottom, a rather barren one: How astonishing that in a time of Revolt and abrogation of all Law but Cannon Law, there should be such Unlawful-ness? Intrepid Veto-of-Scoundrels, narrow-faithful, respect-able, methodic man, work thou in that manner, since happily it is thy manner, and wear thyself away; though ineffectual, not profitless in it—then nor now!—The brave Dame Roland, bravest of all French women, begins to have misgivings: The figure of Danton has too much of the " Sardanapalus charac-ter," at a Republican Rolandin Dinner-table: Clootz, Speaker of Mankind, proses sad stuff about a Universal Republic, or union of all Peoples and Kindreds in one and the same Fra-ternal Bond; of which Bond, how it is to be tied, one unhappily sees not.

It is also an indisputable, unaccountable or accountable fact, that Grains are becoming scarcer and scarcer. Riots for grain, tumultuous Assemblages demanding to have the price of grain fixed, abound far and near. The Mayor of Paris and other poor Mayors are like to have their difficulties. Pétion was re-elected Mayor of Paris; but has declined; being now a Convention Legislator. Wise surely to decline: for,

besides this of Grains and all the rest, there is in these times
an Improvised Insurrectionary Commune passing into an
Elected legal one; getting their accounts settled—not without irritancy! Pétion has declined: nevertheless many do
covet and canvass. After months of scrutinizing, balloting,
arguing and jargoning, one Doctor Chambon gets the post of
honour: who will not long keep it; but be, as we shall see,
literally crushed out of it.[2]

Think also if the private Sansculotte has not his difficulties,
in a time of dearth! Bread, according to the People's-Friend,
may be some " six sous per pound, a day's wages some fifteen "; and grim winter here. How the Poor Man continues
living, and so seldom starves; by miracle! Happily, in these
days, he can enlist, and have himself shot by the Austrians,
in an unusually satisfactory manner: for the Rights of Man.
—But Commandant Santerre, in this so straitened condition
of the flour-market, and state of Equality and Liberty, proposes, through the Newspapers, two remedies, or at least
palliatives: First, that all classes of men should live two days
of the week on potatoes; then, second, that every man should
hang his dog. Hereby, as the Commandant thinks, the saving, which indeed he computes to so many sacks, would be
very considerable. Cheerfuler form of inventive-stupidity
than Commandant Santerre's dwells in no human soul. Inventive-stupidity, imbedded in health, courage, and good-
nature: much to be commended. " My whole strength," he
tells the Convention once, " is, day and night, at the service
of my fellow-citizens: if they find me worthless, they will dismiss me; I will return and brew beer." [3]

Or figure what correspondences a poor Roland, Minister of
the Interior, must have, on this of Grains alone! Free-trade
in Grain, impossibility to fix the Prices of Grain; on the other
hand, clamour and necessity to fix them: Political Economy
lecturing from the Home Office, with demonstration clear as
Scripture—ineffectual for the empty National Stomach. The
Mayor of Chartres, like to be eaten himself, cries to the
Convention; the Convention sends honourable Members in
Deputation; who endeavour to feed the multitude by miraculous spiritual methods; but can not. The multitude, in spite
of all Eloquence, come bellowing round; will have the Grain-
Prices fixed, and at a moderate elevation; or else—the hon-

ourable Deputies hanged on the spot! The honourable Deputies, reporting this business, admit that, on the edge of horrid death, they did fix, or affect to fix the Price of Grain: for which, be it also noted, the Convention, a Convention that will not be trifled with, sees good to reprimand them.[4]

But as to the origin of these Grain-Riots, is it not most probably your secret Royalists again? Glimpses of Priests were discernible in this of Chartres—to the eye of Patriotism. Or indeed may not " the root of it all lie in the Temple Prison, in the heart of a perjured King," well as we guard him?[5] Unhappy perjured King!—And so there shall be Baker's Queues by and by, more sharp-tempered than ever: on every Baker's door-rabbet an iron ring, and coil of rope; whereon, with firm grip, on this side and that, we form our Queue: but mischievous deceitful persons cut the rope, and our Queue becomes a ravelment; wherefore the coil must be made of iron chain.[6] Also there shall be Prices of Grain well fixed; but then no grain purchasable by them: bread not to be had except by Ticket from the Mayor, few ounces per mouth daily; after long swaying, with firm grip, on the chain of the Queue. And Hunger shall stalk direful; and Wrath and Suspicion, whetted to the Preternatural pitch, shall stalk; as those other preternatural " shapes of Gods in their wrathfulness " were discerned stalking, in " glare and gloom of that fire-ocean," when Troy Town fell!—

NOTES

[1] Madame Roland, " Mémoires," ii, 237, etc.
[2] " Dictionnaire des Hommes Marquans," § Chambon.
[3] " Moniteur " (in " Hist. Parl.," xx, 412).
[4] " Hist. Parl.," xx, 431–440.
[5] Ibid., xx, 409.
[6] Mercier, " Nouveau Paris."

CHAPTER III

DISCROWNED

BUT the question more pressing than all on the Legislator, as yet, is this third: What shall be done with King Louis?

King Louis, now King and Majesty to his own family alone, in their own Prison Apartment alone, has, for months past, been mere Louis Capet and the Traitor Veto with the rest of France. Shut in his Circuit of the Temple, he has heard and seen the loud whirl of things; yells of September Massacres, Brunswick war-thunders dying off in disaster and discomfiture, he passive, a spectator merely; waiting whither it would please to whirl with him. From the neighbouring windows, the curious, not without pity, might see him walk daily, at a certain hour, in the Temple Garden, with his Queen, Sister and two Children, all that now belongs to him in this Earth.[1] Quietly he walks and waits; for he is not of lively feelings, and is of a devout heart. The wearied Irresolute has, at least, no need of resolving now. His daily meals, lessons to his Son, daily walk in the Garden, daily game at ombre or daughts, fill up the day: the morrow will provide for itself.

The morrow indeed; and yet How? Louis asks, How? France, with perhaps still more solicitude, asks, How? A King dethroned by insurrection is verily not easy to dispose of. Keep him prisoner, he is a secret centre for the Disaffected, for endless plots, attempts and hopes of theirs. Banish him, he is an open centre for them; his royal war-standard, with what of divinity it has, unrolls itself, summoning the world. Put him to death? A cruel questionable extremity that too: and yet the likeliest in these extreme circumstances, of insurrectionary men, whose own life and death lies staked: accordingly it is said, from the last step of the throne to the first of the scaffold there is short distance.

But, on the whole, we will remark here that this business of Louis looks altogether different now, as seen over Seas and at the distance of forty-four years, from what it looked then, in France, and struggling confused all round one. For indeed it is a most lying thing that same Past Tense always: so beautiful, sad, almost Elysian-sacred, " in the moonlight of Memory," it seems; and seems only. For observe, always one most important element is surreptitiously (we not noticing it) withdrawn from the Past Time: the haggard element of Fear! Not there does Fear dwell, nor Uncertainty, nor Anxiety; but it dwells here; haunting us, tracking us; running like an accursed ground-discord through all the music-tones of our Existence—making the Tense a mere Present one! Just so is it with this of Louis. Why smite the fallen? asks Magnanimity, out of danger now. He is fallen so low this once-high man; no criminal nor traitor, how far from it; but the unhappiest of Human Solecisms: whom if abstract Justice had to pronounce upon, she might well become concrete Pity, and pronounce only sobs and dismissal!

So argues retrospective Magnanimity: but Pusillanimity, present, prospective? Reader, thou hast never lived, for months, under the rustle of Prussian gallows-ropes; never wert thou portion of a National Sahara-waltz, Twenty-five millions running distracted to fight Brunswick! Knights Errant themselves, when they conquered Giants, usually slew the Giants: quarter was only for other Knights Errant, who knew courtesy and the laws of battle. The French Nation, in simultaneous, desperate dead-pull, and as if by miracle of madness, has pulled down the most dread Goliath, huge with the growth of ten centuries; and can not believe, though his giant bulk, covering acres, lies prostrate, bound with peg and packthread, that he will not rise again, man-devouring; that the victory is not partly a dream. Terror has its scepticism; miraculous victory its rage of vengeance. Then as to criminality, is the prostrated Giant, who will devour us of he rise, an innocent Giant? Curate Grégoire, who indeed is now Constitutional Bishop Grégoire, asserts, in the heat of eloquence, that Kingship by the very nature of it is a crime capital; that Kings' Houses are as wild-beasts' dens.[2] Lastly consider this: that there is on record a Trial of Charles First! This printed " Trial of Charles First " is sold and read every-

where at present [3]—Quel spectacle! Thus did the English
People judge their Tyrant, and become the first of Free
Peoples: which feat, by the grace of Destiny, may not France
now rival? Scepticism of terror, rage of miraculous victory,
sublime spectacle to the universe—all things point one fatal
way.

Such leading questions, and their endless incidental ones—
of September Anarchists and Departmental Guard; of Grain-
Riots, plaintive Interior Ministers; of Armies, Hassenfratz
dilapidations; and what is to be done with Louis—beleaguer
and embroil this Convention; which would so gladly make the
Constitution rather. All which questions, too, as we often
urge of such things, are in growth; they grow in every French
head; and can be seen growing also, very curiously, in this
mighty welter of Parliamentary Debate, of Public Business
which the Convention has to do. A question emerges, so
small at first; is put off, submerged; but always re-emerges
bigger than before. It is a curious, indeed an indescribable
sort of growth which such things have.

We perceive, however, both by its frequent re-emergence
and by its rapid enlargement of bulk, that this Question of
King Louis will take the lead of all the rest. And truly, in
that case, it will take the lead in a much deeper sense. For
as Aaron's Rod swallowed all the other serpents; so will the
Foremost Question, whichever may get foremost, absorb all
other questions and interests; and from it and the decision of
it will they all, so to speak, be born, or new-born, and have
shape, physiognomy and destiny corresponding. It was appointed of Fate that, in this wide-weltering, strangely growing, monstrous stupendous imbroglio of Convention Business,
the grand First-Parent of all the questions, controversies,
measures and enterprises which were to be evolved there to
the world's astonishment, should be this Question of King
Louis.

NOTES

[1] Moore, i, 123; ii, 224, etc.
[2] "Moniteur," Séance du 21 Septembre, An. Ier (1792).
[3] Moore's "Journal," ii, 165.

CHAPTER IV

THE LOSER PAYS

THE Sixth of November 1792 was a great day for the Republic: outwardly, over the Frontiers; inwardly, in the Salle de Manége.

Outwardly: for Dumouriez, overrunning the Netherlands, did, on that day, come in contact with Saxe-Teschen and the Austrians; Dumouriez wide-winged, they wide-winged; at and around the village of Jemappes, near Mons. And fire-hail is whistling far and wide there, the great guns playing, and the small; so many green Heights getting fringed and maned with red Fire. And Dumouriez is swept back on this wing, and swept back on that, and is like to be swept back utterly; when he rushes up in person, the prompt Polymetis; speaks a prompt word or two; and then, with clear tenor-pipe, "uplifts the Hymn of the Marseillese, entonna la Marseillaise," [1] ten-thousand tenor or bass pipes joining; or say, some Forty-thousand in all; for every heart leaps at the sound; and so with rhythmic march-melody, waxing ever quicker, to double and to treble quick, they rally, they advance, they rush, death-defying, man-devouring; carry batteries, redoutes, whatsoever is to be carried; and, like the fire-whirlwind, sweep all manner of Austrians from the scene of action. Thus, through the hands of Dumouriez, may Rouget de Lille, in figurative speech, be said to have gained, miraculously, like another Orpheus, by his Marseillese fiddle-strings (fidibus canoris), a Victory of Jemappes; and conquered the Low Countries.

Young General Égalité, it would seem, shone brave among the bravest on this occasion. Doubtless a brave Égalité— whom however does not Dumouriez rather talk of oftener than need were? The Mother Society has her own thoughts. As for the Elder Égalité, he flies low at this time; appears in the Convention for some half-hour daily, with rubicund, preoccupied or impassive quasi-contemptuous countenance; and then takes himself away.[2] The Netherlands are conquered, at least overrun. Jacobin missionaries, your Prolys, Pereiras, follow in the train of the Armies; also Convention Commissioners, melting church-plate, revolutionizing and remodelling — among whom Danton, in brief space, does immensities of business; not neglecting his own wages and trade-profits, it is thought. Hassenfratz dilapidates at home; Dumouriez grumbles and they dilapidate abroad: within the walls there is sinning, and without the walls there is sinning.

But in the Hall of the Convention, at the same hour with this victory of Jemappes, there went another thing forward: Report, of great length, from the proper appointed Committee, on the Crimes of Louis. The Galleries listen breathless; take comfort, ye Galleries: Deputy Valazé, Reporter on this occasion, thinks Louis very criminal; and that, if convenient, he should be tried—poor Girondin Valazé, who may be tried himself, one day! Comfortable so far. Nay, here comes a second Committee-reporter, Deputy Mailhe, with a Legal Argument, very prosy to read now, very refreshing to hear then, That, by the Law of the Country, Louis Capet was only called Inviolable by a figure of rhetoric; but at bottom was perfectly violable, triable; that he can, and even should be tried. This Question of Louis, emerging so often as an angry confused possibility, and submerging again, has emerged now in an articulate shape.

Patriotism growls indignant joy. The so-called reign of Equality is not to be a mere name, then, but a thing! Try Louis Capet? scornfully ejaculates Patriotism. Mean criminals go to the gallows for a purse cut; and this chief criminal, guilty of a France cut; of a France slashed asunder with Clotho-scissors and Civil war; with his victims "twelve-hundred on the Tenth of August alone" lying low in the Catacombs, fattening the passes of Argonne Wood, of Valmy and far Fields; he, such chief criminal, shall not even come to the bar?—For, alas, O Patriotism! add we, it was from of old said, "The loser pays!" It is he who has to pay all scores, run up by whomsoever; on him must all breakages and charges fall; and the twelve-hundred on the Tenth of August are not rebel traitors, but victims and martyrs: such is the law of quarrel.

Patriotism, nothing doubting, watches over this Question of the trial, now happily emerged in an articulate shape; and will see it to maturity, if the gods permit. With a keen solicitude Patriotism watches; getting ever keener, at every new difficulty, as Girondins and false brothers interpose delays; till it get a keenness as of fixed-idea, and will have this Trial and no earthly thing instead of it—if Equality be not a name. Love of Equality; then scepticism of terror, rage of victory, sublime spectacle to the universe: all these things are strong.

But indeed this Question of the Trial, is it not to all persons a most grave one; filling with dubiety many a Legislative head! Regicide? asks the Gironde Respectability. To kill a king, and become the horror of respectable nations and persons? But then also, to save a king; to lose one's footing with the decided Patriot; the undecided Patriot, though never so respectable, being mere hypothetic froth and no footing?—The dilemma presses sore; and between the horns of it you wriggle round and round. Decision is nowhere, save in the Mother Society and her Sons. These have decided, and go forward: the others wriggle round uneasily within their dilemma-horns, and make way nowhither.

NOTES

[1] Dumouriez, " Mémoires," iii, 174.   [2] Moore, ii, 148.

CHAPTER V

STRETCHING OF FORMULAS

BUT how this Question of the Trial grew laboriously, through the weeks of gestation, now that it has been articulated or conceived, were superfluous to trace here. It emerged and submerged among the infinite of questions and embroilments. The Veto of Scoundrels writes plaintive Letters as to Anarchy; " concealed Royalists," aided by Hunger, produce Riots about Grain. Alas! it is but a week ago, these Girondins made a new fierce onslaught on the September Massacres!

For, one day, among the last of October, Robespierre, being summoned to the tribune by some new hint of that old calumny of the Dictatorship, was speaking and pleading there, with more and more comfort to himself; till rising high in heart, he cried out valiantly: " Is there any man here that dare specifically accuse me?" " Moi!" exclaimed one. Pause of deep silence: a lean angry little Figure, with broad bald brow, strode swiftly toward the tribune, taking papers from its pocket: " I accuse thee, Robespierre—I Jean Baptiste Louvet!" The Seagreen became tallowgreen; shrinking to a corner of the tribune. Danton cried, " Speak, Robespierre; there are many good citizens that listen "; but the tongue refused its office. And so Louvet, with a shrill tone, read and recited crime after crime: dictatorial temper, exclusive popularity, bullying at elections, mob-retinue, September Massacres—till all the Convention shrieked again, and had almost indicted the Incorruptible there on the spot. Never did the Incorruptible run such a risk. Louvet, to his dying day, will regret that the Gironde did not take a bolder attitude, and extinguish him there and then.

Not so, however: the Incorruptible, about to be indicted in this sudden manner, could not be refused a week of delay. That week he is not idle; nor is the Mother Society idle—

fierce-tremulous for her chosen son. He is ready at the day
with his written Speech; smooth as a Jesuit Doctor's; and
convinces some. And now? Why now lazy Vergniaud does
not rise with Demosthenic thunder; poor Louvet, unprepared,
can do little or nothing: Barrère proposes that these comparatively despicable " personalities " be dismissed by order of
the day! Order of the day it accordingly is. Barbaroux
can not even get a hearing; not though he rush down to the
Bar, and demand to be heard there as a petitioner.[1] The
Convention, eager for public business (with that first articulate
emergence of the Trial just coming on), dismisses these com-
parative misères and despicabilities: splenetic Louvet must
digest his spleen, regretfully forever: Robespierre, dear to
Patriotism, is dearer for the dangers he has run.

This is the second grand attempt by our Girondin Friends
of Order to extinguish that black-spot in their domain; and
we see they have made it far blacker and wider than before!
Anarchy, September Massacre: it is a thing that lies hideous
in the general imagination; very detestable to the undecided
Patriot, of Respectability: a thing to be harped on as often
as need is. Harp on it, denounce it, trample it, ye Girondin
Patriots—and yet behold, the black-spot will not trample
down; it will only, as we say, trample blacker and wider:
fools, it is no black-spot of the surface, but a well-spring of
the deep! Consider rightly, it is the Apex of the everlasting
Abyss, this black-spot, looking up as water through thin ice
—say, as the region of Nether Darkness through your thin
film of Gironde Regulation and Respectability: trample it
not, lest the film break, and then—!

The truth is, if our Gironde Friends had an understanding
of it, where were French Patriotism, with all its eloquence, at
this moment, had not that same great Nether Deep, of Bedlam,
Fanaticism and Popular wrath and madness, risen unfathom-
able on the Tenth of August? French Patriotism were an
eloquent Reminiscence; swinging on Prussian gibbets. Nay,
where, in few months, were it still, should the same great
Nether Deep subside?—Nay, as readers of Newspapers pretend to recollect, this hatefulness of the September Massacre is
itself partly an after-thought: readers of Newspapers can quote
Gorsas and various Brissotins approving of the September
Massacre, at the time it happened; and calling it a salutary

vengeance.[2] So that the real grief, after all, were it not so much righteous horror, as grief that one's own power was departing? Unhappy Girondins!

In the Jacobin Society, therefore, the decided Patriot complains that here are men who with their private ambitions and animosities will ruin Liberty, Equality, and Brotherhood, all three: they check the spirit of Patriotism; throw stumbling-blocks in its way; and instead of pushing on, all shoulders at the wheel, will stand idle there, spitefully clamouring what foul ruts there are, what rude jolts we give! To which the Jacobin Society answers with angry roar—with angry shriek, for there are Citoyennes too, thick crowded in the galleries here. Citoyennes who bring their seam with them, or their knitting-needles; and shriek or knit as the case needs; famed Tricoteuses, Patriot Knitters; Mère Duchesse, or the like Deborah and Mother of the Faubourgs, giving the key-note. It is a changed Jacobin Society; and a still changing. Where Mother Duchess now sits, authentic Duchesses have sat. High-rouged dames went once in jewels and spangles; now, instead of jewels, you may take the knitting-needles and leave the rouge: the rouge will gradually give place to natural brown, clean washed or even unwashed: and Demoiselle Théroigne herself get scandalously fustigated. Strange enough; it is the same tribune raised in mid-air, where a high Mirabeau, a high Barnave and Aristocrat Lameths once thundered; whom gradually your Brissots, Guadets, Vergniauds, a hotter style of Patriots in bonnet rouge, did displace; red heat, as one may say, superseding light. And now your Brissots in turn, and Brissotins, Rolandins, Girondins, are becoming supernumerary; must desert the sittings, or be expelled: the light of the Mighty Mother is burning not red but blue!—Provincial Daughter Societies loudly disapprove these things; loudly demand the swift reinstatement of such eloquent Girondins, the swift "erasure of Marat, radiation de Marat." The Mother Society, so far as natural reason can predict, seems ruining herself. Nevertheless she has at all crises seemed so; she has a preternatural life in her, and will not ruin.

But, in a fortnight more, this great Question of the Trial, while the fit Committee is assiduously but silently working on it, receives an unexpected stimulus. Our readers remember poor Louis's turn for smith-work: how, in old happier days, a certain Sieur Gamain of Versailles was wont to come over and instruct him in lockmaking—often scolding him, they say, for his numbness. By whom, nevertheless, the royal Apprentice had learned something of that craft. Hapless Apprentice; perfidious Master-Smith! For now, on this 20th of November 1792, dingy Smith Gamain comes over to the Paris Municipality, over to Minister Roland, with hints that he, Smith Gamain, knows a thing; that, in May last, when traitorous Correspondence was so brisk, he and the royal Apprentice fabricated an " Iron Press, Armoire de Fer," cunningly inserting the same in a wall of the royal chamber in the Tuileries; invisible under the wainscot; where doubtless it still sticks! Perfidious Gamain, attended by the proper Authorities, finds the wainscot panel which none else can find; wrenches it up; discloses the Iron Press—full of Letters and Papers! Roland clutches them out; conveys them over in towels to the fit assiduous Committee, which sits hard by. In towels, we say, and without notarial inventory; an oversight on the part of Roland.

Here, however, are Letters enough: which disclose to a demonstration the Correspondence of a traitorous self-preserving Court; and this not with Traitors only, but even with Patriots so-called! Barnave's treason, of Correspondence with the Queen, and friendly advice to her, ever since that Varennes Business, is hereby manifest: how happy that we have him, this Barnave, lying safe in the Prison of Grenoble, since September last, for he had long been suspect! Talleyrand's treason, many a man's treason, if not manifest hereby, is next to it. Mirabeau's treason: wherefore his Bust in the Hall of the Convention " is veiled with gauze," till we ascertain. Alas! it is too ascertainable! His Bust in the Hall of the Jacobins, denounced by Robespierre from the tribune in mid-air, is not veiled, it is instantly broken to shreds; a Patriot mounting swiftly with a ladder, and shivering it down on the floor—it and others: amid shouts.[3] Such is their recompense and amount of wages, at this date: on the principle of supply and demand. Smith Gamain, inadequately recompensed for the present, comes, some fifteen months after, with a humble Petition; setting forth that no sooner was that important Iron Press finished off by him, than (as he now bethinks himself)

Louis gave him a large glass of wine. Which large glass of wine did produce in the stomach of Sieur Gamain the terriblest effects, evidently tending toward death, and was then brought up by an emetic; but has, notwithstanding, entirely ruined the constitution of Sieur Gamain; so that he can not work for his family (as he now bethinks himself). The recompense of which is " Pension of Twelve-hundred Francs," and " honourable mention." So different is the ratio of demand and supply at different times.

Thus, amid obstructions and stimulating furtherances, has the Question of the Trial to grow; emerging and submerging; fostered by solicitous Patriotism. Of the Orations that were spoken on it, of the painfully devised Forms of Process for managing it, the Law Arguments to prove it lawful, and all the infinite floods of Juridical and other ingenuity and oratory, be no syllable reported in this History. Lawyer ingenuity is good: but what can it profit here? If the truth must be spoken, O august Senators, the only Law in this case is: Væ victis, The loser pays! Seldom did Robespierre say a wiser word than the hint he gave to that effect, in his oration, That it was needless to speak of Law; that here, if never elsewhere, our Right was Might. An oration admired almost to ecstasy by the Jacobin Patriot: who shall say that Robespierre is not a thorough-going man; bold in Logic at least? To the like effect, or still more plainly, spake young Saint-Just, the black-haired, mild-toned youth. Danton is on mission, in the Netherlands, during this preliminary work. The rest, far as one reads, welter amid Law of Nations, Social Contract, Juristics, Syllogistics; to us barren as the East wind. In fact, what can be more unprofitable than the sight of Seven-hundred and Forty-nine ingenious men struggling with their whole force and industry, for a long course of weeks, to do at bottom this: To stretch out the old Formula and Law Phraseology, so that it may cover the new, contradictory, entirely uncoverable Thing? Whereby the poor Formula does but crack, and one's honesty along with it! The thing that is palpably hot, burning, wilt thou prove it, by syllogism, to be a freezing-mixture? This of stretching out Formulas till they crack, is, especially in times of swift change, one of the sorrowfulest tasks poor Humanity has.

NOTES

[1] Louvet, "Mémoires" (Paris, 1823), p. 52; "Moniteur" (Séances du 29 Octobre, 5 Novembre, 1792); Moore, ii, 178, etc.

[2] See "Hist. Parl.," xvii, 401; Newspapers by Gorsas and others (cited ibid., 428).

[3] "Journal des Débats des Jacobins" (in "Hist. Parl.," xxii, 296).

CHAPTER VI

AT THE BAR

MEANWHILE, in a space of some five weeks, we have got to another emerging of the Trial, and a more practical one than ever.

On Tuesday eleventh of December, the King's Trial has emerged, very decidedly: into the streets of Paris; in the shape of that green Carriage of Mayor Chambon, within which sits the King himself, with attendants, on his way to the Convention Hall! Attended, in that green carriage, by Mayors Chambon, Procureurs Chaumette; and outside of it by Commandants Santerre, with cannon, cavalry and double row of infantry; all Sections under arms, strong Patrols scouring all streets; so fares he, slowly through the dull drizzling weather: and about two o'clock we behold him, " in walnut-coloured greatcoat, redingote noisette," descending through the Place Vendôme, toward that Salle de Manége; to be indicted, and judicially interrogated. The mysterious Temple Circuit has given up its secret; which now, in this walnut-coloured coat, men behold with eyes. The same bodily Louis who was once Louis the Desired, fares there: hapless King, he is getting now toward port; his deplorable farings and voyagings draw to a close. What duty remains to him henceforth, that of placidly enduring, he is fit to do.

The singular Procession fares on; in silence, says Prudhomme, or amid growlings of the Marseillese Hymn; in silence, ushers itself into the Hall of the Convention, Santerre holding Louis's arm with his hand. Louis looks round him, with composed air, to see what kind of Convention and Parliament it is. Much changed indeed—since February gone two years, when our Constituent, then busy, spread fleur-de-lys velvet for us; and we came over to say a kind word here, and they all started up swearing Fidelity; and all France started up swearing, and made it a Feast of Pikes; which has ended in this! Barrère, who once "wept" looking up from his Editor's-Desk, looks down now from his President's-Chair, with a list of Fifty-seven Questions; and says, dry-eyed: "Louis, you may sit down." Louis sits down: it is the very seat, they say, same timber and stuffing, from which he accepted the Constitution, amid dancing and illumination, autumn gone a year. So much woodwork remains identical; so much else is not identical. Louis sits and listens, with a composed look and mind.

Of the Fifty-seven Questions we shall not give so much as one. They are questions captiously embracing all the main Documents seized on the Tenth of August, or found lately in the Iron Press; embracing all the main incidents of the Revolution History; and they ask, in substance, this: Louis, who wert King, art thou not guilty to a certain extent, by act and written document, of trying to continue King? Neither in the Answers is there much notable. Mere quiet negations, for most part; an accused man standing on the simple basis of No: I do not recognise that document; I did not do that act; or did it according to the law that then was. Whereupon the Fifty-seven Questions, and Documents to the number of a Hundred and Sixty-two, being exhausted in this manner, Barrère finishes, after some three hours, with his: "Louis, I invite you to withdraw."

Louis withdraws, under Municipal escort, into a neighbouring Committee-room; having first, in leaving the bar, demanded to have Legal Counsel. He declines refreshment, in this Committee-room; then, seeing Chaumette busy with a small loaf which a grenadier had divided with him, says, he will take a bit of bread. It is five o'clock; and he had breakfasted but slightly, in a morning of such drumming and alarm. Chaumette breaks his half-loaf: the King eats of the crust; mounts the green Carriage, eating; asks now, What he shall do with the crumb? Chaumette's clerk takes it from him; flings it out into the street. Louis says, It is pity to fling out bread, in a time of dearth. "My grandmother," remarks Chaumette, "used to say to me, Little boy, never waste a crumb of bread; you can not make one." "Monsieur Chaumette," answers Louis, "your grandmother seems to have been a sensible woman."[1] Poor innocent mortal; so quietly he waits the drawing of the lot—fit to do this at least well; Passivity alone, without Activity, sufficing for it! He talks once of travelling over France by and by, to have a geographical and topographical view of it; being from of old fond of geography.—The Temple Circuit again receives him, closes on him; gazing Paris may retire to its hearths and coffee-houses, to its clubs and theatres: the damp Darkness has sunk, and with it the drumming and patrolling of this strange Day.

Louis is now separated from his Queen and Family; given up to his simple reflections and resources. Dull lie these stone walls round him; of his loved ones none with him. "In this state of uncertainty," providing for the worst, he writes his Will: a Paper which can still be read; full of placidity, simplicity, pious sweetness. The Convention, after debate, has granted him Legal Counsel, of his own choosing. Advocate Target feels himself "too old," being turned of fifty-four; and declines. He had gained great honour once, defending Rohan the Necklace-Cardinal; but will gain none here. Advocate Tronchet, some ten years older, does not decline. Nay, behold, good old Malesherbes steps forward voluntarily; to the last of his fields, the good old hero! He is gray with seventy years: he says, " I was twice called to the Council of him who was my Master, when all the world coveted that honour; and I owe him the same service now, when it has become one which many reckon dangerous." These two, with a younger Desèze, whom they will select for pleading, are busy over that Fifty-and-sevenfold Indictment, over the Hundred and Sixty-two Documents; Louis aiding them as he can.

A great Thing is now therefore in open progress; all men, in all lands, watching it. By what Forms and Methods shall the Convention acquit itself, in such manner that there rest not on it even the suspicion of blame? Difficult that will be! The Convention, really much at a loss, discusses and deliberates. All day from morning to night, day after day, the Tribune drones with oratory on this matter; one must stretch the old Formula to cover the new Thing. The Patriots of the Mountain, whetted even keener, clamour for despatch above all; the only good Form will be a swift one. Nevertheless the Convention deliberates; the Tribune drones

—drowned indeed in tenor, and even in treble, from time to time; the whole Hall shrilling up round it into pretty frequent wrath and provocation. It has droned and shrilled wellnigh a fortnight, before we can decide, this shrillness getting even shriller, That on Wednesday 26th of December, Louis shall appear and plead. His Advocates complain that it is fatally soon; which they well might as Advocates: but without remedy; to Patriotism it seems endlessly late.

On Wednesday therefore, at the cold dark hour of eight in the morning, all Senators are at their post. Indeed they warm the cold hour, as we find, by a violent effervescence, such as is too common now; some Louvet or Buzot attacking some Tallien, Chabot; and so the whole Mountain effervescing against the whole Gironde. Scarcely is this done, at nine, when Louis and his three Advocates, escorted by the clang of arms and Santerre's National force, enter the Hall.

Desèze unfolds his papers; honourably fulfilling his perilous office, pleads for the space of three hours. An honourable Pleading, " composed almost overnight "; courageous yet discreet; not without ingenuity, and soft pathetic eloquence: Louis fell on his neck, when they had withdrawn, and said with tears, " Mon pauvre Desèze! " Louis himself, before withdrawing, had added a few words, " perhaps the last he would utter to them ": how it pained his heart, above all things, to be held guilty of that bloodshed on the Tenth of August; or of ever shedding or wishing to shed French blood. So saying, he withdrew from that Hall—having indeed finished his work there. Many are the strange errands he has had thither; but this strange one is the last.

And now, why will the Convention loiter? Here is the Indictment and Evidence; here is the Pleading: does not the rest follow of itself? The Mountain, and Patriotism in general, clamours still louder for despatch; for Permanent-session, till the task be done. Nevertheless a doubting, apprehensive Convention decides that it will still deliberate first; that all Members, who desire it, shall have leave to speak.—To your desks, therefore, ye eloquent Members! Down with your thoughts, your echoes and hearsays of thoughts; now is the time to show one's self; France and the Universe listens! Members are not wanting: Oration, spoken Pamphlet follows

46

spoken Pamphlet, with what eloquence it can: President's List
swells ever higher with names claiming to speak; from day
to day, all days and all hours, the constant Tribune drones—
shrill Galleries supplying, very variably, the tenor and treble.
It were a dull tone otherwise.

The Patriots, in Mountain and Galleries, or taking counsel
nightly in Section-house, in Mother Society, amid their shrill
Tricoteuses, have to watch lynx-eyed; to give voice when
needful; occasionally very loud. Deputy Thuriot, he who was
Advocate Thuriot, who was Elector Thuriot, and from the
top of the Bastille saw Saint-Antoine rising like the ocean;
this Thuriot can stretch a Formula as heartily as most men.
Cruel Billaud is not silent, if you incite him. Nor is cruel
Jean-Bon silent; a kind of Jesuit he too—write him not, as
the Dictionaries too often do, " Jambon," which signifies mere
Ham!

But, on the whole, let no man conceive it possible that
Louis is not guilty. The only question for a reasonable man
is or was: Can the Convention judge Louis? Or must it be
the whole People; in Primary Assembly, and with delay?
Always delay, ye Girondins, false hommes d'état! so bellows
Patriotism, its patience almost failing.—But indeed, if we consider it, what shall these poor Girondins do? Speak their
conviction that Louis is a Prisoner of War; and can not be
put to death without injustice, solecism, peril? Speak such
conviction; and lose utterly your footing with the decided
Patriot! Nay, properly it is not even a conviction, but a
conjecture and dim puzzle. How many poor Girondins are
sure of but one thing: That a man and Girondin ought to
have footing somewhere, and to stand firmly on it; keeping
well with the Respectable Classes! This is what conviction
and assurance of faith they have. They must wriggle painfully between their dilemma-horns.[2]

Nor is France idle, nor Europe. It is a Heart this Convention, as we said, which sends out influences, and receives
them. A King's Execution, call it Martyrdom, call it Punishment, were an influence!—Two notable influences this Convention has already sent forth over all Nations; much to its
own detriment. On the 19th of November, it emitted a Decree, and has since confirmed and unfolded the details of it,

That any Nation which might see good to shake off the
fetters of Despotism was thereby, so to speak, the Sister of
France, and should have help and countenance. A Decree
much noised of by Diplomatists, Editors, International Lawyers; such a Decree as no living Fetter of Despotism nor
Person in Authority anywhere, can approve of! It was Deputy Chambon the Girondin who propounded this Decree—at
bottom perhaps as a flourish of rhetoric.

The second influence we speak of had a still poorer origin:
in the restless loud-rattling slightly-furnished head of one
Jacob Dupont from the Loire country. The Convention is
speculating on a plan of National Education: Deputy Dupont
in his speech says, " I am free to avow, M. le Président, that I
for my part am an Atheist " [3]—thinking the world might like
to know that. The French world received it without commentary; or with no audible commentary, so loud was France
otherwise. The Foreign world received it with confutation,
with horror and astonishment; [4] a most miserable influence
this! And now if to these two were added a third influence
and sent pulsing abroad over all the Earth: that of Regicide?

Foreign Courts interfere in this Trial of Louis; Spain,
England: not to be listened to; though they come, as it were,
at least Spain comes, with the olive-branch in one hand, and
the sword without scabbard in the other. But at home too,
from out of this circumambient Paris and France, what influences come thick-pulsing! Petitions flow in; pleading for
equal justice, in a reign of so-called Equality. The living
Patriot pleads—O ye National Deputies, do not the dead
Patriots plead? The Twelve-hundred that lie in cold obstruc-
tion, do not they plead; and petition, in Death's dumb-show,
from their narrow house there, more eloquently than speech?
Crippled Patriots hop on crutches round the Salle de Manége,
demanding justice. The Wounded of the Tenth of August,
the Widows and Orphans of the Killed petition in a body;
and hop and defile, eloquently mute, through the Hall: one
wounded Patriot, unable to hop, is borne on his bed thither,
and passes shoulder-high, in the horizontal posture. [5] The
Convention Tribune, which has paused at such sight, commences again—droning mere Juristic Oratory. But out of
doors Paris is piping ever higher. Bull-voiced St.-Huruge is
heard; and the hysteric eloquence of Mother Duchess; " Var-

let, Apostle of Liberty," with pike and red cap, flies hastily,
carrying his oratorical folding-stool. Justice on the Traitor!
cries all the Patriot world. Consider also this other cry,
heard loud on the streets: " Give us Bread, or else kill us! "
Bread and Equality; Justice on the Traitor, that we may have
Bread!

The Limited or undecided Patriot is set against the Decided. Mayor Chambon heard of dreadful rioting at the
Théâtre de la Nation : it had come to rioting, and even to fist-
work, between the Decided and the Undecided, touching a
new Drama called "Ami des Lois" (Friend of the Laws).
One of the poorest Dramas ever written; but which had di-
dactic applications in it; wherefore powdered wigs of Friends
of Order and black hair of Jacobin heads are flying there; and
Mayor Chambon hastens with Santerre, in hopes to quell it.
Far from quelling it, our poor Mayor gets so " squeezed," says
the Report, and likewise so blamed and bullied, say we—
that he, with regret, quits the brief Mayoralty altogether, " his
lungs being affected." This miserable "Ami des Lois" is
debated of in the Convention itself; so violent, mutually-
enraged, are the Limited Patriots and the Unlimited.[6]

Between which two classes, are not Aristocrats enough, and
Crypto-Aristocrats, busy? Spies running over from London
with important Packets; spies pretending to run! One of
these latter, Viard was the name of him, pretended to accuse
Roland, and even the Wife of Roland: to the joy of Chabot
and the Mountain. But the Wife of Roland came, being
summoned, on the instant, to the Convention Hall; came, in
her high clearness; and, with few clear words, dissipated this
Viard into despicability and air; all Friends of Order applauding.[7] So, with Theatre-riots, and " Bread, or else kill us ";
with Rage, Hunger, preternatural Suspicion, does this wild
Paris pipe. Roland grows ever more querulous, in his Messages and Letters; rising almost to the hysterical pitch. Marat, whom no power on Earth can prevent seeing into traitors
and Rolands, takes to bed for three days; almost dead, the
invaluable People's-Friend, with heart-break, with fever and
headache: " O Peuple babillard, si tu savais agir, People of
Babblers, if thou couldst but act! "

To crown all, victorious Dumouriez, in these New-year's
days, is arrived in Paris—one fears for no good. He pretends

to be complaining of Minister Pache, and Hassenfratz dilapidations; to be concerting measures for the spring Campaign: one finds him much in the company of the Girondins. Plotting with them against Jacobinism, against Equality, and the Punishment of Louis? We have letters of his to the Convention itself. Will he act the old Lafayette part, this new victorious General? Let him withdraw again; not undenounced.[8]

And still in the Convention Tribune, it drones continually, mere Juristic Eloquence, and Hypothesis without Action; and there are still fifties on the President's List. Nay, these Gironde Presidents give their own party preference: we suspect they play foul with the List; men of the Mountain can not be heard. And still it drones, all through December into January and a New year; and there is no end! Paris pipes round it; multitudinous; ever higher, to the note of the whirlwind. Paris will " bring cannon from Saint-Denis "; there is talk of " shutting the Barriers "—to Roland's horror.

Whereupon, behold, the Convention Tribune suddenly ceases droning: we cut short, be on the List who likes; and make end. On Tuesday next, the Fifteenth of January 1793, it shall go to the Vote, name by name; and one way or other, this great game play itself out!

NOTES

[1] Prudhomme's Newspaper (in " Hist. Parl.," xxi, 314).

[2] See Extracts from their Newspapers, in " Hist. Parl.," xxi, 1–38, etc.

[3] " Moniteur," Séance du 14 Décembre 1792.

[4] Mrs. Hannah More, " Letter to Jacob Dupont " (London, 1793), etc., etc.

[5] " Hist. Parl.," xxii, 131; Moore, etc.

[6] Ibid., xxiii, 31, 48, etc.

[7] " Moniteur," Séance du 7 Décembre 1792.

[8] Dumouriez, " Mémoires," iii, c. 4.

CHAPTER VII

THE THREE VOTINGS

IS Louis Capet guilty of conspiring against Liberty? Shall our Sentence be itself final, or need ratifying by Appeal to the People? If guilty, what Punishment? This is the form agreed to, after uproar and " several hours of tumultuous indecision ": these are the Three successive Questions, whereon the Convention shall now pronounce. Paris floods round their Hall; multitudinous, many-sounding. Europe and all Nations listen for their answer. Deputy after Deputy shall answer to his name: Guilty or Not guilty?

As to the Guilt, there is, as above hinted, no doubt in the mind of Patriot men. Overwhelming majority pronounces Guilt; the unanimous Convention votes for Guilt, only some feeble twenty-eight voting not Innocence, but refusing to vote at all. Neither does the Second Question prove doubtful, whatever the Girondins might calculate. Would not Appeal to the People be another name for civil war? Majority of two to one answers that there shall be no Appeal: this also is settled. Loud Patriotism, now at ten o'clock, may hush itself for the night; and retire to its bed not without hope. Tuesday has gone well. On the morrow comes, What Punishment? On the morrow is the tug of war.

Consider therefore if, on this Wednesday morning, there is an affluence of Patriotism; if Paris stands a-tiptoe, and all Deputies are at their post! Seven-hundred and Forty-nine honourable Deputies; only some twenty absent on mission, Duchâtel and some seven others absent by sickness. Meanwhile expectant Patriotism and Paris standing a-tiptoe have need of patience. For this Wednesday again passes in debate and effervescence; Girondins proposing that a " majority of three-fourths " shall be required; Patriots fiercely resisting

702

them. Danton, who has just got back from mission in the Netherlands, does obtain " order of the day " on this Girondin proposal; nay, he obtains further that we decide sans désemparer, in Permanent-session, till we have done.

And so, finally, at eight in the evening this Third stupendous Voting, by roll-call or appel nominal, does begin. What Punishment? Girondins undecided, Patriots decided, men afraid of Royalty, men afraid of Anarchy, must answer here and now. Infinite Patriotism, dusky in the lamp-light, floods all corridors, crowds all galleries; sternly waiting to hear. Shrill-sounding Ushers summon you by Name and Department; you must rise to the Tribune, and say.

Eye-witnesses have represented this scene of the Third Voting, and of the votings that grew out of it—a scene protracted, like to be endless, lasting, with few brief intervals, from Wednesday till Sunday morning—as one of the strangest seen in the Revolution. Long night wears itself into day, morning's paleness is spread over all faces; and again the wintry shadows sink, and the dim lamps are lit: but through day and night and the vicissitudes of hours, Member after Member is mounting continually these Tribune-steps; pausing aloft there, in the clearer upper light, to speak his Fate-word; then diving down into the dusk and throng again. Like Phantoms in the hour of midnight; most spectral, pandemonial! Never did President Vergniaud, or any terrestrial President, superintend the like. A King's Life, and so much else that depends thereon, hangs trembling in the balance. Man after man mounts; the buzz hushes itself till he have spoken: Death; Banishment; Imprisonment till the Peace. Many say, Death; with what cautious well-studied phrases and paragraphs they could devise, of explanation, of enforcement, of faint recommendation to mercy. Many too say, Banishment; something short of Death. The balance trembles, none can yet guess whitherward. Whereat anxious Patriotism bellows; irrepressible by Ushers.

The poor Girondins, many of them, under such fierce bellowing of Patriotism, say Death; justifying, motivant, that most miserable word of theirs by some brief casuistry and jesuitry. Vergniaud himself says, Death; justifying by jesuitry. Rich Lepelletier Saint-Fargeau had been of the Noblesse, and then of the Patriot Left Side, in the Constituent; and had argued and reported, there and elsewhere, not a little, against Capital Punishment: nevertheless he now says, Death; a word which may cost him dear. Manuel did surely rank with the Decided in August last; but he has been sinking and backsliding ever since September and the scenes of September. In this Convention, above all, no word he could speak would find favour; he says now, Banishment; and in mute wrath quits the place forever—much hustled in the corridors. Philippe Égalité votes, in his soul and conscience, Death: at the sound of which and of whom, even Patriotism shakes its head; and there runs a groan and shudder through this Hall of Doom. Robespierre's vote can not be doubtful; his speech is long. Men see the figure of shrill Sieyès ascend; hardly pausing, passing merely, this figure says, " La Mort sans phrase, Death without phrases"; and fares onward and downward. Most spectral, pandemonial!

And yet if the Reader fancy it of a funereal, sorrowful or even grave character, he is far mistaken: " the Ushers in the Mountain quarter," says Mercier, " had become as Box-keepers at the Opera "; opening and shutting of Galleries for privileged persons, for " D'Orléans Égalité's mistresses," or other high-dizened women of condition, rustling with laces and tricolor. Gallant Deputies pass and repass thitherward, treating them with ices, refreshments and small-talk; the high-dizened heads beck responsive; some have their card and pin, pricking down the Ayes and Noes, as at a game of Rouge-et-Noir. Farther aloft reigns Mère Duchesse with her unrouged Amazons; she can not be prevented making long " Hahas," when the vote is not " La Mort." In these Galleries there is refection, drinking of wine and brandy " as in open tavern, en pleine tabagie." Betting goes on in all coffeehouses of the neighbourhood. But within-doors, fatigue, impatience, uttermost weariness sits now on all visages; lighted up only from time to time by turns of the game. Members have fallen asleep; Ushers come and awaken them to vote: other Members calculate whether they shall not have time to run and dine. Figures rise, like phantoms, pale in the dusky lamp-light; utter from this Tribune, only one word: Death. " Tout est optique," says Mercier, " The World is all an optical shadow." [1] Deep in the Thursday night, when the Voting is done, and Secretaries are summing it up, sick Duchâtel, more spectral than another, comes borne on a chair, wrapped in blankets, in " nightgown and nightcap," to vote for Mercy: one vote it is thought may turn the scale.

Ah, no! In profoundest silence, President Vergniaud, with a voice full of sorrow, has to say: " I declare, in the name of the Convention, that the punishment it pronounces on Louis Capet is that of Death." Death by a small majority of Fifty-three. Nay, if we deduct from the one side, and add to the other, a certain Twenty-six, who said Death but coupled some faintest ineffectual surmise of mercy with it, the majority will be but One.

Death is the sentence: but its execution? It is not exe-cuted yet! Scarcely is the vote declared when Louis's Three Advocates enter; with Protest in his name, with demand for Delay, for Appeal to the People. For this do Desèze and Tronchet plead, with brief eloquence: brave old Malesherbes pleads for it with eloquent want of eloquence, in broken sen-tences, in embarrassment and sobs; that brave time-honoured face, with its gray strength, its broad sagacity and honesty, is mastered with emotion, melts into dumb tears.[2]—They re-ject the Appeal to the People; that having been already set-tled. But as to the Delay, what they call Sursis, it shall be considered; shall be voted for to-morrow: at present we ad-journ. Whereupon Patriotism " hisses " from the Mountain: but a "tyrannical majority " has so decided, and adjourns.

There is still this fourth Vote, then, growls indignant Pa-triotism—this vote, and who knows what other votes, and adjournments of voting; and the whole matter still hovering hypothetical! And at every new vote those Jesuit Girondins, even they who voted for Death, would so fain find a loophole! Patriotism must watch and rage. Tyrannical adjournments there have been; one, and now another at midnight on plea of fatigue—all Friday wasted in hesitation and higgling; in re-counting of the votes, which are found correct as they stood! Patriotism bays fiercer than ever; Patriotism, by long watching, has become red-eyed, almost rabid.

" Delay: yes or no?" men do vote it finally, all Saturday, all day and night. Men's nerves are worn out, men's hearts are desperate; now it shall end. Vergniaud, spite of the baying, ventures to say " Yes, Delay "; though he had voted Death.

Philippe Égalité says, in his soul and conscience, "No." The next Member mounting: "Since Philippe says No, I for my part say Yes, moi je dis Oui." The balance still trembles. Till finally, at three o'clock on Sunday morning, we have: "No Delay," by a majority of Seventy; "Death within four-and-twenty hours!"

Garat, Minister of Justice, has to go to the Temple with this stern message: he ejaculates repeatedly, "Quelle commission affreuse, What a frightful function!"[3] Louis begs for a Confessor; for yet three days of life, to prepare himself to die. The Confessor is granted; the three days and all respite are refused.

There is no deliverance, then? Thick stone walls answer, None. Has King Louis no friends? Men of action, of courage grown desperate, in this his extreme need? King Louis's friends are feeble and far. Not even a voice in the coffee-houses rises for him. At Méot the Restaurateur's no Captain Dampmartin now dines; or sees death-doing whiskerandoes on furlough exhibit daggers of improved structure. Méot's gallant Royalists on furlough are far across the marches; they are wandering distracted over the world: or their bones lie whitening Argonne Wood. Only some weak Priests "leave Pamphlets on all the bourne-stones," this night, calling for a rescue: calling for the pious women to rise; or are taken distributing Pamphlets, and sent to Prison.[4]

Nay, there is one death-doer, of the ancient Méot sort, who, with effort, has done even less and worse: slain a Deputy, and set all the Patriotism of Paris on edge! It was five on Saturday evening when Lepelletier Saint-Fargeau, having given his vote, "No Delay," ran over to Février's in the Palais Royal to snatch a morsel of dinner. He had dined, and was paying. A thickset man "with black hair and blue beard," in a loose kind of frock, stepped up to him; it was, as Février and the bystanders bethought them, one Pâris of the old King's-Guard. "Are you Lepelletier?" asks he.—"Yes."—"You voted in the King's Business—?"—"I voted Death."—"Scélérat, take that!" cries Pâris, flashing out a sabre from under his frock, and plunging it deep in Lepelletier's side. Février clutches him: but he breaks off; is gone.

The voter Lepelletier lies dead; he has expired in great

pain, at one in the morning—two hours before that Vote of " No Delay " was fully summed up. Guardsman Pâris is flying over France; can not be taken; will be found some months after, self-shot in a remote inn.[5]—Robespierre sees reason to think that Prince d'Artois himself is privately in Town; that the Convention will be butchered in the lump. Patriotism sounds mere wail and vengeance : Santerre doubles and trebles all his patrols. Pity is lost in rage and fear; the Convention has refused the three days of life and all respite.

NOTES

[1] Mercier, " Nouveau Paris," vi, 156–159; Montgaillard, iii, 348–387; Moore, etc.

[2] " Moniteur " (in " Hist. Parl.," xxiii, 210). See Boissy d'Anglas, " Vie de Malesherbes," ii, 139.

[3] " Biographie des Ministres," p. 157.

[4] See Prudhomme's Newspaper, " Révolutions de Paris " (in " Hist. Parl.," xxiii, 318).

[5] " Hist. Parl.," xxiii, 275, 318; Félix Lepelletier, " Vie de Michel Lepelletier son Frère," p. 61, etc. Félix, with due love of the miraculous, will have it that the Suicide in the inn was not Pâris, but some double-ganger of his.

CHAPTER VIII

PLACE DE LA RÉVOLUTION

TO this conclusion, then, hast thou come, O hapless Louis! The Son of Sixty Kings is to die on the Scaffold by form of Law. Under Sixty Kings this same form of Law, form of Society, has been fashioning itself together these thousand years; and has become, one way and other, a most strange Machine. Surely, if needful, it is also frightful, this Machine; dead, blind; not what it should be; which, with swift stroke, or by cold slow torture, has wasted the lives and souls of innumerable men. And behold now a King himself, or say rather Kinghood in his person, is to expire here in cruel tortures—like a Phalaris shut in the belly of his own red-heated Brazen Bull! It is ever so; and thou shouldst know it, O haughty tyrannous man: injustice breeds injustice; curses and falsehoods do verily return " always home," wide as they may wander. Innocent Louis bears the sins of many generations: he too experiences that man's tribunal is not in this Earth; that if he had no Higher one, it were not well with him.

A King dying by such violence appeals impressively to the imagination; as the like must do, and ought to do. And yet at bottom it is not the King dying, but the man! Kingship is a coat: the grand loss is of the skin. The man from whom you take his Life, to him can the whole combined world do more? Lally went on his hurdle; his mouth filled with a gag. Miserablest mortals, doomed for picking pockets, have a whole five-act Tragedy in them, in that dumb pain, as they go to the gallows, unregarded; they consume the cup of trembling down to the lees. For Kings and for Beggars, for the justly doomed and the unjustly, it is a hard thing to die. Pity them all: thy utmost pity, with all aids and appliances and throne-and-scaffold contrasts, how far short is it of the thing pitied!

A Confessor has come; Abbé Edgeworth, of Irish extrac-
tion, whom the King knew by good report, has come promptly
on this solemn mission.   Leave the Earth alone, then, thou
hapless King; it with its malice will go its way, thou also
canst go thine.   A hard scene yet remains: the parting with
our loved ones.   Kind hearts, environed in the same grim
peril with us; to be left here!   Let the Reader look with
the eyes of Valet Cléry through these glass-doors, where also
the Municipality watches; and see the cruelest of scenes:

"At half-past eight, the door of the ante-room opened: the
Queen appeared first, leading her Son by the hand; then
Madame Royale and Madame Elisabeth: they all flung themselves into the arms of the King.   Silence reigned for some
minutes; interrupted only by sobs.   The Queen made a movement to lead his Majesty toward the inner room, where M.
Edgeworth was waiting unknown to them: 'No,' said the
King, 'let us go into the dining-room; it is there only that
I can see you.'   They entered there; I shut the door of it,
which was of glass.   The King sat down, the Queen on his
left hand, Madame Elisabeth on his right, Madame Royale
almost in front; the young Prince remained standing between
his Father's legs.   They all leaned toward him, and often held
him embraced.   This scene of wo lasted an hour and three
quarters; during which we could hear nothing; we could see
only that always when the King spoke, the sobbings of the
Princesses redoubled, continued for some minutes; and that
then the King began again to speak." [1]—And so our meetings
and our partings do now end!   The sorrows we gave each
other; the poor joys we faithfully shared, and all our lovings
and our sufferings, and confused toilings under the earthly
Sun, are over.   Thou good soul, I shall never, never through
all ages of Time, see thee any more!—Never!   O Reader,
knowest thou that hard word?

For nearly two hours this agony lasts; then they tear
themselves asunder.   "Promise that you will see us on the
morrow."   He promises: Ah yes, yes; yet once; and go now,
ye loved ones; cry to God for yourselves and me!—It was
a hard scene, but it is over.   He will not see them on the
morrow.   The Queen, in passing through the ante-room,
glanced at the Cerberus Municipals; and, with woman's vehemence, said through her tears, " Vous êtes tous des scélérats."

King Louis slept sound, till five in the morning, when Cléry, as he had been ordered, awoke him. Cléry dressed his hair: while this went forward, Louis took a ring from his watch, and kept trying it on his finger; it was his wedding-ring, which he is now to return to the Queen as a mute fare-well. At half-past six, he took the Sacrament; and continued in devotion, and conference with Abbé Edgeworth. He will not see his Family: it were too hard to bear.

At eight, the Municipals enter: the King gives them his Will, and messages and effects; which they, at first, brutally refuse to take charge of: he gives them a roll of gold pieces, a hundred and twenty-five louis; these are to be returned to Malesherbes, who had lent them. At nine, Santerre says the hour is come. The King begs yet to retire for three minutes. At the end of three minutes, Santerre again says the hour is come. "Stamping on the ground with his right-foot, Louis answers: 'Partons, Let us go.'"—How the rolling of those drums comes in, through the Temple bastions and bulwarks, on the heart of a queenly wife; soon to be a widow! He is gone, then, and has not seen us? A Queen weeps bitterly; a King's Sister and Children. Over all these Four does Death also hover: all shall perish miserably save one; she, as Duchesse d'Angoulême, will live—not happily.

At the Temple Gate were some faint cries, perhaps from voices of pitiful women: "Grâce! Grâce!" Through the rest of the streets there is silence as of the grave. No man not armed is allowed to be there: the armed, did any even pity, dare not express it, each man overawed by all his neighbours. All windows are down, none seen looking through them. All shops are shut. No wheel-carriage rolls, this morning, in these streets but one only. Eighty-thousand armed men stand ranked, like armed statues of men; cannons bristle, cannoneers with match burning, but no word or movement: it is as a city enchanted into silence and stone: one carriage with its escort, slowly rumbling, is the only sound. Louis reads, in his Book of Devotion, the Prayers of the Dying: clatter of this death-march falls sharp on the ear, in the great silence; but the thought would fain struggle heavenward, and forget the Earth.

As the clocks strike ten, behold the Place de la Révolution, once Place de Louis Quinze: the Guillotine, mounted near the old Pedestal where once stood the Statue of that Louis! Far round, all bristles with cannons and armed men: spectators crowding in the rear; D'Orléans Égalité there in cabriolet. Swift messengers, hoquetons, speed to the Townhall, every three minutes: near by is the Convention sitting— vengeful for Lepelletier. Heedless of all, Louis reads his Prayers of the Dying; not till five minutes yet has he finished; then the Carriage opens. What temper he is in? Ten different witnesses will give ten different accounts of it. He is in the collision of all tempers; arrived now at the black Mahlstrom and descent of Death: in sorrow, in indignation, in resignation struggling to be resigned. "Take care of M. Edgeworth," he straitly charges the Lieutenant who is sitting with them: then they two descend.

The drums are beating: "Taisez-vous, Silence!" he cries "in a terrible voice, d'une voix terrible." He mounts the scaffold, not without delay; he is in puce coat, breeches of gray, white stockings. He strips off the coat; stands disclosed in a sleeve-waistcoat of white flannel. The Executioners approach to bind him: he spurns, resists; Abbé Edgeworth has to remind him how the Saviour, in whom men trust, submitted to be bound. His hands are tied, his head bare; the fatal moment is come. He advances to the edge of the Scaffold, "his face very red," and says: "Frenchmen, I die innocent: it is from the Scaffold and near appearing before God that I tell you so. I pardon my enemies; I desire that France——" A General on horseback, Santerre or another, prances out, with uplifted hand: "Tambours!" The drums drown the voice. "Executioners, do your duty!" The Executioners, desperate lest themselves be murdered (for Santerre and his Armed Ranks will strike, if they do not), seize the hapless Louis: six of them desperate, him singly desperate, struggling there; and bind him to their plank. Abbé Edgeworth, stooping, bespeaks him: "Son of Saint Louis, ascend to Heaven." The Axe clanks down; a King's Life is shorn away. It is Monday the 21st of January 1793. He was aged Thirty-eight years four months and twenty-eight days.[2]

Executioner Samson shows the Head: fierce shout of "Vive la République!" rises, and swells; caps raised on bayonets, hats waving: students of the College of Four Nations take it up, on the far Quais; fling it over Paris. D'Orléans

drives off in his cabriolet: the Townhall Councillors rub their
hands, saying, "It is done, It is done." There is dipping of
handkerchiefs, of pike-points in the blood. Headsman Samson, though he afterward denied it,[3] sells locks of the hair:
fractions of the puce coat are long after worn in rings.[4]—And
so, in some half-hour it is done; and the multitude has all
departed. Pastry-cooks, coffee-sellers, milkmen sing out their
trivial quotidian cries: the world wags on, as if this were
a common day. In the coffeehouses that evening, says
Prudhomme, Patriot shook hands with Patriot in a more
cordial manner than usual. Not till some days after, according to Mercier, did public men see what a grave
thing it was.

A grave thing it indisputably is; and will have consequences. On the morrow morning, Roland, so long steeped
to the lips in disgust and chagrin, sends in his demission. His
accounts lie all ready, correct in black-on-white to the uttermost farthing: these he wants but to have audited, that he
might retire to remote obscurity, to the country and his books.
They will never be audited, those accounts; he will never get
retired thither.

It was on Tuesday that Roland demitted. On Thursday
comes Lepelletier St.-Fargeau's Funeral, and passage to the
Pantheon of Great Men. Notable as the wild pageant of a
winter day. The Body is borne aloft, half-bare; the winding-
sheet disclosing the death-wound: sabre and bloody clothes
parade themselves; a "lugubrious music" wailing harsh
næniæ. Oak-crowns shower down from windows; President Vergniaud walks there, with Convention, with Jacobin
Society, and all Patriots of every colour, all mourning
brother-like.

Notable also for another thing this Burial of Lepelletier:
it was the last act these men ever did with concert! All
Parties and figures of Opinion, that agitate this distracted
France and its Convention, now stand, as it were, face to face,
and dagger to dagger; the King's Life, round which they all
struck and battled, being hurled down. Dumouriez, conquering Holland, growls ominous discontent, at the head of
Armies. Men say Dumouriez will have a King; that young
D'Orléans Égalité shall be his King. Deputy Fauchet, in the

"Journal des Amis," curses his day, more bitterly than Job did; invokes the poniards of Regicides, of "Arras Vipers" or Robespierres, of Pluto Dantons, of horrid Butchers Legendre and Simulacra d'Herbois, to send him swiftly to another world than theirs.[5] This is Te-Deum Fauchet, of the Bastille Victory, of the Cercle Social. Sharp was the death-hail rattling round one's Flag-of-Truce, on that Bastille day: but it was soft to such wreckage of high Hope as this; one's New Golden Era going down in leaden dross, and sulphurous black of the Everlasting Darkness!

At home this Killing of a King has divided all friends; and abroad it has united all enemies. Fraternity of Peoples, Revolutionary Propagandism; Atheism, Regicide; total destruction of social order in this world! All Kings, and lovers of Kings, and haters of Anarchy, rank in coalition; as in a war for life. England signifies to Citizen Chauvelin, the Ambassador or rather Ambassador's-Cloak, that he must quit the country in eight days. Ambassador's-Cloak and Ambassador, Chauvelin and Talleyrand, depart accordingly.[6] Talleyrand, implicated in that Iron Press of the Tuileries, thinks it safest to make for America.

England has cast out the Embassy: England declares war —being shocked principally, it would seem, at the condition of the river Scheldt. Spain declares war; being shocked principally at some other thing; which doubtless the Manifesto indicates.[7] Nay, we find it was not England that declared war first, or Spain first; but that France herself declared war first on both of them [8]—a point of immense Parliamentary and Journalistic interest in those days, but which has become of no interest whatever in these. They all declare war. The sword is drawn, the scabbard thrown away. It is even as Danton said, in one of his all-too gigantic figures: "The coalized Kings threatens us; we hurl at their feet, as gage of battle, the Head of a King."

NOTES

[1] Cléry's "Narrative" (London, 1798), cited in Weber, iii, 312.

[2] Newspapers, Municipal Records, etc., etc. (in "Hist. Parl.," xxiii, 298–349); "Deux Amis," ix, 369–373; Mercier, "Nouveau Paris," iii, 3–8.

[3] His Letter in the Newspapers (" Hist. Parl.," ubi suprà).
[4] Forster's " Briefwechsel," i, 473.
[5] " Hist. Parl.," ubi suprà.
[6] " Annual Register " of 1793, pp. 114–128.
[7] March 23d (" Annual Register," p. 161).
[8] February 1st; March 7th (" Moniteur " of these dates).

BOOK XVI

THE GIRONDINS

CHAPTER I

CAUSE AND EFFECT

THIS huge Insurrectionary Movement, which we liken to a breaking-out of Tophet and the Abyss, has swept away Royalty, Aristocracy, and a King's life. The question is, What will it next do; how will it henceforth shape itself? Settle down into a reign of Law and Liberty; according as the habits, persuasions and endeavours of the educated, moneyed, respectable class prescribe? That is to say: the volcanic lava-flood, bursting up in the manner described, will explode and flow according to Girondin Formula and pre-established rule of Philosophy? If so, for our Girondin friends it will be well.

Meanwhile were not the prophecy rather, that as no external force, Royal or other, now remains which could control this Movement, the Movement will follow a course of its own; probably a very original one? Further, that whatsoever man or men can best interpret the inward tendencies it has, and give them voice and activity, will obtain the lead of it? For the rest, that as a thing without order, a thing proceeding from beyond and beneath the region of order, it must work and welter, not as a Regularity but as a Chaos; destructive and self-destructive; always till something that has order arise, strong enough to bind it into subjection again? Which something, we may further conjecture, will not be a Formula, with philosophical propositions and forensic eloquence; but a Reality, probably with a sword in its hand!

As for the Girondin Formula, of a respectable Republic for the Middle Classes, all manner of Aristocracies being now sufficiently demolished, there seems little reason to expect that the business will stop there. Liberty, Equality, Fraternity, these are the words; enunciative and prophetic. Republic for the respectable washed Middle Classes, how can that be the fulfilment thereof? Hunger and nakedness, and nightmare oppression lying heavy on Twenty-five million hearts; this, not the wounded vanities of contradicted philosophies of philosophical Advocates, rich Shopkeepers, rural Noblesse, was the prime mover in the French Revolution; as the like will be in all such Revolutions, in all countries. Feudal Fleur-de-lys had become an insupportably bad marching-banner, and needed to be torn and trampled: but Moneybag of Mammon (for that, in these times, is what the respectable Republic for the Middle Classes will signify) is a still worse, while it lasts. Properly, indeed, it is the worst and basest of all banners and symbols of dominion among men; and indeed is possible only in a time of general Atheism, and Unbelief in anything save in brute Force and Sensualism; pride of birth, pride of office, any known kind of pride being a degree better than purse-pride. Freedom, Equality, Brotherhood: not in the Money-bag, but far elsewhere, will Sansculottism seek these things.

We say therefore that an Insurrectionary France, loose of control from without, destitute of supreme order from within, will form one of the most tumultuous Activities ever seen on this Earth; such as no Girondin Formula can regulate. An immeasurable force, made up of forces manifold, heterogeneous, compatible and incompatible. In plainer words, this France must needs split into Parties; each of which seeking to make itself good, contradiction, exasperation will arise; and Parties on Parties find that they can not work together, can not exist together.

As for the number of Parties, there will, strictly counting, be as many Parties as there are opinions. According to which rule, in this National Convention itself, to say nothing of France generally, the number of Parties ought to be Seven-hundred and Forty-nine; for every unit entertains his opinion. But now, as every unit has at once an individual nature or necessity to follow his own road, and a gregarious nature or necessity to see himself travelling by the side of others—what can there be but dissolutions, precipitations, endless turbulence of attracting and repelling; till once the master-element get evolved, and this wild alchemy arrange itself again?

To the length of Seven-hundred and Forty-nine Parties, however, no Nation was ever yet seen to go. Nor indeed much beyond the length of Two Parties; two at a time—

so invincible is man's tendency to unite, with all the invincible divisiveness he has! Two Parties, we say, are the usual number at one time: let these two fight it out, all minor shades of party rallying under the shade likest them; when the one has fought down the other, then it, in its turn, may divide, self-destructive; and so the process continue, as far as needful. This is the way of Revolutions, which spring up as the French one has done; when the so-called Bonds of Society snap asunder; and all Laws that are not Laws of Nature become naught and Formulas merely.

But, quitting these somewhat abstract considerations, let History note this concrete reality which the streets of Paris exhibit, on Monday the 25th of February 1793. Long before daylight that morning, these streets are noisy and angry. Petitioning enough there has been; a Convention often solicited. It was but yesterday there came a Deputation of Washerwomen with Petition; complaining that not so much as soap could be had; to say nothing of bread, and condiments of bread. The cry of women, round the Salle de Manége, was heard plaintive: " Du pain et du savon, Bread and soap." [1]

And now from six o'clock, this Monday morning, one perceives the Bakers' Queues unusually expanded, angrily agitating themselves. Not the Baker alone, but two Section Commissioners to help him, manage with difficulty the daily distribution of loaves. Soft-spoken assiduous, in the early candle-light, are Baker and Commissioners: and yet the pale chill February sunrise discloses an unpromising scene. Indignant Female Patriots, partly supplied with bread, rush now to the shops, declaring that they will have groceries. Groceries enough: sugar-barrels rolled forth into the street, Patriot Citoyennes weighing it out at a just rate of elevenpence a pound; likewise coffee-chests, soap-chests, nay, cinnamon and cloves-chests, with aquavitæ and other forms of alcohol—at a just rate, which some do not pay; the pale-faced Grocer silently wringing his hands! What help? The distributive Citoyennes are of violent speech and gesture, their long Eumenides-hair hanging out of curl; nay, in their girdles pistols are seen sticking: some, it is even said, have beards— male Patriots in petticoats and mob-cap. Thus, in the street of Lombards, in the street of Five-Diamonds, street of Pulleys, in most streets of Paris does it effervesce, the livelong day; no Municipality, no Mayor Pache, though he was War-Minister lately, sends military against it, or aught against it but persuasive-eloquence, till seven at night, or later.

On Monday gone five weeks, which was the twenty-first of January, we saw Paris, beheading its King, stand silent, like a petrified City of Enchantment: and now on this Monday it is so noisy, selling sugar! Cities, especially Cities in Revolution, are subject to these alternations; the secret courses of civic business and existence effervescing and efflorescing, in this manner, as a concrete Phenomenon to the eye. Of which Phenomenon, when secret existence becoming public effloresces on the street, the philosophical cause and effect is not so easy to find. What, for example, may be the accurate philosophical meaning, and meanings, of this sale of sugar? These things that have become visible in the street of Pulleys and over Paris, whence are they, we say; and whither?—

That Pitt has a hand in it, the gold of Pitt: so much, to all reasonable Patriot men, may seem clear. But then, through what agents of Pitt? Varlet, Apostle of Liberty, was discerned again of late, with his pike and red nightcap. Deputy Marat published in his Journal, this very day, complaining of the bitter scarcity, and sufferings of the people, till he seemed to get wroth: "If your Rights of Man were anything but a piece of written paper, the plunder of a few shops, and a forestaller or two hung up at the door-lintels, would put an end to such things." [2] Are not these, say the Girondins, pregnant indications? Pitt has bribed the Anarchists; Marat is the agent of Pitt: hence this sale of sugar. To the Mother Society, again, it is clear that the scarcity is factitious; is the work of Girondins, and such-like; a set of men sold partly to Pitt; sold wholly to their own ambitions and hard-hearted pedantries; who will not fix the grain-prices, but prate pedantically of free-trade; wishing to starve Paris into violence, and embroil it with the Departments: hence this sale of sugar.

And, alas! if to these two notabilities, of a Phenomenon and such Theories of a Phenomenon, we add this third notability, That the French Nation has believed, for several years now, in the possibility, nay, certainty and near advent, of a universal Millennium, or reign of Freedom, Equality, Fraternity, wherein man should be the brother of man, and sorrow and sin flee away? Not bread to eat, nor soap to wash with; and the reign of Perfect Felicity ready to arrive, due always since the Bastille fell! How did our hearts burn within us, at that Feast of Pikes, when brother flung himself on brother's bosom; and in sunny jubilee, Twenty-five millions burst forth into sound and cannon-smoke! Bright was our Hope then, as sunlight; red-angry is our Hope grown now, as consuming fire. But, O Heavens, what enchantment is it, or devilish legerdemain, of such effect, that Perfect Felicity, always within arm's length, could never be laid hold of, but only in her stead Controversy and Scarcity? This set of traitors after that set! Tremble, ye traitors; dread a People which calls itself patient, long-suffering; but which can not always submit to have its pocket picked, in this way—of a Millennium!

Yes, Reader, here is the miracle. Out of that putrescent rubbish of Scepticism, Sensualism, Sentimentalism, hollow Machiavelism, such a Faith has verily risen; flaming in the heart of a People. A whole People, awakening as it were to consciousness in deep misery, believes that it is within reach of a Fraternal Heaven-on-Earth. With longing arms, it struggles to embrace the Unspeakable; can not embrace it, owing to certain causes.—Seldom do we find that a whole People can be said to have any Faith at all; except in things which it can eat and handle. Whensoever it gets any Faith, its history becomes spirit-stirring, noteworthy. But since the time when steel Europe shook itself simultaneously at the word of Hermit Peter, and rushed toward the Sepulchre where God had lain, there was no universal impulse of Faith that one could note. Since Protestantism went silent, no Luther's voice, no Zisca's drum any longer proclaiming that God's Truth was not the Devil's Lie; and the Last of the Cameronians (Renwick was the name of him; honour to the name of the brave!) sank, shot, on the Castle-hill of Edinburgh, there was no partial impulse of Faith among Nations. Till now, behold, once more, this French Nation believes! Herein, we say, in that astonishing Faith of theirs, lies the miracle. It is a Faith undoubtedly of the more prodigious sort, even among Faiths; and will embody itself in prodigies. It is the soul of that world-prodigy named French Revolution; whereat the world still gazes and shudders.

But, for the rest, let no man ask History to explain by cause and effect how the business proceeded henceforth. This battle of Mountain and Gironde, and what follows, is the battle of Fanaticisms and Miracles; unsuitable for cause and effect. The sound of it, to the mind, is as a hubbub of voices in distraction; little of articulate is to be gathered by long listening and studying; only battle-tumult, shouts of triumph, shrieks of despair. The Mountain has left no Memoirs; the Girondins have left Memoirs, which are too often little other than long-drawn Interjections, of "Woe is me," and "Cursed be ye." So soon as History can philosophically delineate the conflagration of a kindled Fireship, she may try this other task. Here lay the bitumen-stratum, there the brimstone one; so ran the vein of gunpowder, of nitre, terebinth and foul grease: this, were she inquisitive enough, History might partly know. But how they acted and reacted below decks, one fire-stratum playing into the other, by its nature and the art of man, now when all hands ran raging, and the flames lashed high over shrouds and topmast: this let not History attempt.

The Fireship is old France, the old French Form of Life; her crew a Generation of men. Wild are their cries and their ragings there, like spirits tormented in that flame. But, on the whole, are they not gone, O Reader? Their Fireship and they, frightening the world, have sailed away; its flames and its thunders quite away, into the Deep of Time. One thing therefore History will do: pity them all; for it went hard with them all. Not even the seagreen Incorruptible but shall have some pity, some human love, though it takes an effort. And now, so much once thoroughly attained, the rest will become easier. To the eye of equal brotherly pity, innumerable perversions dissipate themselves; exaggerations and execrations fall off, of their own accord. Standing wistfully on the safe shore, we will look, and see, what is of interest to us, what is adapted to us.

NOTES

[1] "Moniteur," etc. ("Hist. Parl.," xxiv, 332-348).
[2] "Hist. Parl.," xxiv, 353-356.

CHAPTER II

CULOTTIC AND SANSCULOTTIC

GIRONDE and Mountain are now in full quarrel; their mutual rage, says Toulongeon, is growing a "pale" rage. Curious, lamentable: all these men have the word Republic on their lips; in the heart of every one of them is a passionate wish for something which he calls Republic: yet see their death-quarrel! So, however, are men made. Creatures who live in confusion; who, once thrown together, can readily fall into that confusion of confusions which quarrel is, simply because their confusions differ from one another; still more because they seem to differ! Men's words are a poor exponent of their thought; nay, their thought itself is a poor exponent of the inward unnamed Mystery, wherefrom both thought and action have their birth. No man can explain himself, can get himself explained; men see not one another, but distorted phantasms which they call one another; which they hate and go to battle with: for all battle is well said to be misunderstanding.

But indeed that similitude of the Fireship; of our poor French brethren, so fiery themselves, working also in an element of fire, was not insignificant. Consider it well, there is a shade of the truth in it. For a man, once committed headlong to republican or any other Transcendentalism, and fighting and fanaticizing amid a Nation of his like, becomes as it were enveloped in an ambient atmosphere of Transcendentalism and Delirium: his individual self is lost in something that is not himself, but foreign though inseparable from him. Strange to think of, the man's cloak still seems to hold the same man: and yet the man is not there, his volition is not there; nor the source of what he will do and devise; instead of the man and his volition there is a piece of Fanaticism and Fatalism incarnated in the shape of him. He, the hapless in-

carnated Fanaticism, goes his road; no man can help him,
he himself least of all. It is a wonderful, tragical predica-
ment—such as human language, unused to deal with these
things, being contrived for the uses of common life, struggles
to shadow out in figures. The ambient element of material
fire is not wilder than this of Fanaticism; nor, though visible
to the eye, is it more real. Volition bursts forth involuntary-
voluntary; rapt along; the movement of free human minds
becomes a raging tornado of fatalism, blind as the winds; and
Mountain and Gironde, when they recover themselves, are
alike astounded to see where it has flung and dropped them.
To such height of miracle can men work on men; the Conscious and the Unconscious blended inscrutably in this our
inscrutable Life; endless Necessity environing Freewill!

The weapons of the Girondins are Political Philosophy,
Respectability, and Eloquence. Eloquence, or call it rhetoric,
really of a superior order; Vergniaud, for instance, turns a
period as sweetly as any man of that generation. The weapons of the Mountain are those of mere Nature: Audacity
and Impetuosity which may became Ferocity, as of men complete in their determination, in their conviction; nay, of men,
in some cases, who as Septemberers must either prevail or
perish. The ground to be fought for is Popularity: further
you may either seek Popularity with the friends of Freedom
and Order, or with the friends of Freedom Simple; to seek it
with both has unhappily become impossible. With the former
sort, and generally with the Authorities of the Departments,
and such as read Parliamentary Debates, and are of Respectability, and of a peace-loving moneyed nature, the Girondins
carry it. With the extreme Patriot again, with the indigent
Millions, especially with the Population of Paris who do not
read so much as hear and see, the Girondins altogether lose
it, and the Mountain carries it.

Egoism, nor meanness of mind, is not wanting on either
side. Surely not on the Girondin side; where in fact the
instinct of self-preservation, too prominently unfolded by circumstances, cuts almost a sorry figure; where also a certain
finesse, to the length even of shuffling and shamming, now
and then shows itself. They are men skilful in Advocate-
fence. They have been called the Jesuits of the Revolution; [1]
but that is too hard a name. It must be owned likewise

that this rude blustering Mountain has a sense in it of what
the Revolution means; which these eloquent Girondins are
totally void of. Was the Revolution made, and fought for,
against the world, these four weary years, that a Formula
might be substantiated; that Society might become methodic,
demonstrable by logic; and the old Noblesse with their pre-
tensions vanish? Or ought it not withal to bring some glimmering of light and alleviation to the Twenty-five Millions,
who sat in darkness, heavy-laden, till they rose with pikes
in their hands? At least and lowest, one would think, it
should bring them a proportion of bread to live on? There
is in the Mountain here and there; in Marat People's-friend;
in the incorruptible Seagreen himself, though otherwise so
lean and formulary, a heartfelt knowledge of this latter fact—
without which knowledge all other knowledge here is naught,
and the choicest forensic eloquence is as sounding brass and
a tinkling cymbal. Most cold, on the other hand, most pat-
ronizing, unsubstantial is the tone of the Girondins toward
" our poorer brethren "—those brethren whom one often hears
of under the collective name of " the masses," as if they were
not persons at all, but mounds of combustible explosive material, for blowing down Bastilles with! In very truth, a Revo-
lutionist of this kind, is he not a Solecism? Disowned by Nature and Art; deserving only to be erased, and disappear!
Surely, to our poorer brethren of Paris, all this Girondin pat-
ronage sounds deadening and killing: if fine-spoken and incon-
trovertible in logic, then all the falser, all the hatefuler in fact.

Nay, doubtless, pleading for Popularity, here among our
poorer brethren of Paris, the Girondin has a hard game to
play. If he gain the ear of the Respectable at a distance, it
is by insisting on September and such-like; it is at the expense
of this Paris where he dwells and perorates. Hard to perorate in such an auditory! Wherefore the question arises:
Could not we get ourselves out of this Paris? Twice or
oftener such an attempt is made. If not we ourselves, thinks
Guadet, then at least our Suppléans might do it. For every
Deputy has his Suppléant, or Substitute, who will take his place
if need be: might not these assemble, say at Bourges, which is
a quiet episcopal Town, in quiet Berri, forty good leagues off?
In that case, what profit were it for the Paris Sansculottery to
insult us; our Suppléans sitting quiet in Bourges, to whom we

could run? Nay, even the Primary electoral Assemblies, thinks Guadet, might be reconvoked, and a New Convention got, with new orders from the Sovereign People; and right glad were Lyons, were Bordeaux, Rouen, Marseilles, as yet Provincial Towns, to welcome us in their turn, and become a sort of Capital Towns; and teach these Parisians reason.

Fond schemes; which all misgo! If decreed, in heat of eloquent logic, to-day, they are repealed, by clamour and passionate wider considerations, on the morrow.[2] Will you, O Girondins, parcel us into separate Republics, then; like the Swiss, like your Americans; so that there be no Metropolis or indivisible French Nation any more? Your Departmental Guard seemed to point that way! Federal Republic? Federalist? Men and Knitting-women repeat Fédéraliste, with or without much Dictionary-meaning; but go on repeating it, as is usual in such cases, till the meaning of it becomes almost magical, fit to designate all mystery of Iniquity; and Fédéraliste has grown a word of Exorcism and Apage-Satanas. But furthermore, consider what " poisoning of public opinion " in the Departments, by these Brissots, Gorsas, Caritat-Condorcet Newspapers! And then also what counter-poisoning, still feller in quality, by a " Père Duchesne " of Hébert, brutalest Newspaper yet published on Earth; by a " Rougiff " of Guffroy; by the "incendiary leaves of Marat"! More than once, on complaint given and effervescence rising, it is decreed that a man can not both be Legislator and Editor; that he shall choose between the one function and the other.[3] But this too, which indeed could help little, is revoked or eluded; remains a pious wish mainly.

Meanwhile, as the sad fruit of such strife, behold, O ye National Representatives, how, between the friends of Law and the friends of Freedom everywhere, mere heats and jealousies have arisen; fevering the whole Republic! Department, Provincial Town is set against Metropolis, Rich against Poor, Culottic against Sansculottic, man against man. From the Southern Cities come Addresses of an almost inculpatory character; for Paris has long suffered Newspaper calumny. Bordeaux demands a reign of Law and Respectability, meaning Girondism, with emphasis. With emphasis Marseilles demands the like. Nay, from Marseilles there come two

Addresses: one Girondin; one Jacobin Sansculottic. Hot
Rebecqui, sick of this Convention-work, has given place to his
Substitute, and gone home; where also, with such jarrings,
there is work to be sick of.

Lyons, a place of Capitalists and Aristocrats, is in still
worse state; almost in revolt. Chalier the Jacobin Town-Coun-
cillor has got, too literally, to daggers-drawn with Nièvre-
Chol the Modératin Mayor; one of your Moderate, perhaps
Aristocrat, Royalist or Federalist Mayors! Chalier, who pilgrimed to Paris "to behold Marat and the Mountain," has
verily kindled himself at their sacred urn: for on the 6th of
February last, History or Rumour has seen him haranguing
his Lyons Jacobins in a quite transcendental manner, with a
drawn dagger in his hand; recommending (they say) sheer
September methods, patience being worn out; and that the
Jacobin Brethren should, impromptu, work the Guillotine
themselves! One sees him still, in Engravings: mounted on
a table; foot advanced, body contorted; a bald, rude, slope-
browed, infuriated visage of the canine-species, the eyes starting from their sockets; in his puissant right-hand the brandished dagger, or horse-pistol, as some give it; other dog-
visages kindling under him—a man not likely to end well!
However, the Guillotine was not got together impromptu,
that day, "on the Pont Saint-Clair," or elsewhere; but indeed
continued lying rusty in its loft: [4] Nièvre-Chol with military
went about, rumbling cannon, in the most confused manner;
and the "nine hundred prisoners" received no hurt. So distracted is Lyons grown, with its cannons rumbling, Convention Commissioners must be sent thither forthwith: if even
they can appease it, and keep the Guillotine in its loft?

Consider finally if, on all these mad jarrings of the Southern Cities, and of France generally, a traitorous Crypto-Royalist class is not looking and watching; ready to strike in, at
the right season! Neither is there bread; neither is there soap:
see the Patriot women selling out sugar, at a just rate of
twenty-two sous per pound! Citizen Representatives, it were
verily well that your quarrels finished, and the reign of Perfect
Felicity began.

NOTES

[1] Dumouriez, "Mémoires," iii, 314.　[3] "Hist. Parl.," xxv, 25, etc.
[2] "Moniteur," 1793, No. 140, etc.　[4] Ibid., xxiv, 385–393; xxvi, 229, etc.

CHAPTER III

GROWING SHRILL

ON the whole, one can not say that the Girondins are wanting to themselves, so far as good-will might go. They prick assiduously into the sore-places of the Mountain; from principle, and also from Jesuitism.

Besides September, of which there is now little to be made except effervescence, we discern two sore-places, where the Mountain often suffers: Marat, and Orléans Égalité. Squalid Marat, for his own sake and for the Mountain's, is assaulted ever and anon; held up to France, as a squalid bloodthirsty Portent, inciting to the pillage of shops; of whom let the Mountain have the credit! The Mountain murmurs, ill at ease: this "Maximum of Patriotism," how shall they either own him or disown him? As for Marat personally, he, with his fixed-idea, remains invulnerable to such things; nay, the People's-friend is very evidently rising in importance, as his befriended People rises. No shrieks now, when he goes to speak; occasional applauses rather, furtherance which breeds confidence. The day when the Girondins proposed to "decree him accused" (décréter d'accusation, as they phrase it) for that February Paragraph, of "hanging up a Forestaller or two at the door-lintels," Marat proposes to have them "decreed insane"; and, descending the Tribune-steps, is heard to articulate these most unsenatorial ejaculations: "Les cochons, les imbécilles, Pigs, idiots!" Oftentimes he croaks harsh sarcasm, having really a rough rasping tongue, and a very deep fund of contempt for fine outsides; and once or twice, he even laughs, nay, "explodes into laughter, rit aux éclats," at the gentilities and superfine airs of these Girondin "men of statesmanship," with their pedantries, plausibilities, pusillanimities: "these two years," says he, "you have been whining about attacks, and plots, and danger from Paris; and you have not a scratch to show for yourselves." [1]—Danton gruffly rebukes him, from time to time: a Maximum of Patriotism whom one can neither own nor disown!

But the second sore-place of the Mountain is this anomalous Monseigneur Equality Prince d'Orléans. Behold these men, says the Gironde; with a whilom Bourbon Prince among them: they are creatures of the D'Orléans Faction; they will have Philippe made King; one King no sooner guillotined than another made in his stead! Girondins have moved, Buzot moved long ago, from principle and also from Jesuitism, that the whole race of Bourbons should be marched forth from the soil of France; this Prince Égalité to bring up the rear. Motions which might produce some effect on the public—which the Mountain, ill at ease, knows not what to do with.

And poor Orléans Égalité himself, for one begins to pity even him, what does he do with them? The disowned of all parties, the rejected and foolishly bedrifted hither and thither, to what corner of Nature can he now drift with advantage? Feasible hope remains not for him: unfeasible hope, in pallid doubtful glimmers, there may still come, bewildering, not cheering or illuminating—from the Dumouriez quarter; and how if not the time-wasted Orléans Égalité, then perhaps the young unworn Chartres Égalité might arise to be a kind of King? Sheltered, if shelter it be, in the clefts of the Mountain, poor Égalité will wait: one refuge in Jacobinism, one in Dumouriez and Counter-Revolution, are there not two chances? However, the look of him, Dame Genlis says, is grown gloomy; sad to see. Sillery also, the Genlis's Husband, who hovers about the Mountain, not on it, is in a bad way. Dame Genlis is come to Raincy, out of England and Bury St. Edmunds, in these days; being summoned by Égalité, with her young charge, Mademoiselle Égalité—that so Mademoiselle might not be counted among Emigrants and hardly dealt with. But it proves a ravelled business: Genlis and charge find that they must return to the Netherlands; must wait on the Frontiers, for a week or two; till Monseigneur, by Jacobin help, get it wound up. "Next morning," says Dame Genlis, "Monseigneur, gloomier than ever, gave me his arm, to lead me to the carriage. I was greatly troubled; Mademoiselle burst into tears; her Father was pale and trembling. After I had got seated, he stood immovable at the carriage-

48

door, with his eyes fixed on me; his mournful and painful look seemed to implore pity—'Adieu, Madame!' said he. The altered sound of his voice completely overcame me; unable to utter a word, I held out my hand; he grasped it close; then turning, and advancing sharply toward the postillions, he gave them a sign, and we rolled away." [2]

Nor are Peace-makers wanting; of whom likewise we mention two; one fast on the crown of the Mountain, the other not yet alighted anywhere: Danton and Barrère. Ingenious Barrère, Old-Constituent and Editor, from the slopes of the Pyrenees, is one of the usefulest men of this Convention, in his way. Truth may lie on both sides, on either side, or on neither side; my friends, ye must give and take: for the rest, success to the winning side! This is the motto of Barrère. Ingenious, almost genial; quick-sighted, supple, graceful; a man that will prosper. Scarcely Belial in the assembled Pandemonium was plausibler to ear and eye. An indispensable man: in the great Art of Varnish he may be said to seek his fellow. Has there an explosion arisen, as many do arise, a confusion, unsightliness, which no tongue can speak of, nor eye look on; give it to Barrère; Barrère shall be Committee-Reporter of it; you shall see it transmute itself into a regularity, into the very beauty and improvement that was needed. Without one such man, we say, how were this Convention bestead! Call him not, as exaggerative Mercier does, "the greatest liar in France": nay, it may be argued there is not truth enough in him to make a real lie of. Call him, with Burke, Anacreon of the Guillotine, and a man serviceable to this Convention.

The other Peace-maker whom we name is Danton. Peace, O peace with one another! cries Danton often enough: Are we not alone against the world; a little band of brothers? Broad Danton is loved by all the Mountain; but they think him too easy-tempered, deficient in suspicion: he has stood between Dumouriez and much censure, anxious not to exasperate our only General: in the shrill tumult Danton's strong voice reverberates, for union and pacification. Meetings there are; dinings with the Girondins: it is so pressingly essential that there be union. But the Girondins are haughty and respectable: this Titan Danton is not a man of Formulas, and there rests on him a shadow of September. "Your Girondins have no confidence in me ": this is the answer a conciliatory Meillan gets from him; to all the arguments and pleadings this conciliatory Meillan can bring, the repeated answer is, " Ils n'ont point de confiance." [3]—The tumult will get even shriller; rage is growing pale.

In fact, what a pang is it to the heart of a Girondin, this first withering probability that the despicable unphilosophic anarchic Mountain, after all, may triumph! Brutal September-berers, a fifth-floor Tallien, " a Robespierre without an idea in his head," as Condorcet says, " or a feeling in his heart ": and yet we, the flower of France, can not stand against them; behold, the sceptre departs from us; from us and goes to them! Eloquence, Philosophism, Respectability avail not: " against Stupidity the very gods fight to no purpose,

" Mit der Dummheit kämpfen Götter selbst vergebens! "

Shrill are the plaints of Louvet; his thin existence all acidified into rage and preternatural insight of suspicion. Wroth is young Barbaroux; wroth and scornful. Silent, like a Queen with the aspic on her bosom, sits the wife of Roland; Roland's Accounts never yet got audited, his name become a byword. Such is the fortune of war, especially of revolution. The great gulf of Tophet and Tenth of August opened itself at the magic of your eloquent voice; and lo now, it will not close at your voice! It is a dangerous thing such magic. The Magician's Famulus got hold of the forbidden Book, and summoned a goblin: " Plait-il, What is your will? " said the goblin. The Famulus, somewhat struck, bade him fetch water: the swift goblin fetched it, pail in each hand; but lo, would not cease fetching it! Desperate, the Famulus shrieks at him, smites at him, cuts him in two; lo, two goblin water-carriers ply; and the house will be swum away in Deucalion Deluges.

NOTES

[1] " Moniteur," Séance du 20 Mai, 1793.
[2] Genlis, " Mémoires " (London, 1825), iv, 118.
[3] " Mémoires de Meillan, Représentant du Peuple " (Paris, 1823), p. 51.

CHAPTER IV

FATHERLAND IN DANGER

OR rather we will say, this Senatorial war might have lasted long; and Party tugging and throttling with Party might have suppressed and smothered one another, in the ordinary bloodless Parliamentary way; on one condition: that France had been at least able to exist, all the while. But this Sovereign People has a digestive faculty, and can not do without bread. Also we are at war, and must have victory; at war with Europe, with Fate and Famine: and behold, in the spring of the year, all victory deserts us.

Dumouriez had his outposts stretched as far as Aix-la-Chapelle, and the beautifulest plan for pouncing on Holland, by stratagem, flat-bottomed boats and rapid intrepidity; wherein too he had prospered so far; but unhappily could prosper no further. Aix-la-Chapelle is lost; Maestricht will not surrender to mere smoke and noise: the flat-bottomed boats have to launch themselves again, and return the way they came. Steady now, ye rapidly intrepid men; retreat with firmness, Parthian-like! Alas! were it General Miranda's fault; were it the War-minister's fault; or were it Dumouriez's own fault and that of Fortune: enough, there is nothing for it but retreat—well if it be not even flight; for already terror-stricken cohorts and stragglers pour off, not waiting for order; flow disastrous, as many as ten thousand of them, without halt till they see France again.[1] Nay, worse: Dumouriez himself is perhaps secretly turning traitor? Very sharp is the tone in which he writes to our Committees. Commissioners and Jacobin Pillagers have done such incalculable mischief; Hassenfratz sends neither cartridges nor clothing; shoes we have, deceptively " soled with wood and pasteboard." Nothing in short is right. Danton and Lacroix, when it was they that were Commissioners, would needs join Belgium to France—

732

of which Dumouriez might have made the prettiest little
Duchy for his own secret behoof! With all these things the
General is wroth; and writes to us in a sharp tone. Who
knows what this hot little General is meditating? Dumouriez
Duke of Belgium or Brabant; and say, Égalité the Younger
King of France: there were an end for our Revolution!—
Committee of Defence gazes, and shakes its head: who except
Danton, defective in suspicion, could still struggle to be of
hope?

And General Custine is rolling back from the Rhine Country; conquered Mentz will be reconquered, the Prussians
gathering round to bombard it with shot and shell. Mentz
may resist, Commissioner Merlin, the Thionviller, "making
sallies, at the head of the besieged"—resist to the death; but
not longer than that. How sad a reverse for Mentz! Brave
Forster, brave Lux planted Liberty-trees, amid Ça-ira-ing
music, in the snow-slush of last winter, there; and made
Jacobin Societies; and got the Territory incorporated with
France; they came hither to Paris, as Deputies or Delegates,
and have their eighteen francs a-day: but see, before once the
Liberty-tree is got rightly in leaf, Mentz is changing into an
explosive crater; vomiting fire, bevomited with fire!

Neither of these men shall again see Mentz; they have
come hither only to die. Forster has been round the Globe;
he saw Cook perish under Owyhee clubs; but like this Paris
he has yet seen or suffered nothing. Poverty escorts him:
from home there can nothing come, except Job's-news; the
eighteen daily francs, which we here as Deputy or Delegate
with difficulty "touch," are in paper assignats, and sink fast
in value. Poverty, disappointment, inaction, obloquy; the
brave heart slowly breaking! Such is Forster's lot. For the
rest, Demoiselle Théroigne smiles on you in the Soirées;
"a beautiful brownlocked face," of an exalted temper; and
contrives to keep her carriage. Prussian Trenck, the poor
subterranean Baron, jargons and jangles in an unmelodious
manner. Thomas Paine's face is red-pustuled, "but the eyes
uncommonly bright." Convention Deputies ask you to dinner: very courteous; and "we all play at plumpsack."[2] "It
is the Explosion and New-creation of a World," says Forster;
"and the actors in it, such small mean objects, buzzing round
one like a handful of flies."—

Likewise there is war with Spain. Spain will advance through the gorges of the Pyrenees; rustling with Bourbon banners, jingling with artillery and menace. And England has donned the red coat; and marches, with Royal Highness of York—whom some once spake of inviting to be our King. Changed that humour now: and ever more changing; till no hatefuler thing walk this Earth than a denizen of that tyrannous Island; and Pitt be declared and decreed, with effervescence, " L'ennemi du genre humain, The enemy of mankind "; and, very singular to say, you make order that no Soldier of Liberty give quarter to an Englishman. Which order, however, the Soldier of Liberty does but partially obey. We will take no Prisoners then, say the Soldiers of Liberty; they shall all be " Deserters " that we take.[3] It is a frantic order; and attended with inconvenience. For surely, if you give no quarter, the plain issue is that you will get none; and so the business become as broad as it was long.—Our " recruitment of Three-hundred Thousand men," which was the decreed force for this year, is like to have work enough laid to its hand.

So many enemies come wending on; penetrating through throats of mountains, steering over the salt sea; toward all points of our territory; rattling chains at us. Nay, worst of all: there is an enemy within our own territory itself. In the early days of March, the Nantes Postbags do not arrive; there arrive only instead of them Conjecture, Apprehension, bodeful wind of Rumour. The bodefulest proves true. Those fanatic Peoples of La Vendée will no longer keep under: their fire of insurrection, heretofore dissipated with difficulty, blazes out anew, after the King's Death, as a wide conflagration; not riot but civil war. Your Cathelineaus, your Stofflets, Charettes, are other men than was thought: behold how their Peasants, in mere russet and hodden, with their rude arms, rude array, with their fanatic Gaelic frenzy and wild-yelling battle-cry of " God and the King! " dash at us like a dark whirlwind; and blow the best-disciplined Nationals we can get into panic and sauve-qui-peut! Field after field is theirs; one sees not where it will end. Commandant Santerre may be sent there; but with non-effect; he might as well have returned and brewed beer.

It has become peremptorily necessary that a National Con-

vention cease arguing, and begin acting. Yield one party of
you to the other, and do it swiftly. No theoretic outlook is
here, but the close certainty of ruin; the very day that is
passing over us must be provided for.

It was Friday the Eighth of March when this Job's-post
from Dumouriez, thickly preceded and escorted by so many
other Job's-posts, reached the National Convention. Blank
enough are most faces. Little will it avail whether our Septemberers be punished or go unpunished; if Pitt and Cobourg
are coming in, with one punishment for us all; nothing now
between Paris itself and the Tyrants but a doubtful Dumouriez, and hosts in loose-flowing loud retreat!—Danton the
Titan rises in this hour as always in the hour of need. Great
is his voice, reverberating from the domes—Citizen-Repre-
sentatives, shall we not, in such crisis of Fate, lay aside dis-
cords? Reputation: O what is the reputation of this man
or of that? "Que mon nom soit flétri; que la France soit
libre: Let my name be blighted; Let France be free!" It is
necessary now again that France rise, in swift vengeance, with
her million right-hands, with her heart as of one man. Instantaneous recruitment in Paris; let every Section of Paris
furnish its thousands; every Section of France! Ninety-six
Commissioners of us, two for each Section of the Forty-eight,
they must go forthwith, and tell Paris what the Country needs
of her. Let Eighty more of us be sent, post-haste, over
France; to spread the fire-cross, to call forth the might of men.
Let the Eighty also be on the road, before this sitting rise.
Let them go, and think what their errand is. Speedy Camp
of Fifty-thousand between Paris and the North Frontier; for
Paris will pour forth her volunteers! Shoulder to shoulder;
one strong universal death-defiant rising and rushing; we shall
hurl back these Sons of Night yet again; and France, in spite
of the world, be free![4]—So sounds the Titan's voice: into
all Section-houses; into all French hearts. Sections sit in
Permanence, for recruitment, enrolment, that very night.
Convention Commissioners, on swift wheels, are carrying the
fire-cross from Town to Town, till all France blaze.

And so there is Flag of "Fatherland in Danger" waving
from the Townhall, Black Flag from the top of Notre-Dame
Cathedral; there is Proclamation, hot eloquence; Paris rushing

out once again to strike its enemies down. That, in such circumstances, Paris was in no mild humour can be conjectured. Agitated streets; still more agitated round the Salle de Manége! Feuillans-Terrace crowds itself with angry Citizens, angrier Citizenesses; Varlet perambulates with portable chair: ejaculations of no measured kind, as to perfidious fine-spoken Hommes d'état, friends of Dumouriez, secret friends of Pitt and Cobourg, burst from the hearts and lips of men. To fight the enemy? Yes, and even to "freeze him with terror, glacer d'effroi": but first to have domestic Traitors punished! Who are they that, carping and quarrelling, in their Jesuitic most moderate way, seek to shackle the Patriotic movement? That divide France against Paris, and poison public opinion in the Departments? That when we ask for bread, and a Maximum fixed-price, treat us with lectures on Free-trade in grains? Can the human stomach satisfy itself with lectures on Free-trade; and are we to fight the Austrians in a moderate manner, or in an immoderate? This Convention must be purged.

"Set up a swift Tribunal for Traitors, a Maximum for Grains": thus speak with energy the Patriot Volunteers, as they defile through the Convention Hall, just on the wing to the Frontiers—perorating in that heroical Cambyses' vein of theirs: beshouted by the Galleries and Mountain; bemurmured by the Right-side and Plain. Nor are prodigies wanting: lo, while a Captain of the Section Poissonnière perorates with vehemence about Dumouriez, Maximum and Crypto-Royalist Traitors, and his troop beat chorus with him, waving their Banner overhead, the eye of a Deputy discerns, in this same Banner, that the cravates or streamers of it have Royal fleurs-de-lys! The Section-Captain shrieks; his troop shriek, horror-struck, and "trample the Banner under foot": seemingly the work of some Crypto-Royalist Plotter? Most probable [5]—perhaps at bottom, only the old Banner of the Section, manufactured prior to the Tenth of August, when such streamers were according to rule! [6]

History, looking over the Girondin Memoirs, anxious to disentangle the truth of them from the hysterics, finds these days of March, especially this Sunday the Tenth of March, play a great part. Plots, plots; a plot for murdering the Girondin Deputies; Anarchists and Secret-Royalists plotting,

in hellish concert, for that end! The far greater part of
which is hysterics. What we do find indisputable is, that
Louvet and certain Girondins were apprehensive they might
be murdered on Saturday, and did not go to the evening
sitting; but held council with one another, each inciting his
fellow to do something resolute, and end these Anarchists: to
which, however, Pétion, opening the window, and finding the
night very wet, answered only, " Ils ne feront rien," and " com-
posedly resumed his violin," says Louvet; [7] thereby, with soft
Lydian tweedledeeing, to wrap himself against eating cares.
Also that Louvet felt especially liable to being killed; that
several Girondins went abroad to seek beds: liable to being
killed; but were not. Further that, in very truth, Journalist
Deputy Gorsas, poisoner of the Departments, he and his
Printer had their houses broken into (by a tumult of Patriots,
among whom redcapped Varlet, American Fournier loom
forth, in the darkness of the rain and riot); had their wives
put in fear; their presses, types, and circumjacent equipments
beaten to ruin; no Mayor interfering in time; Gorsas himself
escaping, pistol in hand, " along the coping of the back wall."
Further, that Sunday, the morrow, was not a workday; and
the streets were more agitated than ever: Is it a new September, then, that these Anarchists intend? Finally, that no
September came—and also that hysterics, not unnaturally, had
reached almost their acme.[8]

Vergniaud denounces and deplores; in sweetly turned
periods. Section Bonconseil, Good-counsel so-named, not
Mauconseil or Ill-counsel as it once was—does a far notabler
thing: demands that Vergniaud, Brissot, Guadet, and other
denunciatory, fine-spoken Girondins, to the number of Twenty-two, be put under arrest! Section Good-counsel, so named
ever since the Tenth of August, is sharply rebuked, like a
Section of Ill-counsel: [9] but its word is spoken, and will not
fall to the ground.

In fact, one thing strikes us in these poor Girondins: their
fatal shortness of vision; nay, fatal poorness of character, for
that is the root of it. They are as strangers to the People
they would govern; to the thing they have come to work in.
Formulas, Philosophies, Respectabilities, what has been written in Books, and admitted by the Cultivated Classes: this inadequate Scheme of Nature's working is all that Nature, let

her work as she will, can reveal to these men. So they perorate and speculate; and call on the Friends of Law, when the
question is not Law or No-Law, but Life or No-Life. Pedants
of the Revolution, if not Jesuits of it! Their Formalism is
great; great also is their Egoism. France rising to fight
Austria has been raised only by plot of the Tenth of March,
to kill Twenty-two of them! This Revolution Prodigy, un-
folding itself into terrific stature and articulation, by its own
laws and Nature's, not by the laws of Formula, has become
unintelligible, incredible as an impossibility, the " waste chaos
of a Dream." A Republic founded on what they call the
Virtues; on what we call the Decencies and Respectabilities:
this they will have, and nothing but this. Whatsoever other
Republic Nature and Reality send, shall be considered as not
sent; as a kind of Nightmare Vision, and thing non-extant;
disowned by the Laws of Nature and of Formula. Alas!
dim for the best eyes is this Reality; and as for these men,
they will not look at it with eyes at all, but only through
" facetted spectacles " of Pedantry, wounded Vanity; which
yield the most portentous fallacious spectrum. Carping and
complaining forever of Plots and Anarchy, they will do one
thing; prove, to demonstration, that the Reality will not translate into their Formula; that they and their Formula are incompatible with the Reality: and, in its dark wrath, the Reality will extinguish it and them! What a man kens he cans.
But the beginning of a man's doom is, that vision be withdrawn from him; that he sees not the reality, but a false
spectrum of the reality; and following that, step darkly, with
more or less velocity, downward to the utter Dark; to Ruin,
which is the great Sea of Darkness, whither all falsehoods,
winding or direct, continually flow!

This Tenth of March we may mark as an epoch in the
Girondin destinies; the rage so exasperated itself, the miscon-
ception so darkened itself. Many desert the sittings; many
come to them armed.[10] An honourable Deputy, setting out
after breakfast, must now, besides taking his Notes, see whether
his Priming is in order.

Meanwhile with Dumouriez in Belgium it fares ever worse.
Were it again General Miranda's fault, or some other's fault,
there is no doubt whatever but the " Battle of Nerwinden," on

the 18th of March, is lost; and our rapid retreat has become a far too rapid one. Victorious Cobourg, with his Austrian prickers, hangs like a dark cloud on the rear of us: Dumouriez never off horseback night or day; engagement every three hours; our whole discomfited Host rolling rapidly inward, full of rage, suspicion, and sauve-qui-peut! And then Dumouriez himself, what his intents may be? Wicked seemingly and not charitable! His despatches to Committee openly denounce a factious Convention, for the woes it has brought on France and him. And his speeches—for the General has no reticence! The execution of the Tyrant this Dumouriez calls the Murder of the King. Danton and Lacroix, flying thither as Commissioners once more, return very doubtful; even Danton now doubts.

Three Jacobin Missionaries, Proly, Dubuisson, Pereira, have flown forth; sped by a wakeful Mother Society: they are struck dumb to hear the General speak. The Convention, according to this General, consists of three-hundred scoundrels and four-hundred imbeciles: France can not do without a King. "But we have executed our King." "And what is it to me," hastily cries Dumouriez, a General of no reticence, "whether the King's name be Ludovicus or Jacobus?" "Or Philippus!" rejoins Proly—and hastens to report progress. Over the Frontiers such hope is there.

NOTES

[1] Dumouriez, iv, 16–73.
[2] Forster's "Briefwechsel," ii, 460, 514, 631.
[3] See Dampmartin, "Evénemens," ii, 213–230.
[4] "Moniteur" (in "Hist. Parl.," xxv, 6).
[5] "Choix des Rapports," xi, 277.
[6] "Hist. Parl.," xxv, 72.
[7] Louvet, "Mémoires," p. 72.
[8] Meillan, pp. 23, 24; Louvet, pp. 71–80.
[9] "Moniteur" (Séance du 12 Mars), 15 Mars.
[10] Meillan, "Mémoires," pp. 24, 85.

CHAPTER V

SANSCULOTTISM ACCOUTRED

LET us look, however, at the grand internal Sansculottism and Revolution Prodigy, whether it stirs and waxes: there and not elsewhere may hope still be for France. The Revolution Prodigy, as Decree after Decree issues from the Mountain, like creative fiats, accordant with the nature of the Thing—is shaping itself rapidly, in these days, into terrific stature and articulation, limb after limb. Last March, 1792, we saw all France flowing in blind terror; shutting town-barriers, boiling pitch for Brigands: happier, this March, that it is a seeing terror; that a creative Mountain exists, which can say fiat! Recruitment proceeds with fierce celerity: nevertheless our Volunteers hesitate to set out, till Treason be punished at home; they do not fly to the frontiers; but only fly hither and thither, demanding and denouncing. The Mountain must speak new fiat and new fiats.

And does it not speak such? Take, as first example, those Comités Révolutionnaires for the arrestment of Persons Suspect. Revolutionary Committee, of Twelve chosen Patriots, sits in every Township of France; examining the Suspect, seeking arms, making domiciliary visits and arrestments— caring, generally, that the Republic suffer no detriment. Chosen by universal suffrage, each in its Section, they are a kind of elixir of Jacobinism; some Forty-four Thousand of them awake and alive over France! In Paris and all Towns, every house-door must have the names of the inmates legibly printed on it, " at a height not exceeding five feet from the ground "; every Citizen must produce his certificatory Carte de Civisme, signed by Section-President; every man be ready to give account of the faith that is in him. Persons Suspect had as well depart this soil of Liberty! And yet departure too is bad: all Emigrants are declared Traitors, their property

become National; they are " dead in Law "—save, indeed, that
for our behoof they shall " live yet fifty years in Law," and
what heritages may fall to them in that time become National
too! A mad vitality of Jacobinism, with Forty-four Thousand
centres of activity, circulates through all fibres of France.

Very notable also is the Tribunal Extraordinaire: [1] decreed
by the Mountain; some Girondins dissenting, for surely such
a Court contradicts every formula—other Girondins assenting,
nay, co-operating, for do not we all hate Traitors, O ye people
of Paris?—Tribunal of the Seventeenth, in Autumn last, was
swift; but this shall be swifter. Five Judges; a standing
Jury, which is named from Paris and the Neighbourhood,
that there be not delay in naming it: they are subject to no
Appeal; to hardly any Law-forms, but must " get themselves
convinced " in all readiest ways; and for security are bound
" to vote audibly "; audibly, in the hearing of a Paris Public.
This is the Tribunal Extraordinaire; which, in few months,
getting into most lively action, shall be entitled Tribunal
Révolutionnaire; as indeed it from the very first has entitled
itself: with a Herman or a Dumas for Judge-President, with
a Fouquier-Tinville for Attorney-General, and a Jury of such
as Citizen Leroi, who has surnamed himself Dix-Août, " Leroi
August-Tenth," it will become the wonder of the world.
Herein has Sansculottism fashioned for itself a Sword of
Sharpness: a weapon magical; tempered in the Stygian hell-
waters; to the edge of it all armour, and defence of strength
or of cunning shall be soft; it shall mow down Lives and
Brazen-gates; and the waving of it shed terror through the
souls of men.

But speaking of an amorphous Sansculottism taking form,
ought we not, above all things, to specify how the Amorphous
gets itself a Head? Without metaphor, this Revolution Government continues hitherto in a very anarchic state. Executive Council of Ministers, Six in number, there is: but they,
especially since Roland's retreat, have hardly known whether
they were Ministers or not. Convention Committees sit supreme over them; but then each Committee as supreme as
the others: Committee of Twenty-one, of Defence, of General
Surety; simultaneous or successive, for specific purposes. The
Convention alone is all-powerful—especially if the Commune
go with it; but is too numerous for an administrative body.

Wherefore, in this perilous quick-whirling condition of the Republic, before the end of March we obtain our small Comité de Salut Public;[2] as it were, for miscellaneous accidental purposes requiring despatch—as it proves, for a sort of universal supervision, and universal subjection. They are to report weekly, these new Committee-men; but to deliberate in secret. Their number is Nine, firm Patriots all, Danton one of them; renewable every month—yet why not re-elect them if they turn out well? The flower of the matter is, that they are but nine; that they sit in secret. An insignificant-looking thing at first, this Committee, but with a principle of growth in it! Forwarded by fortune, by internal Jacobin energy, it will reduce all Committees and the Convention itself to mute obedience, the Six Ministers to Six assiduous Clerks; and work its will on the Earth and under Heaven for a season. A "Committee of Public Salvation" whereat the world still shrieks and shudders.

If we call that Revolutionary Tribunal a Sword, which Sansculottism has provided for itself, then let us call the "Law of the Maximum" a Provender-scrip, or Haversack, wherein, better or worse, some ration of bread may be found. It is true, Political Economy, Girondin free-trade, and all law of supply and demand, are hereby hurled topsyturvy: but what help? Patriotism must live; the "cupidity of farmers" seems to have no bowels. Wherefore this Law of the Maximum, fixing the highest price of grains, is, with infinite effort, got passed;[3] and shall gradually extend itself into a Maximum for all manner of comestibles and commodities: with such scrambling and topsyturvying as may be fancied! For now if, for example, the farmer will not sell? The farmer shall be forced to sell. An accurate Account of what grain he has shall be delivered in to the Constituted Authorities: let him see that he say not too much; for in that case, his rents, taxes and contributions will rise proportionally: let him see that he say not too little; for, on or before a set day, we shall suppose in April, less than one-third of this declared quantity must remain in his barns, more than two-thirds of it must have been thrashed and sold. One can denounce him, and raise penalties.

By such inextricable overturning of all Commercial relations will Sansculottism keep life in; since not otherwise. On the whole, as Camille Desmoulins says once, "while the Sansculottes fight, the Monsieurs must pay." So there come Impôts Progressifs, Ascending Taxes; which consume, with fast-increasing voracity, the "superfluous-revenue" of men: beyond fifty-pounds a-year, you are not exempt; rising into the hundreds, you bleed freely; into the thousands and tens of thousands, you bleed gushing. Also there come Requisitions; there comes "Forced-Loan of a Milliard," some Fifty-Millions Sterling, which of course they that have must lend. Unexampled enough; it has grown to be no country for the Rich, this; but a country for the Poor! And then if one fly, what steads it ? Dead in Law; nay, kept alive fifty years yet, for their accursed behoof! In this manner therefore it goes; topsyturvying, Ça-ira-ing—and withal there is endless sale of Emigrant National-Property, there is Cambon with endless cornucopia of Assignats. The Trade and Finance of Sansculottism; and how, with Maximum and Bakers' queues, with Cupidity, Hunger, Denunciation, and Paper-money, it led its galvanic-life, and began and ended—remains the most interesting of all Chapters in Political Economy: still to be written.

All which things, are they not clean against Formula? O Girondin Friends, it is not a Republic of the Virtues we are getting; but only a Republic of the Strengths, virtuous and other!

NOTES

[1] "Moniteur," No. 70 (du 11 Mars), No. 76, etc.
[2] Ibid., No. 83 (du 24 Mars, 1793), Nos. 86, 98, 99, 100.
[3] Ibid. (du 20 Avril, etc., to 20 Mai, 1793).

CHAPTER VI

THE TRAITOR

BUT Dumouriez, with his fugitive Host, with his King Ludovicus or King Philippus? There lies the crisis; there hangs the question: Revolution Prodigy, or Counter-Revolution?—One wide shriek covers that North-east region. Soldiers, full of rage, suspicion and terror, flock hither and thither; Dumouriez, the many-counselled, never off horseback, knows now no counsel that were not worse than none: the counsel, namely, of joining himself with Cobourg; marching to Paris, extinguishing Jacobinism, and, with some new King Ludovicus or King Philippus, restoring the Constitution of 1791![1]

Is wisdom quitting Dumouriez; the herald of Fortune quitting him? Principle, faith political or other, beyond a certain faith of mess-rooms, and honour of an officer, had him not to quit. At any rate his quarters in the Burgh of Saint-Amand; his head-quarters in the Village of Saint-Amand des Boues, a short way off—have become a Bedlam. National Representatives, Jacobin Missionaries are riding and running; of the "three Towns," Lille, Valenciennes, or even Condé, which Dumouriez wanted to snatch for himself, not one can be snatched; your Captain is admitted, but the Town-gate is closed on him, and then alas! the Prison-gate, and "his men wander about the ramparts." Couriers gallop breathless; men wait, or seem waiting, to assassinate, to be assassinated; Battalions nigh frantic with such suspicion and uncertainty, with " Vive-la-République! " and " Sauve-qui-peut! " rush this way and that—Ruin and Desperation in the shape of Cobourg lying entrenched close by.

Dame Genlis and her fair Princess d'Orléans find this Burgh of Saint-Amand no fit place for them; Dumouriez's protection is grown worse than none. Tough Genlis, one of the toughest women; a woman, as it were, with nine lives in her; whom nothing will beat: she packs her bandboxes; clear for flight in a private manner. Her beloved Princess she will—leave here, with the Prince Chartres Égalité her Brother. In the cold gray of the April morning, we find her accordingly established in her hired vehicle, on the street of Saint-Amand; postillions just cracking their whips to go—when behold the young Princely Brother, struggling hitherward, hastily calling; bearing the Princess in his arms! Hastily he has clutched the poor young lady up, in her very night-gown, nothing saved of her goods except the watch from the pillow: with brotherly despair he flings her in, among the bandboxes, into Genlis's chaise, into Genlis's arms: Leave her not, in the name of Mercy and Heaven! A shrill scene, but a brief one—the postillions crack and go. Ah, whither? Through by-roads and broken hill-passes; seeking their way with lanterns after nightfall; through perils, and Cobourg Austrians, and suspicious French Nationals: finally, into Switzerland; safe though nigh moneyless.[2] The brave young Égalité has a most wild Morrow to look for; but now only himself to carry through it.

For indeed over at that Village named of the Mudbaths, Saint-Amand des Boues, matters are still worse. About four o'clock on Tuesday afternoon, the 2d of April 1793, two Couriers come galloping as if for life; Mon Général! Four National Representatives, War-Minister at their head, are posting hitherward from Valenciennes; are close at hand— with what intents one may guess! While the Couriers are yet speaking, War-Minister and National Representatives, old Camus the Archivist for chief speaker of them, arrive. Hardly has Mon Général had time to order out the Hussar Regiment de Berchigny; that it take rank and wait near by, in case of accident. And so, enter War-Minister Beurnonville, with an embrace of friendship, for he is an old friend; enter Archivist Camus and the other three following him.

They produce Papers, invite the General to the bar of the Convention: merely to give an explanation or two. The General finds it unsuitable, not to say impossible, and that " the service will suffer." Then comes reasoning; the voice of the old Archivist getting loud. Vain to reason loud with this

Dumouriez; he answers mere angry irreverences. And so,
amid plumed staff-officers, very gloomy-looking; in jeopardy
and uncertainty, these poor National messengers debate and
consult, retire and re-enter, for the space of some two hours:
without effect. Whereupon Archivist Camus, getting quite
loud, proclaims, in the name of the National Convention, for
he has the power to do it, That General Dumouriez is arrested:
" Will you obey the National mandate, General? "—" Pas dans
ce moment-ci, Not at this particular moment," answers the
General also aloud; then glancing the other way, utters certain unknown vocables, in a mandatory manner; seemingly
a German word-of-command.³ Hussars clutch the Four
National Representatives, and Beurnonville the War-Minister;
pack them out of the apartment; out of the Village, over the
lines to Cobourg, in two chaises that very night—as hostages,
prisoners; to lie long in Maestricht and Austrian strong-
holds!⁴ Jacta est alea.

This night Dumouriez prints his " Proclamation "; this
night and the morrow the Dumouriez Army, in such darkness
visible, and rage of semi-desperation as there is, shall meditate
what the General is doing, what they themselves will do in it.
Judge whether this Wednesday was of halcyon nature, for any
one! But on the Thursday morning, we discern Dumouriez
with small escort, with Chartres Égalité and a few staff-officers,
ambling along the Condé Highway: perhaps they are for
Condé, and trying to persuade the Garrison there; at all
events, they are for an interview with Cobourg, who waits in
the woods by appointment, in that quarter. Nigh the Village
of Doumet, three National Battalions, a set of men always
full of Jacobinism, sweep past us; marching rather swiftly—
seemingly in mistake, by a way we had not ordered. The
General dismounts, steps into a cottage, a little from the wayside; will give them right order in writing. Hark! what
strange growling is heard; what barkings are heard, loud
yells of " Traitors," of " Arrest ": the National Battalions have
wheeled round, are emitting shot! Mount, Dumouriez, and
spring for life! Dumouriez and Staff strike the spurs in,
deep; vault over ditches, into the fields, which prove to be
morasses; sprawl and plunge for life; bewhistled with curses
and lead. Sunk to the middle, with or without horses, several
servants killed, they escape out of shot-range, to General Mack

the Austrian's quarters. Nay, they return on the morrow, to Saint-Amand and faithful foreign Berchigny; but what boots it? The Artillery has all revolted, is jingling off to Valenciennes; all have revolted, are revolting; except only foreign Berchigny, to the extent of some poor fifteen hundred, none will follow Dumouriez against France and Indivisible Republic: Dumouriez's occupation's gone.[5]

Such an instinct of Frenchhood and Sansculottism dwells in these men: they will follow no Dumouriez nor Lafayette, nor any mortal on such errand. Shriek may be of "Sauve-qui-peut!" but will also be of "Vive-la-République!" New National Representatives arrive; new General Dampierre, soon killed in battle; new General Custine: the agitated Hosts draw back to some Camp of Famars; make head against Cobourg as they can.

And so Dumouriez is in the Austrian quarters; his drama ended, in this rather sorry manner. A most shifty, wiry man; one of Heaven's Swiss; that wanted only work. Fifty years of unnoticed toil and valour; one year of toil and valour, not unnoticed, but seen of all countries and centuries; then thirty other years again unnoticed, of Memoir-writing, English Pension, scheming and projecting to no purpose: Adieu, thou Swiss of Heaven, worthy to have been something else!

His Staff go different ways. Brave young Égalité reaches Switzerland and the Genlis Cottage; with a strong crabstick in his hand, a strong heart in his body: his Princedom is now reduced to that. Égalité the Father sat playing whist, in his Palais Égalité, at Paris, on the 6th day of this same month of April, when a catchpole entered: Citoyen Égalité is wanted at the Convention Committee![6] Examination, requiring Arrestment; finally requiring Imprisonment, transference to Marseilles and the Castle of If! Orléansdom has sunk in the black waters; Palais Égalité, which was Palais Royal, is like to become Palais National.

NOTES

[1] Dumouriez, "Mémoires," iv, c. 7–10.
[2] Genlis, iv, 139.
[3] Dumouriez, iv, 159, etc.
[4] Their Narrative, written by Camus (in Toulongeon, iii, app. 60–87).
[5] "Mémoires," iv, 162–180.   [6] See Montgaillard, iv, 122.

CHAPTER VII

IN FIGHT

OUR Republic, by paper Decree, may be "One and Indivisible"; but what profits it while these things are? Federalists in the Senate, renegadoes in the Army, traitors everywhere! France, all in desperate recruitment since the Tenth of March, does not fly to the frontier, but only flies hither and thither. This defection of contemptuous diplomatic Dumouriez falls heavy on the fine-spoken high-sniffing Hommes d'état whom he consorted with; forms a second epoch in their destinies.

Or perhaps more strictly we might say, the second Girondin epoch, though little noticed then, began on the day when, in reference to this defection, the Girondins broke with Danton. It was the first day of April; Dumouriez had not yet plunged across the morasses to Cobourg, but was evidently meaning to do it, and our Commissioners were off to arrest him; when what does the Girondin Lasource see good to do, but rise, and Jesuitically question and insinuate at great length, whether a main accomplice of Dumouriez had not probably been—Danton! Gironde grins sardonic assent; Mountain holds its breath. The figure of Danton, Levasseur says, while this speech went on, was noteworthy. He sat erect with a kind of internal convulsion struggling to keep itself motionless; his eye from time to time flashing wilder, his lip curling in Titanic scorn.[1] Lasource, in a fine-spoken attorney manner, proceeds: there is this probability to his mind, and there is that; probabilities which press painfully on him, which cast the Patriotism of Danton under a painful shade—which painful shade, he, Lasource, will hope that Danton may find it not impossible to dispel.

"Les Scélérats!" cries Danton, starting up, with clenched right-hand, Lasource having done; and descends from the

Mountain, like a lava-flood: his answer not unready. Lasource's probabilities fly like idle dust; but leave a result
behind them. "Ye were right, friends of the Mountain," begins Danton, "and I was wrong: there is no peace possible
with these men. Let it be war, then! They will not save
the Republic with us: it shall be saved without them; saved
in spite of them." Really a burst of rude Parliamentary eloquence this; which is still worth reading in the old "Moniteur." With fire-words the exasperated rude Titan rives and
smites these Girondins; at every hit the glad Mountain utters
chorus; Marat, like a musical bis, repeating the last phrase.[2]
Lasource's probabilities are gone; but Danton's pledge of
battle remains lying.

A third epoch, or scene in the Girondin Drama, or rather
it is but the completion of this second epoch, we reckon from
the day when the patience of virtuous Pétion finally boiled
over; and the Girondins, so to speak, took up this battle-
pledge of Danton's, and decreed Marat accused. It was the
eleventh of the same month of April, on some effervescence
rising, such as often rose; and President had covered himself,
mere Bedlam now ruling; and Mountain and Gironde were
rushing on one another with clenched right-hands, and even
with pistols in them; when, behold, the Girondin Duperret
drew a sword! Shriek of horror rose, instantly quenching all
other effervescence, at sight of the clear murderous steel;
whereupon Duperret returned it to the leather again—con-
fessing that he did indeed draw it, being instigated by a kind
of sacred madness, " sainte fureur," and pistols held at him;
but that if he parricidally had chanced to scratch the outmost
skin of National Representation with it, he too carried pistols,
and would have blown his brains out on the spot.[3]

But now in such posture of affairs, virtuous Pétion rose,
next morning, to lament these effervescences, this endless
Anarchy invading the Legislative Sanctuary itself; and here,
being growled at and howled at by the Mountain, his patience,
long tried, did, as we say, boil over; and he spake vehemently,
in high key, with foam on his lips; " whence," says Marat, " I
concluded he had got la rage," the rabidity, or dog-madness.
Rabidity smites others rabid: so there rises new foam-lipped
demand to have Anarchists extinguished; and specially to

have Marat put under Accusation. Send a representative to
the Revolutionary Tribunal? Violate the inviolability of a
Representative? Have a care, O Friends! This poor Marat
has faults enough; but against Liberty or Equality, what
fault? That he has loved and fought for it, not wisely but
too well. In dungeons and cellars, in pinching poverty, under
anathema of men; even so, in such fight, has he grown so
dingy, bleared; even so has his head become a Stylites one!
Him you will fling to your Sword of Sharpness; while Cobourg and Pitt advance on us, fire-spitting?

The Mountain is loud, the Gironde is loud and deaf; all
lips are foamy. With " Permanent-Session of twenty-four
hours," with vote by roll-call, and a deadlift effort, the
Gironde carries it: Marat is ordered to the Revolutionary
Tribunal, to answer for that February Paragraph of Fore-
stallers at the door-lintel, with other offences; and, after a
little hesitation, he obeys.[4]

Thus is Danton's battle-pledge taken up; there is, as he
said there would be, " war without truce or treaty, ni trève ni
composition." Wherefore, close now with one another, Formula and Reality, in death-grips, and wrestle it out; both of
you can not live, but only one!

NOTES

[1] " Mémoires de Réné Levasseur " (Bruxelles, 1830), i, 164.
[2] Séance du 1 Avril, 1793 (in " Hist. Parl.," xxv, 24–35).
[3] " Hist. Parl.," xv, 397.
[4] " Moniteur " (du 16 Avril, 1793, et seq.).

CHAPTER VIII

IN DEATH-GRIPS

IT proves what strength, were it only of inertia, there is in established Formulas, what weakness in nascent Realities, and illustrates several things, that this death-wrestle should still have lasted some six weeks or more. National business, discussion of the Constitutional Act, for our Constitution should decidedly be got ready, proceeds along with it. We even change our Locality; we shift, on the Tenth of May, from the old Salle de Manége into our new Hall, in the Palace, once a King's but now the Republic's, of the Tuileries. Hope and ruth, flickering against despair and rage, still struggle in the minds of men.

It is a most dark confused death-wrestle, this of the six weeks. Formalist frenzy against Realist frenzy; Patriotism, Egoism, Pride, Anger, Vanity, Hope and Despair, all raised to the frenetic pitch: Frenzy meets Frenzy, like dark clashing whirlwinds; neither understands the other; the weaker, one day, will understand that it is verily swept down! Girondism is strong as established Formula and Respectability: do not as many as Seventy-two of the Departments, or say respectable Heads of Departments, declare for us? Calvados, which loves its Buzot, will even rise in revolt, so hint the Addresses; Marseilles, cradle of Patriotism, will rise; Bordeaux will rise, and the Gironde Department, as one man; in a word, who will not rise, were our Réprésentation Nationale to be insulted, or one hair of a Deputy's head harmed! The Mountain, again, is strong as Reality and Audacity. To the Reality of the Mountain are not all furthersome things possible? A new Tenth of August, if needful; nay, a new Second of September!—

But, on Wednesday afternoon, Twenty-fourth day of April, year 1793, what tumult as of fierce jubilee is this? It is

Marat returning from the Revolutionary Tribunal! A week
or more of death-peril: and now there is triumphant acquittal; Revolutionary Tribunal can find no accusation against
this man. And so the eye of History beholds Patriotism,
which had gloomed unutterable things all week, break into
loud jubilee, embrace its Marat; lift him into a chair of triumph, bear him shoulder-high through the streets. Shoulder-
high is the injured People's-friend, crowned with an oak-
garland; amid the wavy sea of red night-caps, carmagnole
jackets, grenadier bonnets and female mob-caps; far-sound-
ing like a sea! The injured People's-friend has here reached
his culminating point; he too strikes the stars with his sublime head.

But the Reader can judge with what face President Lasource, he of the " painful probabilities," who presides in this
Convention Hall, might welcome such jubilee-tide, when it
got thither, and the Decreed of Accusation floating on the top
of it! A National Sapper, spokesman on the occasion, says,
the People know their Friend, and love his life as their own;
" whosoever wants Marat's head must get the Sapper's first." [1]
Lasource answered with some vague painful mumblement—
which, says Levasseur, one could not help tittering at.[2] Patriot Sections, Volunteers not yet gone to the Frontiers, come
demanding the " purgation of traitors from your own bosom ";
the expulsion, or even the trial and sentence, of a factious
Twenty-two.

Nevertheless the Gironde has got its Commission of
Twelve; a Commission specially appointed for investigating
these troubles of the Legislative Sanctuary: let Sansculottism
say what it will, Law shall triumph. Old-Constituent Rabaut
Saint-Étienne presides over this Commission: " it is the last
plank whereon a wrecked Republic may perhaps still save
herself." Rabaut and they therefore sit, intent; examining
witnesses; launching arrestments; looking out into a waste
dim sea of troubles—the womb of Formula, or perhaps her
grave! Enter not that sea, O Reader! There are dim deso-
lation and confusion; raging women and raging men. Sections come demanding Twenty-two; for the number first given
by Section Bonconseil still holds, though the names should
even vary. Other Sections, of the wealthier kind, come denouncing such demand; nay, the same Section will demand

to-day, and denounce the demand to-morrow, according as the wealthier sit, or the poorer. Wherefore, indeed, the Girondins decree that all Sections shall close "at ten in the evening"; before the working people come: which Decree remains without effect. And nightly the Mother of Patriotism wails doleful; doleful, but her eye kindling! And Fournier l'Américain is busy, and the two banker Freys, and Varlet Apostle of Liberty; the bull-voice of Marquis St.-Huruge is heard. And shrill women vociferate from all Galleries, the Convention ones and downward. Nay, a "Central Committee" of all the Forty-eight Sections looms forth huge and dubious; sitting dim in the Archevêché, sending Resolutions, receiving them: a Centre of the Sections; in dread deliberation as to a New Tenth of August!

One thing we will specify, to throw light on many: the aspect under which, seen through the eyes of these Girondin Twelve, or even seen through one's own eyes, the Patriotism of the softer sex presents itself. There are Female Patriots, whom the Girondins call Megæras, and count to the extent of eight thousand; with serpent-hair, all out of curl; who have changed the distaff for the dagger. They are of "the Society called Brotherly," Fraternelle, say Sisterly, which meets under the roof of the Jacobins. "Two thousand daggers," or so, have been ordered—doubtless for them. They rush to Versailles, to raise more women; but the Versailles women will not rise.[3]

Nay, behold, in National Garden of Tuileries—Demoiselle Théroigne herself is become as a brown-locked Diana (were that possible) attacked by her own dogs, or she-dogs! The Demoiselle, keeping her carriage, is for Liberty indeed, as she has full well shown; but then for Liberty with Respectability: whereupon these serpent-haired Extreme She Patriots do now fasten on her, tatter her, shamefully fustigate her, in their shameful way; almost fling her into the Garden-ponds, had not help intervened. Help, alas! to small purpose. The poor Demoiselle's head and nervous-system, none of the soundest, is so tattered and fluttered that it will never recover; but flutter worse and worse, till it crack; and within year and day we hear of her in madhouse and strait-waistcoat, which proves permanent!—Such brown-locked Figure did flutter, and inarticulately jabber and gesticulate, little able to speak the ob-

scure meaning it had, through some segment of the Eighteenth
Century of Time. She disappears here from the Revolution
and Public History for evermore.[4]

Another thing we will not again specify, yet again beseech
the Reader to imagine: the reign of Fraternity and Perfection.
Imagine, we say, O Reader, that the Millennium were struggling on the threshold, and yet not so much as groceries could
be had—owing to traitors. With what impetus would a man
strike traitors, in that case! Ah, thou canst not imagine it;
thou hast thy groceries safe in the shops, and little or no hope
of a Millennium ever coming!—But indeed, as to the temper
there was in men and women, does not this one fact say
enough: the height Suspicion had risen to? Preternatural
we often called it; seemingly in the language of exaggeration:
but listen to the cold deposition of witnesses. Not a musical
Patriot can blow himself a snatch of melody from the French
Horn, sitting mildly pensive on the housetop, but Mercier will
recognise it to be a signal which one Plotting Committee is
making to another. Distraction has possessed Harmony herself; lurks in the sound of "Marseillaise" and "Ça-ira."[5]
Louvet, who can see as deep into a millstone as the most, discerns that we shall be invited back to our old Hall of the Manége, by a Deputation; and then the Anarchists will massacre
Twenty-two of us, as we walk over. It is Pitt and Cobourg; the
gold of Pitt.—Poor Pitt! They little know what work he has
with his own Friends of the People; getting them bespied,
beheaded, their habeas-corpuses suspended, and his own Social
Order and strong-boxes kept tight—to fancy him raising mobs
among his neighbours!

But the strangest fact connected with French or indeed
with human Suspicion, is perhaps this of Camille Desmoulins.
Camille's head, one of the clearest in France, has got itself so
saturated through every fibre with Preternaturalism of Suspicion, that looking back on that Twelfth of July 1789, when
the thousands rose round him, yelling responsive at his word
in the Palais-Royal Garden, and took cockades, he finds it
explicable only on this hypothesis, That they were all hired to
do it, and set on by the Foreign and other Plotters. "It was
not for nothing," says Camille with insight, "that this multitude burst up round me when I spoke!" No, not for nothing.
Behind, around, before, it is one huge Preternatural Puppet-

play of Plots; Pitt pulling the wires.[6] Almost I conjecture that I, Camille myself, am a Plot, and wooden with wires.—The force of insight could no further go.

Be this as it will, History remarks that the Commission of Twelve, now clear enough as to the Plots; and luckily having " got the threads of them all by the end," as they say—are launching Mandates of Arrest rapidly in these May days; and carrying matters with a high hand; resolute that the sea of troubles shall be restrained. What chief Patriot, Section-President even, is safe? They can arrest him; tear him from his warm bed, because he has made irregular Section Arrestments! They arrest Varlet Apostle of Liberty. They arrest Procureur-Substitute Hébert, Père Duchesne; a Magistrate of the People, sitting in Townhall; who, with high solemnity of martyrdom, takes leave of his colleagues; prompt he, to obey the Law; and solemnly acquiescent, disappears into prison.

The swifter fly the Sections, energetically demanding him back; demanding not arrestment of Popular Magistrates, but of a traitorous Twenty-two. Section comes flying after Section—defiling energetic, with their Cambyses-vein of oratory: nay, the Commune itself comes, with Mayor Pache at its head; and with question not of Hébert and the Twenty-two alone, but with this ominous old question made new, " Can you save the Republic, or must we do it? " To whom President Max Isnard makes fiery answer: If by fatal chance, in any of those tumults which since the Tenth of March are ever returning, Paris were to lift a sacrilegious finger against the National Representation, France would rise as one man, in never-imagined vengeance, and shortly " the traveller would ask, on which side of the Seine Paris had stood "![7] Whereat the Mountain bellows only louder, and every Gallery; Patriot Paris boiling round.

And Girondin Valazé has nightly conclaves at his house; sends billets, " Come punctually, and well armed, for there is to be business." And Megæra women perambulate the streets, with flags, with lamentable alleleu.[8] And the Convention-doors are obstructed by roaring multitudes: fine-spoken Hommes d'état are hustled, maltreated, as they pass; Marat will apostrophize you, in such death-peril, and say, " Thou too art of them." If Roland ask leave to quit Paris, there is order of the day. What help? Substitute Hébert, Apostle Varlet, must be given back; to be crowned with oak-garlands. The Commission of Twelve, in a Convention overwhelmed with roaring Sections, is broken; then on the morrow, in a Convention of rallied Girondins, is reinstated. Dim Chaos, or the sea of troubles, is struggling through all its elements; writhing and chafing toward some Creation.

NOTES

[1] Séance du 26 Avril, 1793 (in " Moniteur," No. 116).

[2] Levasseur, " Mémoires," i, c. 6.

[3] Buzot, " Mémoires," pp. 69, 84; Meillan, " Mémoires," pp. 192, 195, 196. See " Commission des Douze " (in " Choix des Rapports," xii, 69–131).

[4] " Deux Amis," vii, 77–80; Forster, i, 514; Moore, i, 70. She did not die till 1817; in the Salpêtrière, in the most abject state of insanity; see Esquirol, " Des Maladies Mentales " (Paris, 1838), i, 445–450.

[5] Mercier, " Nouveau Paris," vi, 63.

[6] See " Histoire des Brissotins," par Camille Desmoulins (a Pamphlet of Camille's, Paris, 1793).

[7] " Moniteur," Séance du 25 Mai, 1793.

[8] Meillan, " Mémoires," p. 195; Buzot, pp. 69, 84.

CHAPTER IX

EXTINCT

ACCORDINGLY, on Friday the Thirty-first of May 1793, there comes forth into the summer sunlight one of the strangest scenes. Mayor Pache with Municipality arrives at the Tuileries Hall of Convention; sent for, Paris being in visible ferment; and gives the strangest news.

How, in the gray of this morning, while we sat Permanent in Townhall, watchful for the commonweal, there entered, precisely as on a Tenth of August, some Ninety-six extraneous persons; who declared themselves to be in a state of Insurrection; to be plenipotentiary Commissioners from the Forty-eight Sections, sections or members of the Sovereign People, all in a state of Insurrection; and further, that we, in the name of said Sovereign in Insurrection, were dismissed from office. How we thereupon laid off our sashes, and withdrew into the adjacent Saloon of Liberty. How, in a moment or two, we were called back; and reinstated; the Sovereign pleasing to think us still worthy of confidence. Whereby, having taken new oath of office, we on a sudden find ourselves Insurrectionary Magistrates, with extraneous Committee of Ninety-six sitting by us; and a Citoyen Henriot, one whom some accuse of Septemberism, is made Generalissimo of the National Guard; and, since six o'clock, the tocsins ring, and the drums beat—Under which peculiar circumstances, what would an august National Convention please to direct us to do? [1]

Yes, there is the question! "Break the Insurrectionary Authorities," answer some with vehemence. Vergniaud at least will have " the National Representatives all die at their post "; this is sworn to, with ready loud acclaim. But as to breaking the Insurrectionary Authorities—alas! while we yet debate, what sound is that? Sound of the Alarm-Cannon on

757

the Pont Neuf; which it is death by the Law to fire without order from us!

It does boom off there nevertheless; sending a stound through all hearts. And the tocsins discourse stern music; and Henriot with his Armed Force has enveloped us! And Section succeeds Section, the livelong day; demanding with Cambyses-oratory, with the rattle of muskets, That traitors, Twenty-two or more, be punished; that the Commission of Twelve be irrecoverably broken. The heart of the Gironde dies within it; distant are the Seventy-two respectable Departments, this fiery Municipality is near! Barrère is for a middle course; granting something. The Commission of Twelve declares that, not waiting to be broken, it hereby breaks itself, and is no more. Fain would Reporter Rabaut speak his and its last words; but he is bellowed off. Too happy that the Twenty-two are still left unviolated!—Vergniaud, carrying the laws of refinement to a great length, moves, to the amazement of some, that " the Sections of Paris have deserved well of their country." Whereupon, at a late hour of the evening, the deserving Sections retire to their respective places of abode. Barrère shall report on it. With busy quill and brain he sits, secluded; for him no sleep tonight. Friday the last of May has ended in this manner.

The Sections have deserved well: but ought they not to deserve better? Faction and Girondism is struck down for the moment, and consents to be a nullity; but will it not, at another favourabler moment rise, still feller; and the Republic have to be saved in spite of it? So reasons Patriotism, still Permanent; so reasons the Figure of Marat, visible in the dim Section-world, on the morrow. To the conviction of men!— And so at eventide of Saturday, when Barrère had just got the thing all varnished by the labour of a night and day, and his Report was setting off in the evening mail-bags, tocsin peals out again. Générale is beating; armed men taking station in the Place Vendôme and elsewhere, for the night; supplied with provisions and liquor. There, under the summer stars, will they wait, this night, what is to be seen and to be done, Henriot and Townhall giving due signal.

The Convention, at sound of générale, hastens back to its Hall; but to the number only of a Hundred; and does little business, puts off business till the morrow. The Girondins do

not stir out thither, the Girondins are abroad seeking beds.—
Poor Rabaut, on the morrow morning, returning to his post,
with Louvet and some others, through streets all in ferment,
wrings his hands, ejaculating, " Illa suprema dies!" [2] It has
become Sunday the 2d day of June, year 1793, by the old
style; by the new style, year One of Liberty, Equality, Fraternity. We have got to the last scene of all, that ends this
history of the Girondin Senatorship.

It seems doubtful whether any terrestrial Convention had
ever met in such circumstances as this National one now does.
Tocsin is pealing; Barriers shut; all Paris is on the gaze, or
under arms. As many as a Hundred Thousand under arms
they count: National Force; and the Armed Volunteers, who
should have flown to the Frontiers and La Vendée; but would
not, treason being unpunished; and only flew hither and
thither! So many, steady under arms, environ the National
Tuileries and Garden. There are horse, foot, artillery, sappers
with beards: the artillery one can see with their camp-furnaces
in this National Garden, heating bullets red, and their match
is lighted. Henriot in plumes rides, amid a plumed Staff: all
posts and issues are safe; reserves lie out, as far as the Wood
of Boulogne; the choicest Patriots nearest the scene. One
other circumstance we will note: that a careful Municipality,
liberal of camp-furnaces, has not forgotten provision-carts.
No member of the Sovereign need now go home to dinner;
but can keep rank—plentiful victual circulating unsought.
Does not this People understand Insurrection? Ye, not un-
inventive, Gualches!—

Therefore let a National Representation, " mandatories of
the Sovereign," take thought of it. Expulsion of your Twenty-two, and your Commission of Twelve: we stand here till it
be done! Deputation after Deputation, in ever stronger language, comes with that message. Barrère proposes a middle
course: Will not perhaps the inculpated Deputies consent to
withdraw voluntarily; to make a generous demission and self-
sacrifice for the sake of one's country? Isnard, repentant of
that search on which river-bank Paris stood, declares himself
ready to demit. Ready also is Te-Deum Fauchet; old Dusaulx
of the Bastille, " vieux radoteur, old dotard," as Marat calls
him, is still readier. On the contrary, Lanjuinais the Breton

declares that there is one man who never will demit voluntarily; but will protest to the uttermost, while a voice is left
him. And he accordingly goes on protesting; amid rage and
clangour; Legendre crying at last: "Lanjuinais, come down
from the Tribune, or I will fling thee down, ou je te jette en
bas!" For matters are come to extremity. Nay, they do
clutch hold of Lanjuinais, certain zealous Mountain-men; but
can not fling him down, for he "cramps himself on the railing"; and "his clothes get torn." Brave Senator, worthy of
pity! Neither will Barbaroux demit; he "has sworn to die at
his post, and will keep that oath." Whereupon the Galleries
all rise with explosion; brandishing weapons, some of them;
and rush out, saying: "Allons, then; we must save our country!" Such a Session is this of Sunday the second of June.

Churches fill, over Christian Europe, and then empty themselves; but this Convention empties not, the while: a day of
shrieking contention, of agony, humiliation, and tearing of
coat-skirts; illa suprema dies! Round stand Henriot and his
Hundred Thousand, copiously refreshed from tray and basket:
nay, he is "distributing five francs a-piece," we Girondins
saw it with our eyes; five francs to keep them in heart! And
distraction of armed riot encumbers our borders, jangles at
our Bar; we are prisoners in our own Hall: Bishop Grégoire
could not get out for a besoin actuel without four gendarmes
to wait on him! What is the character of a National Representative become? And now the sunlight falls yellower on
western windows, and the chimney-tops are flinging longer
shadows; the refreshed Hundred Thousand, nor their shadows, stir not! What to resolve on? Motion rises, superfluous
one would think, That the Convention go forth in a body;
ascertain with its own eyes whether it is free or not. Lo,
therefore, from the Eastern Gate of the Tuileries, a distressed
Convention issuing; handsome Hérault Séchelles at their head;
he with hat on, in sign of public calamity, the rest bareheaded—toward the Gate of the Carrousel; wondrous to see:
toward Henriot and his plumed Staff. "In the name of the
National Convention, make way!" Not an inch of way does
Henriot make: "I receive no orders, till the Sovereign, yours
and mine, have been obeyed." The Convention presses on;
Henriot prances back, with his Staff, some fifteen paces. "To
arms! Cannoneers, to your guns!"—flashes out his puissant

sword, as the Staff all do, and the Hussars all do. Cannoneers
brandish the lit match; Infantry present arms—alas! in the
level way, as if for firing! Hatted Hérault leads his distressed
flock, through their pinfold of a Tuileries again; across the
Garden, to the Gate on the opposite side. Here is Feuillans-
Terrace, alas! there is our old Salle de Manége; but neither
at this Gate of the Pont Tournant is there egress. Try the
other; and the other: no egress! We wander disconsolate
through armed ranks; who indeed salute with " Live the Republic! " but also with " Die the Gironde! " Other such sight,
in the year One of Liberty, the westering sun never saw.

And now behold Marat meets us; for he lagged in this
Suppliant Procession of ours: he has got some hundred elect
Patriots at his heels; he orders us, in the Sovereign's name,
to return to our place, and do as we are bidden and bound.
The Convention returns. " Does not the Convention," says
Couthon with a singular power of face, " see that it is free "—
none but friends round it? The Convention, overflowing with
friends and armed Sectioners, proceeds to vote as bidden.
Many will not vote, but remain silent; some one or two protest, in words, the Mountain has a clear unanimity. Commission of Twelve, and the denounced Twenty-two, to whom we
add Ex-Ministers Clavière and Lebrun: these, with some
slight extempore alterations (this or that orator proposing,
but Marat disposing), are voted to be under " Arrestment in
their own houses." Brissot, Buzot, Vergniaud, Guadet, Louvet, Gensonné, Barbaroux, Lasource, Lanjuinais, Rabaut—
Thirty-two, by the tale; all that we have known as Girondins,
and more than we have known. They, " under the safeguard
of the French People "; by and by, under the safeguard of two
Gendarmes each, shall dwell peaceably in their own houses;
as Non-Senators; till further order. Herewith ends Séance
of Sunday the second of June 1793.

At ten o'clock, under mild stars, the Hundred Thousand,
their work well finished, turn homeward. Already yesterday,
Central Insurrection Committee had arrested Madame Roland; imprisoned her in the Abbaye. Roland has fled, no man
knows whither.

Thus fell the Girondins, by Insurrection; and became extinct as a Party: not without a sigh from most Historians.

The men were men of parts, of Philosophic culture, decent behaviour; not condemnable in that they were but Pedants, and had not better parts; not condemnable, but most unfortunate. They wanted a Republic of the Virtues, wherein themselves should be head; and they could only get a Republic of the Strengths, wherein others than they were head.

For the rest, Barrère shall make Report of it. The night concludes with a " civic promenade by torchlight ": [3] surely the true reign of Fraternity is now not far?

NOTES

[1] " Débats de la Convention " (Paris, 1828), iv, 187–223; " Moniteur," Nos. 152–154, 1793.

[2] Louvet, " Mémoires," p. 89.

[3] Buzot, " Mémoires," p. 310. See " Pièces Justificatives," of Narratives, Commentaries, etc., in Buzot, Louvet, Meillan; " Documens Complémentaires," in " Hist. Parl.," xxviii, 1–78.

Book XVII

TERROR

CHAPTER I

CHARLOTTE CORDAY

IN the leafy months of June and July, several French Departments germinate a set of rebellious paper-leaves, named Proclamations, Resolutions, Journals, or Diurnals, " of the Union for Resistance to Oppression." In particular, the Town of Caen, in Calvados, sees its paper-leaf of " Bulletin de Caen " suddenly bud, suddenly establish itself as Newspaper there; under the Editorship of Girondin National Representatives!

For among the proscribed Girondins are certain of a more desperate humour. Some, as Vergniaud, Valazé, Gensonné, " arrested in their own houses," will await with stoical resignation what the issue may be. Some, as Brissot, Rabaut, will take to flight, to concealment; which, as the Paris Barriers are opened again in a day or two, is not yet difficult. But others there are who will rush, with Buzot, to Calvados; or far over France, to Lyons, Toulon, Nantes and elsewhither, and then rendezvous at Caen: to awaken as with war-trumpet the respectable Departments; and strike down an anarchic Mountain Faction; at least not yield without a stroke at it. Of this latter temper we count some score or more, of the Arrested, and of the Not-yet-arrested: a Buzot, a Barbaroux, Louvet, Guadet, Pétion, who have escaped from Arrestment in their own homes; a Salles, a Pythagorean Valady, a Duchâtel, the Duchâtel that came in blanket and nightcap to vote for the life of Louis, who have escaped from danger and likelihood of Arrestment. These, to the number at one time of Twenty-seven, do accordingly lodge here, at the " Intendance, or Departmental Mansion," of the town of Caen in Calvados; welcomed by Persons in Authority; welcomed and defrayed, having no money of their own. And the " Bulletin de Caen " comes forth, with the most animating paragraphs: How the Bordeaux Department, the Lyons Department, this

Department after the other is declaring itself; sixty, or say sixty-nine, or seventy-two [1] respectable Departments either declaring, or ready to declare. Nay, Marseilles, it seems, will march on Paris by itself, if need be. So has Marseilles Town said, That she will march. But on the other hand, that Montélimart Town has said, No thoroughfare; and means even to "bury herself" under her own stone and mortar first—of this be no mention in "Bulletin de Caen."

Such animating paragraphs we read in this new Newspaper; and fervours and eloquent sarcasm: tirades against the Mountain, from the pen of Deputy Salles; which resemble, say friends, Pascal's "Provincials." What is more to the purpose, these Girondins have got a General in chief, one Wimpfen, formerly under Dumouriez; also a secondary questionable General Puisaye, and others; and are doing their best to raise a force for war. National Volunteers, whosoever is of right heart: gather in, ye National Volunteers, friends of Liberty; from our Calvados Townships, from the Eure, from Brittany, from far and near: forward to Paris, and extinguish Anarchy! Thus at Caen, in the early July days, there is a drumming and parading, a perorating and consulting: Staff and Army; Council; Club of Carabots, Anti-Jacobin friends of Freedom, to denounce atrocious Marat. With all which, and the editing of Bulletins, a National Representative has his hands full.

At Caen it is most animated; and, as one hopes, more or less animated in the "Seventy-two Departments that adhere to us." And in a France begirt with Cimmerian invading Coalitions, and torn with an internal La Vendée, this is the conclusion we have arrived at: To put down Anarchy by Civil War! "Durum et durum," the Proverb says, "non faciunt murum." La Vendée burns: Santerre can do nothing there; he may return home and brew beer. Cimmerian bombshells fly all along the North. That Siege of Mentz is become famed—lovers of the Picturesque (as Goethe will testify), washed country-people of both sexes, stroll thither on Sundays, to see the artillery work and counterwork; "you only duck a little while the shot whizzes past." [2] Condé is capitulating to the Austrians; Royal Highness of York, these several weeks, fiercely batters Valenciennes. For, alas! our fortified Camp of Famars was stormed; General Dampierre was killed; General Custine was blamed—and indeed is now come to Paris to give "explanations."

Against all which the Mountain and atrocious Marat must even make head as they can. They, anarchic Convention as they are, publish Decrees, expostulary, explanatory, yet not without severity; they ray-forth Commissioners, singly or in pairs, the olive-branch in one hand, yet the sword in the other. Commissioners come even to Caen; but without effect. Mathematical Romme, and Prieur named of the Côte d'Or, venturing thither, with their olive and sword, are packed into prison: there may Romme lie, under lock and key, " for fifty days "; and meditate his New Calendar, if he please. Cimmeria, La Vendée, and Civil War! Never was Republic One and Indivisible at a lower ebb.—

Amid which dim ferment of Caen and the World, History specially notices one thing: in the lobby of the Mansion de l'Intendance, where busy Deputies are coming and going, a young Lady with an aged valet, taking grave graceful leave of Deputy Barbaroux.[3] She is of stately Norman figure; in her twenty-fifth year; of beautiful still countenance: her name is Charlotte Corday, heretofore styled D'Armans, while Nobility still was. Barbaroux has given her a Note to Deputy Duperret—him who once drew his sword in the effervescence. Apparently she will to Paris on some errand? " She was a Republican before the Revolution, and never wanted energy." A completeness, a decision is in this fair female Figure: " by energy she means the spirit that will prompt one to sacrifice himself for his country." What if she, this fair young Charlotte, had emerged from her secluded stillness, suddenly like a Star; cruel-lovely, with half-angelic, half-dæmonic splendour; to gleam for a moment, and in a moment be extinguished: to be held in memory, so bright-complete was she, through long centuries!—Quitting Cimmerian Coalitions without, and the dim-simmering Twenty-five millions within, History will look fixedly at this one fair Apparition of a Charlotte Corday; will note whither Charlotte moves, how the little Life burns forth so radiant, then vanishes swallowed of the Night.

With Barbaroux's Note of Introduction, and slight stock of luggage, we see Charlotte on Tuesday the 9th of July seated in the Caen Diligence, with a place for Paris. None takes farewell of her, wishes her Good-journey: her Father will find a line left, signifying that she is gone to England, that he must pardon her, and forget her. The drowsy Diligence lum-

bers along; amid drowsy talk of Politics, and praise of the
Mountain; in which she mingles not: all night, all day, and
again all night. On Thursday, not long before noon, we are
at the bridge of Neuilly; here is Paris with her thousand
black domes, the goal and purpose of thy journey! Arrived
at the Inn de la Providence in the Rue des Vieux Augustins,
Charlotte demands a room; hastens to bed; sleeps all afternoon and night, till the morrow morning.

On the morrow morning, she delivers her Note to Duperret.
It relates to certain Family Papers which are in the Minister
of the Interior's hands; which a Nun at Caen, an old Convent-
friend of Charlotte's, has need of; which Duperret shall assist
her in getting: this then was Charlotte's errand to Paris?
She has finished this, in the course of Friday—yet says nothing
of returning. She has seen and silently investigated several
things. The Convention, in bodily reality, she has seen; what
the Mountain is like. The living physiognomy of Marat she
could not see; he is sick at present, and confined to home.

About eight on the Saturday morning, she purchases a
large sheath-knife in the Palais Royal; then straightway, in
the Place des Victoires, takes a hackney-coach: "To the Rue
de l'École de Médecine, No. 44." It is the residence of the
Citoyen Marat!—The Citoyen Marat is ill, and can not be
seen; which seems to disappoint her much. Her business is
with Marat then? Hapless beautiful Charlotte; hapless squalid
Marat! From Caen in the utmost West, from Neuchâtel in
the utmost East, they two are drawing nigh each other; they
two have, very strangely, business together.—Charlotte, returning to her Inn, despatches a short Note to Marat; signifying that she is from Caen, the seat of the rebellion; that she
desires earnestly to see him, and "will put it in his power
to do France a great service." No answer. Charlotte writes
another Note, still more pressing; sets out with it by coach,
about seven in the evening, herself. Tired day-labourers have
again finished their Week; huge Paris is circling and simmering, manifold, according to its vague wont: this one fair
Figure has decision in it; drives straight—toward a purpose.

It is yellow July evening, we say, the thirteenth of the
month; eve of the Bastille day—when " M. Marat," four years
ago, in the crowd of the Pont Neuf, shrewdly required of
that Besenval Hussar-party, which had such friendly disposi-

tions, "to dismount, and give up their arms, then"; and became notable among Patriot men. Four years: what a road he has travelled—and sits now, about half-past seven of the clock, stewing in slipper-bath; sore afflicted; ill of Revolution Fever—of what other malady this History had rather not name. Excessively sick and worn, poor man: with precisely elevenpence-halfpenny of ready-money, in paper; with slipper-bath; strong three-footed stool for writing on, the while; and a squalid—Washerwoman, one may call her: that is his civic establishment in Medical-School Street; thither and not else-whither has his road led him. Not to the reign of Brother-hood and Perfect Felicity; yet surely on the way toward that? —Hark, a rap again! A musical woman's voice, refusing to be rejected: it is the Citoyenne who would do France a service. Marat, recognising from within, cries, "Admit her." Charlotte Corday is admitted.

Citoyen Marat, I am from Caen the seat of rebellion, and wished to speak with you.—Be seated, mon enfant. Now what are the Traitors doing at Caen? What Deputies are at Caen?—Charlotte names some Deputies. "Their heads shall fall within a fortnight," croaks the eager People's-friend, clutching his tablets to write: Barbaroux, Pétion, writes he with bare shrunk arm, turning aside in the bath; Pétion, and Louvet, and—Charlotte has drawn her knife from the sheath; plunges it, with one sure stroke, into the writer's heart. "À moi, chère amie, Help, dear!" no more could the Death-choked say or shriek. The helpful Washerwoman running in, there is no Friend of the People, or Friend of the Washer-woman left; but his life with a groan gushes out, indignant, to the shades below.[4]

And so Marat People's-friend is ended; the lone Stylites has got hurled down suddenly from his Pillar—whitherward He that made him knows. Patriot Paris may sound triple and tenfold, in dole and wail; re-echoed by Patriot France; and the Convention, "Chabot pale with terror, declaring that they are to be all assassinated," may decree him Pantheon Honours, Public Funeral, Mirabeau's dust making way for him; and Jacobin Societies, in lamentable oratory, summing up his character, parallel him to One, whom they think it honour to call "the good Sansculotte"—whom we name not here;[5] also a Chapel may be made, for the urn that holds

his Heart, in the Place du Carrousel; and new-born children
be named Marat; and Lago-di-Como Hawkers bake mountains
of stucco into unbeautiful Busts; and David paint his Picture,
or Death-Scene; and such other Apotheosis take place as the
human genius, in these circumstances, can devise: but Marat
returns no more to the light of this Sun. One sole circumstance we have read with clear sympathy, in the old " Moniteur " Newspaper: how Marat's Brother comes from Neuchâtel
to ask of the Convention, " that the deceased Jean-Paul Marat's
musket be given him." [6] For Marat too had a brother and
natural affections; and was wrapped once in swaddling-
clothes, and slept safe in a cradle like the rest of us. Ye
children of men!—A sister of his, they say, lives still to this
day in Paris.

As for Charlotte Corday, her work is accomplished; the
recompense of it is near and sure. The chère amie, and
neighbours of the house, flying at her, she " overturns some
movables," entrenches herself till the gendarmes arrive; then
quietly surrenders; goes quietly to the Abbaye Prison: she
alone quiet, all Paris sounding, in wonder, in rage or admiration, round her. Duperret is put in arrest, on account of her;
his Papers sealed—which may lead to consequences. Fauchet, in like manner, though Fauchet had not so much as
heard of her. Charlotte, confronted with these two Deputies,
praises the grave firmness of Duperret, censures the dejection
of Fauchet.

On Wednesday morning, the thronged Palais de Justice
and Revolutionary Tribunal can see her face; beautiful and
calm: she dates it " fourth day of the Preparation of Peace."
A strange murmur ran through the Hall, at sight of her; you
could not say of what character.[7] Tinville has his indictments
and tape-papers: the cutler of the Palais Royal will testify
that he sold her the sheath-knife; " All these details are needless," interrupted Charlotte; " it is I that killed Marat." By
whose instigation?—" By no one's." What tempted you,
then? His crimes. " I killed one man," added she, raising
her voice extremely (extrêmement), as they went on with their
questions, " I killed one man to save a hundred thousand; a
villain to save innocents; a savage wild-beast to give repose
to my country. I was a Republican before the Revolution;
I never wanted energy." There is therefore nothing to be

said. The public gazes astonished: the hasty limners sketch
her features, Charlotte not disapproving: the men of law proceed with their formalities. The doom of Death as a murderess. To her Advocate she gives thanks; in gentle phrase,
in high-flown classical spirit. To the Priest they send her
she gives thanks; but needs not any shriving, any ghostly
or other aid from him.

On this same evening therefore, about half-past seven
o'clock, from the gate of the Conciergerie, to a City all on
tiptoe, the fatal Cart issues; seated on it a fair young creature,
sheeted in red smock of Murderess; so beautiful, serene, so
full of life; journeying toward death—alone amid the World.
Many take off their hats, saluting reverently; for what heart
but must be touched? [8] Others growl and howl. Adam Lux,
of Mentz, declares that she is greater than Brutus; that it
were beautiful to die with her: the head of this young man
seems turned. At the Place de la Révolution, the countenance
of Charlotte wears the same still smile. The executioners
proceed to bind her feet; she resists, thinking it meant as an
insult; on a word of explanation, she submits with cheerful
apology. As the last act, all being now ready, they take the
neckerchief from her neck; a blush of maidenly shame over-
spreads that fair face and neck; the cheeks were still tinged
with it when the executioner lifted the severed head, to show
it to the people. " It is most true," says Forster, " that he
struck the cheek insultingly; for I saw it with my eyes: the
Police imprisoned him for it." [9]

In this manner have the Beautifulest and Squalidest come
in collision, and extinguished one another. Jean-Paul Marat
and Marie-Anne Charlotte Corday both, suddenly, are no
more. " Day of the Preparation of Peace? " Alas! how were
peace possible or preparable, while, for example, the hearts
of lovely Maidens, in their convent-stillness, are dreaming
not of Love-paradises and the light of Life, but of Codrus'
sacrifices and Death well-earned? That Twenty-five million
hearts have got to such temper, this is the Anarchy; the soul
of it lies in this: whereof not peace can be the embodiment!
The death of Marat, whetting old animosities tenfold, will be
worse than any life. O ye hapless Two, mutually extinctive,
the Beautiful and the Squalid, sleep ye well—in the Mother's
bosom that bore you both!

This is the History of Charlotte Corday; most definite, most complete; angelic-dæmonic: like a Star! Adam Lux goes home, half-delirious; to pour forth his Apotheosis of her, in paper and print; to propose that she have a statue with this inscription, " Greater than Brutus." Friends represent his danger; Lux is reckless; thinks it were beautiful to die with her.

NOTES

[1] Meillan, pp. 72, 73; Louvet, p. 129.
[2] " Belagerung von Mainz " (Goethe's " Werke," xxx, 278–334).
[3] Meillan, p. 75; Louvet, p. 114.
[4] " Moniteur," Nos. 197–199; " Hist. Parl.," xxviii, 301–305; " Deux Amis," i, 368–374.
[5] See " Éloge funèbre de Jean-Paul Marat," prononcé à Strasbourg (in Barbaroux, pp. 125–131); Mercier, etc.
[6] Séance du 16 Septembre 1793.
[7] " Procès de Charlotte Corday," etc. (" Hist. Parl.," xxviii, 311–338).
[8] " Deux Amis," x, 374–384.
[9] " Briefwechsel," i, 508.

CHAPTER II

IN CIVIL WAR

BUT during these same hours, another guillotine is at work, on another: Charlotte, for the Girondins, dies at Paris to-day; Chalier, by the Girondins, dies at Lyons to-morrow.

From rumbling of cannon along the streets of that City, it has come to firing of them, to rabid fighting: Nièvre Chol and the Girondins triumph—behind whom there is, as everywhere, a Royalist Faction waiting to strike in. Trouble enough at Lyons; and the dominant party carrying it with a high hand! For, indeed, the whole South is astir; incarcerating Jacobins; arming for Girondins: wherefore we have got a " Congress of Lyons "; also a " Revolutionary Tribunal of Lyons," and Anarchists shall tremble. So Chalier was soon found guilty, of Jacobinism, of murderous Plot, " address with drawn dagger on the sixth of February last "; and, on the morrow, he also travels his final road, along the streets of Lyons, " by the side of an ecclesiastic, with whom he seems to speak earnestly "—the axe now glittering nigh. He could weep, in old years, this man, and " fall on his knees on the pavement," blessing Heaven at sight of Federation Programs or the like; then he pilgrimed to Paris, to worship Marat and the Mountain: now Marat and he are both gone—we said he could not end well. Jacobinism groans inwardly, at Lyons; but dare not outwardly. Chalier, when the Tribunal sentenced him, made answer: ". My death will cost this City dear."

Montélimart Town is not buried under its ruins; yet Marseilles is actually marching, under order of a " Lyons Congress "; is incarcerating Patriots; the very Royalists now showing face. Against which a General Cartaux fights, though in small force; and with him an Artillery Major, of

the name of—Napoleon Buonaparte. This Napoleon, to prove
that the Marseillese have no chance ultimately, not only fights
but writes; publishes his "Supper of Beaucaire," a Dialogue
which has become curious.[1] Unfortunate Cities, with their
actions and their reactions! Violence to be paid with violence
in geometrical ratio; Royalism and Anarchism both striking
in—the final net-amount of which geometrical series, what man
shall sum?

The Bar of Iron has never yet floated in Marseilles Harbour; but the body of Rebecqui was found floating, self-
drowned there. Hot Rebecqui, seeing how confusion deep-
ened, and Respectability grew poisoned with Royalism, felt
that there was no refuge for a Republican but death. Rebecqui disappeared: no one knew whither; till, one morning,
they found the empty case or body of him risen to the top,
tumbling on the salt waves;[2] and perceived that Rebecqui
had withdrawn forever.—Toulon likewise is incarcerating Patriots; sending delegates to Congress; intriguing, in case of
necessity, with the Royalists and English. Montpellier, Bordeaux, Nantes: all France, that is not under the swoop of
Austria and Cimmeria, seems rushing into madness and suicidal ruin. The Mountain labours; like a volcano in a burning
volcanic Land. Convention Committees, of Surety, of Salvation, are busy night and day: Convention Commissioners whirl
on all highways; bearing olive-branch and sword, or now perhaps sword only. Chaumette and Municipals come daily to
the Tuileries demanding a Constitution: it is some weeks now
since he resolved, in Townhall, that a Deputation "should go
every day," and demand a Constitution, till one were got;[3]
whereby suicidal France might rally and pacify itself; a thing
inexpressibly desirable.

This then is the fruit your Antianarchic Girondins have
got from that Levying of War in Calvados? This fruit, we
may say; and no other whatsoever. For indeed, before either
Charlotte's or Chalier's head had fallen, the Calvados War
itself had, as it were, vanished, dreamlike, in a shriek! With
"seventy-two Departments" on our side, one might have
hoped better things. But it turns out that Respectabilities,
though they will vote, will not fight. Possession always is
nine points in Law; but in Lawsuits of this kind, one may
say, it is ninety-and-nine points. Men do what they were

wont to do; and have immense irresolution and inertia: they obey him who has the symbols that claim obedience.   Consider what, in modern society, this one fact means: the Metropolis is with our enemies!   Metropolis, Mother-city; rightly so named: all the rest are but as her children, her nurselings. Why, there is not a leathern Diligence, with its post-bags and luggage-boots, that lumbers out from her, but is as a huge life-pulse; she is the heart of all.   Cut short that one leathern Diligence, how much is cut short!—General Wimpfen, looking practically into the matter, can see nothing for it but that one should fall back on Royalism; get into communication with Pitt!   Dark innuendoes he flings out, to that effect: whereat we Girondins start, horror-struck.   He produces as his Second in command a certain " Ci-devant," one Comte Puisaye; entirely unknown to Louvet; greatly suspected by him.

Few wars, accordingly, were ever levied of a more insufficient character than this of Calvados.   He that is curious in such things may read the details of it in the Memoirs of that same Ci-devant Puisaye, the much-enduring man and Royalist: How our Girondin National forces, marching off with plenty of wind-music, were drawn out about the old Château of Brécourt, in the wood-country near Vernon, to meet the Mountain National forces advancing from Paris.   How on the fifteenth afternoon of July, they did meet—and, as it were, shrieked mutually, and took mutually to flight, without loss. How Puisaye thereafter—for the Mountain Nationals fled first, and we thought ourselves the victors—was roused from his warm bed in the Castle of Brécourt; and had to gallop without boots; our Nationals, in the night-watches, having fallen unexpectedly into sauve-qui-peut—and in brief the Calvados War had burnt priming; and the only question now was, Whitherward to vanish, in what hole to hide one's self! [4]

The National Volunteers rush homeward, faster than they came.   The Seventy-two Respectable Departments, says Meillan, " all turned round and forsook us, in the space of four-and-twenty hours."   Unhappy those who, as at Lyons for instance, have gone too far for turning!   " One morning," we find placarded on our Intendance Mansion, the Decree of Convention which casts us Hors la loi, into Outlawry; placarded by our Caen Magistrates—clear hint that we also are to vanish. Vanish indeed: but whitherward? Gorsas has friends in Rennes; he will hide there—unhappily will not lie hid. Guadet, Lanjuinais are on cross roads; making for Bordeaux. To Bordeaux! cries the general voice, of Valour alike and of Despair. Some flag of Respectability still floats there, or is thought to float.

Thitherward therefore; each as he can! Eleven of these ill-fated Deputies, among whom we may count as twelfth, Friend Riouffe the Man of Letters, do an original thing: Take the uniform of National Volunteers, and retreat southward with the Breton Battalion, as private soldiers of that corps. These brave Bretons had stood truer by us than any other. Nevertheless, at the end of a day or two, they also do now get dubious, self-divided; we must part from them; and, with some half-dozen as convoy or guide, retreat by ourselves—a solitary marching detachment, through waste regions of the West.[5]

NOTES

[1] See Hazlitt, ii, 529–541.
[2] Barbaroux, p. 29.
[3] "Deux Amis," x, 345.
[4] "Mémoires de Puisaye" (London, 1803), ii, 142–167.
[5] Louvet, pp. 101–137; Meillan, pp. 81, 241–270.

CHAPTER III

RETREAT OF THE ELEVEN

IT is one of the notablest Retreats, this of the Eleven, that History presents: The handful of forlorn Legislators retreating there, continually, with shouldered firelock and well-filled cartridge-box, in the yellow autumn; long hundreds of miles between them and Bordeaux; the country all getting hostile, suspicious of the truth; simmering and buzzing on all sides, more and more. Louvet has preserved the Itinerary of it; a piece worth all the rest he ever wrote.

O virtuous Pétion, with thy early-white head, O brave young Barbaroux, has it come to this? Weary ways, worn shoes, light purse—encompassed with perils as with a sea! Revolutionary Committees are in every Township; of Jacobin temper; our friends all cowed, our cause the losing one. In the Borough of Moncontour, by ill chance, it is market-day: to the gaping public such transit of a solitary Marching Detachment is suspicious; we have need of energy, of promptitude and luck, to be allowed to march through. Hasten, ye weary pilgrims! The country is getting up; noise of you is bruited day after day, a solitary Twelve retreating in this mysterious manner: with every new day, a wider wave of inquisitive pursuing tumult is stirred up, till the whole West will be in motion. " Cussy is tormented with gout, Buzot is too fat for marching." Riouffe, blistered, bleeding, marches only on tiptoe; Barbaroux limps with sprained ankle, yet even cheery, full of hope and valour. Light Louvet glances hare-eyed, not hare-hearted: only virtuous Pétion's serenity " was but once seen ruffled." [1] They lie in straw-lofts, in woody brakes; rudest paillasse on the floor of a secret friend is luxury. They are seized in the dead of night by Jacobin mayors and tap of drum; get off by firm countenance, rattle of muskets and ready wit.

51   777

Of Bordeaux, through fiery La Vendée and the long geographical spaces that remain, it were madness to think: well if you can get to Quimper on the sea-coast, and take shipping there. Faster, ever faster! Before the end of the march, so hot has the country grown, it is found advisable to march all night. They do it; under the still night-canopy they plod along—and yet behold, Rumour has outplodded them. In the paltry Village of Carhaix (be its thatched huts and bottomless peat-bogs long notable to the Traveller), one is astonished to find light still glimmering: citizens are awake, with rush-lights burning, in that nook of the terrestrial Planet; as we traverse swiftly the one poor street, a voice is heard saying, "There they are, Les voilà qui passent!"[2] Swifter, ye doomed lame Twelve: speed ere they can arm; gain the Woods of Quimper before day, and lie squatted there!

The doomed Twelve do it; though with difficulty, with loss of road, with peril and the mistakes of a night. In Quimper are Girondin friends, who perhaps will harbour the homeless, till a Bordeaux ship weigh. Wayworn, heartworn, in agony of suspense, till Quimper friendship get warning, they lie there, squatted under the thick wet boscage; suspicious of the face of man. Some pity to the brave; to the unhappy! Unhappiest of all Legislators, O when ye packed your luggage, some score or two-score months ago, and mounted this or the other leathern vehicle, to be Conscript Fathers of a regenerated France, and reap deathless laurels—did you think your journey was to lead hither? The Quimper Samaritans find them squatted; lift them up to help and comfort; will hide them in sure places. Thence let them dissipate gradually; or there they can lie quiet, and write Memoirs, till a Bordeaux ship sail.

And thus, in Calvados all is dissipated; Romme is out of prison, meditating his Calendar; ringleaders are locked in his room. At Caen the Corday family mourns in silence: Buzot's House is a heap of dust and demolition; and amid the rubbish sticks a Gallows, with this inscription, "Here dwelt the Traitor Buzot, who conspired against the Republic." Buzot and the other vanished Deputies are hors la loi, as we saw; their lives free to take where they can be found. The worse

fares it with the poor Arrested visible Deputies at Paris.
" Arrestment at home " threatens to become " Confinement in
the Luxembourg "; to end: where? For example, what pale-
visaged thin man is this, journeying toward Switzerland as a
Merchant of Neuchâtel, whom they arrest in the town of
Moulins? To Revolutionary Committee he is suspect. To
Revolutionary Committee, on probing the matter, he is evidently: Deputy Brissot! Back to thy Arrestment, poor
Brissot; or indeed to strait confinement—whither others are
fated to follow. Rabaut has built himself a false-partition,
in a friend's house; lives, in invisible darkness, between two
walls. It will end, this same Arrestment business, in Prison,
and the Revolutionary Tribunal.

Nor must we forget Duperret, and the seal put on his
papers by reason of Charlotte. One Paper is there, fit to
breed wo enough: A secret solemn Protest against that suprema dies of the Second of June! This Secret Protest our
poor Duperret had drawn up, the same week, in all plainness
of speech; waiting the time for publishing it: to which Secret
Protest his signature, and that of other honourable Deputies
not a few, stands legibly appended. And now, if the seals
were once broken, the Mountain still victorious? Such Protesters, your Merciers, Bailleuls, Seventy-three by the tale,
what yet remains of Respectable Girondism in the Convention, may tremble to think!—These are the fruits of levying
civil war.

Also we find, that in these last days of July, the famed
Siege of Mentz is finished: the Garrison to march out with
honours of war; not to serve against the Coalition for a year.
Lovers of the Picturesque, and Goethe standing on the Chaus-
sée of Mentz, saw, with due interest, the Procession issuing
forth, in all solemnity:

" Escorted by Prussian horse came first the French Garrison. Nothing could look stranger than this latter; a column
of Marseillese, slight, swarthy, parti-coloured, in patched
clothes, came tripping on—as if King Edwin had opened the
Dwarf Hill, and sent out his nimble Host of Dwarfs. Next
followed regular troops; serious, sullen; not as if downcast or
ashamed. But the remarkablest appearance, which struck
every one, was that of the Chasers (Chasseurs) coming out
mounted: they had advanced quite silent to where we stood,

when their Band struck up the 'Marseillaise.' This revolutionary Te-Deum has in itself something mournful and bodeful, however briskly played; but at present they gave it in
altogether slow time, proportionate to the creeping step they
rode at. It was piercing and fearful, and a most serious-
looking thing, as these cavaliers, long, lean men, of a certain
age, with mien suitable to the music, came pacing on: singly
you might have likened them to Don Quixote; in mass, they
were highly dignified.

"But now a single troop became notable: that of the Commissioners or Répresentans. Merlin of Thionville, in hussar
uniform, distinguishing himself by wild beard and look, had
another person in similar costume on his left; the crowd
shouted out, with rage, at sight of this latter, the name of a
Jacobin Townsman and Clubbist; and shook itself to seize
him. Merlin drew bridle; referred to his dignity as French
Representative, to the vengeance that should follow any in-
jury done; he would advise every one to compose himself,
for this was not the last time they would see him here." [3]
Thus rode Merlin; threatening in defeat. But what now
shall stem that tide of Prussians setting-in through the
opened Northeast? Lucky if fortified Lines of Weissembourg, and impassabilities of Vosges Mountains confine it
to French Alsace, keep it from submerging the very heart
of the country!

Furthermore, precisely in the same days, Valenciennes
Siege is finished, in the Northwest—fallen, under the red hail
of York! Condé fell some fortnight since. Cimmerian Coalition presses on. "What seems very notable too, on all these
captured French Towns there flies not the Royalist fleur-de-
lys, in the name of a new Louis the Pretender; but the Austrian flag flies; as if Austria meant to keep them for herself!
Perhaps General Custine, still in Paris, can give some explanation of the fall of these strong-places? Mother Society,
from tribune and gallery, growls aloud that he ought to do
it — remarks, however, in a splenetic manner, that "the
Monsieurs of the Palais Royal" are calling Long-life to this
General.

The Mother Society, purged now, by successive "scruti-
nies or épurations," from all taint of Girondism, has become a
great Authority: what we can call shield-bearer or bottle-

holder, nay, call it fugleman, to the purged National Convention itself. The Jacobins Debates are reported in the " Moniteur," like Parliamentary ones.

NOTES

[1] Meillan, pp. 119–137.
[2] Louvet, pp. 138–164.
[3] " Belagerung von Mainz " (Goethe's " Works," xxx, 315).

CHAPTER IV

O NATURE

BUT looking more specially into Paris City, what is this that History, on the 10th of August, Year One of Liberty, " by old-style, year 1793," discerns there? Praised be the Heavens, a new Feast of Pikes!

For Chaumette's " Deputation every day " has worked out its result: a Constitution. It was one of the rapidest Constitutions ever put together; made, some say in eight days, by Hérault Séchelles and others; probably a workmanlike, roadworthy Constitution enough—on which point, however, we are, for some reasons, little called to form a judgment. Workmanlike or not, the Forty-four Thousand Communes of France, by overwhelming majorities, did hasten to accept it; glad of any Constitution whatsoever. Nay, Departmental Deputies have come, the venerablest Republicans of each Department, with solemn message of Acceptance; and now what remains but that our new Final Constitution be proclaimed, and sworn to, in Feast of Pikes? The Departmental Deputies, we say, are come some time ago; Chaumette very anxious about them, lest Girondin Monsieurs, Agio-jobbers, or were it even Filles de joie of a Girondin temper, corrupt their morals.[1] Tenth of August, immortal Anniversary, greater almost than Bastille July, is the Day.

Painter David has not been idle. Thanks to David and the French genius, there steps forth into the sunlight, this day, a Scenic Phantasmagory unexampled—whereof History, so occupied with Real Phantasmagories, will say but little.

For one thing, History can notice with satisfaction, on the ruins of the Bastille, a Statue of Nature; gigantic, spouting water from her two mammelles. Not a Dream this; but a fact, palpable visible. There she spouts, great Nature; dim, before daybreak. But as the coming Sun ruddies the East,

come countless Multitudes, regulated and unregulated; come
Departmental Deputies, come Mother Society and Daughters;
comes National Convention, led on by handsome Hérault;
soft wind-music breathing note of expectation. Lo, as great
Sol scatters his first fire-handful, tipping the hills and chimney-
heads with gold, Hérault is at great Nature's feet (she is
plaster-of-Paris merely); Hérault lifts, in an iron saucer, water
spouted from the sacred breasts; drinks of it, with an eloquent
Pagan Prayer, beginning, " O Nature! " and all the Departmental Deputies drink, each with what best suitable ejaculation
or prophetic-utterance is in him—amid breathings, which become blasts, of wind-music; and the roar of artillery and
human throats: finishing well the first act of this solemnity.

Next are processionings along the Boulevards: Deputies
or Officials bound together by long indivisible tricolor riband;
general " members of the Sovereign " walking pell-mell, with
pikes, with hammers, with the tools and emblems of their
crafts; among which we notice a Plough, and ancient Baucis
and Philemon seated on it, drawn by their children. Many-
voiced harmony and dissonance filling the air. Through
Triumphal Arches enough: at the basis of the first of which,
we descry—whom thinkest thou?—the Heroines of the Insurrection of Women. Strong Dames of the Market, they
sit there (Théroigne too ill to attend, one fears), with oak-
branches, tricolor bedizenment; firm seated on their Cannons.
To whom handsome Hérault, making pause of admiration,
addresses soothing eloquence; whereupon they rise and fall
into the march.

And now mark, in the Place de la Révolution, what other
august Statue may this be; veiled in canvas—which swiftly
we shear off, by pulley and cord? The Statue of Liberty!
She too is of plaster, hoping to become of metal; stands
where a Tyrant Louis Quinze once stood. " Three thousand
birds " are let loose, into the whole world, with labels round
their neck, " We are free; imitate us." Holocaust of Royalist
and ci-devant trumpery, such as one could still gather, is
burnt; pontifical eloquence must be uttered, by handsome
Hérault, and Pagan orizons offered up.

And then forward across the River; where is new enormous Statuary; enormous plaster Mountain; Hercules-Peuple,
with uplifted all-conquering club; " many-headed Dragon of

Girondin Federalism rising from fetid marsh "—needing new eloquence from Hérault. To say nothing of Champ-de-Mars, and Fatherland's Altar there; with urn of slain Defenders, Carpenter's-level of the Law; and such exploding, gesticulating and perorating, that Hérault's lips must be growing white, and his tongue cleaving to the roof of his mouth.[2]

Toward six o'clock let the wearied President, let Paris Patriotism generally sit down to what repast, and social repasts, can be had; and with flowing tankard or light-mantling glass, usher in this New and Newest Era. In fact, is not Romme's New Calendar getting ready? On all house-tops flicker little tricolor Flags, their flagstaff a Pike and Liberty-Cap. On all house-walls—for no Patriot not suspect will be behind another—there stands printed these words: " Republic one and indivisible; Liberty, Equality, Fraternity, or Death!"

As to the New Calendar, we may say here rather than elsewhere that speculative men have long been struck with the inequalities and incongruities of the Old Calendar; that a New one has long been as good as determined on. Maréchal the Atheist, almost ten years ago, proposed a New Calendar, free at least from superstition: this the Paris Municipality would now adopt, in defect of a better; at all events, let us have either this of Maréchal's or a better—the New Era being come. Petitions, more than once, have been sent to that effect; and indeed, for a year past, all Public Bodies, Journalists, and Patriots in general, have dated " First Year of the Republic." It is a subject not without difficulties. But the Convention has taken it up; and Romme, as we say, has been meditating it; not Maréchal's New Calendar, but a better New one of Romme's and our own. Romme, aided by a Monge, a Lagrange and others, furnishes mathematics; Fabre d'Eglantine furnishes poetic nomenclature: and so, on the 5th of October 1793, after trouble enough, they bring forth this New Republican Calendar of theirs, in a complete state; and by Law get it put in action.

Four equal Seasons, Twelve equal Months of Thirty days each; this makes three hundred and sixty days; and five odd days remain to be disposed of. The five odd days we will make Festivals, and name the five Sansculottides, or Days without Breeches. Festival of Genius; Festival of Labour;

of Actions; of Rewards; of Opinion: these are the five Sans-culottides. Whereby the great Circle, or Year, is made complete: solely every fourth year, whilom called Leap-year, we introduce a sixth Sansculottide; and name it Festival of the Revolution. Now as to the day of commencement, which offers difficulties, is it not one of the luckiest coincidences that the Republic herself commenced on the 21st of September; close on the Autumnal Equinox? Autumnal Equinox, at midnight for the meridian of Paris, in the year whilom Christian 1792, from that moment shall the New Era reckon itself to begin. Vendémiaire, Brumaire, Frimaire; or as one might say, in mixed English, Vintagearious, Fogarious, Frostarious: these are our three Autumn months. Nivose, Pluviose, Ventose, or say, Snowous, Rainous, Windous, make our Winter season. Germinal, Floréal, Prairial, or Buddal, Floweral, Meadowal, are our Spring season. Messidor, Thermidor, Fructidor, that is to say (dor being Greek for gift), Reapidor, Heatidor, Fruitidor, are Republican Summer. These Twelve, in a singular manner, divide the Republican Year. Then as to minuter subdivisions, let us venture at once on a bold stroke: adopt your decimal subdivision; and instead of the world-old Week, or Se'ennight, make it a Tennight, or Décade —not without results. There are three Decades, then, in each of the months, which is very regular; and the Décadi, or Tenth-day, shall always be the "Day of Rest." And the Christian Sabbath, in that case? Shall shift for itself!

This, in brief, is the New Calendar of Romme and the Convention; calculated for the meridian of Paris, and Gospel of Jean Jacques: not one of the least afflicting occurrences for the actual British reader of French History—confusing the soul with Messidors, Meadowals; till at last, in self-defence, one is forced to construct some ground-scheme, or rule of Commutation from New-style to Old-style, and have it lying by him. Such ground-scheme, almost worn out in our service, but still legible and printable, we shall now in a Note, present to the reader. For the Romme Calendar, in so many Newspapers, Memoirs, Public Acts, has stamped itself deep into that section of Time: a New Era that lasts some Twelve years and odd is not to be despised.[3] Let the reader, therefore, with such ground-scheme, help himself, where needful, out of New-style into Old-style, called also "slave-style, stile-esclave "—whereof we, in these pages, shall as much as possible use the latter only.

Thus with new Feast of Pikes, and New Era or New Calendar, did France accept her New Constitution: the most Democratic Constitution ever committed to paper. How it will work in practice? Patriot Deputations, from time to time, solicit fruition of it; that it be set a-going. Always, however, this seems questionable; for the moment, unsuitable. Till, in some weeks, Salut Public, through the organ of Saint-Just, makes report, that, in the present alarming circumstances, the state of France is Revolutionary; that her " Government must be Revolutionary till the Peace." Solely as Paper, then, and as a Hope, must this poor new Constitution exist—in which shape we may conceive it lying, even now, with an infinity of other things, in that Limbo near the Moon. Further than paper it never got, nor ever will get.

NOTES

[1] " Deux Amis," xi, 73.
[2] " Choix des Rapports," xii, 432–442.
[3] September 22d of 1792 is Vendémiaire 1st of Year One, and the new months are all of 30 days each; therefore:

		ADD			DAYS
To the number of the day in	Vendémiaire	21	We have the number of the day in	September	30
	Brumaire	21		October	31
	Frimaire	20		November	30
	Nivose	20		December	31
	Pluviose	19		January	31
	Ventose	18		February	28
	Germinal	20		March	31
	Floréal	19		April	30
	Prairial	19		May	31
	Messidor	18		June	30
	Thermidor	18		July	31
	Fructidor	17		August	31

There are 5 Sansculottides, and in leap-year a sixth, to be added at the end of Fructidor. Romme's first Leap-year is " An 4 " (1795, not 1796), which is another troublesome circumstance, every fourth year, from " September 23d " round to " February 29 " again.

The New Calendar ceased on the 1st of January, 1806. See " Choix des Rapports," xiii, 83–99; xix, 199.

CHAPTER V

SWORD OF SHARPNESS

IN fact, it is something quite other than paper theorems, it is iron and audacity that France now needs.

Is not La Vendée still blazing—alas! too literally; rogue Rossignol burning the very corn-mills? General Santerre could do nothing there; General Rossignol, in blind fury, often in liquor, can do less than nothing. Rebellion spreads, grows ever madder. Happily these lean Quixote-figures, whom we saw retreating out of Mentz, "bound not to serve against the Coalition for a year," have got to Paris. National Convention packs them into post-vehicles and conveyances; sends them swiftly, by post, into La Vendée. There valiantly struggling, in obscure battle and skirmish, under rogue Rossignol, let them, unlaureled, save the Republic, and "be cut down gradually to the last man." [1]

Does not the Coalition, like a fire-tide, pour in; Prussia through the opened Northeast; Austria, England through the Northwest? General Houchard prospers no better there than General Custine did: let him look to it! Through the Eastern and the Western Pyrenees Spain has deployed itself; spreads, rustling with Bourbon banners, over the face of the South. Ashes and embers of confused Girondin civil war covered that region already. Marseilles is damped down, not quenched; to be quenched in blood. Toulon, terror-struck, too far gone for turning, has flung itself, ye righteous Powers, into the hands of the English! On Toulon Arsenal there flies a flag—nay, not even the Fleur-de-lys of a Louis Pretender; there flies that accursed St. George's Cross of the English and Admiral Hood! What remnant of sea-craft, arsenals, roperies, war-navy France had, has given itself to these enemies of human nature, "ennemis du genre humain." Beleaguer it, bombard it, ye Commissioners Barras, Fréron,

Robespierre Junior; thou General Cartaux, General Dugommier; above all, thou remarkable Artillery-Major, Napoleon
Buonaparte! Hood is fortifying himself, victualling himself;
means, apparently, to make a new Gibraltar of it.

But lo, in the Autumn night, late night, among the last
of August, what sudden red sunblaze is this that has risen
over Lyons City; with a noise to deafen the world? It is
the Powder-tower of Lyons, nay, the Arsenal with four Pow-
der-towers, which has caught fire in the Bombardment; and
sprung into the air, carrying "a hundred and seventeen
houses" after it. With a light, one fancies, as of the noon
sun; with a roar second only to the Last Trumpet! All living
sleepers far and wide it has awakened. What a sight was that,
which the eye of History saw, in the sudden nocturnal sunblaze! The roofs of hapless Lyons, and all its domes and
steeples made momentarily clear; Rhone and Soane streams
flashing suddenly visible; and height and hollow, hamlet and
smooth stubblefield, and all the region round—heights, alas!
all scarped and counter-scarped, into trenches, curtains, redoubts; blue Artillerymen, little Powder-devilkins, plying their
hell-trade there through the not ambrosial night! Let the
darkness cover it again; for it pains the eye. Of a truth,
Chalier's death is costing the City dear. Convention Commissioners, Lyons Congresses have come and gone; and action
there was and reaction; bad ever growing worse; till it has
come to this; Commissioner Dubois-Crancé, "with seventy-
thousand men, and all the Artillery of several Provinces,"
bombarding Lyons day and night.

Worse things still are in store. Famine is in Lyons, and
ruin and fire. Desperate are the sallies of the besieged; brave
Précy, their National Colonel and Commandant, doing what
is in man: desperate but ineffectual. Provisions cut off; nothing entering our city but shot and shells! The Arsenal has
roared aloft; the very Hospital will be battered down, and the
sick buried alive. A black Flag hung on this latter noble
Edifice, appealing to the pity of the besiegers; for though
maddened, were they not still our brethren? In their blind
wrath, they took it for a flag of defiance, and aimed thitherward the more. Bad is growing ever worse here: and how
will the worse stop, till it have grown worst of all? Commis-

sioner Dubois will listen to no pleading, to no speech, save this only, We surrender at discretion. Lyons contains in it subdued Jacobins; dominant Girondins; secret Royalists. And now, mere deaf madness and cannon-shot, enveloping them, will not the desperate Municipality fly, at last, into the arms of Royalism itself? Majesty of Sardinia was to bring help, but it failed. Emigrant d'Autichamp, in name of the Two Pretender Royal Highnesses, is coming through Switzerland with help; coming, not yet come: Précy hoists the Fleur-de-lys!

At sight of which all true Girondins sorrowfully fling down their arms: Let our Tricolor brethren storm us, then, and slay us in their wrath; with you we conquer not. The famishing women and children are sent forth: deaf Dubois sends them back—rains in mere fire and madness. Our " redoubts of cotton-bags " are taken, retaken; Précy under his Fleur-de-lys is valiant as Despair. What will become of Lyons? It is a siege of seventy days.[2]

Or see, in these same weeks, far in the Western Waters: breasting through the Bay of Biscay, a greasy dingy little Merchant-ship, with Scotch skipper; under hatches whereof sit, disconsolate—the last forlorn nucleus of Girondism, the Deputies from Quimper! Several have dissipated themselves, whithersoever they could. Poor Riouffe fell into the talons of Revolutionary Committee and Paris Prison. The rest sit here under hatches; reverend Pétion with his gray hair, angry Buzot, suspicious Louvet, brave young Barbaroux, and others. They have escaped from Quimper, in this sad craft; are now tacking and struggling; in danger from the waves, in danger from the English, in still worse danger from the French— banished by Heaven and Earth to the greasy belly of this Scotch skipper's Merchant-vessel, unfruitful Atlantic raving round. They are for Bordeaux, if peradventure hope yet linger there. Enter not Bordeaux, O Friends! Bloody Convention Representatives, Tallien and such-like, with their Edicts, with their Guillotine, have arrived there; Respectability is driven under ground; Jacobinism lords it on high. From that Réole landing-place, or Beak of Ambès, as it were, pale Death, waving his Revolutionary Sword of Sharpness, waves you elsewhither!

On one side or the other of that Bec d'Ambès, the Scotch

Skipper with difficulty moors, a dexterous greasy man; with difficulty lands his Girondins—who, after reconnoitering, must rapidly burrow in the Earth; and so, in subterranean ways, in friends' back-closets, in cellars, barn-lofts, in caves of Saint-Emilion and Libourne, stave-off cruel Death.[3] Unhappiest of all Senators!

NOTES

[1] "Deux Amis," xi, 147; xiii, 160–192, etc.
[2] Ibid., 80–143.
[3] Louvet, pp. 180–199.

CHAPTER VI

RISEN AGAINST TYRANTS

AGAINST all which incalculable impediments, horrors and disasters, what can a Jacobin Convention oppose? The uncalculating Spirit of Jacobinism, and Sansculottic sansformulistic Frenzy! Our Enemies press-in on us, says Danton, but they shall not conquer us, " we will burn France to ashes rather, nous brûlerons la France."

Committees, of Sureté, of Salut, have raised themselves " à la hauteur, to the height of circumstances." Let all mortals raise themselves à la hauteur. Let the Forty-four thousand Sections and their Revolutionary Committees stir every fire of the Republic; and every Frenchman feel that he is to do or die. They are the life-circulation of Jacobinism, these Sections and Committees: Danton, through the organ of Barrère and Salut Public, gets decreed, That there be in Paris, by law, two meetings of Section weekly; also that the Poorer Citizen be paid for attending, and have his day's-wages of Forty Sous.[1] This is the celebrated " Law of the Forty Sous "; fiercely stimulant to Sansculottism, to the life-circulation of Jacobinism.

On the twenty-third of August, Committee of Public Salvation, as usual through Barrère, had promulgated, in words not unworthy of remembering, their Report, which is soon made into a Law, of Levy in Mass. " All France, and whatsoever it contains of men or resources, is put under requisition," says Barrère; really in Tyrtæan words, the best we know of his. " The Republic is one vast besieged city." Two-hundred and fifty Forges shall, in these days, be set up in the Luxembourg Garden, and round the outer wall of the Tuileries; to make gun-barrels; in sight of Earth and Heaven! From all hamlets, toward their Departmental Town; from all Departmental Towns, toward the appointed Camp and seat of war, the Sons

791

of Freedom shall march; their banner is to bear: " Le Peuple
Français debout contre les Tyrans, The French People risen
against Tyrants. The young men shall go to the battle; it
is their task to conquer: the married men shall forge arms,
transport baggage and artillery; provide subsistence: the
women shall work at soldier's clothes, make tents; serve in
the hospitals: the children shall scrape old-linen into surgeon's-lint: the aged men shall have themselves carried into
public places, and there, by their words, excite the courage
of the young; preach hatred to Kings and unity to the Republic." [2]   Tyrtæan words; which tingle through all French
hearts.

In this humour, then, since no other serves, will France
rush against its enemies. Headlong, reckoning no cost or
consequence; heeding no law or rule but that supreme law,
Salvation of the People! The weapons are, all the iron that
is in France; the strength is, that of all the men, women, and
children that are in France. There, in their two-hundred and
fifty shed-smithies, in Garden of Luxembourg or Tuileries, let
them forge gun-barrels, in sight of Heaven and Earth.

Nor with heroic daring against the Foreign foe, can black
vengeance against the Domestic be wanting. Life-circulation
of the Revolutionary Committees being quickened by that
Law of the Forty Sous, Deputy Merlin—not the Thionviller,
whom we saw ride out of Mentz, but Merlin of Douai, named
subsequently Merlin Suspect—comes, about a week after, with
his world-famous Law of the Suspect: ordering all Sections,
by their Committees, instantly to arrest all Persons Suspect;
and explaining withal who the Arrestable and Suspect specially are. " Are suspect," says he, " all who by their actions,
by their connections, speakings, writings have "—in short become Suspect.[3]   Nay, Chaumette, illuminating the matter still
further, in his Municipal Placards and Proclamations, will
bring it about that you may almost recognise a Suspect on the
streets, and clutch him there—off to Committee and Prison.
Watch well your words, watch well your looks: if Suspect of
nothing else, you may grow, as came to be a saying, " Suspect
of being Suspect "! For are we not in a state of Revolution?

No frightfuler Law ever ruled in a Nation of men. All
Prisons and Houses of Arrest in French land are getting

crowded to the ridge-tile: Forty-four thousand Committees, like as many companies of reapers or gleaners, gleaning France, are gathering their harvest, and storing it in these Houses. Harvest of Aristocrat tares! Nay, lest the Forty-four thousand, each on its own harvest-field, prove insufficient, we are to have an ambulant "Revolutionary Army": six-thousand strong, under right captains, this shall perambulate the country at large, and strike-in wherever it finds such harvest-work slack. So have Municipality and Mother Society petitioned; so has Convention decreed.[4] Let Aristocrats, Federalists, Monsieurs vanish, and all men tremble: "the Soil of Liberty shall be purged"—with a vengeance!

Neither hitherto has the Revolutionary Tribunal been keeping holiday. Blanchelande, for losing Saint-Domingo; "Conspirators of Orléans," for "assassinating," for assaulting the sacred Deputy Léonard-Bourdon: these with many Nameless, to whom life was sweet, have died. Daily the great Guillotine has its due. Like a black Spectre, daily at even-tide glides the Death-tumbril through the variegated throng of things. The variegated street shudders at it, for the moment; next moment forgets it: The Aristocrats! They were guilty against the Republic; their death, were it only that their goods are confiscated, will be useful to the Republic; "Vive la République!"

In the last days of August fell a notabler head: General Custine's. Custine was accused of harshness, of unskilfulness, perfidiousness; accused of many things: found guilty, we may say, of one thing, unsuccessfulness. Hearing his unexpected Sentence, "Custine fell down before the Crucifix," silent for the space of two hours: he fared, with moist eyes and a look of prayer, toward the Place de la Révolution; glanced upward at the clear suspended axe; then mounted swiftly aloft,[5] swiftly was struck away from the lists of the Living. He had fought in America; he was a proud, brave man; and his fortune led him hither.

On the 2d of this same month, at three in the morning, a vehicle rolled off, with closed blinds, from the Temple to the Conciergerie. Within it were two Municipals; and Marie-Antoinette, once Queen of France! There in that Conciergerie, in ignominious dreary cell, she, secluded from children, kindred, friend and hope, sits long weeks; expecting when the end will be.[6]

52

The Guillotine, we find, gets always a quicker motion, as other things are quickening. The Guillotine, by its speed of going, will give index of the general velocity of the Republic. The clanking of its huge axe, rising and falling there, in horrid systole-diastole, is portion of the whole enormous life-movement and pulsation of the Sansculottic System!—" Orléans Conspirators" and Assaulters had to die, in spite of much weeping and entreating; so sacred is the person of a Deputy. Yet the sacred can become desecrated: your very Deputy is not greater than the Guillotine. Poor Deputy Journalist Gorsas: we saw him hide at Rennes, when the Calvados War burnt priming. He stole, afterward, in August, to Paris; lurked several weeks about the Palais ci-devant Royal; was seen there, one day; was clutched, identified, and without ceremony, being already " out of the Law," was sent to the Place de la Révolution. He died, recommending his wife and children to the pity of the Republic. It is the ninth day of October 1793. Gorsas is the first Deputy that dies on the scaffold; he will not be the last.

Ex-Mayor Bailly is in Prison; Ex-Procureur Manuel. Brissot and our poor Arrested Girondins have become Incarcerated Indicted Girondins; universal Jacobinism clamouring for their punishment. Duperret's Seals are broken! Those Seventy-three Secret Protesters, suddenly one day, are reported upon, are decreed accused; the Convention-doors being " previously shut," that none implicated might escape. They were marched, in a very rough manner, to Prison that evening. Happy those of them who chanced to be absent! Condorcet has vanished into darkness; perhaps, like Rabaut, sits between two walls, in the house of a friend.

NOTES

¹ " Moniteur," Séance du 5 Septembre, 1793.
² " Débats," Séance du 23 Août, 1793.
³ " Moniteur," Séance du 17 Septembre, 1793.
⁴ Ibid., Séances du 5, 9, 11 Septembre.
⁵ " Deux Amis," xi, 148–188.
⁶ See " Mémoires particuliers de la Captivité à la Tour du Temple " (by the Duchesse d'Angoulême, Paris, 21 Janvier, 1817).

CHAPTER VII

MARIE-ANTOINETTE

ON Monday the Fourteenth of October 1793, a Cause
is pending in the Palais de Justice, in the new Revolutionary Court, such as those old stone-walls never
witnessed: the Trial of Marie-Antoinette. The once brightest
of Queens, now tarnished, defaced, forsaken, stands here at
Fouquier-Tinville's Judgment-bar; answering for her life.
The Indictment was delivered her last night.[1] To such changes
of human fortune what words are adequate? Silence alone is
adequate.

There are few Printed things one meets with of such tragic,
almost ghastly, significance as those bald Pages of the " Bulletin du Tribunal Révolutionnaire," which bear title, " Trial of
the Widow Capet." Dim, dim, as in disastrous eclipse; like
the pale kingdoms of Dis! Plutonic Judges, Plutonic Tinville; encircled, nine times, with Styx and Lethe, with Fire-
Phlegethon and Cocytus named of Lamentation! The very
witnesses summoned are like Ghosts: exculpatory, inculpatory,
they themselves are all hovering over death and doom; they
are known, in our imagination, as the prey of the Guillotine.
Tall ci-devant Count d'Estaing, anxious to show himself Patriot, can not escape; nor Bailly, who, when asked If he knows
the Accused, answers with a reverent inclination toward her,
" Ah, yes, I know Madame." Ex-Patriots are here, sharply
dealt with, as Procureur Manuel; ex-Ministers, shorn of their
splendour. We have cold Aristocratic impassivity, faithful to
itself even in Tartarus; rabid stupidity, of Patriot Corporals,
Patriot Washerwomen, who have much to say of Plots, Treasons, August Tenth, old Insurrection of Women. For all now
has become a crime in her who has lost.

Marie-Antoinette, in this her utter abandonment, and hour
of extreme need, is not wanting to herself, the imperial woman.

Her look, they say, as that hideous Indictment was reading, continued calm; " she was sometimes observed moving her fingers, as when one plays on the piano." You discern, not without interest, across that dim Revolutionary Bulletin itself, how she bears herself queenlike. Her answers are prompt, clear, often of Laconic brevity; resolution, which has grown contemptuous without ceasing to be dignified, veils itself in calm words. " You persist, then, in denial? "—" My plan is not denial: it is the truth I have said, and I persist in that." Scandalous Hébert has borne his testimony as to many things: as to one thing, concerning Marie-Antoinette and her little Son —wherewith Human Speech had better not further be soiled. She has answered Hébert; a Juryman begs to observe that she has not answered as to this. " I have not answered," she exclaims with noble emotion, " because Nature refuses to answer such a charge brought against a Mother. I appeal to all the Mothers that are here." Robespierre, when he heard of it, broke out into something almost like swearing at the brutish blockheadism of this Hébert; [2] on whose foul head his foul lie has recoiled. At four o'clock on Wednesday morning, after two days and two nights of interrogating, jury-charging, and other darkening of counsel, the result comes out: sentence of Death. " Have you anything to say? " The Accused shook her head, without speech. Night's candles are burning out; and with her too Time is finishing, and it will be Eternity and Day. This Hall of Tinville's is dark, ill-lighted except where she stands. Silently she withdraws from it, to die.

Two Processions, or Royal Progresses, three-and-twenty years apart, have often struck us with a strange feeling of contrast. The first is of a beautiful Archduchess and Dauphiness, quitting her Mother's City, at the age of Fifteen; toward hopes such as no other Daughter of Eve then had: " On the morrow," says Weber, an eye-witness, " the Dauphiness left Vienna. The whole city crowded out; at first with a sorrow which was silent. She appeared: you saw her sunk back into her carriage; her face bathed in tears; hiding her eyes now with her handkerchief, now with her hands; several times putting out her head to see yet again this Palace of her Fathers, whither she was to return no more. She motioned her regret, her gratitude to the good Nation, which was crowding here to bid her farewell. Then arose not only tears; but piercing cries, on all sides. Men and women alike abandoned themselves to such expression of their sorrow. It was an audible sound of wail, in the streets and avenues of Vienna. The last Courier that followed her disappeared, and the crowd melted away." [3]

The young imperial Maiden of Fifteen has now become a worn discrowned Widow of Thirty-eight; gray before her time: this is the last Procession: " Few minutes after the Trial ended, the drums were beating to arms in all Sections; at sunrise the armed force was on foot, cannons getting placed at the extremities of the Bridges, in the Squares, Crossways, all along from the Palais de Justice to the Place de la Révolution. By ten o'clock, numerous patrols were circulating in the Streets; thirty thousand foot and horse drawn up under arms. At eleven, Marie-Antoinette was brought out. She had on an undress of piqué blanc: she was led to the place of execution, in the same manner as an ordinary criminal; bound, on a Cart; accompanied by a Constitutional Priest in Lay dress; escorted by numerous detachments of infantry and cavalry. These, and the double row of troops all along her road, she appeared to regard with indifference. On her countenance there was visible neither abashment nor pride. To the cries of ' Vive la République ' and ' Down with Tyranny,' which attended her all the way, she seemed to pay no heed. She spoke little to her Confessor. The tricolor Streamers on the housetops occupied her attention, in the Streets du Roule and Saint-Honoré; she also noticed the Inscriptions on the house-fronts. On reaching the Place de la Révolution, her looks turned toward the Jardin National, whilom Tuileries; her face at that moment gave signs of lively emotion. She mounted the Scaffold with courage enough; at a quarter past Twelve, her head fell; the Executioner showed it to the people, amid universal long-continued cries of ' Vive la République! ' " [4]

NOTES

[1] " Procès de la Reine " (" Deux Amis," xi, 251–381).

[2] Villate, " Causes Secrètes de la Révolution de Thermidor " (Paris, 1825), p. 179.

[3] Weber, i, 6.

[4] " Deux Amis," xi, 301.

CHAPTER VIII

THE TWENTY-TWO

WHOM next, O Tinville! The next are of a different colour: our poor Arrested Girondin Deputies. What of them could still be laid hold of; our Vergniaud, Brissot, Fauchet, Valazé, Gensonné; the once flower of French Patriotism, Twenty-two by the tale: hither, at Tinville's Bar, onward from " safeguard of the French People," from confinement in the Luxembourg, imprisonment in the Conciergerie, have they now, by the course of things, arrived. Fouquier-Tinville must give what account of them he can.

Undoubtedly this Trial of the Girondins is the greatest that Fouquier has yet had to do. Twenty-two, all chief Republicans, ranged in a line there; the most eloquent in France; Lawyers too; not without friends in the auditory. How will Tinville prove these men guilty of Royalism, Federalism, Conspiracy against the Republic? Vergniaud's eloquence awakes once more; " draws tears," they say. And Journalists report, and the Trial lengthens itself out day after day; " threatens to become eternal," murmur many. Jacobinism and Municipality rise to the aid of Fouquier. On the 28th of the month, Hébert and others come in deputation to inform a Patriot Convention that the Revolutionary Tribunal is quite " shackled by Forms of Law "; that a Patriot Jury ought to have " the power of cutting short, of terminer les débats, when they feel themselves convinced." Which pregnant suggestion, of cutting short, passes itself, with all despatch, into a Decree.

Accordingly, at ten o'clock on the night of the 30th of October, the Twenty-two, summoned back once more, receive this information, That the Jury feeling themselves convinced have cut short, have brought in their verdict; that the Accused are found guilty, and the Sentence on one and all of them is, Death with confiscation of goods.

Loud natural clamour rises among the poor Girondins; tumult; which can only be repressed by the gendarmes. Valazé stabs himself; falls down dead on the spot. The rest, amid loud clamour and confusion, are driven back to their Conciergerie; Lasource exclaiming, "I die on the day when the People have lost their reason; ye will die when they recover it."[1] No help! Yielding to violence, the Doomed uplift the Hymn of the Marseillese; return singing to their dungeon.

Riouffe, who was their Prison-mate in these last days, has lovingly recorded what death they made. To our notions, it is not an edifying death. Gay satirical Pot-pourri by Ducos; rhymed Scenes of Tragedy, wherein Barrère and Robespierre discourse with Satan; death's eve spent in " singing " and " sallies of gaiety," with " discourses on the happiness of peoples ": these things, and the like of these, we have to accept for what they are worth. It is the manner in which the Girondins make their Last Supper. Valazé, with bloody breast, sleeps cold in death; hears not the singing. Vergniaud has his dose of poison; but it is not enough for his friends, it is enough only for himself; wherefore he flings it from him; presides at this Last Supper of the Girondins, with wild coruscations of eloquence, with song and mirth. Poor human Will struggles to assert itself; if not in this way, then in that.[2]

But on the morrow morning all Paris is out; such a crowd as no man had seen. The Death-carts, Valazé's cold corpse stretched among the yet living Twenty-one, roll along. Bareheaded, hands bound; in their shirt-sleeves, coat flung loosely round the neck: so fare the eloquent of France; bemurmured, beshouted. To the shouts of " Vive la République! " some of them keep answering with counter-shouts of " Vive la République! " Others, as Brissot, sit sunk in silence. At the foot of the scaffold they again strike up, with appropriate variations, the Hymn of the Marseillese. Such an act of music; conceive it well! The yet Living chant there; the chorus so rapidly wearing weak! Samson's axe is rapid; one head per minute, or little less. The chorus is wearing weak; the chorus is worn out—farewell for evermore, ye Girondins. Te-Deum Fauchet has become silent; Valazé's dead head is lopped:

the sickle of the Guillotine has reaped the Girondins all away.
" The eloquent, the young, the beautiful and brave!" exclaims
Riouffe. O Death, what feast is toward in thy ghastly Halls!

Nor, alas! in the far Bordeaux region will Girondism fare
better. In caves of Saint-Emilion, in loft and cellar, the
weariest months roll on; apparel worn, purse empty; wintry
November come; under Tallien and his Guillotine, all hope
now gone. Danger drawing ever nigher, difficulty pressing
ever straiter, they determine to separate. Not unpathetic the
farewell; tall Barbaroux, cheeriest of brave men, stoops to
clasp his Louvet: " In what place soever thou findest my
Mother," cries he, " try to be instead of a son to her: no
resource of mine but I will share with thy Wife, should chance
ever lead me where she is." [3]

Louvet went with Guadet, with Salles and Valadi; Barbaroux with Buzot and Pétion. Valadi soon went southward,
on a way of his own. The two friends and Louvet had a
miserable day and night; the 14th of the November month,
1793. Sunk in wet, weariness, and hunger, they knock, on
the morrow, for help, at a friend's country-house; the faint-
hearted friend refuses to admit them. They stood therefore
under trees, in the pouring rain. Flying desperate, Louvet
thereupon will to Paris. He sets forth, there and then, splash-
ing the mud on each side of him, with a fresh strength gathered from fury or frenzy. He passes villages, finding " the
sentry asleep in his box in the thick rain"; he is gone, before
the man can call after him. He bilks Revolutionary Committees; rides in carriers' carts, covered carts and open; lies
hidden in one, under knapsacks and cloaks of soldiers' wives
on the Street of Orléans, while men search for him; has
hairbreadth escapes that would fill three romances: finally he
gets to Paris to his fair Helpmate; gets to Switzerland, and
waits better days.

Poor Guadet and Salles were both taken, ere long; they
died by the Guillotine in Bordeaux; drums beating to drown
their voice. Valadi also is caught, and guillotined. Barbaroux
and his two comrades weathered it longer, into the summer
of 1794; but not long enough. One July morning, changing
their hiding-place, as they have often to do, " about a league
from Saint-Emilion, they observe a great crowd of country-
people": doubtless Jacobins come to take them? Barbaroux

draws a pistol, shoots himself dead. Alas! and it was not Jacobins; it was harmless villagers going to a village wake. Two days afterward, Buzot and Pétion were found in a Corn-field, their bodies half-eaten by dogs.[4]

Such was the end of Girondism. They arose to regenerate France, these men; and have accomplished this. Alas! whatever quarrel we had with them, has not their cruel fate abolished it? Pity only survives. So many excellent souls of heroes sent down to Hades; they themselves given as a prey of dogs and all manner of birds! But, here too, the will of the Supreme Power was accomplished. As Vergniaud said: "the Revolution, like Saturn, is devouring its own children."

NOTES

[1] Δημοσθένους εἰπόντος, Ἀποκτενοῦσί σε Ἀθηναῖοι, Φωκίων· Ἂν μανῶσιν, εἶπε σὲ δ᾽, ἐάν σωφρονῶσι.—Plut., " Opp.," t. iv, p. 310, ed. Reiske, 1776.

[2] " Mémoires de Riouffe " (in " Mémoires sur les Prisons," Paris, 1823), pp. 48–55.

[3] Louvet, p. 213.

[4] " Recherches Historiques sur les Girondins " (in " Mémoires de Buzot "), p. 107.

Book XVIII

TERROR THE ORDER OF THE DAY

CHAPTER I

RUSHING DOWN

WE are now, therefore, got to that black precipitous Abyss; whither all things have long been tending; where, having now arrived on the giddy verge, they hurl down, in confused ruin; headlong, pellmell, down, down— till Sansculottism have consummated itself; and in this wondrous French Revolution, as in a Doomsday, a World have been rapidly, if not born again, yet destroyed and engulfed. Terror has long been terrible: but to the actors themselves it has now become manifest that their appointed course is one of Terror; and they say, Be it so. " Que la Terreur soit à l'ordre du jour."

So many centuries, say only from Hugh Capet downward, had been adding together, century transmitting it with increase to century, the sum of Wickedness, of Falsehood, Oppression of man by man. Kings were sinners, and Priests were, and People. Open Scoundrels rode triumphant, bediademed, becoronetted, bemitred; or the still fataler species of Secret-Scoundrels, in their fair-sounding formulas, speciosities, respectabilities, hollow within: the race of Quacks was grown many as the sands of the sea. Till at length such a sum of Quackery had accumulated itself as, in brief, the Earth and the Heavens were weary of. Slow seemed the Day of Settlement; coming on, all imperceptible, across the bluster and fanfaronade of Courtierisms, Conquering-Heroisms, Most Christian Grand Monarque-isms, Well-beloved Pompadour-isms: yet behold it was always coming; behold it has come, suddenly, unlooked for by any man! The harvest of long centuries was ripening and whitening so rapidly of late; and now it is grown white, and is reaped rapidly, as it were, in one day. Reaped, in this Reign of Terror; and carried home, to Hades and the Pit!—Unhappy Sons of Adam: it is ever

so; and never do they know it, nor will they know it. With
cheerfully smoothed countenances, day after day, and generation after generation, they, calling cheerfully to one another,
Well-speed-ye, are at work, sowing the wind. And yet, as
God lives, they shall reap the whirlwind: no other thing, we
say, is possible—since God is a Truth, and His World is
a Truth.

History, however, in dealing with this Reign of Terror, has
had her own difficulties. While the Phenomenon continued
in its primary state, as mere " Horrors of the French Revolution," there was abundance to be said and shrieked. With
and also without profit. Heaven knows, there were terrors
and horrors enough: yet that was not all the Phenomenon;
nay, more properly, that was not the Phenomenon at all, but
rather was the shadow of it, the negative part of it. And
now, in a new stage of the business, when History, ceasing to
shriek, would try rather to include under her old Forms of
speech or speculation this new amazing Thing; that so some
accredited scientific Law of Nature might suffice for the unexpected Product of Nature, and History might get to speak of
it articulately, and draw inferences and profit from it; in this
new stage, History, we must say, babbles and flounders perhaps in a still painfuler manner. Take, for example, the latest
Form of speech we have seen propounded on the subject as
adequate to it, almost in these months, by our worthy M.
Roux, in his "Histoire Parlementaire." The latest and the
strangest: that the French Revolution was a dead-lift effort,
after eighteen hundred years of preparation, to realize—the
Christian Religion![1] Unity, Indivisibility, Brotherhood or
Death, did indeed stand printed on all Houses of the Living;
also on Cemeteries, or Houses of the Dead, stood printed, by
order of Procureur Chaumette, " Here is Eternal Sleep ":[2] but
a Christian Religion realized by the Guillotine and Death-
Eternal " is suspect to me," as Robespierre was wont to say,
" m'est suspecte."
Alas! no, M. Roux! A Gospel of Brotherhood, not according to any of the Four old Evangelists, and calling on
men to repent, and amend each his own wicked existence, that
they might be saved; but a Gospel rather, as we often hint,
according to a new Fifth Evangelist Jean-Jacques, calling on

men to amend each the whole world's wicked existence, and
be saved by making the Constitution. A thing different and
distant toto cælo, as they say: the whole breadth of the sky,
and farther if possible!—It is thus, however, that History,
and indeed all human Speech and Reason does yet, what
Father Adam began life by doing: strive to name the new
Thing it sees of Nature's producing—often helplessly enough.

But what if History were to admit, for once, that all the
Names and Theorems yet known to her fall short? That
this grand Product of Nature was even grand, and new, in
that it came not to range itself under old recorded Laws of
Nature at all, but to disclose new ones? In that case, History, renouncing the pretension to name it at present, will
look honestly at it, and name what she can of it! Any ap-
proximation to the right Name has value: were the right
Name itself once here, the Thing is known henceforth; the
Thing is then ours, and can be dealt with.

Now surely not realization, of Christianity or of aught
earthly, do we discern in this Reign of Terror, in this French
Revolution of which it is the consummating. Destruction
rather we discern—of all that was destructible. It is as if
Twenty-five millions, risen at length into the Pythian mood,
had stood up simultaneously to say, with a sound which goes
through far lands and times, that this Untruth of an Existence had become insupportable. O ye Hypocrisies and Speciosities, Royal mantles, Cardinal plush-cloaks, ye Credos,
Formulas, Respectabilities, fair-painted Sepulchres full of dead
men's bones—behold, ye appear to us to be altogether a Lie.
Yet our Life is not a Lie; yet our Hunger and Misery is not
a Lie! Behold, we lift up, one and all, our Twenty-five million
right-hands; and take the Heavens, and the Earth and also
the Pit of Tophet to witness, that either ye shall be abolished,
or else we shall be abolished!

No inconsiderable Oath, truly; forming, as has been often
said, the most remarkable transaction in these last thousand
years. Wherefrom likewise there follow, and will follow, results. The fulfilment of this Oath; that is to say, the black
desperate battle of Men against their whole Condition and
Environment—a battle, alas! withal, against the Sin and Darkness that was in themselves as in others: this is the Reign of
Terror. Transcendental despair was the purport of it, though

not consciously so. False hopes of Fraternity, Political Millennium, and what not, we have always seen: but the unseen heart of the whole, the transcendental despair, was not false; neither has it been of no effect. Despair, pushed far enough, completes the circle, so to speak; and becomes a kind of genuine productive hope again.

Doctrine of Fraternity, out of old Catholicism, does, it is true, very strangely in the vehicle of a Jean-Jacques Evangel, suddenly plump down out of its cloud-firmament; and from a theorem determine to make itself a practice. But just so do all creeds, intentions, customs, knowledges, thoughts, and things, which the French have, suddenly plump down; Catholicism, Classicism, Sentimentalism, Cannibalism; all isms that make up Man in France are rushing and roaring in that gulf; and the theorem has become a practice, and whatsoever can not swim sinks. Not Evangelist Jean-Jacques alone; there is not a Village Schoolmaster but has contributed his quota: do we not "thou" one another, according to the Free Peoples of Antiquity? The French Patriot, in red Phrygian nightcap of Liberty, christens his poor little red infant Cato—Censor, or else of Utica. Gracchus has become Babœuf, and edits Newspapers; Mutius Scævola, Cordwainer of that ilk, presides in the Section Mutius-Scævola: and in brief, there is a world wholly jumbling itself, to try what will swim.

Wherefore we will, at all events, call this Reign of Terror a very strange one. Dominant Sansculottism makes, as it were, free arena; one of the strangest temporary states Humanity was ever seen in. A nation of men, full of wants and void of habits! The old habits are gone to wreck because they were old: men, driven forward by Necessity and fierce Pythian Madness, have, on the spur of the instant, to devise for the want the way of satisfying it. The Wonted tumbles down; by imitation, by invention, the Unwonted hastily builds itself up. What the French National head has in it comes out: if not a great result, surely one of the strangest.

Neither shall the Reader fancy that it was all black, this Reign of Terror: far from it. How many hammermen and squaremen, bakers and brewers, washers and wringers, over this France, must ply their old daily work, let the Government be one of Terror or one of Joy! In this Paris there are

Twenty-three Theatres nightly; some count as many as Sixty Places of Dancing.[3]   The Playwright manufactures—pieces of a strictly Republican character. Ever fresh Novel-garbage, as of old, fodders the Circulating Libraries.[4] The " Cesspool of Agio," now in a time of Paper Money, works with a vivacity unexampled, unimagined; exhales from itself " sudden fortunes," like Aladdin-Palaces : really a kind of miraculous Fata-Morganus, since you can live in them, for a time. Terror is as a sable ground, on which the most variegated of scenes paints itself. In startling transitions, in colours all intensated, the sublime, the ludicrous, the horrible succeed one another; or rather, in crowding tumult, accompany one another.

Here, accordingly, if anywhere, the " hundred tongues," which the old Poets often clamour for, were of supreme service! In defect of any such organ on our part, let the Reader stir up his own imaginative organ : let us snatch for him this or the other significant glimpse of things, in the fittest sequence we can.

NOTES

[1] " Hist. Parl." (Introd.), i, 1 et seq.
[2] " Deux Amis," xii, 78.
[3] Mercier, ii, 124.
[4] " Moniteur " of these months, passim.

CHAPTER II

DEATH

IN the early days of November there is one transient glimpse of things that is to be noted: the last transit to his long home of Philippe d'Orléans Égalité. Philippe was " decreed accused," along with the Girondins, much to his and their surprise; but not tried along with them. They are doomed and dead, some three days, when Philippe, after his long half-year of durance at Marseilles, arrives in Paris. It is, as we calculate, the third of November 1793.

On which same day, two notable Female Prisoners are also put in ward there: Dame Dubarry and Josephine Beauharnais. Dame whilom Countess Dubarry, Unfortunate-female, had returned from London; they snatched her, not only as Exharlot of a whilom Majesty, and therefore Suspect; but as having "furnished the Emigrants with money." Contemporaneously with whom there comes the wife Beauharnais, soon to be the widow: she that is Josephine Tascher Beauharnais; that shall be Josephine Empress Buonaparte—for a black Divineress of the Tropics prophesied long since that she should be a Queen and more. Likewise, in the same hours, poor Adam Lux, nigh turned in the head, who, according to Forster, " has taken no food these three weeks," marches to the Guillotine for his Pamphlet on Charlotte Corday: he " sprang to the scaffold "; said " he died for her with great joy." Amid such fellow-travellers does Philippe arrive. For, be the month named Brumaire year 2 of Liberty, or November year 1793 of Slavery, the Guillotine goes always, Guillotine va toujours.

Enough, Philippe's indictment is soon drawn, his jury soon convinced. He finds himself made guilty of Royalism, Conspiracy and much else; nay, it is a guilt in him that he voted Louis's Death, though he answers, " I voted in my soul and conscience." The doom he finds is death forthwith; this present 6th dim day of November is the last day that Philippe is to see. Philippe, says Montgaillard, thereupon called for breakfast: sufficiency of " oysters, two cutlets, best part of an excellent bottle of claret "; and consumed the same with apparent relish. A Revolutionary Judge, or some official Convention Emissary, then arrived, to signify that he might still do the State some service by revealing the truth about a plot or two. Philippe answered that, on him, in the pass things had come to, the State had, he thought, small claim; that nevertheless, in the interest of Liberty, he, having still some leisure on his hands, was willing, were a reasonable question asked him, to give a reasonable answer. And so, says Montgaillard, he leant his elbow on the mantel-piece, and conversed in an undertone, with great seeming composure; till the leisure was done, or the Emissary went his ways.

At the door of the Conciergerie, Philippe's attitude was erect and easy, almost commanding. It is five years, all but a few days, since Philippe, within these same stone walls, stood up with an air of graciosity, and asked King Louis, " Whether it was a Royal Session, then, or a Bed of Justice? " O Heaven!—Three poor blackguards were to ride and die with him: some say, they objected to such company, and had to be flung in neck and heels;[1] but it seems not true. Objecting or not objecting, the gallows-vehicle gets under way. Philippe's dress is remarked for its elegance; green frock, waistcoat of white piqué, yellow buckskins, boots clear as Warren: his air, as before, entirely composed, impassive, not to say easy and Brummellean-polite. Through street after street; slowly, amid execrations—past the Palais Égalité, whilom Palais Royal! The cruel Populace stopped him there, some minutes: Dame de Buffon, it is said, looked out on him, in Jezebel head-tire; along the ashlar Wall there ran these words in huge tricolor print, " Republic one and indivisible; Liberty, Equality, Fraternity or Death: National Property." Philippe's eyes flashed hellfire, one instant; but the next instant it was gone, and he sat impassive, Brummellean-polite. On the scaffold, Samson was for drawing off his boots: " Tush," said Philippe, " they will come better off after; let us have done, dépêchons-nous! "

So Philippe was not without virtue, then? God forbid that there should be any living man without it! He had the virtue to keep living for five-and-forty years—other virtues perhaps more than we know of. But probably no mortal ever had such things recorded of him: such facts, and also such lies. For he was a Jacobin Prince of the Blood; consider what a combination! Also, unlike any Nero, any Borgia, he lived in the Age of Pamphlets. Enough for us: Chaos has reabsorbed him; may it late or never bear his like again! —Brave young Orléans Égalité, deprived of all, only not deprived of himself, is gone to Coire in the Grisons, under the name of Corby, to teach Mathematics. The Égalité Family is at the darkest depths of the Nadir.

A far nobler Victim follows; one who will claim remembrance from several centuries: Jeanne-Marie Phlipon, the Wife of Roland. Queenly, sublime in her uncomplaining sorrow, seemed she to Riouffe in her Prison. "Something more than is usually found in the looks of women painted itself," says Riouffe,[2] "in those large black eyes of hers, full of expression and sweetness. She spoke to me often, at the Grate: we were all attentive round her, in a sort of admiration and astonishment; she expressed herself with a purity, with a harmony and prosody that made her language like music, of which the ear could never have enough. Her conversation was serious, not cold; coming from the mouth of a beautiful woman, it was frank and courageous as that of a great man." "And yet her maid said: 'Before you, she collects her strength; but in her own room, she will sit three hours sometimes leaning on the window, and weeping.'" She has been in Prison, liberated once, but recaptured the same hour, ever since the first of June: in agitation and uncertainty; which has gradually settled down into the last stern certainty, that of death. In the Abbaye Prison, she occupied Charlotte Corday's apartment. Here in the Conciergerie, she speaks with Riouffe, with Ex-Minister Clavière; calls the beheaded Twenty-two "Nos amis, our Friends"—whom we are soon to follow. During these five months, those "Memoirs" of hers were written, which all the world still reads.

But now, on the 8th of November, "clad in white," says Riouffe, "with her long black hair hanging down to her girdle," she is gone to the Judgment-bar. She returned with a quick step; lifted her finger, to signify to us that she was doomed: her eyes seemed to have been wet. Fouquier-Tinville's questions had been "brutal"; offended female honour flung them back on him, with scorn, not without tears. And now, short preparation soon done, she too shall go her last road. There went with her a certain Lamarche, "Director of Assignat-printing"; whose dejection she endeavoured to cheer. Arrived at the foot of the scaffold, she asked for pen and paper, "to write the strange thoughts that were rising in her":[3] a remarkable request; which was refused. Looking at the Statue of Liberty which stands there, she says bitterly: "O Liberty, what things are done in thy name!" For Lamarche's sake, she will die first; show him how easy it is to die: "Contrary to the order," said Samson.—"Pshaw, you can not refuse the last request of a Lady"; and Samson yielded.

Noble white Vision, with its high queenly face, its soft proud eyes, long black hair flowing down to the girdle; and as brave a heart as ever beat in woman's bosom! Like a white Grecian Statue, serenely complete, she shines in that black wreck of things—long memorable. Honour to great Nature who, in Paris City, in the Era of Noble-Sentiment and Pompadourism, can make a Jeanne Phlipon, and nourish her to clear perennial Womanhood, though but on Logics, Encyclopédies, and the Gospel according to Jean-Jacques! Biography will long remember that trait of asking for a pen "to write the strange thoughts that were rising in her." It is, as a little light-beam, shedding softness, and a kind of sacredness, over all that preceded: so in her too there was an Unnameable; she too was a Daughter of the Infinite; there were mysteries which Philosophism had not dreamt of!—She left long written counsels to her little Girl; she said her Husband would not survive her.

Still crueler was the fate of poor Bailly, First National President, First Mayor of Paris: doomed now for Royalism, Fayettism; for that Red-Flag Business of the Champ-de-Mars —one may say in general, for leaving his Astronomy to meddle with Revolution. It is the 10th of November 1793, a cold, bitter drizzling rain, as poor Bailly is led through the streets; howling Populace covering him with curses, with mud; waving over his face a burning or smoking mockery of a Red Flag. Silent, unpitied, sits the innocent old man. Slow faring through the sleety drizzle, they have got to the Champ-de-

Mars: Not there! vociferates the cursing Populace; such Blood ought not to stain an Altar of the Fatherland: not there; but on that dung-heap by the River-side! So vociferates the cursing Populace; Officiality gives ear to them. The Guillotine is taken down, though with hands numbed by the sleety drizzle; is carried to the River-side; is there set up again, with slow numbness; pulse after pulse still counting itself out in the old man's weary heart. For hours long; amid curses and bitter frost-rain! "Bailly, thou tremblest," said one. "Mon ami, it is for cold," said Bailly, "c'est de froid." Crueler end had no mortal.[4]

Some days afterward, Roland, hearing the news of what happened on the 8th, embraces his kind Friends at Rouen, leaves their kind house which had given him refuge; goes forth, with farewell too sad for tears. On the morrow morning, 16th of the month, "some four leagues from Rouen, Paris-ward, near Bourg-Baudoin, in M. Normand's Avenue," there is seen sitting leant against a tree the figure of a rigorous wrinkled man; stiff now in the rigour of death; a cane-sword run through his heart; and at his feet this writing: "Whoever thou art that findest me lying, respect my remains: they are those of a man who consecrated all his life to being useful; and who has died as he lived, virtuous and honest." "Not fear, but indignation, made me quit my retreat, on learning that my Wife had been murdered. I wished not to remain longer on an Earth polluted with crimes."[5]

Barnave's appearance at the Revolutionary Tribunal was of the bravest; but it could not stead him. They have sent for him from Grenoble; to pay the common smart. Vain is eloquence, forensic or other, against the dumb Clotho-shears of Tinville. He is still but two-and-thirty, this Barnave, and has known such changes. Short while ago, we saw him at the top of Fortune's wheel, his word a law to all Patriots: and now surely he is at the bottom of the wheel; in stormful altercation with a Tinville Tribunal, which is dooming him to die![6] And Pétion, once also of the Extreme Left, and named "Pétion Virtue," where is he? Civilly dead; in the Caves of Saint-Emilion; to be devoured of dogs. And Robespierre, who rode along with him on the shoulders of the people, is in Committee of Salut; civilly alive: not to live always. So giddy-swift whirls and spins this immeasurable tormentum of a Revolution; wild-booming; not to be followed by the eye. Barnave, on the scaffold, stamped with his foot; and looking upward was heard to ejaculate, " This, then, is my reward ! "

Deputy Ex-Procureur Manuel is already gone ; and Deputy Osselin, famed also in August and September, is about to go: and Rabaut, discovered treacherously between his two walls, and the Brother of Rabaut. National Deputies not a few ! And Generals: the memory of General Custine can not be defended by his Son ; his Son is already guillotined. Custine the Ex-Noble was replaced by Houchard the Plebeian: he too could not prosper in the North; for him too there was no mercy; he has perished in the Place de la Révolution, after attempting suicide in Prison. And Generals Biron, Beauharnais, Brunet, whatsoever General prospers not; tough old Lückner, with his eyes grown rheumy; Alsatian Westermann, valiant and diligent in La Vendée: " none of them can," as the Psalmist sings, " his soul from death deliver."

How busy are the Revolutionary Committees; Sections with their Forty Halfpence a-day ! Arrestment on arrestment falls quick, continual; followed by death. Ex-Minister Clavière has killed himself in Prison. Ex-Minister Lebrun, seized in a hay-loft, under the disguise of a working man, is instantly conducted to death.[7] Nay, withal, is it not what Barrère calls " coining money on the Place de la Révolution "? For always the " property of the guilty, if property he have," is confiscated. To avoid accidents, we even make a Law that suicide shall not defraud us; that a criminal who kills himself does not the less incur forfeiture of goods. Let the guilty tremble, therefore, and the suspect, and the rich, and in a word all manner of Culottic men ! Luxembourg Palace, once Monsieur's, has become a huge loathsome Prison; Chantilly Palace too, once Condé's: And their landlords are at Blackenberg, on the wrong side of the Rhine. In Paris are now some Twelve Prisons; in France some Forty-four Thousand: thitherward, thick as brown leaves in Autumn, rustle and travel the suspect; shaken down by Revolutionary Committees, they are swept thitherward, as into their storehouse —to be consumed by Samson and Tinville. " The Guillotine goes not ill, La Guillotine ne va pas mal."

Notes

[1] Forster, ii, 628; Montgaillard, iv, 141–157.
[2] "Mémoires" (sur les "Prisons," i), pp. 55–57.
[3] "Mémoires de Madame Roland" (Introd.), i, 68.
[4] "Vie de Bailly" (in "Mémoires," i), p. 29.
[5] "Mémoires de Madame Roland" (Introd.), i, 88.
[6] Forster, ii, 629.
[7] "Moniteur," 11, 30 Décembre 1793; Louvet, p. 287.

CHAPTER III

DESTRUCTION

THE suspect may well tremble; but how much more the open rebels—the Girondin Cities of the South! Revolutionary Army is gone forth, under Ronsin the Playwright; six thousand strong; " in red nightcap, in tricolor waistcoat, in black-shag trousers, black-shag spencer, with enormous mustachioes, enormous sabre—in carmagnole complète ";[1] and has portable guillotines. Representative Carrier has got to Nantes, by the edge of blazing La Vendée, which Rossignol has literally set on fire: Carrier will try what captives you make; what accomplices they have, Royalist or Girondin: his guillotine goes always, va toujours; and his wool-capped " Company of Marat." Little children are guillotined, and aged men. Swift as the machine is, it will not serve; the Headsman and all his valets sink, worn down with work; declare that the human muscles can no more.[2] Whereupon you must try fusillading; to which perhaps still frightfuler methods may succeed.

In Brest, to like purpose, rules Jean-Bon Saint-André; with an Army of Red Nightcaps. In Bordeaux rules Tallien, with his Isabeau and henchmen; Guadets, Cusseys, Salleses, many fall; the bloody Pike and Nightcap bearing supreme sway; the Guillotine coining money. Bristly fox-haired Tallien, once Able-Editor, still young in years, is now become most gloomy, potent; a Pluto on Earth, and has the keys of Tartarus. One remarks, however, that a certain Senhorina Cabarus, or call her rather Senhora and wedded not yet widowed Dame de Fontenai, brown beautiful woman, daughter of Cabarus the Spanish Merchant—has softened the red bristly countenance; pleading for herself and friends; and prevailing. The keys of Tartarus, or any kind of power, are something to a woman; gloomy Pluto himself is not insensible to love.

Like a new Proserpine, she, by this red gloomy Dis, is gathered; and, they say, softens his stone heart a little.

Maignet, at Orange in the South; Lebon, at Arras in the North, become world's wonders. Jacobin Popular Tribunal, with its National Representative, perhaps where Girondin Popular Tribunal had lately been, rises here and rises there; wheresoever needed. Fouchés, Maignets, Barrases, Frérons scour the Southern Departments; like reapers, with their guillotine-sickle. Many are the labourers, great is the harvest. By the hundred and the thousand, men's lives are cropt; cast like brands into the burning.

Marseilles is taken, and put under martial law: lo, at Marseilles, what one besmutted red-bearded corn-ear is this which they cut—one gross Man, we mean, with copper-studded face; plenteous beard, or beard-stubble, of a tile-colour? By Nemesis and the Fatal Sisters, it is Jourdan Coupe-tête! Him they have clutched, in these martial-law districts; him too, with their "national razor," their rasoir national, they sternly shave away. Low now is Jourdan the Headsman's own head—low as Deshuttes's and Varigny's, which he sent on pikes, in the Insurrection of Women! No more shall he, as a copper Portent, be seen gyrating through the Cities of the South; no more sit judging, with pipes and brandy, in the Ice-tower of Avignon. The all-hiding Earth has received him, the bloated Tilebeard: may we never look upon his like again!—Jourdan one names; the other Hundreds are not named. Alas! they, like confused fagots, lie massed together for us; counted by the cart-load: and yet not an individual fagot-twig of them but had a Life and History; and was cut, not without pangs as when a Kaiser dies!

Least of all cities can Lyons escape. Lyons, which we saw in dread sunblaze, that Autumn night when the Powder-tower sprang aloft, was clearly verging toward a sad end. Inevitable: what could desperate valour and Précy do; Dubois-Crancé, deaf as Destiny, stern as Doom, capturing their "redoubts of cotton-bags": hemming them in, ever closer, with his Artillery-lava? Never would that ci-devant D'Autichamp arrive; never any help from Blankenberg. The Lyons Jacobins were hidden in cellars; the Girondin Municipality waxed pale, in famine, treason, and red fire. Précy drew his sword, and some Fifteen Hundred with him; sprang to saddle, to cut their way to Switzerland. They cut fiercely; and were fiercely cut, and cut down; not hundreds, hardly units of them ever saw Switzerland.[3] Lyons, on the 9th of October, surrenders at discretion; it is become a devoted Town. Abbé Lamourette, now Bishop Lamourette, whilom Legislator, he of the old Baiser-l'Amourette or Delilah-Kiss, is seized here; is sent to Paris to be guillotined: " he made the sign of the cross," they say, when Tinville intimated his death-sentence to him; and died as an eloquent Constitutional Bishop. But wo now to all Bishops, Priests, Aristocrats, and Federalists that are in Lyons! The manes of Chalier are to be appeased; the Republic, maddened to the Sibylline pitch, has bared her right arm. Behold! Representative Fouché, it is Fouché of Nantes, a name to become well known; he with a Patriot company goes duly, in wondrous Procession, to raise the corpse of Chalier. An Ass housed in Priest's cloak, with a mitre on his head, and trailing the Mass-Books, some say the very Bible, at its tail, paces through the Lyons streets: escorted by multitudinous Patriotism, by clangour as of the Pit; toward the grave of Martyr Chalier. The body is dug up, and burnt: the ashes are collected in an Urn; to be worshipped of Paris Patriotism. The Holy Books were part of the funeral pile; their ashes are scattered to the wind. Amid cries of " Vengeance! Vengeance!"—which, writes Fouché, shall be satisfied.[4]

Lyons in fact is a Town to be abolished; not Lyons henceforth, but " Commune Affranchie, Township Freed ": the very name of it shall perish. It is to be razed, this once great City, if Jacobinism prophesy right; and a Pillar to be erected on the ruins, with this Inscription, " Lyons rebelled against the Republic; Lyons is no more." Fouché, Couthon, Collot, Convention Representatives succeed one another: there is work for the hangman; work for the hammerman, not in building. The very Houses of Aristocrats, we say, are doomed. Paralytic Couthon, borne in a chair, taps on the wall, with emblematic mallet, saying, " La Loi te frappe, The Law strikes thee "; masons, with wedge and crowbar, begin demolition. Crash of downfall, dim ruin and dust-clouds fly in the winter wind. Had Lyons been of soft stuff, it had all vanished in those weeks, and the Jacobin prophecy had been fulfilled. But Towns are not built of soap-froth; Lyons Town is built of

stone. Lyons, though it rebelled against the Republic, is
to this day.

Neither have the Lyons Girondins all one neck, that you
could despatch it at one swoop. Revolutionary Tribunal here,
and Military Commission, guillotining, fusillading, do what
they can: the kennels of the Place des Terreaux run red;
mangled corpses roll down the Rhone. Collot d'Herbois, they
say, was once hissed on the Lyons stage: but with what sibila-
tion, of world-catcall or hoarse Tartarean Trumpet, will ye hiss
him now, in this his new character, of Convention Representative—not to be repeated! Two-hundred and nine men are
marched forth over the River, to be shot in mass, by musket
and cannon, in the Promenade of the Brotteaux. It is the
second of such scenes; the first was of some Seventy. The
corpses of the first were flung into the Rhone, but the Rhone
stranded some; so these now, of the second lot, are to be
buried on land. Their one long grave is dug; they stand
ranked, by the loose mould-ridge; the younger of them singing the Marseillaise. Jacobin National Guards give fire; but
have again to give fire, and again; and to take the bayonet
and the spade, for though the doomed all fall, they do not all
die—and it becomes a butchery too horrible for speech. So
that the very Nationals, as they fire, turn away their faces.
Collot, snatching the musket from one such National, and
levelling it with unmoved countenance, says, " It is thus a
Republican ought to fire."

This is the second Fusillade, and happily the last: it is
found too hideous; even inconvenient. There were Two-
hundred and nine marched out; one escaped at the end of
the Bridge: yet behold, when you count the corpses, they are
Two-hundred and ten. Rede us this riddle, O Collot? After
long guessing, it is called to mind that two individuals, here
in the Brotteaux ground, did attempt to leave the rank, protesting with agony that they were not condemned men, that
they were Police Commissaries: which two we repulsed, and
disbelieved, and shot with the rest! [5] Such is the vengeance
of an enraged Republic. Surely this, according to Barrère's
phrase, is Justice " under rough forms, sous des formes
acerbes." But the Republic, as Fouché says, must " march to
Liberty over corpses." Or again, as Barrère has it: " None
but the dead do not come back, Il n'y a que les morts qui ne

reviennent pas." Terror hovers far and wide: "the Guillotine goes not ill."

But before quitting those Southern regions, over which History can cast only glances from aloft, she will alight for a moment, and look fixedly at one point: the Siege of Toulon. Much battering and bombarding, heating of balls in furnaces or farm-houses, serving of artillery well and ill, attacking of Ollioules Passes, Forts Malbosquet, there has been: as yet to small purpose. We have had General Cartaux here, a whilom Painter elevated in the troubles of Marseilles; General Doppet, a whilom Medical man elevated in the troubles of Piemont, who, under Crancé, took Lyons, but can not take Toulon. Finally we have General Dugommier, a pupil of Washington. Convention Représentans also we have had; Barrases, Salicettis, Robespierres the Younger—also an Artillery Chef de brigade, of extreme diligence, who often takes his nap of sleep among the guns; a short, taciturn, olive-complexioned young man, not unknown to us, by name Buonaparte; one of the best Artillery-officers yet met with. And still Toulon is not taken. It is the fourth month now; December, in slave-style; Frostarious or Frimaire, in new-style: and still their cursed Red-Blue Flag flies there. They are provisioned from the Sea; they have seized all heights, felling wood, and fortifying themselves; like the cony, they have built their nest in the rocks.

Meanwhile Frostarious is not yet become Snowous or Nivose, when a Council of War is called; Instructions have just arrived from Government and Salut Public. Carnot, in Salut Public, has sent us a plan of siege: on which plan General Dugommier has this criticism to make, Commissioner Salicetti has that; and criticisms and plans are very various; when that young Artillery-Officer ventures to speak; the same whom we saw snatching sleep among the guns, who has emerged several times in this History—the name of him Napoleon Buonaparte. It is his humble opinion, for he has been gliding about with spy-glasses, with thoughts, That a certain Fort l'Éguillette can be clutched, as with lion-spring, on the sudden; wherefrom, were it once ours, the very heart of Toulon might be battered; the English Lines were, so to speak, turned inside out, and Hood and our Natural Enemies must next day either put to sea, or be burnt to ashes. Commissioners arch their eyebrows, with negatory sniff: who is

this young gentleman with more wit than we all? Brave
veteran Dugommier, however, thinks the idea worth a word;
questions the young gentleman; becomes convinced; and there
is for issue, Try it.

On the taciturn bronze-countenance therefore, things being now all ready, there sits a grimmer gravity than ever, compressing a hotter central-fire than ever. Yonder, thou seest,
is Fort l'Éguillette; a desperate lion-spring, yet a possible
one; this day to be tried!—Tried it is; and found good. By
stratagem and valour, stealing through ravines, plunging fiery
through the fire-tempest, Fort l'Éguillette is clutched at, is
carried; the smoke having cleared, we see the Tricolor fly on
it; the bronze-complexioned young man was right. Next
morning, Hood, finding the interior of his lines exposed, his
defences turned inside out, makes for his shipping. Taking
such Royalists as wished it on board with him, he weighs
anchor; on this 19th of December 1793, Toulon is once more
the Republic's!

Cannonading has ceased at Toulon; and now the guilloting-
ing and fusillading may begin. Civil horrors, truly: but at
least that infamy of an English domination is purged away.
Let there be Civic Feast universally over France: so reports
Barrère, or Painter David; and the Convention assist in a
body.[6] Nay, it is said, these infamous English (with an attention rather to their own interests than to ours) set fire to our
store-houses, arsenals, war-ships in Toulon Harbour, before
weighing; some score of brave war-ships, the only ones we
now had! However, it did not prosper, though the flame
spread far and high; some two ships were burned, not more;
the very galley-slaves ran with buckets to quench. These
same proud Ships, Ship l'Orient and the rest, have to carry
this same young Man to Egypt first: not yet can they be
changed to ashes, or to Sea-Nymphs; not yet to sky-rockets,
O ship l'Orient; nor become the prey of England—before
their time!

And so, over France universally, there is Civic Feast and
high-tide: and Toulon sees fusillading, grapeshotting in mass,
as Lyons saw; and " death is poured out in great floods, vomie
à grands flots "; and Twelve-thousand Masons are requisitioned from the neighbouring country, to raze Toulon from
the face of the Earth. For it is to be razed, so reports Bar-

rère; all but the National Shipping Establishments; and to be called henceforth not Toulon, but "Port of the Mountain." There in black death-cloud we must leave it—hoping only that Toulon too is built of stone; that perhaps even Twelve-thousand Masons can not pull it down, till the fit pass.

One begins to be sick of "death vomited in great floods." Nevertheless, hearest thou not, O Reader (for the sound reaches through centuries), in the dead December and January nights, over Nantes Town—confused noises, as of musketry and tumult, as of rage and lamentation; mingling with the everlasting moan of the Loire waters there? Nantes Town is sunk in sleep; but Représentant Carrier is not sleeping, the wool-capped Company of Marat is not sleeping. Why unmoors that flatbottomed craft, that gabarre; about eleven at night; with Ninety Priests under hatches? They are going to Belle Isle? In the middle of the Loire stream, on signal given, the gabarre is scuttled; she sinks with all her cargo. "Sentence of Deportation," writes Carrier, "was executed vertically." The Ninety Priests, with their ga-barre-coffin, lie deep! It is the first of the Noyades, what we may call Drownages, of Carrier; which have become famous forever.

Guillotining there was at Nantes, till the Headsman sank worn out: then fusillading "in the Plain of Saint-Mauve"; little children fusilladed, and women with children at the breast; children and women, by the hundred and twenty; and by the five hundred, so hot is La Vendée: till the very Jacobins grew sick, and all but the Company of Marat cried, "Hold!" Wherefore now we have got Noyading; and on the 24th night of Frostarious year 2, which is 14th of December 1793, we have a second Noyade; consisting of "a Hundred and Thirty-eight persons." [7]

Or why waste a gabarre, sinking it with them? Fling them out; fling them out, with their hands tied: pour a con-tinual hail of lead over all the space, till the last struggler of them be sunk! Unsound sleepers of Nantes, and the Sea-Villages thereabouts, hear the musketry amid the night-winds; wonder what the meaning of it is. And women were in that gabarre; whom the Red Nightcaps were stripping naked; who begged, in their agony, that their smocks might not be stript from them. And young children were thrown in, their mothers vainly pleading : " Wolflings," answered the Company of Marat, " who would grow to be wolves."

By degrees, daylight itself witnesses Noyades : women and men are tied together, feet and feet, hands and hands ; and flung in : this they call Mariage Républicain, Republican Marriage. Cruel is the panther of the woods, the she-bear bereaved of her whelps : but there is in man a hatred crueler than that. Dumb, out of suffering now, as pale swoln corpses, the victims tumble confusedly seaward along the Loire stream ; the tide rolling them back : clouds of ravens darken the River ; wolves prowl on the shoal-places : Carrier writes, " Quel torrent révolutionnaire, What a torrent of Revolution ! " For the man is rabid ; and the Time is rabid. These are the Noyades of Carrier ; twenty-five by the tale, for what is done in darkness comes to be investigated in sunlight : [8] not to be forgotten for centuries.—We will turn to another aspect of the Consummation of Sansculottism ; leaving this as the blackest.

But indeed men are all rabid ; as the Time is. Representative Lebon, at Arras, dashes his sword into the blood flowing from the Guillotine ; exclaims, " How I like it ! " Mothers, they say, by his orders, have to stand by while the Guillotine devours their children : a band of music is stationed near ; and, at the fall of every head, strikes up its " Ça-ira." [9] In the Burgh of Bedouin, in the Orange region, the Liberty-tree has been cut down overnight. Representative Maignet, at Orange, hears of it ; burns Bedouin Burgh to the last dog-hutch ; guillotines the inhabitants, or drives them into the caves and hills.[10] Republic One and Indivisible ! She is the newest Birth of Nature's waste inorganic Deep, which men name Orcus, Chaos, primeval Night ; and knows one law, that of self-preservation. Tigresse Nationale : meddle not with a whisker of her ! Swift-rending is her stroke ; look what a paw she spreads—pity has not entered into her heart.

Prudhomme, the dull-blustering Printer and Able Editor, as yet a Jacobin Editor, will become a renegade one, and publish large volumes, on these matters, " Crimes of the Revolution " ; adding innumerable lies withal, as if the truth were not sufficient. We, for our part, find it more edifying to know, one good time, that this Republic and National Tigress is a New-Birth ; a Fact of Nature among Formulas, in an Age of Formulas ; and to look, oftenest in silence, how the so genuine

Nature-Fact will demean itself among these.   For the Formulas are partly genuine, partly delusive, supposititious : we call them, in the language of metaphor, regulated modelled shapes ; some of which have bodies and life still in them; most of which, according to a German Writer, have only emptiness, " glass-eyes glaring on you with a ghastly affectation of life, and in their interior unclean accumulation of beetles and spiders !"   But the Fact, let all men observe, is a genuine and sincere one; the sincerest of Facts; terrible in its sincerity, as very Death.   Whatsoever is equally sincere may front it, and beard it; but whatsoever is not?—

NOTES

[1] See Louvet, p. 301.
[2] " Deux Amis," xii, 249–251.
[3] Ibid., xi, 145.
[4] " Moniteur " (du 17 Novembre 1793), etc.
[5] " Deux Amis," xii, 251–262.
[6] " Moniteur," 1793, Nos. 101 (31 Décembre), 95, 96, 98, etc.
[7] " Deux Amis," xii, 266–272; " Moniteur," du 2 Janvier 1794.
[8] " Procès de Carrier " (4 tomes, Paris, 1795).
[9] " Les Horreurs des Prisons d'Arras " (Paris, 1823).
[10] Montgaillard, iv, 200.

CHAPTER IV

CARMAGNOLE COMPLETE

SIMULTANEOUSLY with this Tophet-black aspect, there unfolds itself another aspect, which one may call a Tophet-red aspect, the Destruction of the Catholic Religion; and indeed, for the time being, of Religion itself. We saw Romme's New Calendar establish its Tenth Day of Rest; and asked, what would become of the Christian Sabbath? The Calendar is hardly a month old, till all this is set at rest. Very singular, as Mercier observes: last Corpus-Christi Day 1792, the whole world, and Sovereign Authority itself, walked in religious gala, with a quite devout air—Butcher Legendre, supposed to be irreverent, was like to be massacred in his Gig, as the thing went by. A Gallican Hierarchy, and Church, and Church Formulas seemed to flourish, a little brown-leaved or so, but not browner than of late years or decades; to flourish far and wide, in the sympathies of an unsophisticated People; defying Philosophism, Legislature and the Encyclopédie. Far and wide, alas! like a brown-leaved Vallombrosa: which waits but one whirl-blast of the November wind, and in an hour stands bare! Since that Corpus-Christi Day, Brunswick has come, and the Emigrants, and La Vendée, and eighteen months of Time: to all flourishing, especially to brown-leaved flourishing, there comes, were it never so slowly, an end.

On the 7th of November, a certain Citoyen Parens, Curate of Boissise-le-Bertrand, writes to the Convention that he has all his life been preaching a lie, and is grown weary of doing it; wherefore he will now lay down his Curacy and stipend, and begs that an august Convention would give him something else to live upon. "Mention honorable," shall we give him? Or "reference to Committee of Finances"? Hardly is this got decided, when goose Gobel, Constitutional Bishop of Paris, with his Chapter, with Municipal and Departmental escort in red nightcaps, makes his appearance, to do as Parens has done. Goose Gobel will now acknowledge " no Religion but Liberty "; therefore he doffs his Priest-gear, and receives the Fraternal embrace. To the joy of Departmental Momoro, of Municipal Chaumettes and Héberts, of Vincent and the Revolutionary Army! Chaumette asks, Ought there not, in these circumstances, to be among our intercalary Days Sans-breeches, a Feast of Reason? [1] Proper surely! Let Atheist Maréchal, Lalande, and little Atheist Naigeon rejoice; let Clootz, Speaker of Mankind, present to the Convention his " Evidences of the Mahometan Religion," " a work evincing the nullity of all Religions "—with thanks. There shall be Universal Republic now, thinks Clootz; and " one God only, Le Peuple."

The French nation is of gregarious imitative nature; it needed but a fugle-motion in this matter; and goose Gobel, driven by Municipality and force of circumstances, has given one. What Curé will be behind him of Boissise; what Bishop behind him of Paris? Bishop Grégoire, indeed, courageously declines; to the sound of " We force no one; let Grégoire consult his conscience "; but Protestant and Romish by the hundred volunteer and assent. From far and near, all through November into December, till the work is accomplished, come Letters of renegation, come Curates who " are learning to be Carpenters," Curates with their new-wedded Nuns: has not the day of Reason dawned, very swiftly, and become noon? From sequestered Townships come Addresses, stating plainly, though in Patois dialect, That " they will have no more to do with the black animal called Curay; animal noir appelé Curay." [2]

Above all things, there come Patriotic Gifts, of Church-furniture. The remnant of bells, except for tocsin, descend from their belfries, into the National meltingpot to make cannon. Censers and all sacred vessels are beaten broad; of silver, they are fit for the poverty-stricken Mint; of pewter, let them become bullets, to shoot the " enemies du genre humain." Dalmatics of plush make breeches for him who had none; linen albs will clip into shirts for the Defenders of the Country: old-clothesmen, Jew or Heathen, drive the briskest trade. Chalier's Ass-Procession, at Lyons, was but a type of

what went on, in those same days, in all Towns. In all Towns
and Townships as quick as the guillotine may go, so quick
goes the axe and the wrench: sacristies, lutrins, altar-rails are
pulled down; the Mass-Books torn into cartridge-papers: men
dance the Carmagnole all night about the bonfire. All highways jingle with metallic Priest-tackle, beaten broad; sent to
the Convention, to the poverty-stricken Mint. Good Sainte-
Geneviève's Chasse is let down: alas! to be burst open, this
time, and burnt on the Place de Grève. Saint Louis's Shirt
is burnt—might not a Defender of the Country have had it?
At Saint-Denis Town, no longer Saint-Denis but Franciade,
Patriotism has been down among the Tombs, rummaging;
the Revolutionary Army has taken spoil. This, accordingly,
is what the streets of Paris saw:

"Most of these persons were still drunk, with the brandy
they had swallowed out of chalices—eating mackerel on the
patenas! Mounted on Asses, which were housed with Priests'
cloaks, they reined them with Priests' stoles; they held clutched
with the same hand communion-cup and sacred wafer. They
stopped at the doors of Dramshops; held out ciboriums: and
the landlord, stoup in hand, had to fill them thrice. Next
came Mules high-laden with crosses, chandeliers, censers, holy-
water vessels, hyssops—recalling to mind the Priests of Cybele,
whose panniers, filled with the instruments of their worship,
served at once as storehouse, sacristy, and temple. In such
equipage did these profaners advance toward the Convention.
They enter there, in an immense train, ranged in two rows;
all masked like mummers in fantastic sacerdotal vestments;
bearing on hand-barrows their heaped plunder—ciboriums,
suns, candelabras, plates of gold and silver." [3]

The Address we do not give; for indeed it was in strophes,
sung vivâ voce, with all the parts—Danton glooming considerably, in his place; and demanding that there be prose
and decency in future.[4] Nevertheless the captors of such spolia
opima crave, not untouched with liquor, permission to dance
the Carmagnole also on the spot: whereto an exhilarated Convention can not but accede. Nay, "several Members," continues the exaggerative Mercier, who was not there to witness,
being in Limbo now, as one of Duperret's Seventy-three,
"several Members, quitting their curule chairs, took the hand
of girls flaunting in Priest's vestures, and danced the Carma-

gnole along with them." Such Old-Hallowtide have they, in this year once named of Grace 1793.

Out of which strange fall of Formulas, tumbling there in confused welter, betrampled by the Patriotic dance, is it not passing strange to see a new Formula arise? For the human tongue is not adequate to speak what "triviality run distracted" there is in human nature. Black Mumbo-Jumbo of the woods, and most Indian Wau-waus, one can understand: but this of Procureur Anaxagoras, whilom John-Peter, Chaumette? We will say only: Man is a born idol-worshipper, sight-worshipper, so sensuous-imaginative is he; and also partakes much of the nature of the ape.

For the same day, while this brave Carmagnole-dance has hardly jigged itself out, there arrive Procureur Chaumette and Municipals and Departmentals, and with them the strangest freightage: a New Religion! Demoiselle Candeille, of the Opera; a woman fair to look upon, when well rouged; she, borne on palanquin shoulderhigh; with red woollen nightcap; in azure mantle; garlanded with oak; holding in her hand the Pike of the Jupiter-Peuple, sails in: heralded by white young women girt in tricolor. Let the world consider it! This, O National Convention wonder of the universe, is our New Divinity; Goddess of Reason, worthy, and alone worthy of revering. Her henceforth we adore. Nay, were it too much to ask of an august National Representation that it also went with us to the ci-devant Cathedral called of Notre-Dame, and executed a few strophes in worship of her?

President and Secretaries give Goddess Candeille, borne at due height round their platform, successively the Fraternal kiss; whereupon she, by decree, sails to the right-hand of the President and there alights. And now, after due pause and flourishes of oratory, the Convention, gathering its limbs, does get under way in the required procession toward Notre-Dame —Reason, again in her litter, sitting in the van of them, borne, as one judges, by men in the Roman costume; escorted by wind-music, red nightcaps, and the madness of the world. And so, straightway, Reason taking seat on the high-altar of Notre-Dame, the requisite worship or quasi-worship is, say the Newspapers, executed; National Convention chanting "the 'Hymn to Liberty,' words by Chénier, music by Gossec."

It is the first of the Feasts of Reason; first communion-service of the New Religion of Chaumette.

"The corresponding Festival in the Church of Saint-Eustache," says Mercier, "offered the spectacle of a great tavern. The interior of the choir represented a landscape decorated with cottages and boskets of trees. Round the choir stood tables overloaded with bottles, with sausages, pork-puddings, pastries and other meats. The guests flowed in and out through all doors: whosoever presented himself took part of the good things: children of eight, girls as well as boys, put hand to plate, in sign of Liberty; they drank also of the bottles, and their prompt intoxication created laughter. Reason sat in azure mantle aloft, in a serene manner; Cannoneers, pipe in mouth, serving her as acolytes. And out of doors," continues the exaggerative man, "were mad multitudes dancing round the bonfire of Chapel-balustrades, of Priests' and Canons' stalls; and the dancers—I exaggerate nothing—the dancers nigh bare of breeches, neck and breast naked, stockings down, went whirling and spinning, like those Dust-vortexes, forerunners of Tempest and Destruction." [5] At Saint-Gervais Church, again, there was a terrible "smell of herrings"; Section or Municipality having provided no food, no condiment, but left it to chance. Other mysteries, seemingly of a Cabiric or even Paphian character, we leave under the Veil, which appropriately stretches itself "along the pillars of the aisles"—not to be lifted aside by the hand of History.

But there is one thing we should like almost better to understand than any other: what Reason herself thought of it, all the while. What articulate words poor Mrs. Momoro, for example, uttered; when she had become ungoddessed again, and the Bibliopolist and she sat quiet at home, at supper? For he was an earnest man, Bookseller Momoro; and had notions of Agrarian Law. Mrs. Momoro, it is admitted, made one of the best Goddesses of Reason; though her teeth were a little defective.—And now if the Reader will represent to himself that such visible Adoration of Reason went on "all over the Republic," through these November and December weeks, till the Church woodwork was burnt out, and the business otherwise completed, he will perhaps feel sufficiently what an adoring Republic it was, and without reluctance quit this part of the subject.

Such gifts of Church-spoil are chiefly the work of the Armée Révolutionnaire; raised, as we said, some time ago. It is an army with portable guillotine: commanded by Playwright Ronsin in terrible mustachioes; and even by some uncertain shadow of Usher Maillard, the old Bastille Hero, Leader of the Menads, September Man in Grey! Clerk Vincent of the War-Office, one of Pache's old Clerks, "with a head heated by the ancient orators," had a main hand in the appointments, at least in the staff-appointments.

But of the marchings and retreatings of these Six-thousand no Xenophon exists. Nothing, but an inarticulate hum, of cursing and sooty frenzy, surviving dubious in the memory of ages! They scour the country round Paris; seeking Prisoners; raising Requisitions; seeing that Edicts are executed, that the Farmers have thrashed sufficiently; lowering Church-bells or metallic Virgins. Detachments shoot forth dim, toward remote parts of France; nay, new Provincial Revolutionary Armies rise dim, here and there, as Carrier's Company of Marat, as Tallien's Bordeaux Troop; like sympathetic clouds in an atmosphere all electric. Ronsin, they say, admitted, in candid moments, that his troops were the elixir of the Rascality of the Earth. One sees them drawn up in market-places; travel-splashed, rough-bearded, in carmagnole complète: the first exploit is to prostrate what Royal or Ecclesiastical monument, crucifix or the like, there may be: to plant a cannon at the steeple; fetch down the bell without climbing for it, bell and belfry together. This, however, it is said, depends somewhat on the size of the town: if the town contains much population, and these perhaps of a dubious choleric aspect, the Revolutionary Army will do its work gently, by ladder and wrench; nay, perhaps will take its billet without work at all; and, refreshing itself with a little liquor and sleep, pass on to the next stage.[6] Pipe in cheek, sabre on thigh; in Carmagnole complete!

Such things have been; and may again be. Charles Second sent out his Highland Host over the Western Scotch Whigs: Jamaica Planters got Dogs from the Spanish Main to hunt their Maroons with: France too is bescoured with a Devil's Pack, the baying of which, at this distance of half a century, still sounds in the mind's ear.

NOTES

[1] "Moniteur," Séance du 17 Brumaire (November 7th), 1793.
[2] "Analyse du Moniteur" (Paris, 1801), ii, 280.
[3] Mercier, iv, 134.   See "Moniteur," Séance du 10 Novembre.
[4] See also "Moniteur," Séance du 26 Novembre.
[5] Mercier, iv, 127–146.
[6] "Deux Amis," xii, 62–65.

CHAPTER V

LIKE A THUNDER-CLOUD

BUT the grand and indeed substantially primary and generic aspect of the Consummation of Terror remains still to be looked at; nay, blinkard History has for most part all but overlooked this aspect, the soul of the whole; that which makes it terrible to the Enemies of France. Let Despotism and Cimmerian Coalitions consider. All French men and French things are in a State of Requisition; Fourteen Armies are got on foot; Patriotism, with all that it has of faculty in heart or in head, in soul or body or breeches-pocket, is rushing to the Frontiers, to prevail or die! Busy sits Carnot, in Salut Public; busy, for his share, in "organizing victory." Not swifter pulses that Guillotine, in dread systole-diastole in the Place de la Révolution, than smites the Sword of Patriotism, smiting Cimmeria back to its own borders, from the sacred soil.

In fact, the Government is what we can call Revolutionary; and some men are " à la hauteur," on a level with the circumstances; and others are not à la hauteur—so much the worse for them. But the Anarchy, we may say, has organized itself: Society is literally overset; its old forces working with mad activity, but in the inverse order; destructive and self-destructive.

Curious to see how all still refers itself to some head and fountain; not even an Anarchy but must have a centre to revolve round. It is now some six months since the Committee of Salut Public came into existence; some three months since Danton proposed that all power should be given it, and "a sum of fifty millions," and the "Government be declared Revolutionary." He himself, since that day, would take no hand in it, though again and again solicited; but sits private in his place on the Mountain. Since that day, the Nine, or

833

if they should even rise to Twelve, have become permanent, always re-elected when their term runs out; Salut Public, Sûreté Générale have assumed their ulterior form and mode of operating.

Committee of Public Salvation, as supreme; of General Surety, as subaltern: these, like a Lesser and Greater Council, most harmonious hitherto, have become the centre of all things. They ride this Whirlwind; they, raised by force of circumstances, insensibly, very strangely, thither to that dread height —and guide it, and seem to guide it. Stranger set of Cloud-Compellers the Earth never saw. A Robespierre, a Billaud, a Collot, Couthon, Saint-Just; not to mention still meaner Amars, Vadiers, in Sûreté Générale: these are your Cloud-Compellers. Small intellectual talent is necessary: indeed where among them, except in the head of Carnot, busied organizing victory, would you find any? The talent is one of instinct rather. It is that of divining aright what this great dumb Whirlwind wishes and wills; that of willing, with more frenzy than any one, what all the world wills. To stand at no obstacles; to heed no considerations, human or divine; to know well that, of divine or human, there is one thing needful, Triumph of the Republic, Destruction of the Enemies of the Republic! With this one spiritual endowment, and so few others, it is strange to see how a dumb inarticulately storming Whirlwind of things puts, as it were, its reins into your hand, and invites and compels you to be leader of it.

Hard by sits a Municipality of Paris; all in red nightcaps since the fourth of November last: a set of men fully " on a level with circumstances," or even beyond it. Sleek Mayor Pache, studious to be safe in the middle; Chaumettes, Héberts, Varlets, and Henriot their great Commandant; not to speak of Vincent the War-clerk, of Momoros, Dobsents and such-like: all intent to have Churches plundered, to have Reason adored, Suspects cut down, and the Revolution triumph. Perhaps carrying the matter too far? Danton was heard to grumble at the civic strophes; and to recommend prose and decency. Robespierre also grumbles that, in overturning Superstition, we did not mean to make a religion of Atheism. In fact, your Chaumette and Company constitute a kind of Hyper-Jacobinism, or rabid " Faction des Enragés "; which has given orthodox Patriotism some umbrage, of late months. To

" know a Suspect on the streets " ; what is this but bringing
the Law of the Suspect itself into ill odour ?　Men half-frantic,
men zealous over-much—they toil there, in their red nightcaps, restlessly, rapidly, accomplishing what of Life is allotted
them.

And the Forty-four Thousand other Townships, each with
Revolutionary Committee, based on Jacobin Daughter Society ;
enlightened by the spirit of Jacobinism ; quickened by the
Forty Sous a-day !—The French Constitution spurned always
at anything like Two Chambers ; and yet, behold, has it not
verily got Two Chambers ?　National Convention, elected, for
one ; Mother of Patriotism, self-elected, for another !　Mother
of Patriotism has her Debates reported in the " Moniteur," as
important state-procedures ; which indisputably they are.　A
Second Chamber of Legislature we call this Mother Society—
if perhaps it were not rather comparable to that old Scotch
Body named Lords of the Articles, without whose origination,
and signal given, the so-called Parliament could introduce no
bill, could do no work ?　Robespierre himself, whose words are
a law, opens his incorruptible lips copiously in the Jacobins
Hall.　Smaller Council of Salut Public, Greater Council of
Sûreté Générale, all active Parties, come here to plead ; to
shape beforehand what decision they must arrive at, what
destiny they have to expect.　Now if a question arose, Which
of those Two Chambers, Convention, or Lords of the Articles,
was the stronger ?　Happily they as yet go hand in hand.

As for the National Convention, truly it has become a most
composed Body.　Quenched now the old effervescence ; the
Seventy-three locked in ward ; once noisy Friends of the Girondins sunk all into silent men of the Plain, called even
" Frogs of the Marsh," Crapauds du Marais !　Addresses come,
Revolutionary Church-plunder comes ; Deputations, with prose
or strophes : these the Convention receives.　But beyond this,
the Convention has one thing mainly to do : to listen what
Salut Public proposes, and say, Yea.

Bazire followed by Chabot, with some impetuosity, declared,
one morning, that this was not the way of a Free Assembly.
" There ought to be an Opposition side, a Côté Droit," cried
Chabot : " if none else will form it, I will.　People say to me,
You will all get guillotined in your turn, first you and Bazire,
then Danton, then Robespierre himself." [1]　So spake the Dis-

frocked, with a loud voice: next week, Bazire and he lie in
the Abbaye; wending, one may fear, toward Tinville and the
Axe; and "people say to me"—what seems to be proving
true! Bazire's blood was all inflamed with Revolution Fever;
with coffee and spasmodic dreams.[2]   Chabot, again, how
happy with his rich Jew-Austrian wife, late Fräulein Frey!
But he lies in Prison; and his two Jew-Austrian Brothers-in-
Law, the Bankers Frey, lie with him; waiting the urn of doom.
Let a National Convention, therefore, take warning, and know
its function. Let the Convention, all as one man, set its shoulder to the work; not with bursts of Parliamentary eloquence,
but in quite other and serviceabler ways!

Convention Commissioners, what we ought to call Representatives, "Représentans on mission," fly, like the Herald
Mercury, to all points of the Territory; carrying your behests
far and wide. In their "round hat, plumed with tricolor
feathers, girt with flowing tricolor taffeta; in close frock, tricolor sash, sword and jack-boots," these men are powerfuler
than King or Kaiser. They say to whomso they meet, Do;
and he must do it: all men's goods are at their disposal; for
France is as one huge City in Siege. They smite with Requisitions and Forced-loan; they have the power of life and death.
Saint-Just and Lebas order the rich classes of Strasburg to
"strip-off their shoes," and send them to the Armies, where
as many as "ten-thousand pairs" are needed. Also, that within
four-and-twenty hours, "a thousand beds" be got ready;[3]
wrapt in matting and sent under way. For the time presses!
—Like swift bolts, issuing from the fuliginous Olympus of
Salut Public, rush these men, oftenest in pairs; scatter your
thunder-orders over France; make France one enormous
Revolutionary thunder-cloud.

NOTES

[1] "Débats," du 10 Novembre 1793.
[2] "Dictionnaire des Hommes Marquans," i, 115.
[3] "Moniteur," du 27 Novembre 1793.

CHAPTER VI

DO THY DUTY

ACCORDINGLY, alongside of these bonfires of Church-balustrades, and sounds of fusillading and noyading, there rise quite another sort of fires and sounds: Smithy-fires and Proof-volleys for the manufacture of arms.

Cut off from Sweden and the world, the Republic must learn to make steel for itself; and, by aid of Chemists, she has learnt it. Towns that knew only iron, now know steel: from their new dungeons at Chantilly, Aristocrats may hear the rustle of our new steel furnace there. Do not bells transmute themselves into cannon; iron stancheons into the white-weapon (arme blanche), by sword-cutlery? The wheels of Langres scream, amid their sputtering fire-halo; grinding mere swords. The stithies of Charleville ring with gun-making. What say we, Charleville? Two-hundred and fifty-eight Forges stand in the open spaces of Paris itself; a hundred and forty of them in the Esplanade of the Invalides, fifty-four in the Luxembourg Garden: so many Forges stand; grim Smiths beating and forging at lock and barrel there. The Clock-makers have come, requisitioned, to do the touch-holes, the hard-solder and file-work. Five great Barges swing at anchor on the Seine Stream, loud with boring; the great press-drills grating harsh thunder to the general ear and heart. And deft Stock-makers do gouge and rasp; and all men bestir themselves, according to their cunning—in the language of hope, it is reckoned that " a thousand finished muskets can be delivered daily." [1] Chemists of the Republic have taught us miracles of swift tanning: [2] the cordwainer bores and stitches—not of " wood and pasteboard," or he shall answer it to Tinville! The women sew tents and coats, the children scrape surgeon's lint, the old men sit in the market-places; able men are on march; all men in requisition: from Town to Town flutters, on the Heaven's winds, this Banner, The French People risen against Tyrants.

All which is well. But now arises the question: What is to be done for saltpetre? Interrupted Commerce and the English Navy shut us out from saltpetre; and without saltpetre there is no gunpowder. Republican Science again sits meditative; discovers that saltpetre exists here and there, though in attenuated quantity; that old plaster of walls holds a sprinkling of it—that the earth of the Paris Cellars holds a sprinkling of it, diffused through the common rubbish; that were these dug up and washed, saltpetre might be had. Whereupon, swiftly, see! the Citoyens, with up-shoved bonnet rouge, or with doffed bonnet, and hair toil-wetted; digging fiercely, each in his own cellar, for saltpetre. The Earth-heap rises at every door; the Citoyennes with hod and bucket carrying it up; the Citoyens, pith in every muscle, shovelling and digging: for life and saltpetre. Dig, my braves; and right well speed ye! What of saltpetre is essential the Republic shall not want.

Consummation of Sansculottism has many aspects and tints: but the brightest tint, really of a solar or stellar brightness, is this which the Armies give it. That same fervour of Jacobinism, which internally fills France with hatreds, suspicions, scaffolds and Reason-worship, does, on the Frontiers, show itself as a glorious Pro patria mori. Ever since Dumouriez's defection, three Convention Representatives attend every General. Committee of Salut has sent them; often with this Laconic order only: " Do thy duty, Fais ton devoir." It is strange, under what impediments the fire of Jacobinism, like other such fires, will burn. These Soldiers have shoes of wood and pasteboard, or go booted in hay-ropes, in dead of winter; they skewer a bast mat round their shoulders, and are destitute of most things. What then? It is for Rights of Frenchhood, of Manhood, that they fight: the unquenchable spirit, here as elsewhere, works miracles. " With steel and bread," says the Convention Representative, " one may get to China." The Generals go fast to the guillotine; justly and unjustly. From which what inference? This, among others: That ill-success is death; that in victory alone is life! To conquer or die is no theatrical palabra, in these circumstances, but a practical truth and necessity. All Girondism, Halfness, Compromise is swept away. Forward, ye Soldiers of the Republic, captain and man! Dash, with your Gaelic impetuosity, on Austria, England, Prussia, Spain, Sardinia; Pitt, Cobourg, York, and the Devil and the World! Behind us is but the Guillotine; before us is Victory, Apotheosis and Millennium without end!

See, accordingly, on all Frontiers, how the Sons of Night, astonished after short triumph, do recoil—the Sons of the Republic flying at them, with wild Ça-ira or Marseillese Aux armes, with the temper of cat-o'-mountain, or demon incarnate; which no Son of Night can stand! Spain, which came bursting through the Pyrenees, rustling with Bourbon banners, and went conquering here and there for a season, falters at such cat-o'-mountain welcome; draws itself in again; too happy now were the Pyrenees impassable. Not only does Dugommier, conqueror of Toulon, drive Spain back; he invades Spain. General Dugommier invades it by the Eastern Pyrenees; General Müller shall invade it by the Western. " Shall," that is the word: Committee of Salut Public has said it; Representative Cavaignac, on mission there, must see it done. Impossible! cries Müller.—Infallible! answers Cavaignac. Difficulty, impossibility, is to no purpose. " The Committee is deaf on that side of its head," answers Cavaignac, " n'entend pas de cette oreille là. How many wantest thou of men, of horses, cannons? Thou shalt have them. Conquerors, conquered or hanged, forward we must." [3] Which things also, even as the Representatives spake them, were done. The Spring of the new Year sees Spain invaded: and redoubts are carried, and Passes and Heights of the most scarped description; Spanish Field-officerism struck mute at such cat-o'-mountain spirit, the cannon forgetting to fire.[4] Swept are the Pyrenees; Town after Town flies open, burst by terror or the petard. In the course of another year, Spain will crave Peace; acknowledge its sins and the Republic; nay, in Madrid, there will be joy as for a victory, that even Peace is got.

Few things, we repeat, can be notabler than these Convention Representatives, with their power more than kingly. Nay, at bottom are they not Kings, Able-men, of a sort; chosen from the Seven-hundred and Forty-nine French Kings; with this order, " Do thy duty "? Representative Levasseur, of small stature, by trade a mere pacific Surgeon-Accoucheur, has mutinies to quell; mad hosts (mad at the Doom of Custine) bellowing far and wide; he alone amid them, the one small Representative—small, but as hard as flint, which also carries fire in it! So too, at Hondschooten, far in the afternoon, he declares that the Battle is not lost; that it must be gained; and fights, himself with his own obstetric hand—horse shot under him, or say on foot, " up to the haunches in tide-water "; cutting stoccado and passado there, in defiance of Water, Earth, Air and Fire, the choleric little Representative that he was! Whereby, as natural, Royal Highness of York had to withdraw—occasionally at full gallop; like to be swallowed by the tide: and his Siege of Dunkirk became a dream, realizing only much loss of beautiful siege-artillery and of brave lives.[5]

General Houchard, it would appear, stood behind a hedge on this Hondschooten occasion; wherefore they have since guillotined him. A new General Jourdan, late Sergeant Jourdan, commands in his stead: he, in long-winded Battles of Watigny, " murderous artillery-fire mingling itself with sound of Revolutionary battle-hymns," forces Austria behind the Sambre again; has hopes of purging the soil of Liberty. With hard wrestling, with artillerying and ça-ira-ing, it shall be done. In the course of a new Summer, Valenciennes will see itself beleaguered; Condé beleaguered; whatsoever is yet in the hands of Austria beleaguered and bombarded: nay, by Convention Decree, we even summon them all " either to surrender in twenty-four hours, or else be put to the sword "— a high saying, which, though it remains unfulfilled, may show what spirit one is of.

Representative Drouet as an Old-dragoon, could fight by a kind of second nature: but he was unlucky. Him, in a night-foray at Maubeuge, the Austrians took alive, in October last. They stript him almost naked, he says; making a show of him, as King-taker of Varennes. They flung him into carts; sent him far into the interior of Cimmeria, to " a Fortress called Spitzberg " on the Danube River; and left him there, at an elevation of perhaps a hundred and fifty feet, to his own bitter reflections. Reflections; and also devices! For the indomitable Old-dragoon constructs wing machinery, of Paperkite; saws window-bars; determines to fly down. He

will seize a boat, will follow the River's course; land somewhere in Crim Tartary, in the Black-Sea or Constantinople
region : à la Sindbad ! Authentic History, accordingly, looking
far into Cimmeria, discerns dimly a phenomenon. In the dead
night-watches, the Spitzberg sentry is near fainting with terror : Is it a huge vague Portent descending through the night-
air ? It is a huge National Representative Old-dragoon, descending by Paperkite; too rapidly, alas ! For Drouet had
taken with him " a small provision-store, twenty pounds weight
or thereby "; which proved accelerative : so he fell, fracturing
his leg; and lay there, moaning, till day dawned, till you could
discern clearly that he was not a Portent but a Representative.[6]

Or see Saint-Just, in the Lines of Weissembourg, though
physically of a timid apprehensive nature, how he charges with
his " Alsatian Peasants armed hastily " for the nonce; the solemn face of him blazing into flame; his black hair and tricolor
hat-taffeta flowing in the breeze ! These our Lines of Weissembourg were indeed forced, and Prussia and the Emigrants
rolled through : but we re-force the Lines of Weissembourg;
and Prussia and the Emigrants roll back again still faster—
hurled with bayonet-charges and fiery ça-ira-ing.

Ci-devant Sergeant Pichegru, ci-devant Sergeant Hoche,
risen now to be Generals, have done wonders here. Tall
Pichegru was meant for the Church; was Teacher of Mathematics once, in Brienne School—his remarkablest pupil there
was the Boy Napoleon Buonaparte. He then, not in the
sweetest humour, enlisted, exchanging ferula for musket; and
had got the length of the halberd, beyond which nothing could
be hoped; when the Bastille barriers falling made passage for
him, and he is here. Hoche bore a hand at the literal overturn of the Bastille; he was, as we saw, a Sergeant of the
Gardes Françaises, spending his pay in rushlights and cheap
editions of books. How the Mountains are burst, and many
an Enceladus is disimprisoned; and Captains founding on
Four parchments of Nobility are blown with their parchments
across the Rhine, into Lunar·Limbo !

What high feats of arms, therefore, were done in these
Fourteen Armies; and how, for love of Liberty and hope of
Promotion, lowborn valour cut its desperate way to General-

55

ship; and, from the central Carnot in Salut Public to the out-most drummer on the Frontiers, men strove for their Republic, let Readers fancy. The snows of Winter, the flowers of Sum-mer continue to be stained with warlike blood. Gaelic im-petuosity mounts ever higher with victory; spirit of Jacobin-ism weds itself to national vanity: the Soldiers of the Re-public are becoming, as we prophesied, very Sons of Fire. Barefooted, barebacked: but with bread and iron you can get to China! It is one Nation against the whole world; but the Nation has that within her which the whole world will not conquer. Cimmeria, astonished, recoils faster or slower; all round the Republic there rises fiery, as it were, a magic ring of musket-volleying and ça-ira-ing. Majesty of Prussia, as Majesty of Spain, will by and by acknowledge his sins and the Republic; and make a Peace of Bâle.

Foreign Commerce, Colonies, Factories in the East and in the West, are fallen or falling into the hands of sea-ruling Pitt, enemy of human nature. Nevertheless what sound is this that we hear, on the first of June 1794; sound as of war-thunder borne from the Ocean too, of tone most piercing? War-thunder from off the Brest waters: Villaret-Joyeuse and English Howe, after long manœuvering, have ranked them-selves there; and are belching fire. The enemies of human nature are on their own element; can not be conquered; can not be kept from conquering. Twelve hours of raging can-nonade; sun now sinking westward through the battle-smoke: six French Ships taken, the Battle lost; what Ship soever can still sail, making off! But how is it, then, with that Vengeur Ship, she neither strikes nor makes off? She is lamed, she can not make off; strike she will not. Fire rakes her fore and aft from victorious enemies; the Vengeur is sinking. Strong are ye, Tyrants of the sea; yet we also, are we weak? Lo! all flags, streamers, jacks, every rag of tricolor that will yet run on rope, fly rustling aloft: the whole crew crowds to the upper deck; and with universal soul-maddening yell, shouts " Vive la République! "—sinking, sinking. She staggers, she lurches, her last drunk whirl; Ocean yawns abysmal: down rushes the Vengeur, carrying " Vive la République! " along with her, unconquerable, into Eternity.[7] Let foreign Despots think of that. There is an Unconquerable in man, when he stands on his Rights of Man: let Despots and Slaves and all people know this, and only them that stand on the Wrongs of Man tremble to know it.—So has History written, nothing doubting, of the sunk Vengeur.

—— Reader! Mendez Pinto, Münchausen, Cagliostro, Psalmanazar have been great; but they are not the greatest. O Barrère, Barrère, Anacreon of the Guillotine! must inquisitive pictorial History, in a new edition, ask again, " How is it with the Vengeur," in this its glorious suicidal sinking; and, with resentful brush, dash a bend-sinister of contumelious lamp-black through thee and it? Alas! alas! The Vengeur, after fighting bravely, did sink altogether as other ships do, her captain and above two-hundred of her crew escaping gladly in British boats ; and this same enormous inspiring Feat, and rumour " of sound most piercing," turns out to be an enormous inspiring Non-entity, extant nowhere save, as falsehood, in the brain of Barrère! Actually so.[8] Founded, like the World itself, on Nothing ; proved by Convention Report, by solemn Convention Decree and Decrees, and wooden " Model of the Vengeur " ; believed, bewept, besung by the whole French People to this hour, it may be regarded as Barrère's masterpiece ; the largest, most inspiring piece of blague manufactured, for some centuries, by any man or nation. As such, and not otherwise, be it henceforth memorable.

NOTES

[1] " Choix des Rapports," xiii, 189.

[2] Ibid., xv, 360.

[3] There is, in " Prudhomme," an atrocity à la Captain-Kirk reported of this Cavaignac ; which has been copied into Dictionaries of " Hommes Marquans," of " Biographie Universelle," etc.; which not only has no truth in it, but, much more singular, is still capable of being proved to have none.

[4] " Deux Amis," xiii, 205–230; Toulongeon, etc.

[5] Levasseur, " Mémoires," ii, c. 2–7.

[6] His Narrative (in " Deux Amis," xiv, 177–186).

[7] Compare Barrère (" Choix des Rapports," xvi, 416–421); Lord Howe (" Annual Register " of 1794, p. 86), etc,

[8] Carlyle's " Miscellanies," § Sinking of the Vengeur.

CHAPTER VII

FLAME-PICTURE

IN this manner, mad-blazing with flame of all imaginable tints, from the red of Tophet to the stellar-bright, blazes off this Consummation of Sansculottism.

But the hundredth part of the things that were done, and the thousandth part of the things that were projected and decreed to be done, would tire the tongue of History. Statue of the Peuple Souverain, high as Strasburg Steeple; which shall fling its shadow from the Pont Neuf over Jardin National and Convention Hall—enormous, in Painter David's Head! With other the like enormous Statues not a few: realized in paper Decree. For, indeed, the Statue of Liberty herself is still but Plaster, in the Place de la Révolution. Then Equalization of Weights and Measures, with decimal division; Institutions, of Music and of much else; Institute in general; School of Arts, School of Mars, Elèves de la Patrie, Normal Schools: amid such Gun-boring, Altar-burning, Saltpetre-digging, and miraculous improvements in Tannery!

What, for example, is this that Engineer Chappe is doing, in the Park of Vincennes? In the Park of Vincennes; and onward, they say, in the Park of Lepelletier Saint-Fargeau the assassinated Deputy; and still onward to the Heights of Ecouen and farther, he has scaffolding set up, has posts driven in; wooden arms with elbow-joints are jerking and fugling in the air, in the most rapid mysterious manner! Citoyens ran up, suspicious. Yes, O Citoyens, we are signalling: it is a device this, worthy of the Republic; a thing for what we will call Far-writing without the aid of post-bags; in Greek it shall be named Telegraph.—Télégraphe sacré! answers Citoyenism: For writing to Traitors, to Austria?—and tears it down. Chappe had to escape, and get a new Legislative Decree. Nevertheless he has accomplished it, the indefatigable Chappe:

this his Far-writer, with its wooden arms and elbow-joints, can intelligibly signal; and lines of them are set up, to the North Frontiers and elsewhither. On an Autumn evening of the Year Two, Far-writer having just written that Condé Town has surrendered to us, we send from the Tuileries Convention-Hall this response in the shape of Decree: " The name of Condé is changed to Nord-Libre, North-Free. The Army of the North ceases not to merit well of the country."—To the admiration of men! For lo, in some half hour, while the Convention yet debates, there arrives this new answer: " I inform thee, je t'annonce, Citizen President, that the Decree of Convention, ordering change of the name Condé into North-Free; and the other, declaring that the Army of the North ceases not to merit well of the country; are transmitted and ac-knowledged by Telegraph. I have instructed my Officer at Lille to forward them to North-Free by express. Signed, Chappe." [1]

Or see, over Fleurus in the Netherlands, where General Jourdan, having now swept the soil of Liberty, and advanced thus far, is just about to fight, and sweep or be swept, hangs there not in the Heaven's Vault some Prodigy, seen by Aus-trian eyes and spy-glasses: in the similitude of an enormous Windbag, with netting and enormous Saucer depending from it? A Jove's Balance, O ye Austrian spy-glasses? One saucer-scale of a Jove's Balance; your poor Austrian scale having kicked itself quite aloft, out of sight? By Heaven, answer the spy-glasses, it is a Montgolfier, a Balloon, and they are making signals! Austrian cannon-battery barks at this Mont-golfier; harmless as dog at the Moon: the Montgolfier makes its signals; detects what Austrian ambuscade there may be, and descends at its ease.[2]—What will not these devils incar-nate contrive?

On the whole, is it not, O Reader, one of the strangest Flame-Pictures that ever painted itself; flaming off there, on its ground of Guillotine-black? And the nightly Theatres are Twenty-three; and the Salons de danse are Sixty; full of mere Égalité, Fraternité and Carmagnole. And Section Com-mittee-rooms are Forty-eight; redolent of tobacco and brandy: vigorous with twenty-pence a-day, coercing the Suspect. And the Houses of Arrest are Twelve, for Paris alone; crowded and even crammed. And at all turns, you need your " Cer-tificate of Civism "; be it for going out, or for coming in; nay,

without it you can not, for money, get your daily ounces of
bread. Dusky red-capped Bakers'-queues; wagging themselves; not in silence! For we still live by Maximum, in all
things; waited on by these two, Scarcity and Confusion. The
faces of men are darkened with suspicion; with suspecting,
or being suspect. The streets lie unswept; the ways unmended.
Law has shut her Books; speaks little, save impromptu,
through the throat of Tinville. Crimes go unpunished; not
crimes against the Revolution.[3] "The number of foundling
children," as some compute, "is doubled."

How silent now sits Royalism; sits all Aristocratism; Respectability that kept its Gig! The honour now, and the safety,
is to Poverty, not to Wealth. Your Citizen, who would be
fashionable, walks abroad, with his Wife on his arm, in red-
wool nightcap, black-shag spencer, and carmagnole complete.
Aristocratism crouches low, in what shelter is still left; sub-
mitting to all requisitions, vexations; too happy to escape with
life. Ghastly châteaus stare on you by the wayside; disroofed,
diswindowed; which the National Housebroker is peeling for
the lead and ashlar. The old tenants hover disconsolate, over
the Rhine with Condé; a spectacle to men. Ci-devant Seigneur, exquisite in palate, will become an exquisite Restaurateur Cook in Hamburg; Ci-devant Madame, exquisite in dress,
a successful Marchande des Modes in London. In Newgate-
Street, you meet M. le Marquis, with a rough deal on his
shoulder, adze and jack-plane under arm; he has taken to the
joiner trade; it being necessary to live (faut vivre).[4]—Higher
than all Frenchmen the domestic Stock-jobber flourishes—in
a day of Paper-money. The Farmer also flourishes: "Farmers'
houses," says Mercier, "have become like Pawnbroker's
shops"; all manner of furniture, apparel, vessels of gold and
silver accumulate themselves there: bread is precious. The
Farmer's rent is Paper-money, and he alone of men has bread:
Farmer is better than Landlord, and will himself become
Landlord.

And daily, we say, like a black Spectre, silently through
that Life-tumult, passes the Revolution Cart; writing on the
walls its "Mene, Mene, Thou art weighed, and found wanting!"
A Spectre with which one has grown familiar. Men have
adjusted themselves: complaint issues not from that Death-
tumbril. Weak women and ci-devants, their plumage and

finery all tarnished, sit there; with a silent gaze, as if looking
into the Infinite Black.   The once light lip wears a curl of
irony, uttering no word; and the Tumbril fares along.   They
may be guilty before Heaven, or not; they are guilty, we
suppose, before the Revolution.   Then, does not the Republic
" coin money " of them, with its great axe?   Red Nightcaps
howl dire approval: the rest of Paris looks on; if with a sigh,
that is much: Fellow-creatures whom sighing can not help;
whom black Necessity and Tinville have clutched.

One other thing, or rather two other things, we will still
mention; and no more: The Blond Perukes; the Tannery at
Meudon.   Great talk is of these Perruques blondes: O Reader,
they are made from the Heads of Guillotined women!   The
locks of a Duchess, in this way, may come to cover the scalp
of a Cordwainer; her blonde German Frankism his black Gaelic
poll, if it be bald.   Or they may be worn affectionately, as
relics; rendering one suspect?[5]   Citizens use them, not without
mockery; of a rather cannibal sort.

Still deeper into one's heart goes that Tannery at Meudon;
not mentioned among the other miracles of tanning!   " At
Meudon," says Montgaillard with considerable calmness,
" there was a Tannery of Human Skins; such of the Guillotined
as seemed worth flaying: of which perfectly good wash-leather
was made "; for breeches, and other uses.   The skin of the
men, he remarks, was superior in toughness (consistance) and
quality to shamoy; that of the women was good for almost
nothing, being so soft in texture![6]—History looking back
over Cannibalism, through " Purchas's Pilgrims " and all early
and late Records, will perhaps find no terrestrial Cannibalism
of a sort, on the whole, so detestable.   It is a manufactured,
soft-feeling, quietly elegant sort; a sort perfide!   Alas! then, is
man's civilization only a wrappage, through which the savage
nature of him can still burst, infernal as ever?   Nature still
makes him; and has an Infernal in her as well as a Celestial.

NOTES

[1] " Choix des Rapports," xv, 378, 384.

[2] June 26, 1794 (see " Rapport de Guyton-Morveau sur les Aéro-
stats," in " Moniteur " du 6 Vendémiaire, An 2).

[3] Mercier, v, 25; " Deux Amis," xii, 142–199.

[4] See " Deux Amis," xv, 189–192; " Mémoires de Genlis "; " Found-
ers of the French Republic," etc., etc.

[5] Mercier, ii, 134.   [6] Montgaillard, iv, 290.

Book XIX

THERMIDOR

CHAPTER I

THE GODS ARE ATHIRST

WHAT, then, is this Thing called La Révolution, which, like an Angel of Death, hangs over France, noyading, fusillading, fighting, gun-boring, tanning human skins? La Révolution is but so many Alphabetic Letters; a thing nowhere to be laid hands on, to be clapt under lock and key: where is it? what is it? It is the Madness that dwells in the hearts of men. In this man it is, and in that man; as a rage or as a terror, it is in all men. Invisible, impalpable; and yet no black Azrael, with wings spread over half a continent, with sword sweeping from sea to sea, could be a truer Reality.

To explain, what is called explaining, the march of this Revolutionary Government, be no task of ours. Men can not explain it. A paralytic Couthon, asking in the Jacobins, "What hast thou done to be hanged if Counter-Revolution should arrive?" a sombre Saint-Just, not yet six-and-twenty, declaring that "for Revolutionists there is no rest but in the tomb"; a seagreen Robespierre converted into vinegar and gall; much more an Amar and Vadier, a Collot and Billaud: to inquire what thoughts, predetermination or prevision, might be in the head of these men! Record of their thought remains not; Death and Darkness have swept it out utterly. Nay, if we even had their thought, all that they could have articulately spoken to us, how insignificant a fraction were that of the Thing which realized itself, which decreed itself, on signal given by them! As has been said more than once, this Revolutionary Government is not a self-conscious but a blind fatal one. Each man, enveloped in his ambient-atmosphere of revolutionary fanatic Madness, rushes on, impelled and impelling; and has become a blind brute Force; no rest for him but in the grave! Darkness and the mystery of horrid

cruelty cover it for us, in History; as they did in Nature.
The chaotic Thunder-cloud, with its pitchy black, and its
tumult of dazzling jagged fire, in a world all electric: thou
wilt not undertake to show how that comported itself—what
the secrets of its dark womb were; from what sources, with
what specialties, the lightning it held did, in confused brightness of terror, strike forth, destructive and self-destructive,
till it ended? Like a Blackness naturally of Erebus, which
by will of Providence had for once mounted itself into dominion and the Azure: is not this properly the nature of Sansculottism consummating itself? Of which Erebus Blackness be
it enough to discern that this and the other dazzling fire-bolt,
dazzling fire-torrent, does by small Volition and great Necessity, verily issue—in such and such succession; destructive so
and so, self-destructive so and so: till it end.

Royalism is extinct; "sunk," as they say, "in the mud of
the Loire"; Republicanism dominates without and within:
what, therefore, on the 15th day of March 1794, is this?
Arrestment, sudden really as a bolt out of the Blue, has hit
strange victims: Hébert Père Duchesne, Bibliopolist Momoro,
Clerk Vincent, General Ronsin; high Cordelier Patriots, red-
capped Magistrates of Paris, Worshippers of Reason, Commanders of Revolutionary Army! Eight short days ago, their
Cordelier Club was loud, and louder than ever, with Patriot
denunciations. Hébert Père Duchesne had "held his tongue
and his heart these two months, at sight of Moderates, Crypto-
Aristocrats, Camilles, Scélérats in the Convention itself: but
could not do it any longer; would, if other remedy were not,
invoke the sacred right of Insurrection." So spake Hébert
in Cordelier Session; with vivats, till the roofs rang again.[1]
Eight short days ago; and now already! They rub their eyes:
it is no dream; they find themselves in the Luxembourg.
Goose Gobel too; and they that burnt Churches! Chaumette
himself, potent Procureur, Agent National as they now call it,
who could "recognise the Suspect by the very face of them,"
he lingers but three days; on the third day he too is hurled in.
Most chopfallen, blue, enters the National Agent this Limbo
whither he has sent so many. Prisoners crowd round, gibing
and jeering; "Sublime National Agent," says one, "in virtue
of thy immortal Proclamation, lo there! I am suspect, thou

art suspect, he is suspect, we are suspect, ye are suspect, they are suspect "!

The meaning of these things? Meaning! It is a Plot; Plot of the most extensive ramifications; which, however, Barrère holds the threads of. Such Church-burning and scandalous masquerades of Atheism, fit to make the Revolution odious: where indeed could they originate but in the gold of Pitt? Pitt indubitably, as Preternatural Insight will teach one, did hire this Faction of Enragés, to play their fantastic tricks; to roar in their Cordeliers Club about Moderatism; to print their " Père Duchesne "; worship skyblue Reason in red nightcap; rob Altars—and bring the spoil to us!

Still more indubitable, visible to the mere bodily sight, is this: that the Cordeliers Club sits pale, with anger and terror; and has " veiled the Rights of Man "—without effect. Likewise that the Jacobins are in considerable confusion; busy " purging themselves, s'épurant," as in times of Plot and public Calamity they have repeatedly had to do. Not even Camille Desmoulins but has given offence: nay, there have risen murmurs against Danton himself; though he bellowed them down, and Robespierre finished the matter by " embracing him in the Tribune."

Whom shall the Republic and a jealous Mother Society trust? In these times of temptation, of Preternatural Insight! For there are Factions of the Stranger, " de l'étranger," Factions of Moderates, of Enraged; all manner of Factions: we walk in a world of Plots; strings universally spread, of deadly gins and falltraps, baited by the gold of Pitt! Clootz, Speaker of Mankind so-called, with his " Evidences of Mahometan Religion," and babble of Universal Republic, him an incorruptible Robespierre has purged away. Baron Clootz, and Paine rebellious Needleman lie, these two months, in the Luxembourg; limbs of the Faction de l'étranger. Representative Phélippeaux is purged out: he came back from La Vendée with an ill report in his mouth against rogue Rossignol, and our method of warfare there. Recant it, O Phélippeaux, we entreat thee! Phélippeaux will not recant; and is purged out. Representative Fabre d'Eglantine, famed Nomenclator of Romme's Calendar, is purged out; nay, is cast into the Luxembourg: accused of Legislative Swindling " in regard to moneys of the India Company." There with his Chabots,

Bazires, guilty of the like, let Fabre wait his destiny. And Westermann friend of Danton, he who led the Marseillese on the Tenth of August, and fought well in La Vendée, but spoke not well of rogue Rossignol, is purged out. Lucky, if he too go not to the Luxembourg. And your Prolys, Guzmans, of the Faction of the Stranger, they have gone; Pereyra, though he fled, is gone, "taken in the disguise of a Tavern Cook." I am suspect, thou art suspect, he is suspect!—

The great heart of Danton is weary of it. Danton is gone to native Arcis, for a little breathing-time of peace: Away, black Arachne-webs, thou world of Fury, Terror, and Suspicion; welcome, thou everlasting Mother, with thy spring greenness, thy kind household loves and memories; true art thou, were all else untrue! The great Titan walks silent, by the banks of the murmuring Aube, in young native haunts that knew him when a boy; wonders what the end of these things may be.

But strangest of all, Camille Desmoulins is purged out. Couthon gave as a test in regard to Jacobin purgation the question, "What hast thou done to be hanged if Counter-Revolution should arrive?" Yet Camille, who could so well answer this question, is purged out! The truth is, Camille, early in December last, began publishing a new Journal, or Series of Pamphlets, entitled the "Vieux Cordelier, Old Cordelier." Camille, not afraid at one time to "embrace Liberty on a heap of dead bodies," begins to ask now, Whether among so many arresting and publishing Committees, there ought not to be a "Committee of Mercy"? Saint-Just, he observes, is an extremely solemn young Republican, who "carries his head as if it were a Saint-Sacrament," adorable Hostie, or divine Real-Presence! Sharply enough, this old Cordelier— Danton and he were of the earliest primary Cordeliers—shoots his glittering war-shafts into your new Cordeliers, your Héberts, Momoros, with their brawling brutalities and despicabilities; say, as the Sun-god (for poor Camille is a Poet) shot into that Python Serpent sprung of mud.

Whereat, as was natural, the Hébertist Python did hiss and writhe amazingly; and threaten "sacred right of Insurrection"—and, as we saw, get cast into Prison. Nay, with all the old wit, dexterity and light graceful poignancy, Camille, translating "out of 'Tacitus,' from the Reign of Tiberius," pricks into the Law of the Suspect itself; making it odious! Twice, in the Decade, his wild Leaves issue; full of wit, nay of humour, of harmonious ingenuity and insight—one of the strangest phenomena of that dark time; and smite, in their wild-sparkling way, at various monstrosities, Saint-Sacrament heads, and Juggernaut idols, in a rather reckless manner. To the great joy of Josephine Beauharnais, and the other Five-thousand and odd Suspect, who fill the Twelve Houses of Arrest; on whom a ray of hope dawns! Robespierre, at first approbatory, knew not at last what to think; then thought, with his Jacobins, that Camille must be expelled. A man of true Revolutionary spirit, this Camille; but with the unwisest sallies; whom Aristocrats and Moderates have the art to corrupt! Jacobinism is in uttermost crisis and struggle; enmeshed wholly in plots, corruptibilities, neck-gins and baited falltraps of Pitt ennemi du genre humain. Camille's First Number begins with " O Pitt! "—his last is dated 15 Pluvoise, Year 2, 3d February 1794; and ends with these words of Montezuma's, " Les dieux ont soif, The gods are athirst."

Be this as it may, the Hébertists lie in Prison only some nine days. On the 24th of March, therefore, the Revolution Tumbrils carry through that Life-tumult a new cargo: Hébert, Vincent, Momoro, Ronsin, Nineteen of them in all; with whom, curious enough, sits Clootz, Speaker of Mankind. They have been massed swiftly into a lump, this miscellany of Nondescripts; and travel now their last road. No help. They too must " look through the little window"; they too " must sneeze into the sack, éternuer dans le sac "; as they have done to others, so is it done to them. Sainte-Guillotine, meseems, is worse than the old Saints of Superstition; a man-devouring Saint? Clootz, still with an air of polished sarcasm, endeavours to jest, to offer cheering " arguments of Materialism "; he requested to be executed last, " in order to establish certain principles "—which hitherto, I think, Philosophy has got no good of. General Ronsin too, he still looks forth with some air of defiance, eye of command: the rest are sunk in a stony paleness of despair. Momoro, poor Bibliopolist, no Agrarian Law yet realized—they might as well have hanged thee at Evreux, twenty months ago, when Girondin Buzot hindered them. Hébert Père Duchesne shall never in this world rise in sacred right of insurrection; he sits there low enough, head sunk on breast; Red Nightcaps shouting round him, in frightful parody of his Newspaper Articles, "Grand choler of the Père Duchesne!" Thus perish they; the sack receives all their heads. Through some section of History, Nineteen spectre-chimeras shall flit, squeaking and gibbering; till Oblivion swallow them.

In the course of a week, the Revolutionary Army itself is disbanded; the General having become spectral. This Faction of Rabids, therefore, is also purged from the Republican soil; here also the baited falltraps of that Pitt have been wrenched up harmless; and anew there is joy over a Plot Discovered. The Revolution, then, is verily devouring its own children? All Anarchy, by the nature of it, is not only destructive but self-destructive.

NOTE

[1] "Moniteur," du 17 Ventose (March 7, 1794).

CHAPTER II

DANTON, NO WEAKNESS

DANTON meanwhile has been pressingly sent for from Arcis: he must return instantly, cried Camille, cried Phélippeaux and Friends, who scented danger in the wind. Danger enough! A Danton, a Robespierre, chief-products of a victorious Revolution, are now arrived in immediate front of one another; must ascertain how they will live together, rule together. One conceives easily the deep mutual incompatibility that divided these two: with what terror of feminine hatred the poor seagreen Formula looked at the monstrous colossal Reality, and grew greener to behold him—the Reality, again, struggling to think no ill of a chief-product of the Revolution; yet feeling at bottom that such chief-product was little other than a chief-windbag, blown large by Popular air; not a man, with the heart of a man, but a poor spasmodic incorruptible pedant, with a logic-formula instead of heart; of Jesuit or Methodist-Parson nature; full of sincere-cant, incorruptibility, of virulence, poltroonery; barren as the east-wind! Two such chief-products are too much for one Revolution.

Friends, trembling at the results of a quarrel on their part, brought them to meet. " It is right," said Danton, swallowing much indignation, " to repress the Royalists: but we should not strike except where it is useful to the Republic; we should not confound the innocent and the guilty."—"And who told you," replied Robespierre with a poisonous look, " that one innocent person had perished? "—" Quoi," said Danton, turning round to Friend Pâris self-named Fabricius, Juryman in the Revolutionary Tribunal: " Quoi, not one innocent? What sayest thou of it, Fabricius? " [1]—Friends, Westermann, this Pâris and others urged him to show himself, to ascend the Tribune and act. The man Danton was not prone to

show himself; to act, or uproar for his own safety. A man
of careless, large, hoping nature; a large nature that could
rest: he would sit whole hours, they say, hearing Camille
talk, and liked nothing so well. Friends urged him to fly;
his Wife urged him: " Whither fly?" answered he: " If freed
France cast me out, there are only dungeons for me elsewhere. One carries not his country with him at the sole of
his shoe!" The man Danton sat still. Not even the arrestment of Friend Hérault, a member of Salut, yet arrested by
Salut, can rouse Danton.—On the night of the 30th March
Juryman Pâris came rushing in; haste looking through his
eyes: A clerk of the Salut Committee had told him Danton's
warrant was made out, he is to be arrested this very night!
Entreaties there are and trepidation, of poor Wife, of Pâris
and Friends; Danton sat silent for a while; then answered,
" Ils n'oseraient, They dare not "; and would take no measures.
Murmuring " They dare not," he goes to sleep as usual.

And yet, on the morrow morning, strange rumour spreads
over Paris City: Danton, Camille, Phélippeaux, Lacroix have
been arrested overnight! It is verily so: the corridors of the
Luxembourg were all crowded, Prisoners crowding forth to
see this giant of the Revolution enter among them. " Messieurs," said Danton politely, " I hoped soon to have got you
all out of this: but here I am myself; and one sees not where
it will end."—Rumour may spread over Paris: the Convention
clusters itself into groups; wide-eyed, whispering " Danton
arrested!" Who, then, is safe? Legendre, mounting the
Tribune, utters, at his own peril, a feeble word for him; moving that he be heard at that Bar before indictment; but Robespierre frowns him down: " Did you hear Chabot or Bazire?
Would you have two weights and measures?" Legendre
cowers low: Danton, like the others, must take his doom.

Danton's Prison-thoughts were curious to have; but are
not given in any quantity: indeed few such remarkable men
have been left so obscure to us as this Titan of the Revolution. He was heard to ejaculate: " This time twelvemonth,
I was moving the creation of that same Revolutionary Tribunal. I crave pardon for it of God and man. They are all
Brothers Cain; Brissot would have had me guillotined as
Robespierre now will. I leave the whole business in a frightful
welter (gâchis épouvantable): not one of them understands

anything of government. Robespierre will follow me; I drag
down Robespierre. O, it were better to be a poor fisherman
than to meddle with governing of men.—Camille's young beautiful Wife, who had made him rich not in money alone, hovers
round the Luxembourg, like a disembodied spirit, day and
night. Camille's stolen letters to her still exist; stained with
the marks of his tears.[2] " I carry my head like a Saint-Sacrament? " so Saint-Just was heard to mutter: " perhaps he will
carry his like a Saint-Denis."

Unhappy Danton, thou still unhappier light Camille, once
light Procureur de la Lanterne, ye also have arrived, then, at
the Bourne of Creation, where, like Ulysses Polytlas at the
limit and utmost Gades of his voyage, gazing into that dim
Waste beyond Creation, a man does see the Shade of his
Mother, pale, ineffectual—and days when his Mother nursed
and wrapped him are all-too sternly contrasted with this day!
Danton, Camille, Hérault, Westermann, and the others, very
strangely massed up with Bazires, Swindler Chabots, Fabre
d'Eglantines, Banker Freys, a most motley Batch, " Fournée,"
as such things will be called, stand ranked at the Bar of Tinville. It is the 2d of April 1794. Danton has had but three
days to lie in Prison; for the time presses.

What is your name? place of abode? and the like, Fouquier asks; according to formality. " My name is Danton,"
answers he; " a name tolerably known in the Revolution: my
abode will soon be Annihilation (dans le Néant); but I shall
live in the Pantheon of History." A man will endeavour to
say something forcible, be it by nature or not! Hérault men-
tions epigrammatically that he " sat in this Hall, and was
detested of Parlementeers." Camille makes answer, " My age
is that of the bon Sansculotte Jésus; an age fatal to Revolutionists." O Camille, Camille! And yet in that Divine Transaction, let us say, there did lie, among other things, the fatalest
Reproof ever uttered here below to Worldly Right-honourable-
ness; " the highest fact," so devout Novalis calls it, " in the
Rights of Man." Camille's real age, it would seem, is thirty-
four. Danton is one year older.

Some five months ago, the Trial of the Twenty-two Girondins was the greatest that Fouquier had then done. But
here is a still greater to do; a thing which tasks the whole

faculty of Fouquier; which makes the very heart of him waver.
For it is the voice of Danton that reverberates now from
these domes; in passionate words, piercing with their wild
sincerity, winged with wrath. Your best Witnesses he shivers
into ruin at one stroke. He demands that the Committee-men
themselves come as Witnesses, as Accusers; he "will cover
them with ignominy." He raises his huge stature, he shakes
his huge black head, fire flashes from the eyes of him—piercing
to all Republican hearts: so that the very Galleries, though
we filled them by ticket, murmur sympathy; and are like to
burst down and raise the People, and deliver him! He complains loudly that he is classed with Chabots, with swindling
Stockjobbers; that his Indictment is a list of platitudes and
horrors. "Danton hidden on the 10th of August?" reverberates he, with the roar of a lion in the toils: "where are
the men that had to press Danton to show himself, that day?
Where are these high-gifted souls of whom he borrowed energy? Let them appear, these Accusers of mine: I have all
the clearness of my self-possession when I demand them. I
will unmask the three shallow scoundrels," les trois plats coquins, Saint-Just, Couthon, Lebas, "who fawn on Robespierre,
and lead him toward his destruction. Let them produce themselves here; I will plunge them into Nothingness, out of which
they ought never to have risen." The agitated President agi-
tates his bell; enjoins calmness, in a vehement manner: "What
is it to thee how I defend myself?" cries the other: "the
right of dooming me is thine always. The voice of a man
speaking for his honour and his life may well drown the jingling of thy bell!" Thus Danton, higher and higher; till the
lion-voice of him "dies away in his throat": speech will not
utter what is in that man. The Galleries murmur ominously;
the first day's Session is over.

O Tinville, President Herman, what will ye do? They
have two days more of it, by strictest Revolutionary Law.
The Galleries already murmur. If this Danton were to burst
your mesh-work!—Very curious indeed to consider. It turns
on a hair: and what a hoitytoity were there, Justice and Culprit changing places; and the whole History of France running changed! For in France there is this Danton only that
could still try to govern France. He only, the wild amorphous
Titan—and perhaps that other olive-complexioned individual,

the Artillery-Officer at Toulon, whom we left pushing his fortune in the South?

On the evening of the second day, matters looking not better but worse and worse, Fouquier and Herman, distraction in their aspect, rush over to Salut Public. What is to be done? Salut Public rapidly concocts a new Decree; whereby if men "insult Justice," they may be "thrown out of the Debates." For indeed, withal, is there not "a Plot in the Luxembourg Prison"? Ci-devant General Dillon, and others of the Suspect, plotting with Camille's Wife to distribute assignats; to force the Prisons, overset the Republic? Citizen Laflotte, himself Suspect but desiring enfranchisement, has reported said Plot for us—a report that may bear fruit! Enough, on the morrow morning, an obedient Convention passes this Decree. Salut rushes off with it to the aid of Tinville, reduced now almost to extremities. And so, "Hors de Débats, Out of the Debates, ye insolents! Policemen, do your duty!" In such manner, with a dead-lift effort Salut, Tinville, Herman, Leroi Dix-Août, and all stanch jurymen setting heart and shoulder to it, the Jury becomes "sufficiently instructed"; Sentence is passed, is sent by an Official, and torn and trampled on: Death this day. It is the 5th of April 1794. Camille's poor Wife may cease hovering about this Prison. Nay, let her kiss her poor children; and prepare to enter it, and to follow!—

Danton carried a high look in the Death-cart. Not so Camille: it is but one week, and all is so topsyturvied; angel Wife left weeping; love, riches, revolutionary fame, left all at the Prison-gate; carnivorous Rabble now howling round. Palpable, and yet incredible; like a madman's dream! Camille struggles and writhes; his shoulders shuffle the loose coat off them, which hangs knotted, the hands tied: "Calm, my friend," said Danton; "heed not that vile canaille (laissez là cette vile canaille)." At the foot of the Scaffold, Danton was heard to ejaculate: "O my Wife, my well-beloved, I shall never see thee more, then!"—but, interrupting himself: "Danton, no weakness!" He said to Hérault-Séchelles stepping forward to embrace him: "Our heads will meet there," in the Headsman's sack. His last words were to Samson the Headsman himself: "Thou wilt show my head to the people; it is worth showing."

So passes, like a gigantic mass of valour, ostentation, fury, affection and wild revolutionary force and manhood, this Danton, to his unknown home. He was of Arcis-sur-Aube; born of " good farmer-people " there. He had many sins; but one worst sin he had not, that of Cant. No hollow Formalist, deceptive and self-deceptive, ghastly to the natural sense, was this; but a very Man: with all his dross he was a Man; fiery real, from the great fire-bosom of Nature herself. He saved France from Brunswick; he walked straight his own wild road, whither it led him. He may live for some generations in the memory of men.

NOTES

[1] " Biographie des Ministres," § Danton.
[2] " Aperçus sur Camille Desmoulins " (in " Vieux Cordelier," Paris, 1825), pp. 1–29.

CHAPTER III

THE TUMBRILS

NEXT week, it is still but the 10th of April, there comes a new Nineteen; Chaumette, Gobel, Hébert's Widow, the Widow of Camille: these also roll their fated journey; black Death devours them. Mean Hébert's Widow was weeping, Camille's Widow tried to speak comfort to her. O ye kind Heavens, azure, beautiful, eternal behind your tempests and Time-clouds, is there not pity in store for all! Gobel, it seems, was repentant; he begged absolution of a Priest; died as a Gobel best could. For Anaxagoras Chaumette, the sleek head now stripped of its bonnet rouge, what hope is there? Unless Death were "an eternal sleep"? Wretched Anaxagoras, God shall judge thee, not I.

Hébert, therefore, is gone, and the Hébertists; they that robbed Churches, and adored blue Reason in red nightcap. Great Danton, and the Dantonists; they also are gone. Down to the catacombs; they are become silent men! Let no Paris Municipality, no Sect or Party of this hue or that, resist the will of Robespierre and Salut. Mayor Pache, not prompt enough in denouncing these Pitt Plots, may congratulate about them now. Never so heartily; it skills not! His course likewise is to the Luxembourg. We appoint one Fleuriot-Lescot Interim-Mayor in his stead: an "architect from Belgium," they say, this Fleuriot; he is a man one can depend on. Our new Agent-National is Payan, lately Juryman; whose cynosure also is Robespierre.

Thus then, we perceive, this confusedly electric Erebus-cloud of Revolutionary Government has altered its shape somewhat. Two masses, or wings, belonging to it; an over-electric mass of Cordelier Rabids, and an under-electric of Dantonist Moderates and Clemency-men—these two masses, shooting bolts at one another, so to speak, have annihilated one another.

For the Erebus-cloud, as we often remark, is of suicidal nature;
and, in jagged irregularity, darts its lightning withal into itself.
But now these two discrepant masses being mutually annihilated, it is as if the Erebus-cloud had got to internal composure; and did only pour its hellfire lightning on the World
that lay under it. In plain words, Terror of the Guillotine
was never terrible till now. Systole, diastole, swift and ever
swifter goes the Axe of Samson. Indictments cease by degrees
to have so much as plausibility: Fouquier chooses from the
Twelve Houses of Arrest what he calls Batches, "Fournées,"
a score or more at a time; his Jurymen are charged to make
feu de file, file-firing till the ground be clear. Citizen Laflotte's
report of Plot in the Luxembourg is verily bearing fruit!
If no speakable charge exist against a man, or Batch of men,
Fouquier has always this: a Plot in the Prison. Swift and ever
swifter goes Samson; up, finally to threescore and more at
a Batch. It is the highday of Death: none but the Dead
return not.

O dusky D'Espréménil, what a day is this the 22d of April,
thy last day! The Palais Hall here is the same stone Hall,
where thou, five years ago, stoodest perorating, amid endless
pathos of rebellious Parlement, in the gray of the morning;
bound to march with D'Agoust to the Isles of Hières. The
stones are the same stones: but the rest, Men, Rebellion,
Pathos, Peroration, see, it has all fled, like a gibbering troop of
ghosts, like the phantasms of a dying brain. With D'Espréménil, in the same line of Tumbrils, goes the mournfulest
medley. Chapelier goes, ci-devant popular President of the
Constituent; whom the Menads and Maillard met in his carriage, on the Versailles Road. Thouret likewise, ci-devant
President, father of Constitutional Law-acts; he whom we
heard saying, long since, with a loud voice, "The Constituent
Assembly has fulfilled its mission!" And the noble old Malesherbes, who defended Louis and could not speak, like a gray
old rock dissolving into sudden water: he journeys here now,
with his kindred, daughters, sons, and grandsons, his Lamoi-
gnons, Châteaubriands; silent, toward Death.—One young
Châteaubriand alone is wandering amid the Natchez, by the
roar of Niagara Falls, the moan of endless forests: Welcome
thou great Nature, savage, but not false, not unkind, un-
motherly; no Formula thou, or rabid jangle of Hypothesis,

Parliamentary Eloquence, Constitution-building and the Guillotine; speak thou to me, O Mother, and sing my sick heart thy mystic everlasting lullaby-song, and let all the rest be far!—

Another row of Tumbrils we must notice: that which holds Elisabeth, the Sister of Louis. Her Trial was like the rest; for Plots, for Plots. She was among the kindliest, most innocent of women. There sat with her, amid four-and-twenty others, a once timorous Marchioness de Crussol; courageous now; expressing toward her the liveliest loyalty. At the foot of the Scaffold, Elisabeth with tears in her eyes thanked this Marchioness; said she was grieved she could not reward her. " Ah, Madame, would your Royal Highness deign to embrace me, my wishes were complete ! "—" Right willingly, Marquise de Crussol, and with my whole heart." [1] Thus they: at the foot of the Scaffold. The Royal Family is now reduced to two: a girl and a little boy. The boy, once named Dauphin, was taken from his Mother while she yet lived; and given to one Simon, by trade a Cordwainer, on service then about the Temple-Prison, to bring him up in principles of Sansculottism. Simon taught him to drink, to swear, to sing the carmagnole. Simon is now gone to the Municipality: and the poor boy, hidden in a tower of the Temple, from which in his fright and bewilderment and early decrepitude he wishes not to stir out, lies perishing, " his shirt not changed for six months "; amid squalor and darkness, lamentably [2]—so as none but poor Factory Children and the like are wont to perish, and not be lamented!

The Spring sends its green leaves and bright weather, bright May, brighter than ever: Death pauses not. Lavoisier, famed Chemist, shall die and not live: Chemist Lavoisier was Farmer-General Lavoisier too, and now " all the Farmers-General are arrested "; all, and shall give an account of their moneys and incomings; and die for " putting water in the tobacco " they sold.[3] Lavoisier begged a fortnight more of life, to finish some experiments: but " the Republic does not need such "; the axe must do its work. Cynic Chamfort, reading these inscriptions of " Brotherhood or Death," says, " it is a Brotherhood of Cain ": arrested, then liberated; then about to be arrested again, this Chamfort cuts and slashes himself with frantic uncertain hand; gains, not without difficulty, the refuge of death. Condorcet has lurked deep, these many months; Argus-eyes watching and searching for him. His concealment is become dangerous to others and himself; he has to fly again, to skulk, round Paris, in thickets and stone-quarries. And so at the Village of Clamars, one bleared May morning, there enters a Figure ragged, rough-bearded, hunger-stricken; asks breakfast in the tavern there. Suspect, by the look of him! "Servant out of place, sayest thou?" Committee-President of Forty-Sous finds a Latin Horace on him: "Art not thou one of those Ci-devants that were wont to keep servants? Suspect!" He is haled forthwith, breakfast unfinished, toward Bourg-la-Reine, on foot: he faints with exhaustion; is set on a peasant's horse; is flung into his damp prison-cell: on the morrow, recollecting him, you enter; Condorcet lies dead on the floor. They die fast, and disappear: the Notabilities of France disappear, one after one, like lights in a Theatre, which you are snuffing out.

Under which circumstances, is it not singular, and almost touching, to see Paris City drawn out, in the meek May nights, in civic ceremony, which they call "Souper Fraternel," Brotherly Supper? Spontaneous, or partially spontaneous, in the twelfth, thirteenth, fourteenth nights of this May month, it is seen. Along the Rue Saint-Honoré, and main Streets and Spaces, each Citoyen brings forth what of supper the stingy Maximum has yielded him, to the open air; joins it to his neighbour's supper; and with common table, cheerful light burning frequent, and what due modicum of cut-glass and other garnish and relish is convenient, they eat frugally together, under the kind stars.[4] See it, O Night! With cheerfully pledged wine-cup, hobnobbing to the Reign of Liberty, Equality, Brotherhood, with their wives in best ribbons with their little ones romping round, the Citoyens, in frugal Love-feast, sit there. Night in her wide empire sees nothing similar. O my brothers, why is the reign of Brotherhood not come! It is come, it shall have come, say the Citoyens frugally hobnobbing.—Ah me! these everlasting stars, do they not look down "like glistening eyes, bright with immortal pity, over the lot of man"!—

One lamentable thing, however, is that individuals will attempt assassination—of Representatives of the People. Representative Collot, Member even of Salut, returning home, "about one in the morning," probably touched with liquor, as he is apt to be, meets on the stairs the cry "Scélérat!" and also the snap of a pistol: which latter flashes in the pan; disclosing to him, momentarily, a pair of truculent saucer-eyes, swart grim-clenched countenance; recognisable as that of our little fellow-lodger, Citoyen Amiral, formerly "a clerk in the Lotteries." Collot shouts "Murder!" with lungs fit to awaken all the Rue Favart; Amiral snaps a second time; a second time flashes in the pan; then darts up into his apartment; and, after there firing, still with inadequate effect, one musket at himself and another at his captor, is clutched and locked in Prison.[5] An indignant little man this Amiral, of Southern temper and complexion, of "considerable muscular force." He denies not that he meant to "purge France of a Tyrant"; nay, avows that he had an eye to the Incorruptible himself, but took Collot as more convenient!

Rumour enough hereupon; heaven-high congratulation of Collot, fraternal embracing, at the Jacobins and elsewhere. And yet, it would seem, the assassin mood proves catching. Two days more, it is still but the 23d of May, and toward nine in the evening, Cécile Rénault, Paper-dealer's daughter, a young woman of soft blooming look, presents herself at the Cabinet-maker's in the Rue Saint-Honoré; desires to see Robespierre. Robespierre can not be seen; she grumbles irreverently. They lay hold of her. She has left a basket in a shop hard by: in the basket are female change of raiment and two knives! Poor Cécile, examined by Committee, declares she "wanted to see what a tyrant was like"; the change of raiment was "for my own use in the place I am surely going to."—"What place?"—"Prison; and then the Guillotine," answered she.—Such things come of Charlotte Corday; in a people prone to imitation, and monomania! Swart choleric men try Charlotte's feat, and their pistols miss fire; soft blooming young women try it, and, only half-resolute, leave their knives in a shop.

O Pitt, and ye Faction of the Stranger, shall the Republic never have rest; but be torn continually by baited springes, by wires of explosive spring-guns? Swart Amiral, fair young Cécile, and all that knew them, and many that did not know them, lie locked, waiting the scrutiny of Tinville.

NOTES

[1] Montgaillard, iv, 200.

[2] Duchesse d'Angoulême, "Captivité à la Tour du Temple," pp. 37–71.

[3] "Tribunal Révolutionnaire" du 8 Mai, 1794 ("Moniteur," No. 231).

[4] "Tableaux de la Révolution," § Soupers Fraternels; Mercier, ii, 150.

[5] Riouffe, p. 73; "Deux Amis," xii, 298–302.

CHAPTER IV

MUMBO-JUMBO

BUT on the day they call Décadi, New-Sabbath, 20 Prairial, 8th June by old style, what thing is this going forward in the Jardin National, whilom Tuileries Garden? All the world is there, in holiday clothes:[1] foul linen went out with the Hébertists; nay, Robespierre, for one, would never once countenance that; but went always elegant and frizzled, not without vanity even—and had his room hung round with seagreen Portraits and Busts. In holiday clothes, we say, are the innumerable Citoyens and Citoyennes: the weather is of the brightest; cheerful expectation lights all countenances. Juryman Vilate gives breakfast to many a Deputy, in his official Apartment, in the Pavilion ci-devant of Flora; rejoices in the bright-looking multitudes, in the brightness of leafy June, in the auspicious Décadi, or New-Sabbath. This day, if it please Heaven, we are to have, on improved Anti-Chaumette principles: a new Religion.

Catholicism being burned out, and Reason-worship guillotined, was there not need of one? Incorruptible Robespierre, not unlike the Ancients, as Legislator of a free people, will now also be Priest and Prophet. He has donned his sky-blue coat, made for the occasion; white silk waistcoat broidered with silver, black silk breeches, white stockings, shoe-buckles of gold. He is President of the Convention; he has made the Convention decree, so they name it, décréter the " Existence of the Supreme Being," and likewise " ce principe consolateur of the Immortality of the Soul." These consolatory principles, the basis of rational Republican Religion, are getting decreed; and here, on this blessed Décadi, by help of Heaven and Painter David, is to be our first act of worship.

See, accordingly, how after Decree passed, and what has been called " the scraggiest Prophetic Discourse ever uttered by man "—Mahomet Robespierre, in sky-blue coat and black breeches, frizzled and powdered to perfection, bearing in his hand a bouquet of flowers and wheat-ears, issues proudly from the Convention Hall; Convention following him, yet, as is remarked, with an interval. Amphitheatre has been raised, or at least Monticule or Elevation; hideous Statues of Atheism, Anarchy and such-like, thanks to Heaven and Painter David, strike abhorrence into the heart. Unluckily, however, our Monticule is too small. On the top of it not half of us can stand; wherefore there arises indecent shoving, nay, treasonous irreverent growling. Peace, thou Bourdon de l'Oise; peace, or it may be worse for thee!

The seagreen Pontiff takes a torch, Painter David handing it; mouths some other froth-rant of vocables, which happily one can not hear; strides resolutely forward, in sight of expectant France; sets his torch to Atheism and Company, which are but made of pasteboard steeped in turpentine. They burn up rapidly; and, from within, there rises " by machinery," an incombustible Statue of Wisdom, which, by ill hap, gets besmoked a little; but does stand there visible in as serene attitude as it can.

And then? Why, then, there is other Processioning, scraggy Discoursing, and—this is our Feast of the Être Suprême; our new Religion, better or worse, is come!—Look at it one moment, O Reader, not two. The shabbiest page of Human Annals: or is there, that thou wottest of, one shabbier? Mumbo-Jumbo of the African woods to me seems venerable beside this new Deity of Robespierre; for this is a conscious Mumbo-Jumbo, and knows that he is machinery. O seagreen Prophet, unhappiest of windbags blown nigh to bursting, what distracted Chimera among realities art thou growing to! This then, this common pitch-link for artificial fireworks of turpentine and pasteboard; this is the miraculous Aaron's Rod thou wilt stretch over a hag-ridden hell-ridden France, and bid her plagues cease? Vanish, thou and it!— " Avec ton Être Suprême," said Billaud, " tu commences m'embêter: With thy Être Suprême thou beginnest to be a bore to me." [2]

Catherine Théot, on the other hand, " an ancient serving-maid seventy-nine years of age," inured to Prophecy and the Bastille from of old, sits in an upper room in the Rue de Contrescarpe, poring over the Book of Revelation, with an eye to Robespierre; finds that this astonishing thrice-potent Maximilien really is the Man spoken of by Prophets, who is to make the Earth young again. With her sit devout old Marchionesses, ci-devant honourable women; among whom Old-Constituent Dom Gerle, with his addle head, can not be wanting. They sit there, in the Rue de Contrescarpe; in mysterious adoration: Mumbo is Mumbo, and Robespierre is his Prophet. A conspicuous man this Robespierre. He has his volunteer Bodyguard of Tappe-durs, let us say Strike-sharps, fierce Patriots with feruled sticks; and Jacobins kissing the hem of his garment. He enjoys the admiration of many, the worship of some; and is well worth the wonder of one and all.

The grand question and hope, however, is: Will not this Feast of the Tuileries Mumbo-Jumbo be a sign perhaps that the Guillotine is to abate? Far enough from that! Precisely on the second day after it, Couthon, one of the " three shallow scoundrels," gets himself lifted into the Tribune; produces a bundle of papers. Couthon proposes that, as Plots still abound, the Law of the Suspect shall have extension, and Arrestment new vigour and facility. Further, that as in such case business is like to be heavy, our Revolutionary Tribunal too shall have extension; be divided, say, into Four Tribunals, each with its President, each with its Fouquier or Substitute of Fouquier, all labouring at once, any remnant of shackle or dilatory formality be struck off: in this way it may perhaps still overtake the work. Such is Couthon's Decree of the Twenty-second Prairial, famed in those times. At hearing of which decree, the very Mountain gasped, awestruck; and one Ruamps ventured to say that if it passed without adjournment and discussion, he, as one Representative, " would blow his brains out." Vain saying! The Incorruptible knit his brows; spoke a prophetic fateful word or two; the Law of Prairial is Law; Ruamps glad to leave his rash brains where they are. Death then, and always Death! Even so. Fouquier is enlarging his borders; making room for Batches of a Hundred and fifty at once— getting a Guillotine set up of improved velocity, and to work under cover, in the apartment close by. So that Salut itself has to intervene, and forbid him: " Wilt thou demoralize the Guillotine?" asks Collot reproachfully, " démoraliser le supplice!"

There is indeed danger of that; were not the Republican faith great, it were already done. See, for example, on the 17th of June, what a Batch, Fifty-four at once! Swart Amiral is here, he of the pistol that missed fire; young Cécile Rénault, with her father, family, entire kith and kin; the Widow of D'Espréménil; old M. de Sombreuil of the Invalides, with his Son—poor old Sombreuil, seventy-three years old, his Daughter saved him in September, and it was but for this. Faction of the Stranger, fifty-four of them! In red shirts and smocks as Assassins and Faction of the Stranger, they flit along there; red baleful Phantasmagory, toward the land of Phantoms.

Meanwhile will not the people of the Place de la Révolution, the inhabitants along the Rue Saint-Honoré, as these continual Tumbrils pass, begin to look gloomy? Republicans too have bowels. The Guillotine is shifted, then again shifted; finally set up at the remote extremity of the South-east:[3] Suburbs Saint-Antoine and Saint-Marceau, it is to be hoped, if they have bowels, have very tough ones.

NOTES

[1] Vilate, " Causes Secrètes de la Révolution du 9 Thermidor."

[2] See Vilate, " Causes Secrètes." (Vilate's Narrative is very curious; but is not to be taken as true, without sifting; being, at bottom, in spite of its title, not a Narrative but a Pleading.)

[3] Montgaillard, iv, 237.

CHAPTER V

THE PRISONS

IT is time now, however, to cast a glance into the Prisons. When Desmoulins moved for his Committee of Mercy, these Twelve Houses of Arrest held five-thousand persons. Continually arriving since then, there have now accumulated twelve-thousand. They are Ci-devants, Royalists; in far greater part, they are Republicans, of various Girondin, Fayettish, Un-Jacobin colour. Perhaps no human Habitation or Prison ever equalled in squalor, in noisome horror, these Twelve Houses of Arrest. There exist records of personal experience in them. " Mémoires sur les Prisons "; one of the strangest Chapters in the Biography of Man.

Very singular to look into it: how a kind of order rises up in all conditions of human existence; and wherever two or three are gathered together, there are formed modes of existing together, habitudes, observances, nay gracefulnesses, joys! Citoyen Coittant will explain fully how our lean dinner, of herbs and carrion, was consumed not without politeness and place-aux-dames: how Seigneur and Shoeblack, Duchess and Doll-Tearsheet, flung pell-mell into a heap, ranked themselves according to method: at what hour " the Citoyennes took to their needlework "; and we, yielding the chairs to them, endeavoured to talk gallantly in a standing posture, or even to sing and harp more or less. Jealousies, enmities, are not wanting; nor flirtations, of an effective character.

Alas! by degrees, even needlework must cease: Plot in the Prison rises, by Citoyen Laflotte and Preternatural Suspicion. Suspicious Municipality snatches from us all implements; all money and possession, of means or metal, is ruthlessly searched for, in pocket, in pillow and paillasse, and snatched away: red-capped Commissaries entering every cell. Indignation, temporary desperation, at robbery of its very thimble, fills the gentle heart. Old Nuns shriek shrill discord; demand to be

killed forthwith. No help from shrieking! Better was that
of the two shifty male Citizens, who, eager to preserve an
implement or two, were it but a pipe-picker, or needle to
darn hose with, determined to defend themselves: by tobacco.
Swift then, as your fell Red Caps are heard in the Corridor
rummaging and slamming, the two Citoyens light their pipes,
and begin smoking. Thick darkness envelops them. The Red
Nightcaps, opening the cell, breathe but one mouthful; burst
forth into chorus of barking and coughing. " Quoi, Messieurs," cry the two Citoyens, " you don't smoke? Is the pipe
disagreeable? Est-ce que vous ne fumez pas?" But the Red
Nightcaps have fled, with slight search: " Vous n'aimez pas
la pipe?" cry the Citoyens, as their door slams-to again.[1] My
poor brother Citoyens, O surely, in a reign of Brotherhood,
you are not the two I would guillotine!

Rigour grows, stiffens into horrid tyranny; Plot in the
Prison getting ever rifer. This Plot in the Prison, as we
said, is now the stereotype formula of Tinville: against whomsoever he knows no crime, this is a ready-made crime. His
Judgment-bar has become unspeakable; a recognised mockery; known only as the wicket one passes through, toward
Death. His Indictments are drawn out in blank; you insert
the Names after. He has his moutons, detestable traitor
jackals, who report and bear witness; that they themselves
may be allowed to live—for a time. His Fournées, says the
reproachful Collot, " shall in no case exceed threescore";
that is his maximum. Nightly come his Tumbrils to the
Luxembourg, with the fatal Roll-call; list of the Fournée of
to-morrow. Men rush toward the Grate; listen, if their name
be in it? One deep-drawn breath, when the name is not in;
we live still one day! And yet some score or scores of names
were in. Quick these, they clasp their loved ones to their heart,
one last time; with brief adieu, wet-eyed or dry-eyed, they
mount, and are away. This night to the Conciergerie; through
the Palais misnamed of Justice, to the Guillotine to-morrow.

Recklessness, defiant levity, the Stoicism if not of strength
yet of weakness, has possessed all hearts. Weak women and
Ci-devants, their locks not yet made into blond perukes, their
skins not yet tanned into breeches, are accustomed to " act the
Guillotine" by way of pastime. In fantastic mummery, with
towel-turbans, blanket-ermine, a mock Sanhedrim of Judges

sits, a mock Tinville pleads; a culprit is doomed, is guillotined by the oversetting of two chairs. Sometimes we carry
it further: Tinville himself, in his turn, is doomed, and not
to the Guillotine alone. With blackened face, hirsute, horned,
a shaggy Satan snatches him not unshrieking; shows him,
with outstretched arm and voice, the fire that is not quenched,
the worm that dies not; the monotony of Hell-pain, and the
" What hour? " answered by, " It is Eternity." [2]

And still the Prisons fill fuller, and still the Guillotine goes
faster. On all high roads march flights of Prisoners, wending
toward Paris. Not Ci-devants now; they, the noisy of them,
are mown down; it is Republicans now. Chained two and
two they march; in exasperated moments singing their " Marseillaise." A hundred and thirty-two men of Nantes, for instance, march toward Paris, in these same days: Republicans,
or say even Jacobins to the marrow of the bone; but Jacobins
who had not approved Noyading.[3] " Vive la République! "
rises from them in all streets of towns: they rest by night in
unutterable noisome dens, crowded to choking; one or two
dead on the morrow. They are wayworn, weary of heart; can
only shout: " Live the Republic! " we, as under horrid enchantment, dying in this way for it!

Some Four-hundred Priests, of whom also there is record,
ride at anchor " in the roads of the Isle of Aix," long months;
looking out on misery, vacuity, waste Sands of Oleron and the
ever-moaning brine. Ragged, sordid, hungry; wasted to
shadows: eating their unclean ration on deck, circularly, in
parties of a dozen, with finger and thumb; beating their scandalous clothes between two stones; choked in horrible mias-
mata, closed under hatches, seventy of them in a berth, through
night; so that the " aged Priest is found lying dead in the
morning, in the attitude of prayer "![4]—How long, O Lord!

Not for ever; no. All Anarchy, all Evil, Injustice, is, by
the nature of it, dragon's-teeth; suicidal, and can not endure.

NOTES

[1] " Maison d'Arrêt de Port-Libre," par Coittant, etc. (" Mémoires
sur les Prisons," ii).

[2] Montgaillard, iv, 218; Riouffe, p. 273.

[3] " Voyage de Cent Trente-deux Nantais " (" Prisons," ii, 288–335).

[4] " Relation de ce qu'ont souffert pour la Religion les Prêtres dé-
portés en 1794, dans la rade de l'île d'Aix " (ib., ii, 387–485).

CHAPTER VI

TO FINISH THE TERROR

IT is very remarkable, indeed, that since the Être-Suprême Feast, and the sublime continued harangues on it, which Billaud feared would become a bore to him, Robespierre has gone little to Committee; but held himself apart, as if in a kind of pet. Nay, they have made a Report on that old Catherine Théot, and her Regenerative Man spoken of by the Prophets; not in the best spirit. This Théot mystery they affect to regard as a Plot; but have evidently introduced a vein of satire, of irreverent banter, not against the Spinster alone, but obliquely against her Regenerative Man! Barrère's light pen was perhaps at the bottom of it: read through the solemn snuffling organs of old Vadier of the Sûreté Générale, the Théot Report had its effect; wrinkling the general Republican visage into an iron grin. Ought these things to be?

We note further, that among the Prisoners in the Twelve Houses of Arrest, there is one whom we have seen before. Senhora Fontenai, born Cabarus, the fair Proserpine whom Representative Tallien Pluto-like did gather at Bordeaux, not without effect on himself! Tallien is home, by recall, long since, from Bordeaux; and in the most alarming position. Vain that he sounded, louder even than ever, the note of Jacobinism, to hide past shortcomings: the Jacobins purged him out; two times has Robespierre growled at him words of omen from the Convention Tribune. And now his fair Cabarus, hit by denunciation, lies Arrested, Suspect, in spite of all he could do!—Shut in horrid pinfold of death, the Senhora smuggles out to her red-gloomy Tallien the most pressing entreaties and conjurings: Save me; save thyself. Seest thou not that thy own head is doomed; thou with a too fiery audacity; a Dantonist withal; against whom lie grudges? Are ye not all doomed, as in the Polyphemus

Cavern: the fawningest slave of you will be but eaten last!—
Tallien feels with a shudder that it is true. Tallien has had
words of omen, Bourdon has had words, Fréron is hated and
Barras: each man "feels his head if it yet stick on his
shoulders."

Meanwhile Robespierre, we still observe, goes little to Convention, not at all to Committee; speaks nothing except to
his Jacobin House of Lords, amid his bodyguard of Tappe-
durs. These "forty-days," for we are now far in July, he has
not showed face in Committee; could only work there by his
three shallow scoundrels, and the terror there was of him.
The Incorruptible himself sits apart; or is seen stalking in
solitary places in the fields, with an intensely meditative air;
some say, "with eyes red-spotted," [1] fruit of extreme bile: the
lamentablest seagreen Chimera that walks the Earth that July!
O hapless Chimera—for thou too hadst a life, and heart of
flesh—what is this that the stern gods, seeming to smile all
the way, have led and let thee to! Art not thou he, who,
few years ago, was a young Advocate of promise; and gave up
the Arras Judgeship rather than sentence one man to die?—

What his thoughts might be? His plans for finishing the
Terror? One knows not. Dim vestiges there flit of Agrarian
Law: a victorious Sansculottism become Landed Proprietor;
old Soldiers sitting in National Mansions, in Hospital Palaces
of Chambord and Chantilly; peace bought by victory; breaches
healed by Feast of Être Suprême—and so, through seas of
blood, to Equality, Frugality, worksome Blessedness, Fraternity, and Republic of the virtues. Blessed shore, of such a
sea of Aristocrat blood: but how to land on it? Through
one last wave: blood of corrupt Sansculottists; traitorous or
semi-traitorous Conventionals, rebellious Talliens, Billauds, to
whom with my Être Suprême I have become a bore; with
my Apocalyptic Old Woman a laughing-stock!—So stalks he,
this poor Robespierre, like a seagreen ghost, through the
blooming July. Vestiges of schemes flit dim. But what his
schemes or his thoughts were will never be known to man.

New Catacombs, some say, are digging for a huge simultaneous butchery. Convention to be butchered, down to the
right pitch, by General Henriot and Company: Jacobin House
of Lords made dominant; and Robespierre Dictator. [2] There
is actually, or else there is not actually, a List made out;

which the Hairdresser has got eye on, as he frizzled the Incorruptible locks. Each man asks himself, Is it I?

Nay, as Tradition and rumour of Anecdote still convey it, there was a remarkable bachelor's dinner, one hot day, at Barrère's. For doubt not, O Reader, this Barrère and others of them gave dinners; had "country-house at Clichy," with elegant enough sumptuosities, and pleasures high-rouged.[3] But at this dinner we speak of, the day being so hot, it is said, the guests all stript their coats, and left them in the drawing-room: from the dinner-table Carnot glided out, driven by a necessity, needing of all things paper; groped in Robespierre's pocket; found a list of Forty, his own name among them—and tarried not at the wine-cup that day!—Ye must bestir yourselves, O Friends; ye dull Frogs of the Marsh, mute ever since Girondism sank under, even you now must croak or die! Councils are held, with word and beck; nocturnal, mysterious as death. Does not a feline Maximilien stalk there; voiceless as yet; his green eyes red-spotted; back bent, and hair up? Rash Tallien, with his rash temper and audacity of tongue; he shall bell the cat. Fix a day; and be it soon, lest never!

Lo, before the fixed day, on the day which they call Eighth of Thermidor, 26th July 1794, Robespierre himself reappears in Convention; mounts to the Tribune! The biliary face seems clouded with new gloom: judge whether your Talliens, Bourdons, listened with interest. It is a voice bodeful of death or of life. Longwinded, unmelodious as the screech-owl's, sounds that prophetic voice: Degenerate condition of Republican spirit; corrupt Moderatism; Sûreté, Salut Committees themselves infected; backsliding on this hand and on that; I, Maximilien, alone left incorruptible, ready to die at a moment's warning. For all which what remedy is there? The Guillotine; new vigour to the all-healing Guillotine; death to traitors of every hue! So sings the prophetic voice; into its Convention sounding-board. The old song this: but to-day, O Heavens, has the sounding-board ceased to act? There is not resonance in this Convention; there is, so to speak, a gasp of silence; nay, a certain grating of one knows not what!—Lecointre, our old Draper of Versailles, in these questionable circumstances, sees nothing he can do so safe as rise, "insidiously" or not insidiously, and move, according to established wont, that the Robespierre Speech be "printed and sent to the Departments." Hark: gratings, even of dissonance! Honourable Members hint dissonance; Committee-Members, inculpated in the Speech, utter dissonance, demand " delay in printing." Ever higher rises the note of dissonance; enquiry is even made by Editor Fréron: " What has become of the Liberty of Opinions in this Convention? " The Order to print and transmit, which had got passed, is rescinded. Robespierre, greener than ever before, has to retire, foiled; discerning that it is mutiny, that evil is nigh!

Mutiny is a thing of the fatalest nature in all enterprises whatsoever; a thing so incalculable, swift-frightful: not to be dealt with in fright. But mutiny in a Robespierre Convention, above all—it is like fire seen sputtering in the ship's powder-room! One death-defiant plunge at it, this moment, and you may still tread it out: hesitate till next moment— ship and ship's captain, crew and cargo are shivered far; the ship's voyage has suddenly ended between sea and sky. If Robespierre can, to-night, produce his Henriot and Company, and get his work done by them, he and Sansculottism may still subsist some time; if not, probably not. Oliver Cromwell, when that Agitator Sergeant stept forth from the ranks, with plea of grievances, and began gesticulating and demonstrating, as the mouthpiece of Thousands expectant there— discerned, with those truculent eyes of his, how the matter lay; plucked a pistol from his holsters; blew Agitator and Agitation instantly out. Noll was a man fit for such things.

Robespierre, for his part, glides over at evening to his Jacobin House of Lords; unfolds there, instead of some adequate resolution, his woes, his uncommon virtues, incorruptibilities; then, secondly, his rejected screech-owl Oration—reads this latter over again; and declares that he is ready to die at a moment's warning. Thou shalt not die! shouts Jacobinism from its thousand throats. " Robespierre, I will drink the hemlock with thee," cries Painter David, " Je boirai la cigue avec toi "—a thing not essential to do, but which, in the fire of the moment, can be said.

Our Jacobin sounding-board, therefore, does act! Applauses heaven-high cover the rejected Oration; fire-eyed fury lights all Jacobin features: Insurrection a sacred duty; the Convention to be purged; Sovereign People under Henriot and Municipality; we will make a new June-Second of it: To your tents, O Israel! In this key pipes Jacobinism; in sheer tumult of revolt. Let Tallien and all Opposition men make off. Collot d'Herbois, though of the supreme Salut, and so lately near shot, is elbowed, bullied; is glad to escape alive. Entering Committee-room of Salut, all dishevelled, he finds sleek sombre Saint-Just there, among the rest; who in his sleek way asks, " What is passing at the Jacobins?"—" What is passing?" repeats Collot, in the unhistrionic Cambyses vein: " What is passing? Nothing but revolt and horrors are passing. Ye want our lives; ye shall not have them." Saint-Just stutters at such Cambyses oratory; takes his hat to withdraw. That Report he had been speaking of, Report on Republican Things in General we may say, which is to be read in Convention on the morrow, he can not show it them, at this moment: a friend has it; he, Saint-Just, will get it, and send it, were he once home. Once home, he sends not it, but an answer that he will not send it; that they will hear it from the Tribune to-morrow.

Let every man, therefore, according to a well-known good-advice, " pray to Heaven, and keep his powder dry!" Paris on the morrow, will see a thing. Swift scouts fly dim or invisible, all night, from Sûreté and Salut; from conclave to conclave; from Mother Society to Townhall. Sleep, can it fall on the eyes of Talliens, Frérons, Collots? Puissant Henriot, Mayor Fleuriot, Judge Coffinhal, Procureur Payan, Robespierre and all the Jacobins are getting ready.

NOTES

[1] " Deux Amis," xii, 347–373. [2] " Ibid., 350–358.
[3] See Vilate.

CHAPTER VII

GO DOWN TO

TALLIEN'S eyes beamed bright, on the morrow, Ninth of Thermidor, "about nine o'clock," to see that the Convention had actually met. Paris is in rumour: but at least we are met, in Legal Convention here; we have not been snatched seriatim; treated with a Pride's Purge at the door. "Allons, brave men of the Plain," late Frogs of the Marsh! cried Tallien with a squeeze of the hand, as he passed in; Saint-Just's sonorous voice being now audible from the Tribune, and the game of games begun.

Saint-Just is verily reading that Report of his; green Vengeance, in the shape of Robespierre, watching nigh. Behold, however, Saint-Just has read but few sentences, when interruption rises, rapid crescendo; when Tallien starts to his feet, and Billaud, and this man starts and that—Tallien, a second time, with his: " Citoyens, at the Jacobins last night, I trembled for the Republic. I said to myself, if the Convention dare not strike the Tyrant, then I myself dare; and with this I will do it, if need be," said he, whisking out a clear-gleaming Dagger, and brandishing it there; the Steel of Brutus, as we call it. Whereat we all bellow, and brandish, impetuous acclaim. "Tyranny! Dictatorship! Triumvirate!" And the Salut Committee-men accuse, and all men accuse, and uproar, and impetuously acclaim. And Saint-Just is standing motionless, pale of face; Couthon ejaculating, "Triumvir?" with a look at his paralytic legs. And Robespierre is struggling to speak, but President Thuriot is jingling the bell against him, but the Hall is sounding against him like an Æolus-Hall: and Robespierre is mounting the Tribune-steps and descending again; going and coming, like to choke with rage, terror, desperation —and mutiny is the order of the day! [1]

O President Thuriot, thou that wert Elector Thuriot, and

from the Bastille battlements sawest Saint-Antoine rising like
the Ocean-tide, and hast seen much since, sawest thou ever the
like of this? Jingle of bell, which thou jinglest against Robespierre, is hardly audible amid the Bedlam storm; and men
rage for life. "President of Assassins," shrieks Robespierre,
"I demand speech of thee for the last time!" It can not be
had. "To you, O virtuous men of the Plain," cries he, finding
audience one moment, "I appeal to you!" The virtuous men
of the Plain sit silent as stones. And Thuriot's bell jingles,
and the Hall sounds like Æolus's Hall. Robespierre's frothing
lips are grown "blue"; his tongue dry, cleaving to the roof
of his mouth. "The blood of Danton chokes him," cry they.
"Accusation! Decree of Accusation!" Thuriot swiftly puts
that question. Accusation passes; the incorruptible Maximilien is decreed Accused.

"I demand to share my Brother's fate, as I have striven to
share his virtues," cries Augustin, the Younger Robespierre:
Augustin also is decreed. And Couthon, and Saint-Just, and
Lebas, they are all decreed; and packed forth—not without
difficulty, the Ushers almost trembling to obey. Triumvirate
and Company are packed forth, into Salut Committee-room;
their tongue cleaving to the roof of their mouth. You have
but to summon the Municipality; to cashier Commandant
Henriot, and launch Arrest at him; to regulate formalities;
hand Tinville his victims. It is noon: the Æolus-Hall has
delivered itself; blows now victorious, harmonious, as one
irresistible wind.

And so the work is finished? One thinks so; and yet it is
not so. Alas! there is yet but the first-act finished; three or
four other acts still to come; and an uncertain catastrophe!
A huge City holds in it so many confusions: seven hundred
thousand human heads; not one of which knows what its
neighbour is doing, nay not what itself is doing.—See, accordingly, about three in the afternoon, Commandant Henriot,
how instead of sitting cashiered, arrested, he gallops along the
Quais, followed by Municipal Gendarmes, "trampling down
several persons"! For the Townhall sits deliberating, openly
insurgent: Barriers to be shut; no Gaoler to admit any Prisoner this day—and Henriot is galloping toward the Tuileries,
to deliver Robespierre. On the Quai de la Ferraillerie, a
young Citoyen, walking with his wife, says aloud: "Gendarmes,

that man is not your Commandant; he is under arrest." The Gendarmes strike down the young Citoyen with the flat of their swords.[2]

Representatives themselves (as Merlin the Thionviller), who accost him, this puissant Henriot flings into guard-houses. He bursts toward the Tuileries Committee-room, " to speak with Robespierre ": with difficulty, the Ushers and Tuileries Gendarmes, earnestly pleading and drawing sabre, seize this Henriot; get the Henriot Gendarmes persuaded not to fight; get Robespierre and Company packed into hackney-coaches, sent off under escort, to the Luxembourg and other Prisons. This, then, is the end? May not an exhausted Convention adjourn now, for a little repose and sustenance, " at five o'clock "?

An exhausted Convention did it; and repented it. The end was not come; only the end of the second-act. Hark, while exhausted Representatives sit at victuals—tocsin bursting from all steeples, drums rolling, in the summer evening: Judge Coffinhal is galloping with new Gendarmes, to deliver Henriot from Tuileries Committee-room; and does deliver him! Puissant Henriot vaults on horseback; sets to haranguing the Tuileries Gendarmes; corrupts the Tuileries Gendarmes too; trots off with them to Townhall. Alas! and Robespierre is not in Prison: the Gaoler showed his Municipal order, durst not, on pain of his life, admit any Prisoner; the Robespierre Hackney-coaches, in this confused jangle and whirl of uncertain Gendarmes, have floated safe—into the Townhall! There sit Robespierre and Company, embraced by Municipals and Jacobins in sacred right of Insurrection; redacting Proclamations; sounding tocsins; corresponding with Sections and Mother Society. Is not here a pretty enough third-act of a natural Greek Drama; catastrophe more uncertain than ever?

The hasty Convention rushes together again, in the ominous nightfall: President Collot, for the chair is his, enters with long strides, paleness on his face; claps-on his hat; says with solemn tone: " Citoyens, armed Villains have beset the Committee-rooms, and got possession of them. The hour is come, to die at our post! " " Oui," answer one and all: " We swear it! " It is no rodomontade, this time, but a sad fact and necessity; unless we do at our posts, we must verily die. Swift

therefore, Robespierre, Henriot, the Municipality, are declared
Rebels; put Hors la Loi, Out of Law. Better still, we appoint Barras Commandant of what Armed-force is to be had;
send Missionary Representatives to all Sections and quarters,
to preach, and raise force; will die at least with harness on
our back.

What a distracted City; men riding and running, reporting and hearsaying; the Hour clearly in travail—child not
to be named till born! The poor Prisoners in the Luxembourg hear the rumour; tremble for a new September. They
see men making signals to them, on skylights and roofs,
apparently signals of hope; can not in the least make out
what it is.[3] We observe, however, in the eventide, as usual,
the Death-tumbrils faring Southeastward, through Saint-
Antoine, toward their Barrier du Trône. Saint-Antoine's
tough bowels melt; Saint-Antoine surrounds the Tumbrils;
says, It shall not be. O Heavens, why should it! Henriot
and Gendarmes, scouring the streets that way, bellow, with
waved sabres, that it must. Quit hope, ye poor Doomed!
The Tumbrils move on.

But in this set of Tumbrils there are two other things
notable: one notable person; and one want of a notable
person. The notable person is Lieutenant-General Loiserolles, a nobleman by birth and by nature; laying down his
life here for his son. In the Prison of Saint-Lazare, the night
before last, hurrying to the Grate to hear the Death-List read,
he caught the name of his son. The son was asleep at the
moment. "I am Loiserolles," cried the old man: at Tinville's
bar, an error in the Christian name is little; small objection
was made.—The want of the notable person, again, is that
of Deputy Paine! Paine has sat in the Luxembourg since
January; and seemed forgotten; but Fouquier had pricked
him at last. The Turnkey, List in hand, is marking with chalk
the outer doors of to-morrow's Fournée. Paine's outer door
happened to be open, turned back on the wall; the Turnkey
marked it on the side next him, and hurried on: another
Turnkey came, and shut it; no chalk-mark now visible, the
Fournée went without Paine. Paine's life lay not there.—

Our fifth-act, of this natural Greek Drama, with its natural
unities, can only be painted in gross; somewhat as that antique Painter, driven desperate, did the foam. For through

this blessed July night, there is clangour, confusion very great, of marching troops; of Sections going this way, Sections going that; of Missionary Representatives reading Proclamations by torchlight; Missionary Legendre, who has raised force somewhere, emptying out the Jacobins, and flinging their key on the Convention table: "I have locked their door; it shall be Virtue that reopens it." Paris, we say, is set against itself, rushing confused, as Ocean-currents do; a huge Mahlstrom, sounding there, under cloud of night. Convention sits permanent on this hand; Municipality most permanent on that. The poor prisoners hear tocsin and rumour: strive to bethink them of the signals apparently of hope. Meek continual Twilight streaming up, which will be Dawn and a To-morrow, silvers the Northern hem of Night; it wends and wends there, that meek brightness, like a silent prophecy, along the great ring-dial of the Heaven. So still, eternal! and on Earth all is confused shadow and conflict; dissidence, tumultuous gloom and glare; and " Destiny as yet sits wavering, and shakes her doubtful urn."

About three in the morning the dissident Armed-forces have met. Henriot's Armed-force stood ranked in the Place de Grève; and now Barras's, which he has recruited, arrives there; and they front each other, cannon bristling against cannon. Citoyens! cries the voice of Discretion loudly enough, Before coming to bloodshed, to endless civil-war, hear the Convention Decree read: " Robespierre and all rebels Out of Law!"—Out of Law? There is terror in the sound. Unarmed Citoyens disperse rapidly home. Municipal Cannoneers, in sudden whirl, anxiously unanimous, range themselves on the Convention side, with shouting. At which shout, Henriot descends from his upper room, far gone in drink as some say; finds his Place de Grève empty; the cannon's mouth turned toward him; and on the whole—that it is now the catastrophe!

Stumbling in again, the wretched drunk-sobered Henriot announces: "All is lost!" "Misérable, it is thou that hast lost it!" cry they; and fling him, or else he flings himself, out of window: far enough down; into masonwork and horror of cesspool; not into death but worse. Augustin Robespierre follows him; with the like fate. Saint-Just, they say, called on Lebas to kill him; who would not. Couthon crept under a table; attempting to kill himself; not doing it.—On entering that Sanhedrim of Insurrection, we find all as good as extinct; undone, ready for seizure. Robespierre was sitting on a chair, with pistol-shot blown through not his head but his under-jaw; the suicidal hand had failed.[4] With prompt zeal, not without trouble, we gather these wrecked Conspirators; fish up even Henriot and Augustin, bleeding and foul; pack them all, rudely enough, into carts; and shall, before sunrise, have them safe under lock and key. Amid shoutings and embracings.

Robespierre lay in an anteroom of the Convention Hall, while his Prison-escort was getting ready; the mangled jaw bound up rudely with bloody linen: a spectacle to men. He lies stretched on a table, a deal-box his pillow; the sheath of the pistol is still clenched convulsively in his hand. Men bully him, insult him: his eyes still indicate intelligence; he speaks no word. " He had on the sky-blue coat he had got made for the Feast of the Être Suprême "—O Reader, can thy hard heart hold out against that? His trousers were nankeen; the stockings had fallen down over the ankles. He spake no word more in this world.

And so, at six in the morning, a victorious Convention adjourns. Report flies over Paris as on golden wings; penetrates the Prisons; irradiates the faces of those that were ready to perish: turnkeys and moutons, fallen from their high estate, look mute and blue. It is the 28th day of July, called 10th of Thermidor, year 1794.

Fouquier had but to identify; his Prisoners being already Out of Law. At four in the afternoon, never before were the streets of Paris seen so crowded. From the Palais de Justice to the Place de la Révolution, for thither again go the Tumbrils this time, it is one dense stirring mass; all windows crammed; the very roofs and ridge-tiles budding forth human Curiosity, in strange gladness. The Death-tumbrils, with their motley Batch of Outlaws, some Twenty-three or so, from Maximilien to Mayor Fleuriot and Simon the Cordwainer, roll on. All eyes are on Robespierre's Tumbril, where he, his jaw bound in dirty linen, with his half-dead Brother and half-dead Henriot, lie shattered; their " seventeen hours " of agony about to end. The Gendarmes point their swords at him, to show the people which is he. A woman springs on the Tumbril;

THE MORNING OF THE TENTH OF
THERMIDOR, 1794.

Photogravure from a painting by Étienne Lucien Mélingue.

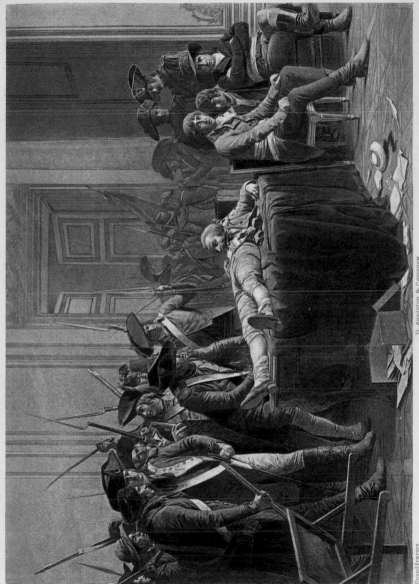

clutching the side of it with one hand, waving the other Sibyl-like; and exclaims: " The death of thee gladdens my very heart, m'enivre de joie"; Robespierre opened his eyes; " Scélérat, go down to Hell, with the curses of all wives and mothers! "—At the foot of the scaffold, they stretched him on the ground till his turn came. Lifted aloft, his eyes again opened; caught the bloody axe. Samson wrenched the coat off him; wrenched the dirty linen from his jaw: the jaw fell powerless, there burst from him a cry—hideous to hear and see. Samson, thou canst not be too quick!

Samson's work done, there bursts forth shout on shout of applause. Shout, which prolongs itself not only over Paris, but over France, but over Europe, and down to this generation. Deservedly, and also undeservedly. O unhappiest Advocate of Arras, wert thou worse than other Advocates? Stricter man, according to his Formula, to his Credo and his Cant, of pro-bities, benevolences, pleasures-of-virtue, and such-like, lived not in that age. A man fitted, in some luckier settled age, to have become one of those incorruptible barren Pattern-Figures and have had marble-tablets and funeral-sermons. His poor landlord, the Cabinet-maker in the Rue Saint-Honoré, loved him; his Brother died for him. May God be merciful to him and to us!

This is the end of the Reign of Terror; new glorious Revolution named of Thermidor; of Thermidor 9th, year 2; which being interpreted into old slave-style means 27th of July 1794. Terror is ended; and death in the Place de la Révolution, were the " Tail of Robespierre " once executed; which service Fouquier, in large Batches, is swiftly managing.

NOTES

[1] " Moniteur," Nos. 311, 312; " Débats," iv, 421–442; " Deux Amis," xii, 390–411.

[2] " Précis des Evénemens du Neuf Thermidor," par C. A. Méda, ancien Gendarme (Paris, 1825).

[3] " Mémoires sur les Prisons," ii, 277.

[4] Méda, p. 384. (Méda asserts that it was he who, with infinite courage though in a lefthanded manner, shot Robespierre. Méda got promoted for his services of this night; and died General and Baron. Few credited Méda in what was otherwise incredible.)

Book XX

VENDÉMIAIRE

CHAPTER I

DECADENT

HOW little did anyone suppose that here was the end not of Robespierre only, but of the Revolution System itself! Least of all did the mutinying Committee-men suppose it; who had mutinied with no view whatever except to continue the National Regeneration with their own heads on their shoulders. And yet so it verily was. The insignificant stone they had struck out, so insignificant anywhere else, proved to be the Keystone; the whole arch-work and edifice of Sansculottism began to loosen, to crack, to yawn; and tumbled piecemeal, with considerable rapidity, plunge after plunge; till the Abyss had swallowed it all, and in this upper world Sansculottism was no more.

For despicable as Robespierre himself might be, the death of Robespierre was a signal at which great multitudes of men, struck dumb with terror heretofore, rose out of their hiding-places; and, as it were, saw one another, how multitudinous they were; and began speaking and complaining. They are countable by the thousand and the million; who have suffered cruel wrong. Ever louder rises the plaint of such a multitude; into a universal sound, into a universal continuous peal, of what they call Public Opinion. Camille had demanded a " Committee of Mercy," and could not get it; but now the whole Nation resolves itself into a Committee of Mercy: the Nation has tried Sansculottism, and is weary of it. Force of Public Opinion! What King or Convention can withstand it? You in vain struggle: the thing that is rejected as " calumnious " to-day must pass as veracious with triumph another day: gods and men have declared that Sansculottism can not be. Sansculottism, on that Ninth night of Thermidor suicidally " fractured its under-jaw "; and lies writhing, never to rise more.

Through the next fifteen months, it is what we may call

the death-agony of Sansculottism.   Sansculottism, Anarchy
of the Jean-Jacques Evangel, having now got deep enough,
is to perish in a new singular system of Culottism and Arrangement.   For Arrangement is indispensable to man; Arrangement, were it grounded only on that old primary Evangel
of Force, with Sceptre in the shape of Hammer!   Be there
method, be there order, cry all men; were it that of the Drill-
sergeant!   More tolerable is the drilled Bayonet-rank, than
that undrilled Guillotine, incalculable as the wind.—How
Sansculottism, writhing in death-throes, strove some twice, or
even three times, to get on its feet again; but fell always,
and was flung resupine the next instant; and finally breathed
out the life of it, and stirred no more: this we are now, from
a due distance, with due brevity, to glance at; and then—O
Reader!—Courage, I see land!

Two of the first acts of the Convention, very natural for it
after this Thermidor, are to be specified here: the first is,
renewal of the Governing Committees.   Both Sûreté Générale
and Salut Public, thinned by the Guillotine, need filling up:
we naturally fill them up with Talliens, Frérons, victorious
Thermidorian men.   Still more to the purpose, we appoint
that they shall, as Law directs, not in name only but in deed,
be renewed and changed from period to period; a fourth
part of them going out monthly.   The Convention will no
more lie under bondage of Committees, under terror of death;
but be a free Convention; free to follow its own judgment,
and the Force of Public Opinion.   Not less natural is it to
enact that Prisoners and Persons under Accusation shall have
right to demand some "Writ of Accusation," and see clearly
what they are accused of.   Very natural acts: the harbingers
of hundreds not less so.

For now Fouquier's trade, shackled by Writ of Accusation,
and legal proof, is as good as gone; effectual only against
Robespierre's Tail.   The Prisons give up their Suspect; emit
them faster and faster.   The Committees see themselves besieged with Prisoners' friends; complain that they are hindered
in their work: it is as with men rushing out of a crowded
place; and obstructing one another.   Turned are the tables:
Prisoners pouring out in floods; Jailors, Moutons and the
Tail of Robespierre going now whither they were wont to

send!—The Hundred and thirty-two Nantese Republicans, whom we saw marching in irons, have arrived; shrunk to Ninety-four, the fifth man of them choked by the road. They arrive: and suddenly find themselves not pleaders for life, but denouncers to death. Their Trial is for acquittal and more. As the voice of a trumpet, their testimony sounds far and wide, mere atrocities of a Reign of Terror. For a space of nineteen days; with all solemnity and publicity. Representative Carrier, Company of Marat; Noyadings, Loire Marriages, things done in darkness, come forth into light: clear is the voice of these poor resuscitated Nantese; and Journals, and Speech, and universal Committee of Mercy reverberate it loud enough, into all ears and hearts. Deputation arrives from Arras; denouncing the atrocities of Representative Lebon. A tamed Convention loves its own life: yet what help? Representative Lebon, Representative Carrier must wend toward the Revolutionary Tribunal; struggle and delay as we will, the cry of a Nation pursues them louder and louder. Them also Tinville must abolish—if indeed Tinville himself be not abolished.

We must note, moreover, the decrepit condition into which a once omnipotent Mother Society has fallen. Legendre flung her keys on the Convention table, that Thermidor night; her President was guillotined with Robespierre. The once mighty Mother came, some time after, with a subdued countenance, begging back her keys: the keys were restored her; but the strength could not be restored her; the strength had departed for ever. Alas! one's day is done. Vain that the Tribune in mid-air sounds as of old: to the general ear it has become a horror, and even a weariness. By and by, Affiliation is prohibited: the mighty Mother sees herself suddenly childless; mourns as so hoarse a Rachel may.

The Revolutionary Committees, without Suspects to prey upon, perish fast; as it were, of famine. In Paris the old Forty-eight of them are reduced to Twelve; their Forty sous are abolished: yet a little while, and Revolutionary Committees are no more. Maximum will be abolished; let Sansculottism find food where it can.[1] Neither is there now any Municipality, any centre at the Townhall. Mayor Fleuriot and Company perished; whom we shall not be in haste to replace. The Townhall remains in a broken submissive state; knows not well what it is growing to; knows only that it is grown weak, and must obey. What if we should split Paris into, say, a Dozen separate Municipalities; incapable of concert! The Sections were thus rendered safe to act with—or indeed might not the Sections themselves be abolished? You had then merely your Twelve manageable pacific Townships, without centre or subdivision: [2] and sacred right of Insurrection fell into abeyance!

So much is getting abolished; fleeting swiftly into the Inane. For the Press speaks, and the human tongue; Journals, heavy and light, in Philippic and Burlesque: a renegade Fréron, a renegade Prudhomme, loud they as ever, only the contrary way. And Ci-devants show themselves, almost parade themselves; resuscitated as from death-sleep; publish what death-pains they have had. The very Frogs of the Marsh croak with emphasis. Your protesting Seventy-three shall, with a struggle, be emitted out of Prison, back to their seats; your Louvets, Isnards, Lanjuinais, and wrecks of Girondism, recalled from their haylofts, and caves in Switzerland, will resume their place in the Convention: [3] natural foes of Terror!

Thermidorian Talliens, and mere foes of Terror, rule in this Convention, and out of it. The compressed Mountain shrinks silent more and more. Moderatism rises louder and louder: not as a tempest, with threatenings; say rather, as the rushing of a mighty organ-blast, and melodious deafening Force of Public Opinion, from the Twenty-five million windpipes of a Nation all in Committee of Mercy: which how shall any detached body of individuals withstand?

NOTES

[1] December 24, 1794 (" Moniteur," No. 97).
[2] October, 1795 (Dulaure, viii, 454–456).
[3] " Deux Amis," xiii, 3–39.

CHAPTER II

LA CABARUS

HOW, above all, shall a poor National Convention withstand it? In this poor National Convention, broken, bewildered by long terror, perturbations and guillotinement, there is no Pilot, there is not now even a Danton, who could undertake to steer you anywhither, in such press of weather. The utmost a bewildered Convention can do, is to veer, and trim, and try to keep itself steady; and rush, undrowned, before the wind. Needless to struggle; to fling helm a-lee, and make 'bout ship! A bewildered Convention sails not in the teeth of the wind; but is rapidly blown round again. So strong is the wind, we say; and so changed; blowing fresher and fresher, as from the sweet Southwest; your devastating Northeasters, and wild Tornado-gusts of Terror, blown utterly out! All Sansculottic things are passing away; all things are becoming Culottic.

Do but look at the cut of clothes; that light visible Result, significant of a thousand things which are not so visible. In winter 1793, men went in red nightcap; Municipals themselves in sabots; the very Citoyennes had to petition against such headgear. But now in this winter 1794, where is the red nightcap? With the things beyond the Flood. Your moneyed Citoyen ponders in what most elegant style he shall dress himself; whether he shall not even dress himself as the Free Peoples of Antiquity. The more adventurous Citoyenne has already done it. Behold her, that beautiful adventurous Citoyenne: in costume of the Ancient Greeks, such Greek as Painter David could teach; her sweeping tresses snooded by glittering antique fillet; bright-dyed tunic of the Greek women; her little feet naked, as in Antique Statues, with mere sandals, and winding-strings of riband—defying the frost!

There is such an effervescence of Luxury. For your Emigrant Ci-devants carried not their mansions and furnitures out of the country with them; but left them standing here: and in the swift changes of property, what with money coined on the Place de la Révolution, what with Army-furnishings, sales of Emigrant Domains and Church Lands and King's Lands, and then with the Aladdin's-lamp of Agio in a time of Paper-money, such mansions have found new occupants. Old wine, drawn from Ci-devant bottles, descends new throats. Paris has swept itself, relighted herself; Salons, Soupers not Fraternal, beam once more with suitable effulgence, very singular in colour. The fair Cabarus is come out of Prison; wedded to her red-gloomy Dis, whom they say she treats too loftily: fair Cabarus gives the most brilliant soirées. Round her is gathered a new Republican Army, of Citoyennes in sandals; Ci-devants or other: what remnants soever of the old grace survive are rallied there. At her right-hand, in this cause, labours fair Josephine the Widow Beauharnais, though in straitened circumstances: intent, both of them, to blandish-down the grimness of Republican austerity, and recivilize mankind.

Recivilize, even as of old they were civilized: by witchery of the Orphic fiddle-bow, and Euterpean rhythm; by the Graces, by the Smiles! Thermidorian Deputies are there in those soirées: Editor Fréron, Orateur du Peuple; Barras, who has known other dances than the Carmagnole. Grim Generals of the Republic are there; in enormous horse-collar neckcloth, good against sabre-cuts; the hair gathered all into one knot, " flowing down behind, fixed with a comb." Among which latter do we not recognise, once more, that little bronze-complexioned Artillery-Officer of Toulon, home from the Italian Wars! Grim enough; of lean, almost cruel aspect: for he has been in trouble, in ill health; also in ill favour, as a man promoted, deservingly or not, by the Terrorists and Robespierre Junior. But does not Barras know him? Will not Barras speak a word for him? Yes—if at any time it will serve Barras so to do. Somewhat forlorn of fortune, for the present, stands that Artillery-Officer; looks, with those deep earnest eyes of his, into a future as waste as the most. Taciturn; yet with the strangest utterances in him, if you awaken him, which smite home, like light or lightning—on the whole, rather dangerous? A " dissocial " man? Dissocial

enough; a natural terror and horror to all Phantasms, being
himself of the genus Reality! He stands here, without work
or outlook, in this forsaken manner—glances nevertheless, it
would seem, at the kind glance of Josephine Beauharnais;
and, for the rest, with severe countenance, with open eyes, and
closed lips, waits what will betide.

That the Balls, therefore, have a new figure this winter, we
can see. Not Carmagnoles, rude "whirlblasts of rags," as
Mercier called them, "precursors of storm and destruction";
no, soft Ionic motions; fit for the light sandal and antique
Grecian tunic! Efflorescence of Luxury has come out: for
men have wealth; nay, new-got wealth; and under the Terror
you durst not dance, except in rags. Among the innumerable
kinds of Balls, let the hasty reader mark only this single one:
the kind they call Victim Balls, Bals à Victime. The dancers,
in choice costume, have all crape round the left arm: to be
admitted, it needs that you be a Victime; that you have lost
a relative under the Terror, Peace to the Dead; let us dance
to their memory! For in all ways one must dance.

It is very remarkable, according to Mercier, under what
varieties of figure this great business of dancing goes on.
"The women," says he, "are Nymphs, Sultanas; sometimes
Minervas, Junos, even Dianas. In lightly-unerring gyrations
they swim there; with such earnestness of purpose; with perfect silence, so absorbed are they. What is singular," continues he, "the onlookers are as it were mingled with the
dancers; form, as it were, a circumambient element round the
different contre-dances, yet without deranging them. It is
rare, in fact, that a Sultana in such circumstances experiences
the smallest collision. Her pretty foot darts down, an inch
from mine; she is off again; she is as a flash of light: but soon
the measure recalls her to the point she set out from. Like
a glittering comet she travels her ellipse; revolving on herself,
as by a double effect of gravitation and attraction." [1] Looking
forward a little way, into Time, the same Mercier discerns
Merveilleuses in "flesh-coloured drawers" with gold circlets;
mere dancing Houris of an artificial Mahomet's-Paradise:
much too Mahometan. Montgaillard, with his splenetic eye,
notes a no less strange thing; that every fashionable Citoyenne
you meet is in an interesting situation. Good Heavens, every?

Mere pillows and stuffing! adds the acrid man—such in a time
of depopulation by war and guillotine, being the fashion.[2]
No further seek its merits to disclose.

Behold also, instead of the old grim Tappe-durs of Robespierre, what new street-groups are these? Young men habited
not in black-shag Carmagnole spencer, but in superfine habit
carré, or spencer with rectangular tail appended to it; " square-
tailed coat," with elegant anti-guillotinish specialty of collar;
" the hair plaited at the temples," and knotted back, long-
flowing, in military wise: young men of what they call the
Muscadin or Dandy species! Fréron, in his fondness, names
them Jeunesse Dorée, Golden or Gilt Youth. They have
come out, these Gilt Youths, in a kind of resuscitated state;
they wear crape round the left arm, such of them as were
Victims. More, they carry clubs loaded with lead; in an angry
manner: any Tappe-dur, or remnant of Jacobinism they may
fall in with, shall fare the worse. They have suffered much:
their friends guillotined; their pleasures, frolics, superfine collars ruthlessly repressed: 'ware now the base Red Nightcaps
who did it! Fair Cabarus and the Army of Greek sandals
smile approval. In the Théâtre Feydeau, young Valour in
square-tailed coat eyes Beauty in Greek sandals, and kindles
by her glances: Down with Jacobinism! No Jacobin hymn
or demonstration, only Thermidorian ones, shall be permitted
here: we beat down Jacobinism with clubs loaded with lead.

But let any one who has examined the Dandy nature, how
petulant it is, especially in the gregarious state, think what
an element, in sacred right of insurrection, this Gilt Youth
was! Broils and battery; war without truce or measure!
Hateful is Sansculottism, as Death and Night. For indeed
is not the Dandy cullotic, habilatory, by law of existence;
" a cloth-animal; one that lives, moves, and has his being in
cloth "?

So goes it, waltzing, bickering; fair Cabarus, by Orphic
witchery, struggling to recivilize mankind. Not unsuccessfully,
we hear. What utmost Republican grimness can resist Greek
sandals, in Ionic motion, the very toes covered with gold
rings?[3] By degrees the indisputablest new-politeness rises;
grows, with vigour. And yet, whether even to this day, that
inexpressible tone of society known under the old Kings, when

Sin had "lost all its deformity" (with or without advantage
to us), and airy Nothing had obtained such a local habitation
and establishment as she never had—be recovered? Or even,
whether it be not lost beyond recovery?[4]—Either way, the
world must contrive to struggle on.

NOTES

[1] Mercier, " Nouveau Paris," iii, 138, 153.
[2] Montgaillard, iv, 436-442.
[3] Montgaillard, Mercier (ubi suprà).
[4] De Staël, " Considérations," iii, c. 10, etc.

CHAPTER III

QUIBERON

BUT, indeed, do not these long-flowing hair-queues of a Jeunesse Dorée in semi-military costume betoken, unconsciously, another still more important tendency? The Republic, abhorrent of her Guillotine, loves her Army.

And with cause. For, surely, if good fighting be a kind of honour, as it is in its season; and be with the vulgar of men, even the chief kind of honour; then here is good fighting, in good season, if there ever was. These sons of the Republic, they rose, in mad wrath, to deliver her from Slavery and Cimmeria. And have they not done it? Through Maritime Alps, through gorges of Pyrenees, through Low Countries, Northward along the Rhine-valley, far is Cimmeria hurled back from the sacred Motherland. Fierce as fire, they have carried her Tricolor over the faces of all her enemies—over scarped heights, over cannon-batteries, it has flown victorious, winged with rage. She has " Eleven hundred-thousand fighters on foot," this Republic: " at one particular moment she had," or supposed she had, " Seventeen-hundred thousand." [1] Like a ring of lightning, they, volleying and ca-ira-ing, begirdle her from shore to shore. Cimmerian Coalition of Despots recoils, smitten with astonishment and strange pangs.

Such a fire is in these Gaelic Republican men; high-blazing; which no Coalition can withstand! Not scutcheons, with four degrees of nobility; but ci-devant Sergeants, who have had to clutch Generalship out of the cannon's throat, a Pichegru, a Jourdan, a Hoche lead them on. They have bread, they have iron; " with bread and iron you can get to China." —See Pichegru's soldiers, this hard winter, in their looped and windowed destitution, in their " straw-rope shoes and cloaks of bast-mat," how they overrun Holland, like a demon-host, the ice having bridged all waters; and rush shouting from victory to victory! Ships in the Texel are taken by hussars on horseback: fled is York; fled is the Stadtholder, glad to escape to England, and leave Holland to fraternize.[2] Such a Gaelic fire, we say, blazes in this People, like the conflagration of grass and dry-jungle; which no mortal can withstand—for the moment.

And even so it will blaze and run, scorching all things; and, from Cadiz to Archangel, mad Sansculottism, drilled now into Soldiership, led on by some " armed Soldier of Democracy " (say, that monosyllabic Artillery-Officer), will set its foot cruelly on the necks of its enemies; and its shouting and their shrieking shall fill the world!—Rash Coalized Kings, such a fire have ye kindled; yourselves fireless, your fighters animated only by drill-sergeants, mess-room moralities and the drummer's cat! However, it is begun, and will not end: not for the matter of twenty years. So long, this Gaelic fire, through its successive changes of colour and character, will blaze over the face of Europe, and afflict and scorch all men— till it provoke all men; till it kindle another kind of fire, the Teutonic kind, namely; and be swallowed up, so to speak, in a day! For there is a fire comparable to the burning of dry-jungle and grass; most sudden, high-blazing: and another fire which we liken to the burning of coal, or even of anthracite coal; difficult to kindle, but then which no known thing will put out. The ready Gaelic fire, we can remark further— and remark not in Pichegrus only, but in innumerable Voltaires, Racines, Laplaces, no less; for a man, whether he fight, or sing, or think, will remain in the same unity of a man—is admirable for roasting eggs, in every conceivable sense. The Teutonic anthracite again, as we see in Luthers, Leibnitzes, Shakspeares, is preferable for smelting metals. How happy is our Europe that has both kinds!

But be this as it may, the Republic is clearly triumphing. In the spring of the year, Mentz Town again sees itself besieged; will again change master: did not Merlin the Thionviller, " with wild beard and look," say it was not for the last time they saw him there? The Elector of Mentz circulates among his brother Potentates this pertinent query, Were it not advisable to treat of Peace? Yes! answers many an Elector from the bottom of his heart. But, on the other hand, Austria hesitates; finally refuses, being subsidied by Pitt. As to Pitt, whoever hesitate, he, suspending his Habeas-corpus, suspending his Cash-payments, stands inflexible—spite of foreign reverses; spite of domestic obstacles, of Scotch National Conventions and English Friends of the People, whom he is obliged to arraign, to hang, or even to see acquitted with jubilee: a lean inflexible man. The Majesty of Spain, as we predicted, makes Peace; also the Majesty of Prussia: and there is a Treaty of Bâle.[3] Treaty with black Anarchists and Regicides! Alas! what help? You can not hang this Anarchy; it is like to hang you: you must needs treat with it.

Likewise, General Hoche has even succeeded in pacificating La Vendée. Rogue Rossignol and his " Infernal Columns " have vanished: by firmness and justice, by sagacity and industry, General Hoche has done it. Taking " Movable Columns," not infernal; girdling-in the Country; pardoning the submissive, cutting down the resistive, limb after limb of the Revolt is brought under. La Rochejacquelin, last of our Nobles, fell in battle; Stofflet himself makes terms; Georges-Cadoudal is back to Brittany, among his Chouans: the frightful gangrene of La Vendée seems veritably extirpated. It has cost, as they reckon in round numbers, the lives of a Hundred-thousand fellow-mortals; with noyadings, conflagratings by infernal column, which defy arithmetic. This is the La Vendée War.[4]

Nay, in few months, it does burst-up once more, but once only—blown upon by Pitt, by our Ci-devant Puisaye of Calvados, and others. In the month of July 1795, English Ships will ride in Quiberon roads. There will be debarkation of chivalrous Ci-devants, of volunteer Prisoners-of-war—eager to desert; of fire-arms, Proclamations, clothes-chests, Royalists and specie. Whereupon also, on the Republican side, there will be rapid stand-to-arms; with ambuscade marchings by Quiberon beach, at midnight; storming of Fort Penthièvre; war-thunder mingling with the roar of the nightly main; and such a morning light as has seldom dawned: debarkation hurled back into its boats, or into the devouring billows, with wreck and wail—in one word, a Ci-devant Puisaye as totally ineffectual here as he was in Calvados, when he rode from Vernon Castle without boots.[5]

Again, therefore, it has cost the lives of many a brave man. Among whom the whole world laments the brave Son

of Sombreuil. Ill-fated family! The father and younger son
went to the guillotine; the heroic daughter languishes, reduced to want, hides her woes from History: the elder son
perishes here; shot by military tribunal as an Emigrant;
Hoche himself can not save him. If all wars, civil and other,
are misunderstandings, what a thing must right-understand-
ing be!

NOTES

[1] Toulongeon, iii, c. 7; v, c. 10 (p. 194).

[2] January 19, 1795 (Montgaillard, iv, 287–311).

[3] April 5, 1795 (Montgaillard, iv, 319).

[4] "Histoire de la Guerre de la Vendée," par M. le Comte de Vau-
ban; "Mémoires de Madame de la Rochejacquelin," etc.

[5] "Deux Amis," xiv, 94–106; Puisaye, "Mémoires," iii–vii.

CHAPTER IV

LION NOT DEAD

THE Convention, borne on the tide of Fortune toward foreign Victory, and driven by the strong wind of Public Opinion toward Clemency and Luxury, is rushing fast; all skill of pilotage is needed, and more than all, in such a velocity.

Curious to see, how we veer and whirl, yet must ever whirl round again, and scud before the wind. If, on the one hand, we re-admit the Protesting Seventy-three, we, on the other hand, agree to consummate the Apotheosis of Marat; lift his body from the Cordeliers Church, and transport it to the Pantheon of Great Men—flinging out Mirabeau to make room for him. To no purpose: so strong blows Public Opinion! A Gilt Youthhood, in plaited hair-tresses, tears down his Busts from the Théâtre Feydeau; tramples them under foot; scatters them, with vociferation, into the Cesspool of Montmartre.[1] Swept is his Chapel from the Place du Carrousel; the Cesspool of Montmartre will receive his very dust. Shorter godhood had no divine man. Some four months in this Pantheon, Temple of All the Immortals; then to the Cesspool, grand Cloaca of Paris and the World! "His Busts at one time amounted to four thousand." Between Temple of All the Immortals and Cloaca of the World, how are poor human creatures whirled!

Furthermore the question arises, When will the Constitution of Ninety-three, of 1793, come into action? Considerate heads surmise, in all privacy, that the Constitution of Ninety-three will never come into action. Let them busy themselves to get ready a better.

Or, again, where now are the Jacobins? Childless, most decrepit, as we saw, sat the mighty Mother; gnashing not teeth, but empty gums, against a traitorous Thermidorian

904

Convention and the current of things. Twice were Billaud, Collot and Company accused in Convention, by a Lecointre, by a Legendre; and the second time, it was not voted calumnious. Billaud from the Jacobin tribune says, " The lion is not dead; he is only sleeping." They ask him in Convention, What he means by the awakening of the lion? And bickerings, of an extensive sort, arose in the Palais-Égalité between Tappe-durs and the Gilt Youthhood; cries of " Down with the Jacobins, the Jocoquins," " coquin " meaning scoundrel! The Tribune in mid-air gave battle-sound; answered only by silence and uncertain gasps. Talk was, in Government Committees, of " suspending " the Jacobin Sessions. Hark, there!—it is in Allhallow-time, or on the Hallow-eve itself, month ci-devant November, year once named of Grace 1794, sad eve for Jacobinism—volley of stones dashing through our windows, with jingle and execration! The female Jacobins, famed Tricoteuses with knitting-needles, take flight; are met at the doors by a Gilt Youthhood and " mob of four thousand persons "; are hooted, flouted, hustled; fustigated in a scandalous manner, cotillons retroussés—and vanish in mere hysterics. Sally out, ye male Jacobins! The male Jacobins sally out; but only to battle, disaster and confusion. So that armed Authority has to intervene: and again on the morrow to intervene; and suspend the Jacobin Session for ever and a day.[2]— Gone are the Jacobins; into invisibility; in a storm of laughter and howls. Their Place is made a Normal School, the first of the kind seen; it then vanishes into a " Market of Thermidor Ninth "; into a Market of Saint-Honoré, where is now peaceable chaffering for poultry and greens. The solemn temples, the great globe itself; the baseless fabric! Are not we such stuff, we and this world of ours, as Dreams are made of?

Maximum being abrogated, Trade was to take its own free course. Alas! Trade, shackled, topsyturvied in the way we saw, and now suddenly let-go again, can for the present take no course at all: but only reel and stagger. There is, so to speak, no Trade whatever for the time being. Assignats, long sinking, emitted in such quantities, sink now with an alacrity beyond parallel. " Combien? " said one, to a Hackney-coachman, " What fare? " " Six thousand livres," answered he: some three hundred pounds sterling, in Paper-money.[3] Pressure of Maximum withdrawn, the things it compressed like-

wise withdraw. "Two ounces of bread per day" is the modicum allotted: wide-waving, doleful are the Bakers' Queues;
Farmers' houses are become pawnbrokers' shops.

One can imagine, in these circumstances, with what humour Sansculottism growled in its throat " La Cabarus"; be-
held Ci-devants return dancing, the Thermidor effulgence of
recivilization, and Balls in flesh-coloured drawers. Greek
tunics and sandals; hosts of Muscadins parading, with their
clubs loaded with lead—and we here, cast out, abhorred,
"picking offals from the street"; [4] agitating in Baker's Queue
for our two ounces of bread! Will the Jacobin lion, which
they say is meeting secretly "at the Archevêché, in bonnet
rouge with loaded pistols," not awaken? Seemingly, not.
Our Collot, our Billaud, Barrère, Vadier, in these last days
of March 1795, are found worthy of Déportation, of Banishment beyond seas; and shall, for the present, be trundled off
to the Castle of Ham. The lion is dead—or writhing in
death-throes!

Behold, accordingly, on the day they call Twelfth of Germinal (which is also called First of April, not a lucky day),
how lively are these streets of Paris once more! Floods of
hungry women, of squalid hungry men; ejaculating, "Bread,
bread, and the Constitution of Ninety-three!" Paris has risen,
once again, like the Ocean-tide; is flowing toward the Tuileries, for Bread and a Constitution. Tuileries Sentries do
their best; but it serves not: the Ocean-tide sweeps them away;
inundates the Convention Hall itself; howling, "Bread and
the Constitution!"

Unhappy Senators, unhappy People, there is yet, after all
toils and broils, no Bread, no Constitution. "Du pain, pas
tant de longs discours, Bread, not bursts of Parliamentary
eloquence!" so wailed the Menads of Maillard, five years ago
and more; so wail ye to this hour. The Convention, with
unalterable countenance, with what thought one knows not,
keeps its seat in this waste howling chaos; rings its storm-bell
from the Pavilion of Unity. Section Lepelletier, old Filles
Saint-Thomas, who are of the money-changing species; these
and Gilt Youthhood fly to the rescue: sweep chaos forth
again, with levelled bayonets. Paris is declared "in a state
of siege." Pichegru, Conqueror of Holland, who happens to

be here, is named Commandant, till the disturbance end.   He, in one day so to speak, ends it.   Accomplishes the transfer of Billaud, Collot and Company; dissipating all opposition " by two cannon-shots," blank cannon-shots, and the terror of his name; and thereupon, announcing, with a Laconicism which should be imitated, " Representatives, your decrees are executed," [5] lays down his Commandantship.

This Revolt of Germinal, therefore, has passed, like a vain cry.   The Prisoners rest safe in Ham, waiting for ships; some nine-hundred " chief Terrorists of Paris " are disarmed.   Sansculottism, swept forth with bayonets, has vanished, with its misery, to the bottom of Saint-Antoine and Saint-Marceau. —Time was when Usher Maillard with Menads could alter the course of Legislation; but that time is not.   Legislation seems to have got bayonets; Section Lepelletier takes its firelock, not for us!   We retire to our dark dens; our cry of hunger is called a Plot of Pitt; the Saloons glitter, the flesh-coloured Drawers gyrate as before.   It was for " The Cabarus," then, and her Muscadins and Money-changers that we fought? It was for Balls in flesh-coloured drawers that we took Feudalism by the beard, and did and dared, shedding our blood like water?   Expressive Silence, muse thou their praise!—

NOTES

[1] " Moniteur," du 25 Septembre, 1794, du 4 Février, 1795.

[2] " Moniteur," Séances du 10–12 Novembre, 1794; " Deux Amis," xiii, 43–49.

[3] Mercier, ii, 94. (" 1st February, 1796: at the Bourse of Paris, the gold louis," of 20 francs in silver, " costs 5,300 francs in assignats." Montgaillard, iv, 419.)

[4] Fantin Desodoards, " Histoire de la Révolution," vii, c. 4.

[5] " Moniteur," Séance du 13 Germinal (April 2d), 1795.

CHAPTER V

LION SPRAWLING ITS LAST

REPRESENTATIVE Carrier went to the Guillotine, in December last; protesting that he acted by orders. The Revolutionary Tribunal, after all it has devoured, has now only, as Anarchic things do, to devour itself. In the early days of May, men see a remarkable thing: Fouquier-Tinville pleading at the Bar once his own. He and his chief Jurymen, Leroi August-Tenth, Juryman Vilate, a Batch of Sixteen; pleading hard, protesting that they acted by orders: but pleading in vain. Thus men break the axe with which they have done hateful things; the axe itself having grown hateful. For the rest, Fouquier died hard enough: "Where are thy Batches?" howled the people.—"Hungry canaille," asked Fouquier, "is thy Bread cheaper, wanting them?"

Remarkable Fouquier; once but as other Attorneys and Law-beagles, which hunt ravenous on this Earth, a well-known phasis of human nature; and now thou art and remainest the most remarkable Attorney that ever lived and hunted in the Upper Air! For, in this terrestrial Course of Time, there was to be an Avatar of Attorneyism; the Heavens had said, Let there be an Incarnation, not divine, of the venatory Attorney-spirit which keeps its eye on the bond only—and lo, this was it; and they have attorneyed it in its turn. Vanish, then, thou rat-eyed Incarnation of Attorneyism; who at bottom wert as other Attorneys, and too hungry sons of Adam! Juryman Vilate had striven hard for life, and published, from his Prison, an ingenious Book, not unknown to us; but it would not stead: he also had to vanish; and this his Book of the "Secret Causes of Thermidor," full of lies, with particles of truth in it undiscoverable otherwise, is all that remains of him.

Revolutionary Tribunal has done; but vengeance has not

done. Representative Lebon, after long struggling, is handed
over to the ordinary Law Courts, and by them guillotined.
Nay, at Lyons and elsewhere, resuscitated Moderatism, in its
vengeance, will not wait the slow process of Law; but bursts
into the Prisons, sets fire to the Prisons; burns some threescore imprisoned Jacobins to dire death, or chokes them " with
the smoke of straw." There go vengeful truculent " Companies of Jesus," " Companies of the Sun "; slaying Jacobinism wherever they meet with it; flinging it into the Rhone-
stream; which once more bears seaward a horrid cargo.[1]
Whereupon, at Toulon, Jacobinism rises in revolt; and is like
to hang the National Representatives.—With such action and
reaction, is not a poor National Convention hard bestead? It
is like the settlement of winds and waters, of seas long tornado-
beaten; and goes on with jumble and with jangle. Now flung
aloft, now sunk in trough of the sea, your Vessel of the Republic has need of all pilotage and more.

What Parliament that ever sat under the Moon had such a
series of destinies as this National Convention of France? It
came together to make the Constitution; and instead of that,
it has had to make nothing but destruction and confusion: to
burn-up Catholicisms, Aristocratisms; to worship Reason and
dig Saltpetre; to fight Titanically with itself and with the whole
world. A Convention decimated by the guillotine; above the
tenth man has bowed his neck to the axe. Which has seen
Carmagnoles danced before it, and patriotic strophes sung
amid Church-spoils; the wounded of the Tenth of August
defile in handbarrows; and, in the Pandemonial Midnight,
Égalité's dames in tricolor drink lemonade, and spectrum of
Sieyès mount, saying, Death sans phrase. A Convention
which has effervesced, and which has congealed; which has
been red with rage, and also pale with rage; sitting with pistols
in its pocket, drawing sword (in a moment of effervescence):
now storming to the four winds, through a Danton-voice,
Awake, O France, and smite the tyrants; now frozen mute
under its Robespierre, and answering his dirge-voice by a
dubious gasp. Assassinated, decimated; stabbed at, shot at,
in baths, on streets and staircases; which has been the nucleus
of Chaos. Has it not heard the chimes at midnight? It has
deliberated, beset by a Hundred-thousand armed men with ar-
tillery-furnaces and provision-carts. It has been betocsined,

bestormed; overflooded by black deluges of Sansculottism; and has heard the shrill cry, "Bread and Soap!" For, as we say, it was the nucleus of Chaos: it sat as the centre of Sansculottism; and had spread its pavilion on the waste Deep, where is neither path nor landmark, neither bottom nor shore. In intrinsic valour, ingenuity, fidelity, and general force and manhood, it has perhaps not far surpassed the average of Parliaments; but in frankness of purpose, in singularity of position, it seeks its fellow. One other Sansculottic submersion, or at most two, and this wearied vessel of a Convention reaches land.

Revolt of Germinal Twelfth ended as a vain cry; moribund Sansculottism was swept back into invisibility. There it has lain moaning, these six weeks: moaning, and also scheming. Jacobins disarmed, flung forth from their Tribune in mid-air, must needs try to help themselves, in secret conclave under ground. Lo therefore, on the First day of the month Prairial, 20th of May 1795, sound of the générale once more; beating sharp ran-tan, "To arms, To arms!"

Sansculottism has risen, yet again, from its death-lair; waste, wild-flowing, as the unfruitful Sea. Saint-Antoine is afoot: "Bread and the Constitution of Ninety-three," so sounds it; so stands it written with chalk on the hats of men. They have their pikes, their firelocks; Paper of Grievances; standards; printed Proclamation, drawn-up in quite official manner —considering this, and also considering that, they, a much-enduring Sovereign People, are in Insurrection; will have Bread and the Constitution of Ninety-three. And so the Barriers are seized, and the générale beats, and tocsins discourse discord. Black deluges overflow the Tuileries; spite of sentries, the Sanctuary itself is invaded: enter, to our Order of the Day, a torrent of dishevelled women, wailing, "Bread! Bread!" President may well cover himself; and have his own tocsin rung in "the Pavilion of Unity"; the ship of the State again labours and leaks; overwashed, near to swamping, with unfruitful brine.

What a day, once more! Women are driven out: men storm irresistibly in; choke all corridors, thunder at all gates. Deputies, putting forth head, obtest, conjure; Saint-Antoine rages, "Bread and Constitution." Report has risen that the "Convention is assassinating the women": crushing and

rushing, clangour and furor! The oak doors have become
as oak tambourines, sounding under the axe of Saint-Antoine;
plaster-work crackles, wood-work booms and jingles; door
starts up—bursts-in Saint-Antoine with frenzy and vociferation, with Rag-standards, printed Proclamation, drum-music:
astonishment to eye and ear. Gendarmes, loyal Sectioners
charge through the other door; they are re-charged; musketry exploding: Saint-Antoine can not be expelled. Obtest-
ing Deputies obtest vainly: Respect the President; approach
not the President! Deputy Féraud, stretching out his hands,
baring his bosom scarred in the Spanish wars, obtests vainly;
threatens and resists vainly. Rebellious Deputy of the Sovereign, if thou have fought, have not we too? We have no
Bread, no Constitution! They wrench poor Féraud; they
tumble him, trample him, wrath waxing to see itself work:
they drag him into the corridor, dead or near it; sever his
head, and fix it on a pike. Ah, did an unexampled Convention want this variety of destiny, too, then? Féraud's bloody
head goes on a pike. Such a game has begun; Paris and
the Earth may wait how it will end.

And so it billows free through all Corridors; within and
without, far as the eye reaches, nothing but Bedlam, and the
great Deep broken loose! President Boissy d'Anglas sits like
a rock: the rest of the Convention is floated "to the upper
benches"; Sectioners and Gendarmes still ranking there to
form a kind of wall for them. And Insurrection rages; rolls
its drums; will read its Paper of Grievances, will have this
decreed, will have that. Covered sits President Boissy; un-
yielding, like a rock in the beating of seas. They menace
him, level muskets at him, he yields not; they hold up Féraud's
bloody head to him, with grave stern air he bows to it, and
yields not.

And the Paper of Grievances can not get itself read for
uproar: and the drums roll, and the throats bawl; and Insurrection, like sphere-music, is inaudible for very noise: Decree us this, Decree us that. One man we discern bawling
" for the space of an hour at all intervals," " Je demande
l'arrestation des coquins et des lâches." Really one of the most
comprehensive Petitions ever put up; which indeed, to this
hour, includes all that you can reasonably ask Constitution of
the Year One, Rotten-Borough, Ballot-Box, or other miracu-

lous Political Ark of the Covenant to do for you to the end
of the world! I also demand arrestment of the Knaves and
Dastards, and nothing more whatever.—National Representation, deluged with black Sansculottism, glides out; for help
elsewhere, for safety elsewhere; here is no help.

About four in the afternoon, there remain hardly more
than some Sixty Members: mere friends, or even secret lead-
ers; a remnant of the Mountain-crest, held in silence by Thermidorian thraldom. Now is the time for them; now or never
let them descend, and speak! They descend, these Sixty, invited by Sansculottism: Romme of the New Calendar, Ruhl
of the Sacred Phial, Goujon, Duquesnoy, Soubrany, and the
rest. Glad Sansculottism forms a ring for them; Romme takes
the President's chair; they begin resolving and decreeing.
Fast enough now comes Decree after Decree, in alternate brief
strains, or strophe and antistrophe—what will cheapen bread,
what will awaken the dormant lion. And at every new decree, Sansculottism shouts " Decreed, decreed!" and rolls its
drums.

Fast enough; the work of months in hours—when see, a
Figure enters, whom in the lamp-light we recognise to be
Legendre; and utters words: fit to be hissed out! And then
see, Section Lepelletier or other Muscadin Section enters, and
Gilt Youth, with levelled bayonets, countenances screwed to
the sticking-place! Tramp, tramp, with bayonets gleaming
in the lamp-light: what can one do, worn down with long
riot, grown heartless, dark, hungry, but roll back, but rush
back, and escape who can? The very windows need to be
thrown up, that Sansculottism may escape fast enough.
Money-changer Sections and Gilt Youth sweep them forth,
with steel besom, far into the depths of Saint-Antoine. Triumph once more! The Decrees of that Sixty are not so much
as rescinded; they are declared null and non-extant. Romme,
Ruhl, Goujon and the ringleaders, some thirteen in all, are
decreed Accused. Permanent-session ends at three in the
morning.[2] Sansculottism once more flung resupine, lies
sprawling; sprawling its last.

Such was the First of Prairial, 20th of May 1795. Second
and Third of Prairial, during which Sansculottism still
sprawled, and unexpectedly rang its tocsin, and assembled in
arms, availed Sansculottism nothing. What though with our

Rommes and Ruhls, accused but not yet arrested, we make a new " True National Convention " of our own, over in the East; and put the others Out of Law? What though we rank in arms and march? Armed Force and Muscadin Sections, some thirty-thousand men, environ that old False Convention: we can but bully one another; bandying nicknames, " Muscadins," against " Blood-drinkers, Buveurs de Sang." Féraud's Assassin, taken with the red hand, and sentenced, and now near to Guillotine and Place de Grève, is retaken; is carried back into Saint-Antoine—to no purpose. Convention Sectionaries and Gilt Youth come, according to Decree, to seek him; nay, to disarm Saint-Antoine! And they do disarm it: by rolling of cannon, by springing upon enemy's cannon; by military audacity, and terror of the Law. Saint-Antoine surrenders its arms; Santerre even advising it, anxious for life and brewhouse. Féraud's Assassin flings himself from a high roof: and all is lost.[3]

Discerning which things, old Ruhl shot a pistol through his old white head; dashed his life in pieces, as he had done the Sacred Phial of Rheims. Romme, Goujon and the others stand ranked before a swiftly-appointed, swift Military Tribunal. Hearing the sentence, Goujon drew a knife, struck it into his breast, passed it to his neighbour Romme; and fell dead. Romme did the like; and another all-but did it; Roman-death rushing on there, as in electric-chain, before your Bailiffs could intervene! The Guillotine had the rest.

They were the Ultimi Romanorum. Billaud, Collot and Company are now ordered to be tried for life; but are found to be already off, shipped for Sinamarri, and the hot mud of Surinam. There let Billaud surround himself with flocks of tame parrots; Collot take the yellow fever, and drinking a whole bottle of brandy, burn up his entrails.[4] Sansculottism sprawls no more. The dormant lion has become a dead one; and now, as we see, any hoof may smite him.

NOTES

[1] " Moniteur," du 27 Juin, du 31 Août, 1795; " Deux Amis," xiii, 121-129.

[2] " Deux Amis," xiii, 129-146.

[3] Toulongeon, v, 297; " Moniteur," Nos. 244-246.

[4] " Dictionnaire des Hommes Marquans," §§ Billaud, Collot.

CHAPTER VI

GRILLED HERRINGS

SO dies Sansculottism, the body of Sansculottism; or is changed. Its ragged Pythian Carmagnole-dance has transformed itself into a Pyrrhic, into a dance of Cabarus Balls. Sansculottism is dead; extinguished by new isms of that kind, which were its own natural progeny; and is buried, we may say, with such deafening jubilation and disharmony of funeral-knell on their part, that only after some half-century or so does one begin to learn clearly why it ever was alive.

And yet a meaning lay in it: Sansculottism verily was alive, a New-Birth of Time; nay, it still lives, and is not dead but changed. The soul of it still lives; still works far and wide, through one bodily shape into another less amorphous, as is the way of cunning Time with his New-Births—till, in some perfected shape, it embrace the whole circuit of the world! For the wise man may now everywhere discern that he must found on his manhood, not on the garnitures of his manhood. He who, in these Epochs of our Europe, founds on garnitures, formulas, culottisms of what sort soever, is founding on old cloth and sheepskin, and can not endure. But as for the body of Sansculottism, that is dead and buried —and, one hopes, need not reappear, in primary amorphous shape, for another thousand years.

It was the frightfulest thing ever born of Time? One of the frightfulest. This Convention, now grown Anti-Jacobin, did, with an eye to justify and fortify itself, publish Lists of what the Reign of Terror had perpetrated: Lists of Persons Guillotined. The Lists, cries splenetic Abbé Montgaillard, were not complete. They contain the names of, How many persons thinks the Reader?—Two-thousand, all but a few. There were above Four-thousand, cries Montgaillard: so many were guillotined, fusilladed, noyaded, done to dire death; of

914

whom Nine-hundred were women.[1]   It is a horrible sum of
human lives, M. l'Abbé—some ten times as many shot rightly
on a field of battle, and one might have had his Glorious-
Victory with Te-Deum.   It is not far from the two-hundredth
part of what perished in the entire Seven-Years War.   By
which Seven-Years War, did not the great Fritz wrench
Silesia from the great Theresa; and a Pompadour, stung by
epigrams, satisfy herself that she could not be an Agnès Sorel?
The head of man is a strange vacant sounding-shell, M.
l'Abbé; and studies Cocker to small purpose.

But what if History somewhere on this Planet were to hear
of a Nation, the third soul of whom had not, for thirty weeks
each year, as many third-rate potatoes as would sustain him?[2]
History, in that case, feels bound to consider that starvation
is starvation; that starvation from age to age presupposes
much; History ventures to assert that the French Sansculotte of Ninety-three, who, roused from long death-sleep, could
rush at once to the frontiers, and die fighting for an immortal
Hope and Faith of Deliverance for him and his, was but the
second-miserablest of men!   The Irish Sans-potato, had he
not senses, then, nay a soul?   In his frozen darkness, it was
bitter for him to die famishing; bitter to see his children
famish.   It was bitter for him to be a beggar, a liar and a
knave.   Nay, if that dreary Greenland-wind of benighted
Want, perennial from sire to son, had frozen him into a kind
of torpor and numb callosity, so that he saw not, felt not—
was this, for a creature with a soul in it, some assuagement;
or the cruelest wretchedness of all?

Such things were; such things are; and they go on in
silence peaceably—and Sansculottisms follow them.   History,
looking back over this France through long times, back to
Turgot's time for instance, when dumb Drudgery staggered
up to its King's Palace, and in wide expanse of sallow faces,
squalor and winged raggedness, presented hieroglyphically its
Petition of Grievances; and for answer got hanged on a " new
gallows forty feet high "—confesses mournfully that there is
no period to be met with, in which the general Twenty-five
Millions of France suffered less than in this period which they
name Reign of Terror!   But it was not the Dumb Millions
that suffered here; it was the Speaking Thousands, and Hundreds, and Units; who shrieked and published, and made

the world ring with their wail, as they could and should:
that is the grand peculiarity. The frightfulest Births of Time
are never the loud-speaking ones, for these soon die; they
are the silent ones, which can live from century to century!
Anarchy, hateful as Death, is abhorrent to the whole nature
of man; and so must itself soon die.

Wherefore let all men know what of depth and of height
is still revealed in man; and with fear and wonder, with just
sympathy and just antipathy, with clear eye and open heart,
contemplate it and appropriate it; and draw innumerable inferences from it. This inference, for example, among the
first: That " if the gods of this lower world will sit on their
glittering thrones, indolent as Epicurus' gods, with the living
Chaos of Ignorance and Hunger weltering uncared-for at their
feet, and smooth Parasites preaching, Peace, peace, when there
is no peace," then the dark Chaos, it would seem, will rise—
has risen, and, O Heavens, has it not tanned their skins into
breeches for itself? That there be no second Sansculottism
in our Earth for a thousand years, let us understand well
what the first was; and let Rich and Poor of us go and do
otherwise.—But to our tale.

The Muscadin Sections greatly rejoice; Cabarus Balls
gyrate: the well-nigh insoluble problem, Republic without
Anarchy, have not we solved it?—Law of Fraternity or Death
is gone: chimerical Obtain-who-need has become practical
Hold-who-have. To anarchic Republic of the Poverties there
has succeeded orderly Republic of the Luxuries; which will
continue as long as it can.

On the Pont au Change, on the Place de Grève, in long
sheds, Mercier, in these summer evenings, saw working men
at their repast. One's allotment of daily bread has sunk to an
ounce and a half. " Plates containing each three grilled herrings, sprinkled with shorn onions, wetted with a little vinegar;
to this add some morsel of boiled prunes, and lentils swimming in a clear sauce: at these frugal tables, the cook's grid-
iron hissing near by, and the pot simmering on a fire between
two stones, I have seen them ranged by the hundred; consuming, without bread, their scant messes, far too moderate
for the keenness of their appetite and the extent of their
stomach." [3] Seine water, rushing plenteous by, will supply
the deficiency.

O Man of Toil, thy struggling and thy daring, these six long years of insurrection and tribulation, thou hast profited nothing by it, then? Thou consumest thy herring and water, in the blessed gold-red evening. O why was the Earth so beautiful, becrimsoned with dawn and twilight, if man's dealings with man were to make it a vale of scarcity, of tears, not even soft tears? Destroying of Bastilles, discomfiting of Brunswicks, fronting of Principalities and Powers, of Earth and Tophet, all that thou hast dared and endured—it was for a Republic of the Cabarus Saloons? Patience; thou must have patience: the end is not yet.

NOTES

[1] Montgaillard, iv, 241.
[2] "Report of the Irish Poor-Law Commission," 1836.
[3] "Nouveau Paris," iv, 118.

CHAPTER VII

THE WHIFF OF GRAPESHOT

IN fact, what can be more natural, one may say inevitable, as a Post-Sansculottic transitionary state, than even this? Confused wreck of a Republic of the Poverties, which ended in Reign of Terror, is arranging itself into such composure as it can. Evangel of Jean-Jacques, and most other Evangels, becoming incredible, what is there for it but return to the old Evangel of Mammon? Contrat-Social is true or untrue, Brotherhood is Brotherhood or Death; but money always will buy money's worth: in the wreck of human dubitations, this remains indubitable, that Pleasure is pleasant. Aristocracy of Feudal Parchment has passed away with a mighty rushing; and now, by a natural course, we arrive at Aristocracy of the Moneybag. It is the course through which all European Societies are, at this hour, travelling. Apparently a still baser sort of Aristocracy? An infinitely baser; the basest yet known.

In which, however, there is this advantage, that, like Anarchy itself, it can not continue. Hast thou considered how Thought is stronger than Artillery-parks, and (were it fifty years after death and martyrdom, or were it two thousand years) writes and unwrites Acts of Parliament, removes mountains; models the World like soft clay? Also how the beginning of all Thought, worth the name, is Love; and the wise head never yet was, without first the generous heart? The Heavens cease not their bounty; they send us generous hearts into every generation. And now what generous heart can pretend to itself, or be hoodwinked into believing, that Loyalty to the Moneybag is a noble Loyalty? Mammon, cries the generous heart out of all ages and countries, is the basest of known Gods, even of known Devils. In him what glory is there, that ye should worship him? No glory dis-

cernible; not even terror: at best, detestability, ill-matched
with despicability!—Generous hearts, discerning, on this hand,
wide-spread Wretchedness, dark without and within, moisten-
ing its ounce-and-half of bread with tears; and, on that hand,
mere Balls in flesh-coloured drawers, and inane or foul glitter
of such sort—can not but ejaculate, can not but announce:
Too much, O divine Mammon; somewhat too much!—The
voice of these, once announcing itself, carries fiat and pereat
in it, for all things here below.

Meanwhile we will hate Anarchy as Death, which it is;
and the things worse than Anarchy shall be hated more.
Surely Peace alone is fruitful.   Anarchy is destruction; a
burning up, say, of Shams and Insupportabilities; but which
leaves Vacancy behind.   Know this also, that out of a world
of Unwise nothing but an Unwisdom can be made.   Arrange
it, constitution-build it, sift it through ballot-boxes as thou
wilt, it is and remains an Unwisdom—the new prey of new
quacks and unclean things, the latter end of it slightly better
than the beginning.   Who can bring a wise thing out of men
unwise?   Not one.   And so Vacancy and general Abolition
having come for this France, what can Anarchy do more?
Let there be Order, were it under the Soldier's Sword; let
there be Peace, that the bounty of the Heavens be not spilt;
that what of Wisdom they do send us bring fruit in its season!
—It remains to be seen how the quellers of Sansculottism
were themselves quelled, and sacred right of Insurrection was
blown away by gunpowder; wherewith this singular eventful
History called French Revolution ends.

The Convention, driven such a course by wild wind, wild
tide, and steerage and non-steerage, these three years, has become weary of its own existence, sees all men weary of it;
and wishes heartily to finish.   To the last it has to strive with
contradictions: it is now getting fast ready with a Constitution, yet knows no peace.   Sieyès, we say, is making the
Constitution once more; has as good as made it.   Warned
by experience, the great Architect alters much, admits much.
Distinction of Active and Passive Citizen, that is, Money-
qualification for Electors: nay, Two Chambers, " Council of
Ancients," as well as " Council of Five-hundred "; to that
conclusion have we come!   In a like spirit, eschewing that

fatal self-denying ordinance of your Old Constituents, we enact not only that actual Convention Members are re-eligible,
but that Two-thirds of them must be re-elected. The Active
Citizen Electors shall for this time have free choice of only
One-third of their National Assembly. Such enactment, of
Two-thirds to be re-elected, we append to our Constitution; we
submit our Constitution to the Townships of France, and say,
" Accept both, or reject both." Unsavoury as this appendix
may be, the Townships, by overwhelming majority, accept and
ratify. With Directory of Five; with Two good Chambers,
double-majority of them nominated by ourselves, one hopes
this Constitution may prove final. March it will; for the legs
of it, the re-elected Two-thirds, are already here, able to march.
Sieyès looks at his paper-fabric with just pride.

But now see how the contumacious Sections, Lepelletier
foremost, kick against the pricks. Is it not manifest infraction
of one's Elective Franchise, Rights of Man, and Sovereignty
of the People, this appendix of re-electing your Two-thirds?
Greedy tyrants, who would perpetuate yourselves!—For the
truth is, victory over Saint-Antoine, and long right of Insurrection, has spoiled these men. Nay, spoiled all men. Consider, too, how each man was free to hope what he liked;
and now there is to be no hope, there is to be fruition,
fruition of this.

In men spoiled by long right of Insurrection, what confused ferments will rise, tongues once begun wagging! Journalists declaim, your Lacretelles, Laharpes; Orators spout.
There is Royalism traceable in it, and Jacobinism. On the
West Frontier, in deep secrecy, Pichegru, durst he trust his
Army, is treating with Condé: in these Sections, there spout
wolves in sheep's clothing, masked Emigrants and Royalists.[1]
All men, as we say, had hoped, each that the Election would
do something for his own side: and now there is no Election, or only the third of one. Black is united with white
against this clause of the Two-thirds; all the Unruly of France,
who see their trade thereby near ending.

Section Lepelletier, after Addresses enough, finds that such
clause is a manifest infraction; that it, Lepelletier for one,
will simply not conform thereto; and invites all other free
Sections to join it, " in central Committee," in resistance to
oppression.[2] The Sections join it, nearly all; strong with

their Forty-thousand fighting men. The Convention therefore may look to itself! Lepelletier, on this 12th day of
Vendémiaire, 4th of October 1795, is sitting in open contra-
vention, in its Convent of Filles Saint-Thomas, Rue Vivienne,
with guns primed. The Convention has some Five-thousand
regular troops at hand; Generals in abundance; and a Fifteen-
hundred of miscellaneous persecuted Ultra-Jacobins, whom in
this crisis it has hastily got together and armed, under the
title of " Patriots of Eighty-nine." Strong in Law, it sends its
General Menou to disarm Lepelletier.

General Menou marches accordingly, with due summons
and demonstration; with no result. General Menou, about
eight in the evening, finds that he is standing ranked in the
Rue Vivienne, emitting vain summonses; with primed guns
pointed out of every window at him; and that he can not
disarm Lepelletier. He has to return, with whole skin, but
without success; and be thrown into arrest, as " a traitor."
Whereupon the whole Forty-thousand join this Lepelletier
which can not be vanquished: to what hand shall a quaking
Convention now turn? Our poor Convention, after such
voyaging, just entering harbour, so to speak, has struck on
the bar—and labours there frightfully, with breakers roaring
round it, Forty-thousand of them, like to wash it, and its
Sieyès Cargo and the whole future of France, into the deep!
Yet one last time, it struggles, ready to perish.

Some call for Barras to be made Commandant; he conquered in Thermidor. Some, what is more to the purpose,
bethink them of the Citizen Buonaparte, unemployed Artillery-Officer, who took Toulon. A man of head, a man of
action: Barras is named Commandant's-Cloak; this young
Artillery-Officer is named Commandant. He was in the Gallery at the moment, and heard it; he withdrew, some half-hour,
to consider with himself: after a half-hour of grim compressed
considering, to be or not to be, he answers " Yea."

And now, a man of head being at the centre of it, the whole
matter gets vital. Swift, to Camp of Sablons; to secure the
Artillery, there are not twenty men guarding it! A swift Adjutant, Murat is the name of him, gallops; gets thither some
minutes within time, for Lepelletier was also on march that
way: the Cannon are ours. And now beset this post, and
beset that; rapid and firm: at Wicket of the Louvre, in Cul-

de-sac Dauphin, in Rue Saint-Honoré, from Pont-Neuf all along the north Quays, southward to Pont ci-devant Royal—rank round the Sanctuary of the Tuileries, a ring of steel discipline; let every gunner have his match burning, and all men stand to their arms!

Thus there is Permanent-session through the night; and thus at sunrise of the morrow, there is seen sacred Insurrection once again: vessel of State labouring on the bar; and tumultuous sea all round her, beating générale, arming and sounding—not ringing tocsin, for we have left no tocsin, but our own in the Pavilion of Unity. It is an imminence of shipwreck, for the whole world to gaze at. Frightfully she labours, that poor ship, within cable-length of port; huge peril for her. However, she has a man at the helm. Insurgent messages, received and not received; messenger admitted blindfolded; counsel and counter-counsel: the poor ship labours!—Vendémiaire 13th, year 4: curious enough, of all days, it is the 5th day of October, anniversary of that Menad-march, six years ago; by sacred right of Insurrection we are got thus far.

Lepelletier has seized the Church of Saint-Roch; has seized the Pont-Neuf, our piquet there retreating without fire. Stray shots fall from Lepelletier; rattle down on the very Tuileries Staircase. On the other hand, women advance dishevelled, shrieking, "Peace!" Lepelletier behind them waving his hat in sign that we shall fraternize. Steady! The Artillery-Officer is steady as bronze; can, if need were, be quick as lightning. He sends eight-hundred muskets with ball-cartridges to the Convention itself; honourable Members shall act with these in case of extremity: whereat they look grave enough. Four of the afternoon is struck.[3] Lepelletier, making nothing by messengers, by fraternity or hat-waving, bursts out, along the Southern Quai Voltaire, along streets and passages, treble-quick, in huge veritable onslaught! Whereupon, thou bronze Artillery-Officer—? "Fire!" say the bronze lips. And roar and thunder, roar and again roar, continual, volcano-like, goes his great gun, in the Cul-de-sac Dauphin against the Church of Saint-Roch; go his great guns on the Pont-Royal; go all his great guns—blow to air some two-hundred men, mainly about the Church of Saint-Roch! Lepelletier can not stand such horse-play; no Sectioner can stand it; the Forty-thousand yield on all sides, scour toward covert. "Some hundred or so of them gathered about the Théâtre de la République; but," says he, " a few shells dislodged them.   It was all finished at six."

The Ship is over the bar, then; free she bounds shoreward—amid shouting and vivats!   Citoyen Buonaparte is " named General of the Interior, by acclamation"; quelled Sections have to disarm in such humour as they may; sacred right of Insurrection is gone for ever!   The Sieyès Constitution can disembark itself and begin marching.   The miraculous Convention Ship has got to land—and is there, shall we figuratively say, changed, as Epic Ships are wont, into a kind of Sea Nymph, never to sail more; to roam the waste Azure, a Miracle in History!

" It is false," says Napoleon, " that we fired first with blank charge; it had been a waste of life to do that."   Most false: the firing was with sharp and sharpest shot: to all men it was plain that here was no sport; the rabbets and plinths of Saint-Roch Church show splintered by it to this hour.—Singular: in old Broglie's time, six years ago, this Whiff of Grapeshot was promised; but it could not be given then; could not have profited then.   Now, however, the time is come for it, and the man; and behold, you have it; and the thing we specifically call French Revolution is blown into space by it, and become a thing that was!—

NOTES

[1] Napoleon, Las Cases (" Choix des Rapports," xvii, 398–411).
[2] " Deux Amis," xiii, 375–406.
[3] " Moniteur," Séance du 5 Octobre 1795.

CHAPTER VIII

FINIS

HOMER'S Epos, it is remarked, is like a Bas-Relief sculpture: it does not conclude, but merely ceases. Such, indeed, is the Epos of Universal History itself. Directorates, Consulates, Emperorships, Restorations, Citizen-Kingships succeed this Business in due series, in due genesis one out of the other. Nevertheless the First-parent of all these may be said to have gone to air in the way we see. A Babœuf Insurrection, next year, will die in the birth; stifled by the Soldiery. A Senate, if tinged with Royalism, can be purged by the Soldiery; and an Eighteenth of Fructidor transacted by the mere show of bayonets.[1] Nay, Soldiers' bayonets can be used à posteriori on a Senate, and make it leap out of window—still bloodless; and produce an Eighteenth of Brumaire.[2] Such changes must happen: but they are managed by intriguings, caballings, and then by orderly word of command; almost like mere changes of Ministry. Not in general by sacred right of Insurrection, but by milder methods growing ever milder, shall the events of French History be henceforth brought to pass.

It is admitted that this Directorate, which owned, at its starting, these three things, an " old table, a sheet of paper, and an inkbottle," and no visible money or arrangement whatever,[3] did wonders: that France, since the Reign of Terror hushed itself, has been a new France, awakened like a giant out of torpor; and has gone on, in the Internal Life of it, with continual progress. As for the External form and forms of Life, what can we say, except that out of the Eater there comes Strength; out of the Unwise there comes not Wisdom! —Shams are burnt up; nay, what as yet is the peculiarity of France, the very Cant of them is burnt up. The new Realities are not yet come: ah no, only Phantasms, Paper models, ten-

INSTALLATION OF THE COUNCIL OF STATE,
DECEMBER 25, 1799.

Photogravure from a painting by Louis Charles Auguste Couder.

tative Prefigurements of such! In France there are now Four
Million Landed Properties; that black portent of an Agrarian
Law is, as it were, realized. What is still stranger, we understand all Frenchmen have " the right of duel "; the Hackney-coachman with the Peer, if insult be given: such is the
law of Public Opinion. Equality at least in death! The Form
of Government is by Citizen King, frequently shot at, not
yet shot.

On the whole, therefore, has it not been fulfilled what was
prophesied, ex postfacto indeed, by the Arch-quack Cagliostro,
or another? He, as he looked in rapt vision and amazement
into these things, thus spake: ⁴ " Ha! What is this? Angels,
Uriel, Anachiel, and ye other Five; Pentagon of Rejuvenes-
cence; Power that destroyedst Original Sin; Earth, Heaven,
and thou Outer Limbo, which men name Hell! Does the
Empire of Imposture waver? Burst there, in starry sheen,
updarting, Light-rays from out of its dark foundations; as it
rocks and heaves, not in travail-throes but in death-throes?
Yea, Light-rays, piercing, clear, that salute the Heavens—lo,
they kindle it; their starry clearness becomes as red Hellfire!
" Imposture is in flames, Imposture is burnt up: one red
sea of Fire, wild-billowing, enwraps the World; with its fire-
tongue licks at the very Stars. Thrones are hurled into it,
and Dubois Mitres, and Prebendal Stalls that drop fatness,
and—ha! what see I?—all the Gigs of Creation: all, all! Wo
is me! Never since Pharaoh's Chariots, in the Red Sea of
water, was there wreck of Wheel-vehicles like this in the Sea
of Fire. Desolate, as ashes, as gases, shall they wander in
the wind.
" Higher, higher yet flames the Fire-Sea; crackling with
new dislocated timber; hissing with leather and prunella.
The metal Images are molten; the marble Images become
mortar-lime; the stone Mountains sulkily explode. Respectability, with all her collected Gigs inflamed for funeral pyre,
wailing, leaves the Earth: not to return save under new Avatar. Imposture how it burns, through generations: how it
is burnt up; for a time. The World is black ashes—which,
ah, when will they grow green? The Images all run into
amorphous Corinthian brass; all Dwellings of men destroyed;
the very mountains peeled and riven, the valleys black and

dead: it is an empty World! Wo to them that shall be born then!——A King, a Queen (ah me!) were hurled in; did rustle once; flew aloft, crackling, like paper-scroll. Iscariot Égalité was hurled in; thou grim De Launay, with thy grim Bastille; whole kindreds and peoples; five millions of mutually destroying Men. For it is the End of the dominion of Imposture (which is Darkness and opaque Fire-damp); and the burning up, with unquenchable fire, of all the Gigs that are in the Earth." This Prophecy, we say, has it not been fulfilled, is it not fulfilling?

And so here, O Reader, has the time come for us two to part. Toilsome was our journeying together; not without offence; but it is done. To me thou wert as a beloved shade, the disembodied or not yet embodied spirit of a Brother. To thee I was but as a Voice. Yet was our relation a kind of sacred one; doubt not that! For whatsoever once sacred things become hollow jargons, yet while the Voice of Man speaks with Man, hast thou not there the living fountain out of which all sacrednesses sprang, and will yet spring? Man, by the nature of him, is definable as " an incarnated Word." Ill stands it with me if I have spoken falsely: thine also it was to hear truly. Farewell.

NOTES

[1] " Moniteur," du 4 Septembre, 1797.
[2] November 9, 1799 (" Choix des Rapports," xvii, 1–96).
[3] Bailleul, " Examen critique des Considérations Mad. de Staël," ii, 275.
[4] " Diamond Necklace " (Carlyle's " Miscellanies ").

INDEX

Volume II begins with page 489

Abbaye Prison, Gardes Françaises liberated by mob, 173; September massacre, 629, 634, 637.

Actions, Festival of, 785.

Agoust, Captain d', arrests Parlementeers, 104, 199.

Aiguillon, Duke d', 4, 16, 22, 31.

Aintrigues, Count d', 120, 147.

Aix, riots in, 414.

Altar of the Fatherland in Champ-de-Mars, 347, 354; riot at, 486.

" Ami des Lois," play, riot over, 700.

" Ami-du-Peuple," newspaper, 238.

" Ami-du-Roi," newspaper, 238.

Amiral, attempts to assassinate Collot d'Herbois, 867; guillotined, 872.

Ancients, Council of, 919.

Anglas, Boissy d', President of Convention, 911.

Anglomania, prevalence of, 50.

Angoulême, Duchesse d', in flight to Varennes, 459; parts from her father, 709.

Angremont, Collenot d', guillotined, 611.

Ankarström, assassin of the King of Sweden, 525.

Antoinette, Marie, at death of Louis XV, 23; picture of the times, 31, 33; diamond necklace affair, 59; in procession of States-General, 149; unpopularity of, 226; Flandre's dinner, 250; Insurrection of Women, 279, 283, 287; procession from Versailles, 290; in the Tuileries, 296; and the Lorraine Federate, 351; meets Mirabeau, 417; Mirabeau's estimate, 418, 431; plans for flight, 415, 419; flight to Varennes, 453 et seq.; return to Paris, 481; secret correspondence, 520; burns Lamotte's " Mémoires," 535; Insurrection of June 20th, 556; Insurrection of August 10th, 590; transferred to the Temple, 601; in the Temple, 682; September massacre, 632; farewell to the king, 709; removed to Conciergerie, 793; account of her farewell to Austria, 795; trial, 795; sentenced, 796; guillotined, 797.

Argonne, campaign in, 623, 652.

Aristocrats, preference given to, in French army, 368; condition of, in 1794, 846; see Royalists.

Arles, aristocrat rising in, 512.

Armagnacs, massacre of the, 645.

Army, French, disaffection in the, 306; in 1792, 529, 549, 612, 621, 678; after flight of Dumouriez,

747; in 1793, 735, 833; victories of 1793-'94, 838; strength and popularity in 1795, 900.

Army, Revolutionary, 793, 817; and the Church spoils, 828, 831; disbanded, 856.

Arras, Lebon and his guillotine in, 824.

Artois, Prince d', 34; emigrates, 204; at Coblentz, 525.

Assembly, Constituent, limitations of, 218, 221; August 4th, 222; right and left side, 223; raises money by Patriotic Gift, 244; Insurrection of Women, 261, 266, 273, 275, 278, 289, 291; in Riding-Hall, 299; issues Assignats, 301; visited by Louis, 327; on Federation, 342; abolition of titles, 344; at Feast of Pikes, 354; on Franklin's death, 357; revolt of the army, 371, 376, 380; thanks Bouille, 391; debates Orleans's regency, 409; "sword in hand," 410; Castries riot, 412; king's flight to Varennes, 460, 484; sends deputation to Avignon, 509; completes the Constitution, 491; dissolved, 495.

Assembly, Legislative, first French Parliament, 493; The Book of the Law, 499; "Baiser de Lamourette," 505; powerless, 533, 581; deputations to, 536; declares war, 545; Insurrection of June 20th, 555; Lafayette pleads against Jacobins, 562; declares Country in Danger, 567, 572; accuses the Marseillese, 581; Insurrection of August 10th, 583, 599; death throes, 607; September massacre, 641; dissolved, 659.

Assembly, National, in the Tennis-court, 164; Royal session, 166; joined by clergy and nobles, 168; under Broglie's cannon, 170, 185; on Bastille night, 200; visited by Louis, 202; becomes Constituent Assembly, 218, 221.

Assignats, issue authorized by Assembly, 301.

Aubriot, Sieur, after king's capture, 479.

Aubry, Lieutenant-Colonel, 531.

Auch, Martin d', Loyalist, in Versailles Tennis-court, 165.

Augeard, Sieur, plots of, 306.

August Tenth, 1792, Insurrection of, 583.

Austrian Committee, so-called, 522.

Avignon, riot in, 414; massacre in, 507 et seq.; Brigands of, 508; massacre in, 627.

Babœuf Insurrection, 924.

Bachaumont, journalist, 58.

Bailliages, Grand, attempt to establish, 101, 108.

Bailly, Astronomer, 131; Deputy for Paris, 145; President of the Assembly, 162, 163; Mayor of Paris, 203, 209, 235; Insurrection of Women, 262; welcomes Versailles procession, 292; Drapeau Rouge, 309; in Champ-de-Mars, 349; arrests Nanci deputies, 380; petition riot in Champ-de-Mars, 488; decline in popularity, 538; in prison, 794; at trial of Marie Antoinette, 795; guillotined, 813.

Baker, hanged, 309.

Bakers' French in tail at, 234, 253, 256, 681.

Bâle, treaty of, 902.

Balloon, invented by Montgolfier,

52; used by the French in warfare, 845.

Balsamo, Joseph, 59; on French Revolution, 925.

Barbaroux, and Marat, 308; in Paris, 513; and Roland, 553; calls for Marseillese, 554, 568; in Convention, 651, 677; Girondin, 731; refuses to withdraw, 760; arrested, 761; in Caen, 765; and Charlotte Corday, 767; in retreat with the eleven Girondins, 777; in Bordeaux, 789; shoots himself, 800.

Bardy, Abbé Louis, massacred, 635.

Barentin, Keeper of Seals, 161.

Barnave, at Grenoble, 107; in States-General, 144; in Constitutional Trio, 224; in Constituent Assembly, 299; in Jacobins, 323; duel with Cazalès, 411; king's return to Paris, 482; and Louis, 519; correspondence with the Queen, 691; trial and execution, 814.

Barras, Paul François, in National Convention, 652; bombards Toulon, 787, 821; during the Terror, 818; commandant on Thermidor 10th, 884; at soirées of La Cabarus, 896.

Barrère, loyalist editor, 238, 319; at trial of Louis, 695; peacemaker in Convention, 730, 758; in Salut Public, 791; on the Terror, 815; on the sinking of the Vengeur, 843; Hébertist plot, 853; dinner-party, 878; deported, 906.

Bartholomew massacre, 645.

"Bastille Dévoilée," by Linguet, 58.

Bastille, meaning of name, 134; attack on the, 190; Quéret-Démery, 199; demolished, 210; key of, sent to Washington, 210; dancing on ruins of, 357.

Bazire, 312; in Legislative Assembly, 502; summoned by Larivière, 564; in Convention, 835; imprisoned, 836, 854; trial, 859.

Beauharnais, General, guillotined, 815.

Beauharnais, Josephine, imprisoned, 810; at soirées of La Cabarus, 896.

Beaumarchais, Caron de, lawsuit of, 44; "Mariage de Figaro," estimate of, 61, 619; to get arms from Holland, 613; attempted arrest of, 618.

Beaumont, Archbishop, Christophe de, 16, 18, 39.

Beaurepaire, General, suicide in Verdun, 621.

Bed of Justice, 85.

Bedouin, liberty-tree cut down, 824.

Béfort, riots in, 414.

Bentham, Jeremy, in National Convention, 609.

Berline, the new, see Fersen.

Berthier, Intendant, son-in-law of Foulon, 204; massacred, 209.

Berthier, Commandant, at Versailles, 421.

Besançon, riot in, 127.

Besenval, on the Court of Louis XVI, 67; on Calonne's dismissal, 77; Commandant of Paris, in riot in Rue Saint-Antoine, 132; on corruption of the guards, 173; in Champ-de-Mars, 179, 184; apparition appears to, 179; decamps, 200; and Louis, 226.

Beurnonville, War-Minister, and Dumouriez, 745.

Billaud-Varennes, in municipal council, 538; in Jacobins, 541; encourages September massacre, 642; trial of Louis, 698; in Salut Public, 834; deported, 906.

Bill-stickers, Heralds' College of, 320, 402.

Biron, General, guillotined, 815.

Blanchelande, guillotined, 793.

Bonnemère, Aubin, at attack on Bastille, 191, 193.

Bordeaux, in sympathy with the Girondins, 726, 751, 765; disaffection in, 774; last of the Girondins, 800; during the Terror, 817.

Boston tea-party, 8.

Bouillé, 363; in America, 47; in Metz, 373, 379; at Nanci, 386 et seq.; hope of French royalty, 415, 418; flight to Varennes, 453 et seq., 479.

Bouillé, Junior, at Varennes, 475.

Bourdon, 312.

Boyer-Fonfrède, 336.

Boyer, M., Captain of Bully-killers, 413.

Brest, galley-slaves at, revolt of, 304; condition of shipping in 1791, 517; during the Terror, 817; naval battle near, 842.

Breteuil, Home-Secretary, 79, 101, 161.

Breton Club, organized, 107; becomes Jacobins Club, 323.

Bretons, deputations of, 107.

Brézé, Marquis de, Supreme Usher, 135, 159; and National Assembly, 163 et seq.

Brienne, Comte de, War-Minister, 111, 114.

Brienne, Loménie, Archbishop of Toulouse, antiprotestant legislation, 39; in the Notables, 76;
appointed Controller and Prime Minister, 79; edicts of, 82; arrests Parlement of Paris, 87; school-fellow of Turgot and Morellet, 90; sick, 98; plot thwarted by D'Espréménil, 101; worn out, 109; invites Necker to take the Controllership, 110; dismissed, 111; death of, 112; effigy burnt, 113.

Brigands, 129, 206, 531.

Brissac, Duke de, commander of King's Constitutional Guard, 492, 535.

Brissot, Jean Pierre, editor of "Moniteur," 138, 235; in London, 406; in Legislative Assembly, 501, 536; in Jacobins, 540; favours regency, 566; pelted in Assembly, 572; arrested, 761; flies, 756; attempts escape, 779; trial with the Girondins, 798; guillotined, 799.

Brittany, troubles in, 107, 127.

Broglie, Marshal, declines seat in Plenary Court, 108, 159; at Versailles, 171; his Ministry dismissed, 203; at Coblentz, 525.

Brunet, General, guillotined, 815.

Brunout, M., 271.

Brunswick, Duke of, preparations against France, 549, 553, 566; manifesto, 573; invades France, 612; takes Verdun, 621; in Argonne, 652; retreats, 660.

Buffon, Madame de, wife of the naturalist, 95; at Orleans's execution, 811.

Bully-killers, 413.

Bunker Hill, battle of, 8.

Buttafuoco, Napoleon's letter to, 370.

Buzot, in Convention, 650; arrested, 761; in Caen, 765; in retreat with the eleven Girondins, 777;

house demolished, 778; in Bordeaux, 789; found dead, 801.

Cabanis, physician to Mirabeau, 435.

Cabarus, Mme., and Tallien, 817; arrested, 876; soirées given by, 896.

Caen, troubles in, 516; harbours Girondins, 765; expels Girondins, 775.

Cagliostro, see Balsamo.

Ça-ira, composed, 326.

Calendar, new, adopted, 784, 826.

Calonne, M. de, Financier, Controller-General of Finance, 70 et seq.; Convocation of the Notables, 72; dismissed, 77; dispute with Necker, 75; flight of, 543.

Calvados, in sympathy with Girondins, 751; uprising in, 765, 774.

Cambon in Legislative Assembly, 503.

Campan, Mme., "Memoirs," 25 et passim; and flight of Royal Family, 453 et seq.

Campan, Usher, 416, 448.

Camus, Archivist, 504; and Dumouriez, 745.

Candeille, Mlle., "Goddess of Reason," 829.

Cannon-fever described by Goethe, 656.

Cannon, Siamese, 182, 192; wooden, 613.

Carhaix, Girondins in, 778.

Carmagnole, costume, 817; danced in Assembly Hall, 828.

Carnot, Captain Hippolyte, in Legislative Assembly, 502; in Salut Public, 821, 833; makes discovery at Barrère dinner, 878.

Carpentras besieged by Jourdan, 509.

Carra, editor, 238; on the King's flight, 419; in Convention, 650.

Carrier, 312; in Convention, 651; in Nantes, 817; "Noyades" of, 823, 824; guillotined, 893, 908.

Cartaux, General, sent against Marseillese, 773; at Toulon, 788, 821.

Castries, Duke de, duel with Charles Lameth, 411; forced to flee, 413; at Coblentz, 525.

Cavaignac, Convention Representative, insists on invasion of Spain, 839.

Cazalès, Royalist, 144; in Constituent Assembly, 223, 299; attempts to leave France, 289; duel with Barnave, 411; at Coblentz, 525.

Cazotte, 544; imprisoned, 617; September massacre, 632.

Cercle Social organized by Fauchet, 405.

Cerutti, funeral oration for Mirabeau, 437.

Cevennes, royalist revolt in, 530.

Chabot, in Legislative Assembly, 502; summoned by Larivière, 564; in Convention, 835; imprisoned, 836, 853; trial, 859.

Chabray, Louison, 270, 276, 280.

Chalier, Jacobin, in Lyons, 727; executed, 773; body exhumed and burned, 819.

Chambon, Doctor, Mayor of Paris, 680, 700; at trial of Louis, 694.

Chamfort, Cynic, 120; commits suicide, 865.

Champ-de-Mars, preparation for Feast of Pikes, 342, 347.

Champs Elysées, Menads in, 260; dancing in, 357.

Chantilly, steel furnaces at, 837.

Chapelier guillotined, 864.

Chappe's telegraph, 844.

Chapt-Rastignac, Abbé de, massacred, 634.

Charles I of England, trial of, 683.

Charleville, gun-making at, 837.

Chartres, grain-riots in, 680.

Châteaubriand guillotined, 864.

Château-Vieux, Swiss Regiment at Nanci, 366, 378, 382; to the galleys, 392, 517; liberated, 546.

Châtelet Prison, September massacre, 630.

Chaumette, "Anaxagoras," 311, 321, 610; at trial of Louis, 694; demands Constitution, 774, 782; Law of the Suspect, 792; worship of Reason, 829; arrested, 852; guillotined, 863.

Chauvelin dismissed by England, 713.

Chénier, Joseph, in Jacobins, 540.

Chepy, Judge at La Force in September massacre, 637.

Chesterfield, Lord, comment on the political condition of France, 15.

Choiseul, Duke, dismissal of, 4.

Choiseul, Duke de, nephew, 454, 465, 474, 478.

Choisi, General, at Avignon, 511.

Clavière, 138, 313; Minister of Finance, 542; recalled, 600; arrested, 761; in prison, 812; suicides, 815.

Clergy, French, in States-General, 148, 157; joins Third-Estate, 159, 163, 166; disposal of property of, 244, 301; ejectment of Dissidents, 414, 446; permitted to marry, 533; religious costume abolished, 535; on abolishment of religion, 827.

Clermont, night of the King's

flight, 473; threatened by Brunswick, 622.

Cléry, valet to Louis, 709.

Clootz, Anacharsis, Baron de, 315; in Jacobins, 323; "Foreigner's Committee," 341, 343; in Convention, 650; at Madame Roland's, 679; "Evidences of the Mahometan Religion," 827; in prison, 853; guillotined, 855.

Clubs, Paris, in 1788, 120; impetus given by States-General, 157, 160; in 1790, 322; in 1791, 404.

Clugny, M. de, Controller-General, 48.

Coblentz, Royalist emigrants at, 525, 545, 566; Brunswick at, 573.

Cobourg, Austrian General, 739; and Dumouriez, 746.

Cockades, black, 249, 253; green, 177, 181; tricolor, 181, 205; tricolor, in Saint-Domingo, 516; white (Bourbon), 251; wool, 545.

Coffinhal, Judge, delivers Henriot, 883.

Coigny, Duke de, quarrels with Louis, 67, 68.

Committee of Public Salvation (Salut Public), 627; attitude toward September massacre, 642; Circular of, 645; in supreme authority, 833, 741; declares government revolutionary, 786; trial of Danton, 861.

Commune, Council General of the, 601, 607.

Conciergerie, September massacre, 630.

Condé, Prince de, 18; emigrates, 203.

Condé, town, falls into the hands of Austria, 780; invested by the French, 840; surrenders, 845.

Condorcet, Marquis, 138, 235; in

Legislative Assembly, 501; in National Convention, 671; in hiding, 794; dies in prison, 866.

Constitution, First French, difficulties in the way of making the, 218; completed, 491; will not march, 505, 519, 533; burst in pieces, 601.

Constitution of 1793, committee to make, 671; completed, 782.

Constitution of 1795, 919.

Constitution, Municipal, of Paris, 318.

Contrat Social, see Rousseau.

Convention, National, 607; membership, 651; in session, 659; objects, 671; trial of Louis, 682, 694; parties, 718; "Bread and Soap" petition, 719; struggle of Mountain and Gironde, 723 et seq.; recruiting of troops, 735; Insurrection of June 2d, 759; completes Constitution, 782; celebrates Feast of Pikes, 1793, 782; Reason worship, 829; controlled by Salut Public, 835; Representatives on mission, 836, 838; turning against Robespierre, 878; Thermidor 9th, 1794, 881; after death of Robespierre, 892, 895; Insurrection of Germinal, 906; remarkable nature of, 906; Insurrection of Prairial, 910; makes new Constitution, 919.

Corday, Charlotte, leaves Caen, 767; arrives in Paris, 768; assassinates Marat, 769; trial, 770; guillotined, 771.

Cordeliers Club, 325, 404, 447, 852.

Cordeliers District, Danton President of, 239.

"Courrier de l'Europe" edited by De Morande, 58.

Court, Plenary, attempt to establish, 101, 108.

Couthon, in Legislative Assembly, 502; in National Convention, 659; in Lyons, 819; in Salut Public, 834; decree of Prairial, 871; accused, 882; escapes, 883; guillotined, 886.

Covenant, Scotch, 334, 339.

Crussol, Marchioness de, guillotined, 865.

Cuissa massacred at La Force, 635.

Cussy in retreat with the eleven Girondins, 777.

Custine, General, takes Mentz, 665; reverses on the Rhine, 733; replaces Dampierre, 747; questioned by the Jacobins, 780; guillotined, 793; son guillotined, 815.

D'Alembert, 32.

Damas, Colonel, Comte de, in Clermont, 473.

Dampierre, General, killed in battle, 747, 766.

Dampmartin, Captain, in Paris, 131; on disaffection in the army, 370; on eagerness of country-people for news, 403; at Avignon, 511.

Danton, Jacques, procession of States-General, 139; President of Cordeliers District, 239, 254, 312; evades arrest, 318; in Cordeliers Club, 325; in the Departmental Council, 430; "Mirabeau of the Sansculottes," 501; elected to Municipal Council, 538; in Jacobins, 541; favours deposition, 566; and the Marseillese, 582; Minister of Justice, 600, 611, 625; searches for arms, 616; speech to the Convention,

626; attitude toward September massacre, 647; in Convention, 651, 659; at Madame Roland's, 679; at trial of Louis, 703; on King's death, 713; peace-maker in Convention, 730, 735; Commissioner to Dumouriez, 739; in Salut Public, 742; breaks with the Girondins, 748; Law of the Forty Sous, 791; rebukes presenters of church plate, 828; retires to Arcis, 854; recalled, 857; and Robespierre, 857; arrested, 858; on trial, 859; guillotined, 861.

Dauphiné, Revolution in, 229, 232.

David, in Convention, 651; statues of Nature, Liberty, and the People, 782; Feast of Etre Suprême, 870.

Deane, Silas, ambassador to France, 46.

Delessarts, 536; before court of Orleans, 542.

Denoue, Commandant, at Nanci, 382.

Desèze, defence of Louis, 696, 705.

Deshuttes killed at Versailles, 282, 284.

Desilles, Captain, in Nanci, 389.

Deslons, Captain, at Varennes, 479.

Desmoulins, Camille, at procession of States-General, 139; in Palais Royal, 177; as an editor, 238, 320; "Attorney-General of the Lamp-Iron," 238; in Cordeliers Club, 325; in Jacobins, 540; in Convention, 650; on plots, 754; expelled from Jacobins, 854; arrested, 858; trial, 859; guillotined, 861.

Desmoulins, wife of, and his imprisonment, 859, 861; guillotined, 863.

Diderot, 32.

Dietrich, Mayor of Strasburg, 232.

Dillon, Theobald, killed by his own men, 549.

Directory of Five, 920.

Doppet, General, at Toulon, 821.

Douai, Parlement of, alone registers Loménie's edicts, 107; riots in, 414.

"Drapeau Rouge," 309; in Champ-de-Mars, 488.

Drouet, Jean Baptiste, discovers King's flight, 469; rewarded, 495; in Convention, 622; captured by Austrians, 840.

Dubarry, Countess, and Louis XV, 4, 16, 22, 31; imprisoned, 810.

Dubois, Captain of the Watch, 115.

Dubois-Crancé bombards Lyons, 788, 818.

Duchâtel, at trial of Louis, 704; in Caen, 765.

Ducos, in Legislative Assembly, 501; trial with the Girondins, 799; guillotined, 799.

Duelling, spread of, 410.

Dufourny, 313.

Dugommier, General, at Toulon, 788, 821; invades Spain, 839.

Duhamel murdered, 580.

Dumas, President of Revolutionary Tribunal, 741.

Dumont, at Bastille ruins, 210; on Mirabeau, 300, 433; Patriot ministry, 542.

Dumouriez, General, at Compiègne, 4; comes to Paris, 312; news of the King's flight, 462; in Niort, 515; called to Paris, 530; Foreign Minister, 542;

turned out, 551; refuses to obey summons by Lückner, 566; reviews army, 621; plans campaign in Argonne, 623; in Argonne, 652; in Paris, confronted by Marat, 664; in the Netherlands, 665, 678; at Jemappes, 685; distrust of, 700, 712; reverses in Holland, 732; and Convention deputies, 738; in Saint-Amand, 744; escapes to the Austrians, 746.

Duperret, Girondin, draws sword in National Convention, 749; and Charlotte Corday, 768; arrested, 779; papers examined, 794.

Dupont, atheist declaration, 699.

Duport, Adrian, in Parlement of Paris, 83; in Constitutional Trio, 224; in Constituent Assembly, 299.

Duportail, Minister, 418.

Duquesnoy, in Insurrection of Prairial, 912; guillotined, 913.

Durosoy guillotined, 611.

Dusaulx, attempt to check September massacre, 641; Girondin, consents to withdraw, 759.

Edgeworth, Abbé, King's confessor, 709.

Editors, Paris (1789), 237; (1789–'90), 319.

Eglantine, Fabre d', in Convention, 651; furnishes names for new calendar, 784; imprisoned, 853; trial, 859.

Elie, Captain, 139; at attack on Bastille, 192, 193; at Hôtel-de-Ville, 198.

Elisabeth, Princess, from Versailles, 290; in flight to Varennes, 459; farewell to Louis, 709; guillotined, 865.

Emigrants, outlawed, 534; laws in regard to, 740; means of support, 846; see Nobles.

England, war with, 713, 734.

Escuyer, Patriot l', in Avignon, 509.

Espréménil, Duval d', in Parliament of Paris, 83, 86; at Royal Session, 94; crucifix, 98; discovers Loménie's plot, 101; arrest, 103–106; turned royalist, 147; in Constituent Assembly, 223, 307; Day of Poniards, 427; guillotined, 864; widow guillotined, 872.

Estain, Prussian flight through, 663.

Estaing, Count d', 248; an Insurrection of Women, 273; at the trial of Marie Antoinette, 795.

Estate, Third, in 1614, 119; deputies of, in 1789, 131, 135, 137; policy of inertia, 156; declares itself National Assembly, 162, 168.

Etampes, Mayor of, massacred, 516, 547.

Etoile, beginning of Federation at, 334.

" Faublas, Chevalier de," by Louvet, estimate of, 62.

Fauchet, Claude, Abbé, at attack on Bastille, 193; blesses tricolor, 234; preaches on Franklin's death, 357; organizes Cercle Social, 405; in Legislative Assembly, 501, 535; on Louis's death, 713; consents to withdraw, 759; arrested, 770; trial with the Girondins, 798; guillotined, 799.

Faussigny, " Sword in hand " speech in Assembly, 410.

Favras, Chevalier, execution of, 306.

Federation, beginning at Etoile, 334; of the Champ-de-Mars, 338, 339, 347, 353; deputies to, 341, 351, 353; of 1792, 564, 571; of 1793, 782.

Féraud, in Convention, 651; massacred, 911.

Fersen, Count, and flight of Royal Family, 454 et seq.

Feudalism abolished by Assembly, 223.

Feuillans Club, 325, 404; extinguished, 539.

Février, restaurateur in Palais Royal, 706.

"Figaro," by Beaumarchais, estimate of, 61; popularity, 619.

Flanders, Louis XV in, 7.

Flandre, Régiment de, reception to, at Versailles, 248.

Flesselles, Paris provost, 174, 180, 181, 184, 192; shot, 198.

Fleuriot, Mayor of Paris, 863; guillotined, 886.

Fleury, Joly de, Controller-General of Finance, 68.

Fontenai, Mme., see Cabarus.

Forster, and French soldiers, 665; in Mentz, 733.

Fouché in Lyons during the Terror, 818, 819.

Foulon, unpopularity of, 70; nicknamed, 93; advises grass for the people, 114; minister, 177; mock-funeral, 204; massacre, 207.

Fournier, "l'Américain," 313; conveys Orleans prisoners to Versailles, 646.

Fourqueux, Controller-General of Finance, 78.

Foy, Café de, revolutionary meeting-place, 173, 177, 238, 245.

Franklin, Benjamin, ambassador to France, 46; funeral sermon by Fauchet, 357; bust in Jacobins, 540.

Fréron, editor, 319; bombards Toulon, 787; during the Terror, 818; at soirées of La Cabarus, 896.

Fréteau, Commère, "Goody," at Royal Session, 94; arrested, 95; released, 98.

Freys, the, Bankers, 313; imprisoned, 836; trial, 859.

Fronsac, Duke d', son of Richelieu, 18.

Furlough, yellow, 373.

Gamain, Sieur, locksmith, 33; informs on Louis, 690.

Garat, Minister of Justice, announces sentence to Louis, 706.

Genius, Festival of, 784; staff of, 520, 529.

Genlis, Mme., 316; and d'Orleans, 729; leaves Saint-Amand, 744.

Gensonné, in Legislative Assembly, 501; arrested, 761, 765; trial with the Girondins, 798; guillotined, 799.

Georget at attack on Bastille, 192.

Gérard, Farmer, Rennes deputy, 145.

Gerle, Dom, 331; at Catherine Théot's, 871.

Gerville, Cahier de, 536.

Germinal Twelfth, 1795, Insurrection of, 906.

Gibraltar, besieged, 47.

Girondins, origin of the, 501, 671; on trial of Louis, 687, 698; accuse Robespierre, 688; struggle with the Mountain, 723; theories and influence, 717, 724; accuse Marat, 726, 728, 749; and Orleans, 729; Barrère and

Danton as peacemakers, 730; fear assassination, 736; break with Danton, 748; Commission of Twelve, 752; arrested, 761; prepare for war, 765; driven from Caen, 775; retreat of the eleven, 777; in Bordeaux, 789, 800; arrest of Duperret's protesters, 794; trial and execution of twenty-two, 798; " Frogs of the Marsh," 835.

Gobel, " goose," in Constituent Assembly, 299; Episcopal mandement, 436; renounces religion, 826; arrested, 852; guillotined, 863.

Goethe, with Brunswick in Argonne, 655; on flight of the Prussian army, 661; on Mentz siege, 766; evacuation of Mentz, 779.

Goguelat, engineer, 454, 465, 469, 474, 478, 520; and the Queen, 530, 543.

Gondran, Captain, of Gardes Françaises, 284.

Gorsas, journalist, 451; in Convention, 650; to Rennes, 776; guillotined, 794.

Goujon, Insurrection of Prairial, 912; suicides, 913.

Gouvion, M. de, Major-General, Insurrection of Women, 257, 261; Commandant of National Guards at Tuileries, 454, 456, 460; death and honours, 549.

Grain-riots, 679.

Grave, Chevalier de, War Minister, 542, 545.

Grégoire, Curé, 148; in Convention, 650, 659; Constitutional Bishop, 683; refuses to renounce religion, 827.

Grenoble, riots in, 107, 127.

Guadet, in Legislative Assembly,

501, 536; proposes removal of Convention, 725; arrested, 761; in Caen, 765; to Bordeaux, 776; guillotined in Bordeaux, 800.

Guard, Body, at Versailles, 282; Constitutional, 491; disbanded, 535; Departmental, proposed, 675.

Guard, French, at arrest of the parlementeers, 104; at Réveillon riot, 132; refuse to fire, 168, 172; at Palais Royal, 173; fire on Royal-Allemand, 179; at attack on Bastille, 192; after fall of Bastille, 199; at Versailles, 279, 284; on Day of Poniards, 425; farewell and last appearance of, 492.

Guard, National (1789), 183; Lafayette elected General, 203; formation of, 206; authorized by Assembly, 222; under Lafayette, 246; at Versailles, 249; Insurrection of Women, 262; at Tuileries, 296; at Nanci, 383 et seq.; and King's return to Paris, 481; in 1791, 497; reorganization in 1792, 538; proposals (1792) vetoed by Louis, 550; in Insurrection of August 10th, 584; and September massacre, 642.

Guards, Swiss, at Réveillon riot, 132; in Bastille, 190, 195; at Versailles, 248, 253; disaffection, 366; in Insurrection of August 10th, 584; massacre of the, 595; September massacre, 631.

Guillotin, Doctor, called by Paris Parlement, 128; invents the guillotine, 145; in deputation to King, 267, 275.

Guillotine, the, invention of, 145; comes into use, 611.

Gustav, King, of Sweden, assassinated, 454, 525.
Guzman comes to Paris, 313.

Hassenfratz in the War-Office, 679.
Haugwitz, Count, in Estain, 663.
Hébert, 312; arrested, 755; released, 756; accuses Queen at trial, 796; trial of the Girondins, 798; arrested, 852; guillotined, 855; widow guillotined, 863.
Henri IV prophesies social millennium, 11.
Henriot, 312; General of National Guard, 757, 760; to order Insurrection, 879; to deliver Robespierre and Convention prisoners, 882; attempts suicide, 885; guillotined, 886.
Herbois, Collot d', hissed in Lyons, 311; in Jacobins, 541; in National Convention, 650, 659; Lyons massacres, 820; in Salut Public, 834; attempted assassination, 867; deported, 906; death of, 913.
Héritier, Jérôme l', shot at Versailles, 282.
Herman, President of Revolutionary Tribunal, 741.
Hoche, Lazare, Sergeant of the Gardes Françaises, 173; General, career of, 841, 900; pacifies La Vendée, 902.
Hondschooten, Battle of, Duke of York defeated, 840.
Hood, English Admiral at Toulon, 787; abandons Toulon, 822.
Hôtel des Invalides plundered, 189.
Hôtel-de-Ville, after fall of Bastille, 198; death of Foulon and

Berthier, 209; Insurrection of Women, 257.
Houchard, General, reverses of, 787; at Hondschooten, 840; guillotined, 815.
Howe, Lord, beats French navy, 842.
Hozier, Sieur d', magnetic vellum, 332.
Huguenin, Patriot, 536; in Insurrection of June 20th, 556.
Hulin, Captain, 139; at attack on Bastille, 192.

Inisdal, Count d', plots flight of Royal Family, 416.
Insurrection, art of, 255; of Women, 256; of June 20th, 553; of August 10th, 576, 583; of June 2d, 757; of Thermidor Ninth and Tenth, 881; of Germinal, 906; of Prairial, 910; of Vendémiaire, 920; Babœuf, 924.
Isnard, Max, 336; in Legislative Assembly, 501, 536, 554; answers the insurrectionists, 755; consents to withdraw, 759; recalled, 894.

Jacob, Jean Claude, " Eldest of Men," 345.
Jacobins' Society, origin in the Breton Club, 107, 323; daughter societies, 324; in Nanci, 377, 392; in 1791, 404; power of the, 539; Lafayette's letter to the, 553; Lafayette's attempt to suppress the, 562; changes in the, 690; influence over Convention, 780; a second legislative chamber, 835; purging the, 853; applaud Robespierre, 879 ; closed by Legendre, 885; decline of the, 893; last of the, 904.

Jalès, Royalist camp of, 304, 507, 530.

Jaucourt in Legislative Assembly, 502.

Jay, Dame le, bookseller, 319.

Jean-Bon, trial of Louis, 698.

Jemappes, victory at, 685.

Joly, Napoleon's publisher at Dôle, 370.

Jones, Paul, equipment of the "Bon Homme Richard," 46; and French Revolution, 314, 342; death of, 572.

Jounneau in September massacre, 641.

Jourdan, Coupe-tête, 139; Insurrection of Women, 269, 284; in the South, 304; in Avignon, 508 et seq.; guillotined, 818.

Jourdan, General, succeeds Houchard, 840; in the Netherlands, 845, 900.

Jourgniac, see Saint-Méard.

Julien, Sieur Jean, pilloried, 625.

June 20, 1792, Insurrection of, 553.

June 2, 1793, Insurrection of, 757.

Kaunitz, Prince, 313; denounces Jacobins, 539.

Kellermann, Dumouriez' second at Valmy, 657.

Klopstock in National Convention, 609.

Korff, Baroness de, Dame de Tourzel, in flight to Varennes, 455, 458.

Labour, Festival of, 784.

La Chenaye, Baudin de, massacred, 636.

Lacroix, in Legislative Assembly, 502; Commissioner to Dumouriez, 739; arrested, 858.

Lafarge, President of the Jacobins, 615.

Lafayette, in America, 47; demands States-General, 81; in procession of States-General, 147; Vice-President of National Assembly, 186, 200; General of National Guard, 203, 209; "Scipio-Americanus," 235; Patrollotism, 246; October 5, 1789, 262; arrival at Versailles, 278, 285; swears the Guards, 288; in Feuillans Club, 325; Sieur Motier, 344; in Champ-de-Mars, 349; at Feast of Pikes, 354; and Bouillé, 364; at Castries riot, 412; at Vincennes riot, 423; Day of Poniards, 426; and St. Cloud incident, 447, 448; at flight from the Tuileries, 456, 460; at petition riot in Champ-de-Mars, 487; proposes revolutionary amnesty, 492; lays down command, 497; decline in popularity, 538, 549, 550; letter to the Jacobins, 553; before the Assembly, 562; and the army, 566; attempt to suppress Jacobins, 572; leaves France, 602.

Laflotte, prison plots, 861.

La Force Prison, September massacre, 630, 635.

Lagrange and new calendar, 784.

Lally, death of, 88; see Tollendal.

Lamarche, Director of Printing, guillotined, 813.

Lamballe, Princess de, 33; flight of, 464; and royalist intriguers, 522; imprisoned, 618; massacred, 631.

Lambesc, Prince, attacks Bust-procession, 178.

Lameth, brothers, in America, 47; in procession of States-General, 147; in Constituent Assembly, 224, 299; in Jacobins, 323.

Charles, duel with de Castries, 411; Théodore, in First Parliament, 502.

Lamoignon, Keeper of Seals, 77, 79, 93; dismissed, 114; burned in effigy, 115; guillotined, 864.

Lamotte, Countess, diamond necklace, 59, 72; escapes, 97; "Mémoires," 535; in London, 617.

Lamotte, M. de, in prison, 617, 635.

Lamourette, Abbé, kiss of, 505, 563; guillotined, 819.

Lanjuinais, Girondin, bravery in Convention, 759; arrested, 761; to Bordeaux, 776; recalled, 894.

Lanterne, death by the, 208.

Laperouse, voyage of, 47.

Laporte guillotined, 611.

Larivière, Juge-de-Paix, imprisoned, 563.

La Rochefoucault, Duke de, 147; President of Directory, 564; massacred, 646.

Lasource, accuses Danton, 748; President of the Convention, 752; arrested, 761; trial with the Girondins, 799; guillotined, 799.

Lataille, master of tennis-court at Versailles, 495.

Launay, Marquis de, Governor of Bastille, 186, 190, 194; massacred, 197.

Lautrec and Charles Lameth, 411.

La Vendée, war in, 303, 414, 614, 734, 766, 787; during the Terror, 817; war ended, 902.

Lavergne, Commandant at Longwi, disgraced, 615.

Lavoisier guillotined, 865.

Lazare, Maison de Saint, plundered, 182.

Lebas, accused, 882; escapes, 883; guillotined, 886.

Le Blanc, Boniface, landlord at Varennes, 476; family takes to the woods, 622.

Lebon, in Convention, 651; in Arras during the Terror, 818, 824; guillotined, 893, 909.

Lebrun, arrested, 761; guillotined, 815.

Lechapelier, Deputy, and Insurrection of Women, 261.

Lecointre, draper, 139; Major of National Guard, 250; at Versailles, 266; Insurrection of Women, 273; in Legislative Assembly, 503.

Lefevre, Abbé, distributes powder, 198, 234; in procession, 203; nearly hanged, 258, 259.

Legendre, 550; in Insurrection of June 20th, 556; in Convention, 651; defends Danton, 858; closes Jacobins, 885; suppresses Insurrection of Prairial, 912.

Lenfant, Abbé, on Protestant edict, 98; massacred, 634.

Lepelletier, see St.-Fargeau.

Lepelletier Section, assists in suppressing Insurrection of Germinal, 906; suppresses Insurrection of Prairial, 912; opposes new Constitution, 920; riots, 921; suppressed by Napoleon, 921.

Leroi, "August-Tenth," juryman in Revolutionary Tribunal, 741; guillotined, 908.

"Lettres-de-Cachet," Mirabeau and his, 59; used by Loménie against Parlement of Paris, 95.

Levaseur, in Convention, 651; Representative, at Battle of Hondschooten, 840.

Liancourt, Duke de, 147; announces revolution to Louis XVI, 200; offers to receive Louis into Normandy, 564.

Liberty, Cap of, 544; statue of, 783.

Ligne, Prince de, death of, 653.

Lille, siege of, 658, 660.

Linguet, "Bastille Dévoilée," 58; editor of "Annales," 138; in Legislative Assembly, 535.

Loiserolles, Lieutenant-General, sacrifice for his son, 884.

Longchamp previous to the Revolution, 50.

Longwi surrendered, 612.

Louis XIV, "L'Etat c'est moi," 10; strikes Louvois, 226.

Louis XV, the well-beloved, 3; in Flanders, 7; the peasant of Senart, 20; last illness, 3 et seq.

Louis XVI, at death of Louis XV, 23; character of the early reign of, 31, 33; answer to the Petition of Grievances, 36; hissed, 89; Royal Session of Parlement of Paris, 93; receives the Deputies at Versailles, 135; in procession of States-General, 149; opens States-General, 150; royal session after Tennis-Court Oath, 166; hears news of the fall of Bastille, 200; visits National Assembly, 202; to Paris, 204; and his valet, 226; Insurrection of Women, 266, 275, 278, 283, 287; procession from Versailles, 290; in the Tuileries, 296; visits Assembly, 327; at Champ-de-Mars digging, 349; at Feast of Pikes, 354; in the cellars of the Luxembourg, 421; Day of Poniards, 426; plans for flight, 248, 415, 419, 430, 450; indecision of, 430, 431, 561; prohibited from St. Cloud, 447; flight to Varennes,

453 et seq.; return to Paris, 481; completion and acceptation of the Constitution, 491; as head of the Constitution, 519; reconciliation with Orleans, 521; and the veto, 533, 550; asks Assembly to declare war, 545; and Insurrection of June 20th, 556; deposition demanded, 566, 581; Federation of 1792, 571; last Levee, 582; Insurrection of August 10th, 585 et seq.; deposed, 600; transferrred to the Temple, 601; in the Temple, 682; informer Gamain, 691; trial before the Convention, 694 et seq.; sentenced, 705; guillotined, 708 et seq.

Louis Philippe, door-keeper at Jacobins, 324; at Valmy, 658; bravery at Jemappes, 685; and his sister, 745; escapes with Dumouriez, 746; to Switzerland, 747; teaching mathematics, 812.

Loustalot, editor, 237, 319.

Louvet, 138; "Chevalier de Faublas," estimate of, 62; as an editor, 320; controverts Robespierre in Jacobins, 541; in Jacobins, 544; in National Convention, 650; accuses Robespierre, 688; Girondin, 731; arrested, 761; in Caen, 765; in retreat with the eleven Girondins, 777; in Bordeaux, 789; escapes to Switzerland, 800; recalled, 894.

Lückner, Supreme General, 364, 549; summons Dumouriez, 566; guillotined, 815.

Lunéville, Malseigne flies to, 384.

Lux, Adam, on death of Charlotte Corday, 771; guillotined, 810.

Luxembourg, gun-making in the, 791, 837.

Lyons, Federation at, 336; disorder in, 727; in sympathy with the Girondins, 765; uprising in, Chalier executed, 773; besieged, 788; surrendered, 818; to be demolished, 819; massacres in, 820; revolt against the Jacobins in, 909.

Mâcon, Révolution in, 232.
Maignet in Orange during the Terror, 818, 824.
Mailhe, report on right to try Louis, 686.
Maillard, Stanislas, in procession of States-General, 139; at the attack on the Bastille, 194, 195; at the Hôtel-de-Ville, 257; leads women to Versailles, 259, 280; addresses the Assembly, 267; in September massacre, 630; in Revolutionary Army, 831.
Maillé, Camp-Marshal, in Insurrection of August 10th, 584; massacred, 638.
Maillebois, Sieur, plots of, 306.
Mailly, Supreme General, 364.
Malesherbes, in the King's Council, 90; defends Louis, 696, 705; guillotined, 864.
Malouet, 144.
Malseigne, M. de, Inspector, sent to Nanci, 381; at Nanci, 382 et seq.; at Coblentz, 525.
Mandat, Commandant, in Insurrection of August 10th, 584; assassinated, 588.
Manuel, in municipal council, 538; in Jacobins, 541; suspended, 563; in Insurrection of August 10th, 586, 589; in September massacre, 610, 637, 642; in Convention, 650, 659; trial of Louis, 704; in prison, 794; at trial of

Marie Antoinette, 795; guillotined, 815.
Marat, Company of, with Carrier in Nantes, 817, 823.
Marat, Jean Paul, horseleech to Prince d'Artois, 51; at procession of States-General, 139; at attack on Bastille, 194; editor and dweller in garrets, 237; arrested, 246; to Versailles, 254; how to accomplish the Revolution, 307; attempts to arrest, 318; editor, 311, 320; would hang Mirabeau, 402; bust in Jacobins, 540; in Legendre's cellar, 577; in Insurrection of August 10th, 586; member of the Commune, 610; in Salut Public, 627; September massacre, 642; September circular, 645; in Convention, 651, 676; confronts Dumouriez, 664; and the Girondins, 726, 728; accused by Girondins, 749; acquitted by Revolutionary Tribunal, 752; orders Convention to return, 761; assassinated by Charlotte Corday, 768; buried with honours, 769; body thrown out of the Pantheon, 904.
Maréchal suggests new calendar, 784.
" Marseillaise " composed by Rouget de Lille, 569.
Marseilles, armed against Brigands, 171; in sympathy with Girondins, 726, 751, 765, 773; trouble in, 787; under martial law, 818.
Marseillese, the six hundred, summoned by Barbaroux, 554; leave Marseilles, 568; arrive in Paris, 579; in Insurrection of August 10th, 591; garrison of Mentz, 779.

Maton de la Varenne, imprisoned, 618; on September massacre, 635.

Mauconseil Section, declares on deposition, 581; suggests arrest of Girondins, 737.

Maupeou, banisher of Parlements, 4, 31.

Maurepas, 31, 33, 39; Prime Minister, character and government, 42 et seq.; death of, 66.

Maury, Abbé, 148; in Constituent Assembly, 224, 299, 307, 410; attempt to leave France, 289; effigy digs in Champ-de-Mars, 349; Cardinal, 497; at Coblentz, 525.

Maximum, Law of, 742.

Meillan, Girondin, and Danton, 731; at Caen, 775.

Memmay, M., of Quincey, explosion of rustics, 231.

Menou fails to disarm Lepelletier section, 921.

Mentz, occupied by French, 665; recaptured, 733; besieged, 766, 779; retaken by the French, 901.

Menus, Salle des, set aside for States-General, 131, 135; States-General opened in, 150.

Méot, Restaurateur, Royalist meeting-place, 417, 706.

Mercier, editor, 238; procession from Versailles, 291; on September massacre, 644; in Convention, 650.

Merlin of Douai, Law of the Suspect, 792.

Merlin of Thionville, in Legislative Assembly, 502, 535; summoned by Larivière, 564; in Mentz, 733; evacuation of Mentz, 780.

Mesmer, Doctor, practice exposed by Academy of Science, 53.

Mestre-de-Camp, Regiment in revolt at Nanci, 378, 380, 382.

Métra, the Newsman, 321.

Metz, revolt of the army under Bouillé in, 373.

Meudon, tannery of Human Skins at, 847.

Miomandre de Saint-Marie, Insurrection of Women, 283; rewarded, 416.

Mirabeau, Comte, character and early life, 59, 140; pamphlets, 73, 142; at convocation of the Notables, 74; expelled by Provence noblesse, 127; cloth shop, 128; Deputy for Aix, 128; greatest of Frenchmen, 140, 143; at Royal Session, silences de Brézé, 166; groaned at in Assembly, 157; his newspaper suppressed, 160; at Bastille ruins, 210; popularity of, 224; on Orleans and Robespierre, 224; Insurrection of Women, 261; October 5, 6, 280, 291; defends the veto, 300; courage of, 300; newspapers, 319; in Jacobins, 323; on abolition of titles, 344; on reorganizing the army, 371; Marat advises hanging, 402; and Orleans, 408; answers to the duellists, 410; meets the Queen, 417; power in Assembly, 424; hope of Royalty, 430; capacity for work, 433; sickness and death, 433 et seq.; last sayings of, 435; public funeral, 437; bust in Jacobins, 540; bust thrown out at Jacobins, 691; body removed from the Pantheon, 769.

Mirabeau, Marquis, on the state of France in 1775, 36; family troubles of, 59; and his son, 140; death of, 186; his prophecies, 228.

Mirabeau, Viscomte, nicknamed Tonneau, 147, 169; in Constituent Assembly, 223, 307; death of, 440.

Miranda, engineer, 313; General, with Dumouriez in Holland, 732, 739.

Miroménil, Keeper of Seals, 76, 77.

Moleville, Bertrand de, in Rennes, 107; he tries journalism, 320; becomes Marine-Minister, 517; his advice to Louis, 519; and to the Assembly, 536; in hiding, 612.

Momoro, editor, 311, 830; Agrarian Law, 610; arrested, 852; guillotined, 855.

Momoro, Madame, Goddess of Reason, 830.

Monarchic Club, 325, 404.

Monge, Minister, 600; and new calendar, 784.

"Moniteur," newspaper, 238, 319; reports Jacobin Debates, 781; quoted passim.

Monsabert, Goeslard de, President of Paris Parlement, 101; arrest of, 103–106.

Montélimart, Federation ceremonies at, 335.

Montesquiou, General, occupies Savoy, 665.

Montgaillard on September massacre, 642.

Montgolfier invents the balloon, 52.

Montmartre, employment of the destitute on, 235; fortified, 613.

Montmédi, Bouillé's preparations at, 453, 465.

Montmorin, Foreign-Secretary, 79, 536; massacred, 631.

Montpellier, disaffection in, 774.

Morande, De, editor of "Courrier de l'Europe," 58, 138; imprisoned, 617.

More, Hannah, on Philippe Orleans, 316.

Morellet, Abbé, 237; school-fellow of Turgot and Brienne, 90.

Moret, Mayor of, detains the King's aunts, 420.

Moton, a watchmaker, saves Abbé Sicard, 629.

Moucheton, M. de, 272, 274.

Moudon, Abbé, confessor of Louis XV, 17, 22.

Mounier, in Grenoble, 107; in procession of States-General, 144; in Constituent Assembly, 223; President of the Assembly, 261, 266, 278; in deputation to the King, 267, 270, 276.

Mountain, the, 502; struggle with Girondins, 723; theories and influence, 724; vulnerable points, 728; last of the, 913.

Müller, General, invades Spain, 839.

Murat, Napoleon's adjutant, 921.

Naigeon, Atheist, 316.

Nanci, affairs in, 377; revolt of army in, 304, 382 et seq., 546.

Nantes, Petition of Grievances, 144; receives news of the King's flight, 462; disaffection in, 774; Carrier and "Company of Marat," 817; massacres in, 823.

Napoleon Bonaparte, studies mathematics in Brienne, 109; in Corsica, 415; Sublieutenant in Auxonne, 370; in Insurrection of August 10th, 595; on the Marseillese, 774; at Toulon, 788, 821; at soirées of La Cabarus, 986; suppresses riot of Lepelletier, 921.

Narbonne, Louis de, assists in flight of King's aunts, 420; War-Minister, 522, 529, 542; escapes to England, 616.

Nature, worship of, 782.

Necker, Controller-General, 48; dispute with Calonne, 75; refuses Loménie's offer of the Controllership, 110; recalled, 113; difficulty as to States-General, 122; in procession of States-General, 149; as conciliator of the orders, 161; popularity, 167; dismissed, 176; recalled, 203; returns in triumph, 227, 232; withdraws with difficulty, 391.

Necklace, Diamond, 55, 59, 72.

Needham, English sympathizer, 313.

Nemours, Dupont de, Secretary of the Notables, 74.

Nerwinden, Battle of, 738.

Newspapers in 1789, 237; in 1789–'90, 319; in 1791, 402; manuscript, 58; placard, 320, 402.

Nièvre-Chol, Mayor of Lyons, 727, 773.

Nismes, riot in, 414.

Nobles, under Louis XV, 12; join Third-Estate, 168; first emigration of, 203; second emigration, 289; forced to flee, 229, 233, 400; at Coblentz, 525, 545; with Brunswick in Argonne, 653; see Aristocrats.

Notables, Calonne's Convocation of the, 72; meet at Versailles, 74; dismissed, 80; reconvoked, 122; dismissed, 123.

Notre-Dame, States-General Deputies at, 136, 150; Te Deum shot in, 203; adoption of tricolor flag, 235; worship of Reason in, 829.

"Noyades" of Carrier, 823, 824.

Oath, Tennis-Court, 164; National, renewed, 328; Federation, 333.

Ogé, leader of Insurrection in Saint-Domingo, 516.

Opinion, Festival of, 785.

Orleans, Duke d', 18.

Orleans, High Court of, established, 533.

Orleans, Philippe d', 18, 19; aspires to be admiral, 47, 74; wealth and character, 51; at Royal Session of Parlement of Paris, 94; arrested, 95; released, 98; "Deliberations," 121; in procession of States-General, 147; joins Third-Estate, 168; Mirabeau's opinion of, 224; Insurrection of Women, 290; returns from England, 316; regency debated in Assembly, 409; last appearance at court, 521; declaration of war, 545; called Egalité, 652; in Convention, 685; trial of Louis, 704; at execution of Louis, 711; decline in popularity, 729; arrest and imprisonment, 747; brought to Paris, 810; trial and execution, 810.

Ormesson, d', Controller-General of Finance, 68; his uncle on States-General, 84.

Osselin, Deputy, guillotined, 815.

Pache, 313; War-Minister, 678, 701; Mayor of Paris, 720, 755, 757, 834; imprisoned, 863.

Paine, Thomas, 314; advises a Republic, 461; in National Convention, 609, 652, 671, 733; in prison, 853; escapes death, 884.

Palais-Royal, changes in the, 52; popularity of, 120, 160; Patriot crowds in, 168, 171, 176, 253;

public speaking in the, 238; burns the Pope in effigy, 451.

Pan, Mallet du, 520.

Panis, 610; September circular, 645.

Pantheon, the, 437.

Parens, Curate, renounces religion, 826.

Pâris, assassin of St.-Fargeau, 706.

Pâris, friend of Danton, 857.

Paris, Ville de, French warship, 46, 47.

Parlement of Douai, alone registers Loménie's edicts, 107.

Parlement of Paris, 31, 65; on registering edicts, 83, 85, 93; Bed of Justice, 85; arrested, 87; in Troyes, 90; Royal Session, 93; Loménie's plots to tame, 100; oath and declaration of, 103; dismissed, 106; reinstated, 120; unpopular, 120; summons Doctor Guillotin, 128; abolished, 129, 302.

Parlements, Provincial, 87, 96, 99; refuse to register Loménie's edicts, 107; abolished, 302.

Patrollotism, 246.

Pau, village in Béarn, riot in, 108.

"Paul et Virginie," by Saint-Pierre, estimate of, 62, 108.

Payan, Agent-National, 863.

Peltier escapes to England, 617.

"Père Duchene," see Hébert.

Pereyra, 313.

Perpignan, riots in, 414, 516.

Perruques blondes, 847.

Pétion, 144; in Constituent Assembly, 299; and king's return to Paris, 482; in London, 497; Mayor of Paris, 430, 538; and Insurrection of June 20, 554; attempt to suspend, 563; Federation of 1792, 571; welcomes Marseillese, 579; in Insurrection of August 10th, 584; and September massacre, 642; in National Convention, 650; President of Convention, 659; refuses mayorship, 679; in Caen, 765; in retreat with the eleven Girondins, 777; in Bordeaux, 789; found dead, 801, 814.

Pétion - National - Pique christened, 547.

Petition of Grievances, 36.

Petit-Jean, magnetic vellum, 332.

Phélippeaux, expelled from Jacobins, 853; arrested, 858.

Philosophism, 14, 32, 237, 316; influence on the Church, 39, 60.

Pichegru, General, career of, 841; victories in Holland, 900; puts down Insurrection of Germinal, 906.

Pikes, Feast of, 339 et seq.; effect on discipline of army, 373; in 1792, 564, 571; in 1793, 782.

Pilnitz, Convention at, 524.

Pin, Latour du, War-Minister, 380; unpopularity, 391.

Pitt, 525, 720; "enemy of mankind," 734; inflexibility of, 902.

Pius VI, Pope, burned in effigy, 451.

Poissonnière, Section, in the Convention Hall, 736.

Polignac, Duchess de, 33, 226.

Polignac, Duke de, 67; emigrates, 203, 226.

Pompignan, Lafranc de, President of the Assembly, 185; minister, 227.

Poniards, Royalist, 417; day of, 422.

Prairial First to Third, 1795, Insurrection of, 910.

Précy, commander in Lyons, 788; cuts his way out, 818.

Prefeln, Goupil de, 408.

Priestley, 609; declines election to National Convention, 651.

Prieur imprisoned at Caen, 767.

Prisons, state of, under the Terror, 815, 873.

Proly, 313; Jacobin, and Dumouriez, 739.

Prophecy, revival of, 331.

Protestants emancipated, 93.

Prudhomme, editor, 237, 311, 319; on " Crimes of the Revolution," 824.

Prussia, Fritz of, and French Princes, 658, 660.

Puisaye, General, in Caen, 766, 775; at Quiberon, 902.

Quéret-Démery, letter found in Bastille, 199.

Quiberon, Battle of, 902.

Quimper, Girondins in, 778, 789.

Rabaut, St. Etienne, French reformer, 144; in Constituent Assembly, 299; in Convention, 650; President of Commission of Twelve, 752; arrested, 761; flies, 765; in hiding, 779, 794; discovered and guillotined, 815.

Raynal, Abbé, 58; letter to Assembly, 237.

Reason, Goddess of, 829.

Rebecqui, in Arles, 512; in Convention, 651, 677; retires, 727; drowns himself, 774.

Reding, Swiss, massacred, 634.

Religion, Christian, the, and French Revolution, 10, 12, 806; abolished, 826; a new, 869.

Remy, Cornet, in Clermont, 473.

Rénault, Cécile, attempts to assassinate Robespierre, 867; guillotined, 872.

Rennes, riot in, 107, 127.

Réole at attack on Bastille, 193.

Repaire, Tardivet du, bravery at Versailles, 283; rewarded, 416.

Representatives on mission, power and intrepidity of, 836, 839.

Resson, Sieur, Jacobin patriot, 562.

Réveillon, paper manufacturer, 52; warehouses burnt by mob, 131.

Revolution, French, causes of, 14, 38, 60, 99; beginning of the, 228; meaning of, 215; Lord Chesterfield on, 15; not a revolt, 200; attitude of Europe toward, 523; accomplishment of Marat's plan for the, 308; Festival of the, 785.

" Révolutions de Paris," newspaper, 237, 319.

Rewards, Festival of, 785.

Richelieu, at death of Louis XV, 18, 23; death of, 116.

Riouffe, in retreat with the eleven Girondins, 776, 777; taken to Paris, 789; on death of the Girondins, 799; on Madame Roland's imprisonment, 812.

Riquettis, the, origin and characteristics of, 140.

Rivarol, editor, 238; " sold and not paid," 301; " staff of genius," 520, 529.

Robespierre, Maximilien, early life and character, 143; in procession of States-General, 143; in Jacobins, 323; Public Accuser, 429; and flight to Varennes, 462; in Constituent Assembly, 307, 408, 495; retires to Arras, 497; influence in Jacobins, 541; in Insurrection of August 10th, 586, 601; in improvised Commune, 610; and September massacre, 643; in Convention, 650, 676; accused by the Girondins, 688; trial of Louis, 704; in Salut Public, 814, 834; and Danton, 857; attempt to assassinate, 867; " Etre Suprême," 869; withdraws, 876; foiled in Convention, 878; accused, 882; escapes, 883; attempts suicide, 886; guillotined, 886.

Robespierre, Augustin, at Toulon, 788, 821; accused, 882; escapes, 883; attempts suicide, 885; guillotined, 886.

Rochambeau, in America, 47; Marshal of Strasburg, 232; Supreme General, 364; quits the service, 549.

Roche-Aymon, Grand Almoner of Louis XV, 17, 23, 55.

Rœderer, Procureur-Syndic, 554; in Insurrection of August 10th, 584.

Rohan, Louis de, Diamond Necklace Cardinal, 55, 59, 72.

Roland, at Lyons Federation, 337; in Paris, 513; minister, 542, 550; letter and dismissal, 551; recalled, 600; prepares for National Convention, 608; attitude toward September massacre, 642; and Pache, 678; misgivings of, 679; ill, 700; wishes to retire, 712; flees from Paris, 761; commits suicide, 814.

Roland, Madame, at Lyons Federation, 337; in Paris, 463; and Barbaroux, 513; character of, 543; accused by Viard, 700; and the struggle of the Girondins, 731; arrested, 761; trial and execution, 812.

Romme, in Convention, 651; imprisoned in Caen, 767; set at liberty, 778; invents new calendar, 784; in Insurrection of Prairial, 912; suicides, 913.

Romœuf, in pursuit of the King, 462, 464; arrives at Varennes, 479.

Ronsin, 312; commands Revolutionary Army, 817, 831; arrested, 852; guillotined, 855.

Rossignol, 312; causes arrest of Maton de la Varenne, 618; in La Vendée, 787, 853.

Rouget de Lille, Colonel, composer of " The Marseillaise," 569.

Rousseau, Jean Jacques, Contrat Social of, 56, 330; Gospel of, 222, 329, 400, 496, 806; statue decreed, 495.

Roussière, Fence-master at Nanci, 379.

Roux, M., on the Reign of Terror, 806.

Royalists, plots for King's flight, 347, 415, 419, 445, 450; Day of Poniards, 425; see Nobles.

Royou, editor, 238, 319; burned in effigy, 451.

Ruamps rebukes Couthon, 871.

Ruhl, in Legislative Assembly, 503; in Insurrection of Prairial, 912; suicides, 913.

Sabatier de Cabre, at Royal Session, 94; arrested, 95; released, 98.

Saint-Antoine, riot in Rue, 131; at attack on Bastille, 190; after fall of Bastille, 200; Insurrection of Women, 263, 269; hangs a Baker, 309.

Saint-Cloud, Louis prohibited from going to, 447.

Saint-Denis, Mayor of, hanged, 235.

Saint-Domingo, rebellion in, 304, 516.

Saint-Fargeau, Lepelletier, " Michel Lepelletier," 344; in Convention, 652; trial of Louis, 703; assassinated, 706; funeral of, 712.

Saint-Huruge, Marquis, 205; harangues in Palais Royal, 239; petitions Assembly, 245; "Father Adam," Insurrection of Women, 269; burns Pope's effigy, 451; leads Insurrection of June 20th, 556.

Saint-Just, in Convention, 651; in Salut Public, 834; at Weissembourg, 841; criticised by Camille Desmoulins, 854; accused, 882; escapes, 883; guillotined, 886.

Saint-Louis, Church of, Assembly of States-General at, 136.

Saint-Meard, Jourgniac de, imprisoned, 618; on September massacre, 630, 634.

Saint-Méry, Moreau de, after fall of Bastille, 199; nominates Lafayette, 203; Deputy for St. Domingo, 292; in fight with Marseillese, 580.

Saint-Pierre, " Paul et Virginie," estimate of, 62, 108.

Sainte-Menehould, alarms at, 466, 469; threatened by Brunswick, 622.

Salles, in Caen, 765; guillotined in Bordeaux, 800.

Salicetti at Toulon, 821.

Salm, Regiment de, at Metz, 374; at Nanci, 387.

Saltpetre, digging cellars for, 838.

Salut Public, Comité de, see Committee.

Samson, executioner of Louis, 711, 813, 815; and Danton, 861; executioner of Robespierre, 887.

Sansculotte, Gilbert, gives name to Sansculottism, 417.

Sansculottism, 215; effects of, 233;

growth of, 243, 295, 308, 538; how named, 417.

Santerre, brewer of Saint-Antoine, 139; at attack on Bastille, 193; colonel of National Guard, 380; at the Tuileries, 417; at Vincennes riot, 424; leads Insurrection of June 20th, 556; in Insurrection of August 10th, 588; and September massacre, 642; how to relieve famine, 680; at trial of Louis, 694; at Theatre riot, 700; at execution of Louis, 710; in La Vendée, 734, 766, 787.

Sausse, Procureur of Varennes, 476; flies, 622.

Savardin, Bonne, plots of, 306.

Savonnières, M. de, 271.

Savoy occupied by the French, 665.

Séchelles, Herault de, in National Convention, 671; leads Convention out, 760; and Constitution of 1793, 671; Feast of Pikes, 1793, 783; arrested, 858; trial, 859; guillotined, 861.

September massacre, 625; investigated by National Convention, 675.

Sergent, " Agate," 643; September circular, 645.

Servan, War-Minister, 542, 545, 550.

Siamese cannon, 182; at attack on Bastille, 192.

Sicard, Abbé, imprisoned, 618; in September massacre, 628, 637.

Sieyès, Abbé, comes to Paris, 120; Constitution-builder, 146, 218, 224, 299; at Champ-de-Mars, digging, 349; in Convention, 651; to make new Constitution, 671; trial of Louis, 704; and Constitution of 1795, 919.

Sillery, Marquis, 316; in Convention, 729.

Simon, the Cordwainer, guillotined, 886; and the Dauphin, 865.

Simoneau, Mayor of Etampes, massacred, 516, 547.

Sombreuil, Governor of Hôtel des Invalides, 186, 189; called before Assembly, 534; imprisoned, 617; acquitted by September tribunal, 632; guillotined, 872; son of, shot as an emigrant, 903.

Sorbonne, declining influence of the, 12.

Soubrany in Insurrection of Prairial, 912; guillotined, 913.

Spain, war with, 734; invaded by the French, 839; peace with, 839.

Staël, Madame de, 48; at States-General procession, 138; on Mirabeau, 140; influence for Narbonne, 522; petitions Manuel and Tallien, 616.

States-General of 1614, 119; demanded by Lafayette, 81; promised in Parlement of Paris, 94; D'Ormesson on, 99; date announced, 110; election of Deputies, 125; Deputies assemble, 131; procession, 136; opened, 150; the Third Estate, 155; separation of the orders, 156.

Strasburg, riot in, 232.

Suard, Ex-Censor, 316.

Suffren, Admiral, 47.

Sugar riot, 719.

Sulleau, editor, massacred, 589.

Supper, Fraternal, 866.

Suspect, arrest of the, 616; laws in regard to the, 740; Law of the, 792.

Suspicion, unparalleled growth of, 290.

Talleyrand-Périgord, Bishop, 148, 203; at Feast of Pikes, 355; excommunicated, 451; in London, 497; letters of, discovered, 691; to America, 713.

Tallien, editor, 311; in municipal assembly, 538, 610; in Convention, 650; in Bordeaux, 789, 800, 817; and Mme. Cabarus, 817; expelled from Jacobins, 876; on Ninth of Thermidor, 881; after death of Robespierre, 892, 894.

Talma, actor, Marat-Dumouriez incident, 664.

Tardivet, see Repaire.

Target refuses to defend Louis, 696.

Tassin, M., 253.

Telegraph, Chappe's, invented, 844.

Tennis-Court, session and oath, 164; club of, 342; owner rewarded, 495.

Terray, Abbé, dissolute financier, 5, 31.

Terror, Reign of, character of the, 805; number of deaths during the, 914.

Théot, Catherine, prophecies in regard to Robespierre, 870.

Thermidor Ninth and Tenth, 1794, 881.

Théroigne, Demoiselle, at procession of States-General, 138; Insurrection of Women, 259, 269; imprisoned, 481; speaks in Jacobins, 540; in Insurrection of August 10th, 584, 588; soirées of, 733; insane, 753.

Thionville, siege of, 658, 660.

Thouret, in Constituent Assembly, 299; dissolves Assembly, 495; guillotined, 864.

Thouvenot, General, called to consultation by Dumouriez, 623.

Thuriot, at attack on Bastille, 190, 194; in Legislative Assembly, 503; and trial of Louis, 698; Convention President on Ninth of Thermidor, 881.

Tinville, Fouquier, 312; in Jacobins, 323; Attorney-General in Revolutionary Tribunal, 741; trial of Marie Antoinette, 795; trial of Girondins, 798; brutal at trial of Madame Roland, 813; trial of Danton, 859; execution by batches, 864, 871, 874; guillotined, 908.

Tollendal, Lally, in procession of States-General, 147; speech at Hôtel-de-Ville, 202.

Torné, Bishop, in Legislative Assembly, 535.

Toulon, disaffection in, 774; in the hands of the English, 787; siege of, 821; abandoned by the English, 822; massacres in, 822.

Toulongeon, Marquis, 290; in Constituent Assembly, 299; on the Jacobins, 540.

Tournay, Louis, at attack on Bastille, 191.

Tourzel, Dame de, in flight to Varennes, 458; imprisoned, 618.

Trenck, Frederick Baron, 313; in Paris, 733.

Tribunal, September, 630; Revotionary, formed, 741; acquits Marat, 752; trial of Marie Antoinette, 795; trial of Girondins, 798; trial of Danton, 859.

Tricolor, adoption of the, 235.

Tronchet defends Louis, 696, 705.

Troyes, Parlement of Paris at, 88, 90.

Tuileries, Royal Family arrive in, 292, 295; on June 20th, 554; on August 10th, 592; gun-making at the, 791.

Turgot, Controller-General, 31, 43; school-fellow of Loménie Brienne, 90.

Udon, Madame d', 513, 530, 542.

United States, Congress in, 225; embassy to Louis XVI, 46; assert liberty, 8.

Usez, riot in, 414.

Vadier deported, 906.

Vaison, Mayor of, buried alive, 509.

Valadi, Marquis, in Caen, 765; Valadi, 138; becomes an officer of the Gardes Françaises, 173; he is guillotined, 800.

Valazé, in Legislative Assembly, 501; reports on right to try Louis, 686; Girondin, holds conferences, 755; arrested, 765; trial with the Girondins, 798; kills himself, 799.

Valenciennes, taken by the English, 780; invested by French, 840.

Valmy, battle at, 656; retreat of the Prussians from, 660.

Varennes, flight of the Royal Family checked at, 475 et seq.; threatened by Brunswick, 622.

Varigny killed at Versailles, 282, 284.

Varlet, Apostle of Liberty, 720, 736, 737, 753; arrested, 755; released, 756.

Vellum, magnetic, 332.

Vendémiaire, 13, 1795, Insurrection of, 920.

Vengeur, sinking of the, 842.

Verdun, besieged and surrendered, 614, 621; flight of Prussian army through, 661.

Vergennes, M. de, Prime Minister, 66; death of, 76.

Vergniaud, in Legislative Assembly, 501, 536; in Insurrection of June 20th, 1792, 557; President of Assembly on August 10th, 599; trial of Louis, 703; arrested, 761, 765; trial with Girondins, 798; guillotined, 799.

Vermond, Abbé de, Queen's reader, 76, 79.

Versailles, opening of States-General at, 135; National Assembly at, 170; on Bastille night, 198, 200; bodyguard at, 248; Insurrection of Women, 259, 265; vacated by Royal Family, 288; Orléans prisoners massacred in, 646.

Veto, question of the, 245; Louis XVI's exercise of the, 533.

Viard, spy, accuses Madame Roland, 700.

Vilate guillotined, 908.

Villedeuil, Controller-General of Finance, 78.

Vincennes, Castle of, disturbance at, 422.

Vincent, arrested, 852; guillotined, 855.

Voltaire, 32; visit to Paris, 44.

Washington, Key of Bastille sent to, 210.

Watigny, Battle of, 840.

Weber, at Insurrection of Women, 280, 287; procession from Versailles, 291, 292; in National Guard, 579; on Marie Antoinette's farewell to Austria, 796.

Weissembourg, French successes at, 841.

Westermann, in Insurrection of August 10th, 588; expelled from Jacobins, 854; tried with Danton, guillotined, 815, 859.

Wimpfen, General, at Caen, 766, 775.

Women, Insurrection of, 256.

York, Duke of, commander of English troops, 734; takes Valenciennes, 780.

Young, Arthur, on French Revolution, 231; on Royal Family at Tuileries, 296.

THE END